"[A] magnificent, superbly researched hist
Oriskany. Betrayed by politicians and sen
win war, the men in the cockpits had on
ism, superb leadership—and each other.
whole bloody tragedy. I could again hear the engines whine, smell the
jet exhaust, see the faces in the ready rooms, feel the deck jump as the
catapults fired, and see the flak and surface-to-air missiles."

—STEPHEN COONTS, *New York Times* best-selling author of
Flight of the Intruder

"This is a superb and exciting book that blends the political and cultural
happenings of the time with the real-time war in the air. It rekindles
memories of flying off the ship, of the flight deck crews, friendships and
missions carried out with valor and professionalism. It makes one very
proud to be a member of the navy and to be a naval aviator. I cannot recommend this book highly enough."

—CDR DOUG SIEGFRIED, USN (Ret) Tailhook Association
Historian, *The Hook*

"A gripping introduction to the naval air war in Vietnam."

—MICHAEL HANKINS, *Michigan War Studies Review*

"A splendid and dramatic picture of the period that the USS *Oriskany*
was in action ... thanks to [Peter Fey's] in-depth research and as a fascinating story teller."

—*Aviation Book Reviews*

"[Fey] brings skills unmatched in telling this most compelling story. Com-
bining first-person narratives with primary and secondary sources results
in a powerful presentation. For the price, I recommend this book to
everyone. Military aviators and, indeed, members of all services can learn
valuable lessons in leadership, sacrifice, and camaraderie from *Bloody Sixteen*'s story. Aviation enthusiasts, history buffs, and anyone seeking a better understanding of Vietnam and its impact on service members and
their families will find much to consider. A fascinating, uplifting, and,
at times, heartbreaking story."

—GOLDA ELDRIDGE, *Air Power History*

"[Fey's] writing style is engaging and easy to understand. Furthermore, *Bloody Sixteen* is an excellent study of how leadership quality was the decisive factor during the worst of times. *Bloody Sixteen* is well researched and will be a welcome addition to readers' libraries. A fitting tribute to the USS *Oriskany* and its air wing, I highly recommend this book to those readers interested in the Vietnam War, air warfare, or combat leadership."

—ROBERT J. RIELLY, *Military Review: The Professional Journal of the U.S. Army*

"Peter Fey's narrative of USS *Oriskany* and Carrier Air Wing 16 personalizes the Vietnam era with insight into the costs and effects. The political and cultural aspects are well handled, including the efforts of POW-MIA families to buck the Johnson administration's reluctance to address those concerns. Fey's description of the atmosphere at the Naval Air Station Lemoore, California, is particularly relevant. Few authors—other than someone who has swum in that pool—would understand it so well."

—BARRETT TILLMAN, author of *On Wave and Wing: The 100 Year Quest to Perfect the Aircraft Carrier*

"A great read in providing a window to view the navy's aviation community coming together to carry out an impossible mission under politically imposed rules of engagement. *Bloody Sixteen* is a great mix of social, political, and naval history."

—CHARLES H. BOGART, *Journal of America's Military Past*

Bloody Sixteen

BLOODY SIXTEEN

The USS *Oriskany* and
Air Wing 16 during the Vietnam War

PETER FEY

Potomac Books
An imprint of the University of Nebraska Press

Library of Congress Cataloging-in-Publication Data
Names: Fey, Peter, (Naval Commander), author.
Title: Bloody sixteen: the USS Oriskany and Air Wing 16 during the Vietnam War / Peter Fey.
Other titles: USS Oriskany and Air Wing 16 during the Vietnam War
Description: [Lincoln, Nebraska]: Potomac Books, an imprint of the University of Nebraska Press, 2018. | Includes bibliographical references and index.
Identifiers: LCCN 2017041404
ISBN 9781612349794 (cloth: alk. paper)
ISBN 9781640123106 (paperback)
ISBN 9781640120075 (epub)
ISBN 9781640120082 (mobi)
ISBN 9781640120099 (pdf)
Subjects: LCSH: Operation Rolling Thunder, 1965–1968. | Vietnam War, 1961–1975—Naval operations, American. | Orskany (Aircraft carrier: CVA 34) | Aircraft carriers—United States.
Classification: LCC DS557.8.O654 F49 2018 |
DDC 959.7/0434—dc23
LC record available at https://lccn.loc.gov/2017041404

Set in Sabon Next Pro by E. Cuddy.

To my father. A scout in the United States Cavalry, he also survived the Vietnam War. He talked very little about his experiences. When he did, it was often of the naval aviators who saved his troop. I grew up in awe of these men, because if my own father held them in such regard, that was good enough for me. Because of him, I chose to follow in the footsteps of giants.

Contents

Illustrations

Preface

To this day it stuns me that their own countrymen missed the story of
their service, lost in the bitter confusion of the war itself. . . . That boomer
elites can canonize this sort of conduct of their father's generation
while ignoring their own is more than a simple oversight—it
is a conscious, continuing tragedy.

—Senator Jim Webb, "Heroes of the Vietnam Generation"

MY INTEREST IN THIS story began with my attendance at the annual
Tailhook convention in September 2001. The infamous 1991 Tailhook
convention happened the year I graduated from high school, and news
stories of the scandal were still etched in my brain ten years later as I
weighed the decision to go. It was with some trepidation that I went.
I'm glad I did.

Imagine my surprise as my roommate and I stepped away from the
registration booth to be met (more like accosted) by a grandfatherly
man with a prosthetic right arm. This man proceeded to question us,
pressing us for details about our naval service and flying from ships at
sea before telling us to buy his book. Being the stereotypical, egotistical young aviators, we laughed off his sales attempt and walked away
to join another conversation. Fortunately, we came to our senses and
doubled back to learn more. Maybe the old man knew more than he
was letting on.

Little did we know, we had just met Wynn Foster, aka Captain
Hook. After pressing him for details, we stood spellbound as he
regaled us with stories about flying from the USS *Oriskany* (CVA-
34) during the Vietnam War. Needless to say, we both bought copies of his book, *Captain Hook: A Pilot's Tragedy and Triumph in the
Vietnam War*, and left in awe. I consider myself lucky to have met

him that night and even more fortunate to have been able to correspond with him throughout the years before his death in 2013. I enjoyed meeting him at each Tailhook convention. Wynn piqued my already high interest in aviation history. The more I studied, the more impressed I became. The saga of the naval aviators flying from *Oriskany* during the early Vietnam years is the stuff from which legends are born.

Without doubt, readers familiar with the topic will point out that it has been covered in great detail. So why another book about the *Oriskany*? Zalin Grant wrote a *New York Times* best seller entitled *Over the Beach*. Why not provide us with a history of the USS *Kitty Hawk* (CVA-63), which served gallantly during the same period? My simple and honest answer is this. I wrote this book for the men of the *Oriskany* and her embarked Carrier Air Wing 16 (CVW-16) because they asked me to.

Shortly after I met Wynn Foster, the September 11 attacks occurred. I soon found myself frequently deployed to both Afghanistan and Iraq. In the midst of it all, I was given ten months during which I was able to write a short master's thesis on the topic. It was warmly received by these men, but I believed I could do much better. Even though I was an outsider, I belonged to that small fraternity of naval aviators, and they began to open up to me. They began to provide information and relate stories that no doubt they had repressed for many years. I attended reunions, collecting photos and more sea stories as word spread, and these aviators shared even more. Time passed, and I was deployed again and again. The gentle prodding to get their story told started to become none too gentle. These men are not getting any younger. As I write this, the senior leaders are in their eighties. Even the youngest men are now in their late sixties.

What became clear is that there was much more to their stories than had been told before. *Oriskany* and CVW-16 made three deployments to Vietnam between April 1965 and January 1968. Each deployment coincided with the most dangerous phases of Operation Rolling Thunder; the Johnson administration's "slow squeeze" meant that *Oriskany* arrived on station just as previous restrictions were lifted and bombing raids increased. As a result, *Oriskany*'s pilots bore the burden as they ventured into heavily defended areas previously declared off limits at a time when the summer monsoons provided the clearest skies over North Vietnam. As this was the best time frame for flight operations, the numbers of sorties flown increased dramatically. The air wing suffered dearly. During 1965 CVW-16 spent 141 days on the line, losing twenty-three aircraft. During 1966 the air wing lost twenty-five aircraft during an eighty-seven-day line period. This cruise was cut short due to a tragic fire on 26 October 1966 that killed forty-four men, including twenty-four aviators and the air wing commander. A shortage of aircraft carriers meant *Oriskany* had only seven months for repairs before deploying again in 1967. The air wing's worst losses were sustained during the June 1967 to January 1968 deployment, when it lost over half of its assigned aircraft and over a third of its assigned pilots. *Oriskany*'s losses accounted for almost 20 percent of the navy's total losses during 1967, the highest loss rate of any carrier air wing during the Vietnam War. Unfortunately, these numbers don't account for the numerous aircraft that were damaged on each mission, adding to the strain on already overtasked sailors.

With the benefit of time, this book is my attempt to tell Air Wing 16's story. While its involvement during this tumultuous period in America's history has a familiar resonance, it is the experiences of this air wing that make it unique. These aviators experienced the highest of highs and lowest of lows in a three-year period. How and why that happened is the real story. These men, who were mostly volunteers answering the call of their country, endured a great deal and at great cost to themselves and their families. I'm forever grateful to them for opening up to me and allowing me to dredge up what are, for most of these men, unpleasant memories of a period they would rather put behind them. It was a terribly confusing and extremely deadly time. Their story and their service are often lost in the bitter confusion of the war itself. I have attempted to retell their story to the best of my ability. During the course of researching this book, one of the pilots nearly broke down while relating to me his thoughts as he visited the Vietnam Veterans Memorial in Washington DC. "Is this all there is?" he asked. "Names on a wall?!" My response is an emphatic "No!" There's much, much more. This book is for these men. It is their story, one that needs to be told.

Finally, a note on names, translations, and sources. Here and throughout the book, I have used local dates and times. I have used the period Western spelling for Vietnamese place-names, for example, Hanoi instead of Ha Noi, Phuc Yen instead of Phúc Yên, Haiphong instead of Hai Phong, and Saigon instead of Ho Chi Minh City. Any errors are mine and mine alone.

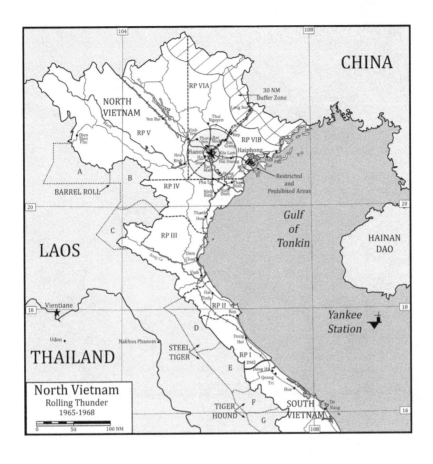

MAP 1. North Vietnam and Southeast Asia during Operation Rolling Thunder, 1965–68. Created by the author.

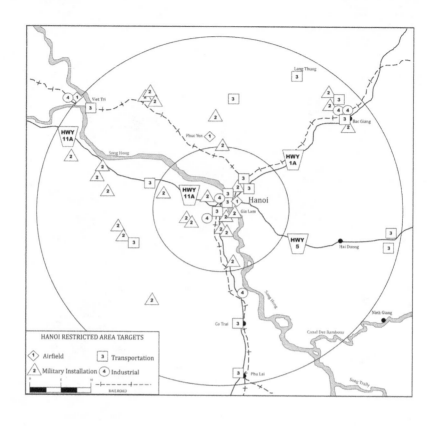

MAP 2. Targets within the restricted and prohibited areas around Hanoi.
Created by the author.

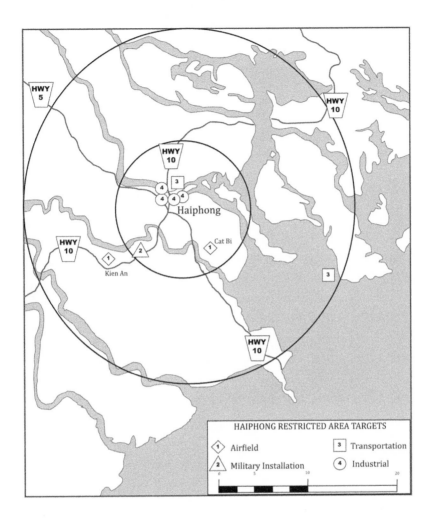

MAP 3. Targets within the restricted and prohibited areas around the port city of Haiphong. Created by the author.

Acknowledgments

I AM INDEBTED TO the following men, who graciously corresponded with me or allowed me to interview them. In many cases, they reached out to me, and each man welcomed me not only into his home but into his life: Jim Abbott, Bob Arnold, John Bittick, John Braly, Tom Brown III, Arne Bruflat, Carl Bruntlett, Gary Case, Dan Clarke, Ed Davis, John Davis, Larry Duthie, James Ellis, Paul Engle, Hal Farley, Larry Feldhaus, Wynn Foster, Ted Franks, Dick Haman, Tom Howard, Jack Jeffords, Dave Johnson, Ken Kreutzmann, John Laughter, Lonny McClung, Tom McClard, Bunny Marks, Tom Maxwell, Jim Mueller, Pat Patrick, Bob Pearl, Don Purdy, Ed Rasimus, Bob Rasmussen, Randy Rime, John Roosen, Harry Sampson, Dick Schaffert, Dick Schulte, Dave Sheeley, Bill Span, Wayne Steward, Cal Swanson, Thad Taylor, Jim Waldron, and Denny Wisely.

Abbreviations

AAA	antiaircraft artillery
AEW	airborne early warning
AGM	air-to-ground missile
BARCAP	barrier combat air patrol
BDA	bomb damage assessment
B/N	bombardier/navigator
CAG	Commander Air Group
CAP	combat air patrol
CAS	close air support
CIA	Central Intelligence Agency
CINCPAC	Commander in Chief Pacific Command
CINCPACFLT	Commander in Chief Pacific Fleet
COD	carrier onboard delivery (C-1A)
CSAR	combat search and rescue
CTF	Carrier Task Force
CVG/CVW	Carrier Air Group / Carrier Air Wing
DIA	Defense Intelligence Agency
ECM	electronic countermeasures
ELINT	electronic intelligence
FAC	forward air control
GCI	ground-controlled intercept
ICC	International Control Commission
JCS	Joint Chiefs of Staff
KIA	killed in action
LOX	liquid oxygen
LWR	launch warning receiver
LZ	landing zone
MACV	Military Assistance Command, Vietnam
MCAS	Marine Corps Air Station

MIA	missing in action
NAS	Naval Air Station
NATO	North Atlantic Treaty Organization
NSC	National Security Council
OBA	oxygen breathing apparatus
OINC	officer-in-charge
ORI	operational readiness inspection
PAVN	People's Army of Vietnam
PIRAZ	Positive Identification Radar Advisory Zone
PJ	Pararescueman
PLA	People's Liberation Army (China)
POL	petroleum, oil, and lubricants
POW	prisoner of war
PVO-Strany	Protivo Vozdushnaya Oborona Strany
RESCAP	rescue combat air patrol
RHAW	radar homing and warning
ROE	rules of engagement
RP	Route Package
RTCC	Rolling Thunder Coordination Committee
RWR	radar warning receiver
SAM	surface-to-air missile
SAR	search and rescue
TARCAP	target combat air patrol
TFS	Tactical Fighter Squadron
TFW	Tactical Fighter Wing
UHT	unit horizontal tail
UNREP	underway replenishment
VPAF	Vietnamese People's Air Force
WBLC	waterborne logistics craft
WESTPAC	Western Pacific

Bloody Sixteen

Part 1

Setting the Stage

Wars cannot be fought the same way bureaucrats haggle over
apportionments. The toll of human life in battle does not lend itself
to cost/benefit analysis. One's plan of action on the international
chessboard cannot be built on compromise businesslike decisions
among factions. To design a country's strategy along a middle course for
bureaucratic reasons is to aim at what Winston Churchill
has called the bull's eye of disaster.

—James Stockdale, CAG-16, *A Vietnam Experience*

1

Rolling Thunder and the Numbers Game

THROUGHOUT THE UNITED STATES' involvement in Vietnam, President Lyndon B. Johnson was divided about how to proceed. Thrust into the role of president after the assassination of John F. Kennedy, Johnson became consumed by the prospect that he would face an election less than a year after taking the presidential oath of office. For Johnson in 1964, politics overshadowed any sense of urgency, initiative, or imagination in the evaluation of America's strategic options in Vietnam. As President Johnson saw it, he had only inherited the presidency and was "simply a trustee who would not command a real political mandate to determine major policy questions unless he prevailed in a national election."[1] Because winning the presidential election was Johnson's overarching goal, he could not permit the situation in Vietnam to deteriorate to a deeper level of crisis. The impending election further constrained Johnson from either escalating the American commitment or embarking on a strategic withdrawal.[2] Thus politics became the enemy of strategy in 1964, a theme that would have dire consequences.

Compounding President Johnson's self-imposed political constraints was the fact that he relied heavily on the advice of his staff, which he inherited from President Kennedy. A product of the Ivy League, Kennedy had filled his staff positions with what were known as "the whiz kids" or "the best and the brightest," essentially, the educated elite of East Coast schools. These men included McGeorge Bundy, the former dean of faculty at Harvard who became Kennedy's national security advisor, and Robert McNamara, a Harvard graduate and CEO of Ford Motor Company before becoming the secretary of defense. A rift between the civilian and military advisors began during the Kennedy administration over both the Bay of Pigs invasion and the Cuban missile crisis. President Johnson's dependence on Kennedy's staff turned this rift into an outright divide between the military leadership and the administration. Because of service parochialism and interservice squabbling, the Joint Chiefs of Staff (JCS) were continually undercut and outmaneuvered by McNamara and other civilian advisors.[3]

Despite the misgivings of the JCS, both Bundy and McNamara sold Johnson on the use of force in gradual responses to show American resolve in the face of Communist aggression and to punish North Vietnam for its continued support of the insurgency in South Vietnam. The first test of this policy came on 29 March, when Viet Cong guerrillas detonated a bomb outside the American Embassy in Saigon.[4] Although Johnson took no action, he ordered the Joint Chiefs, the National Security Council (NSC), and the Military Assistance Command, Vietnam (MACV) to prepare contingency plans for future action against North Vietnam. This plan, produced by Adm. Ulysses S. Grant Sharp, the commander in chief of Pacific Forces (CINCPAC), was forwarded to the JCS and became known as OPLAN 37-64.

OPLAN 37-64 was a three-phase approach, with gradual military force applied to stop the infiltration of North Vietnamese supplies into South Vietnam. The purpose of phase 1 was to deny Viet Cong sanctuaries in Laos and Cambodia. Phase 2 called for reprisal strikes against North Vietnam in addition to an increase in a highly classified program known as OPLAN 34A. These covert operations began in 1961 and continued under President Johnson. During OPLAN 34A, small patrol boats inserted teams into North Vietnam and bombarded coastal facilities. Phase 3 called for strategic bombing of ninety-four military and industrial targets selected by the JCS, though this phase was intended as a last resort. Phase 1 began almost immediately in May 1964 as both air force and navy aircraft began armed reconnaissance flights over Laos in what was termed Operation Yankee Team. Operation Yankee Team convinced President Johnson and his advisors of the viability of gradual, limited application of military power.[5]

The Johnson administration continued to apply gradual pressure during the summer months of 1964; however, election year politics remained their primary concern. Concurrent with OPLAN 34A raids, the navy conducted electronic surveillance operations. Code-named Desoto, these patrols were conducted by destroyers operating in international waters along the coast of North Vietnam.[6] Although the two operations were independent of one another, the attacks carried out by South Vietnamese patrol boats provoked responses by the North Vietnamese that were monitored by the American destroyers, thus providing intelligence on North Vietnamese military capabilities. The pace of these operations doubled in July 1964 as President Johnson sought to keep the situation in South Vietnam from degrading further. Less than three weeks after the Republican National Convention in July, the Gulf of Tonkin incident occurred. The incident brought Johnsonian politics to the forefront and presented itself as the perfect vehicle for Johnson to ride from August through Election Day.[7]

The Gulf of Tonkin incident was in fact two separate incidents. The first occurred on 2 August, as USS *Maddox* (DD731) conducted a Desoto patrol off Hon Me Island. The destroyer was attacked by three North Vietnamese patrol boats. During the ensuing battle, aircraft from USS *Ticonderoga* (CVA-14) sank one of the patrol boats, and the other two escaped. Desoto patrols continued, and in response to the attacks, President Johnson ordered another destroyer, USS *Turner Joy* (DD951), to accompany *Maddox*. On the night of 4 August, the second incident occurred. While both destroyers claimed to have been attacked, the hostile shapes seen on radar scopes were nothing more than returns caused by severe weather. Much controversy surrounded the events of this evening, and while declassified documents have shown that the second attack never took place, the results were far-reaching. Many high-ranking officials from the Central Intelligence Agency (CIA), the Department of State, and the Pentagon could not correlate the evidence assembled by McNamara as supporting a Vietnamese attack. Despite their doubts, people in both the intelligence and defense communities kept their silence. As much as anything else, they were aware that President Johnson would brook no uncertainty that could undermine his position.[8] The first incident set the stage, allowing Johnson to show his restraint in the face of perceived Communist aggression. The second attack allowed him to show his firm resolve. The president ordered retaliatory strikes and went on national television to announce his response. As a result, on 7 August Congress passed a joint resolution, commonly referred to as the Tonkin Gulf Resolution, with only two dissenting votes. The resolution gave President Johnson power to use military force in any way he saw fit against

Communist aggression in Vietnam without the benefit of a declaration of war. The political support he gained also led to Johnson's overwhelming victory in the 1964 presidential election.

Even with the resolution in Johnson's favor, it took another Communist attack for Washington to escalate the war. Following a Viet Cong attack against U.S. advisors in Pleiku in February 1965, Bundy, with the support of Ambassador Maxwell Taylor and Gen. William Westmoreland, recommended a reprisal strike against North Vietnam known as Flaming Dart I. The Viet Cong responded in kind by blowing up a hotel in Qui Nhon, South Vietnam, where American servicemen were billeted. More retaliatory air strikes followed in Flaming Dart II. What Bundy and his advisors sought to engineer was a perpetual bombing campaign, which they described as a generalized and continuing program of "graduated and sustained reprisal." Despite internal studies indicating that coercive bombing was an ineffectual strategy, Bundy and his team persisted. They ignored war game simulations and estimates from the CIA, the Defense Intelligence Agency (DIA), and the State Department that concluded that a bombing campaign would fail to weaken Hanoi's determination to support the insurgency.[9] Flaming Dart proved tactically inconsequential, as Communist forces in South Vietnam continued the insurgency with little concern for American reprisal. More importantly, the limitations imposed on these early strikes, which were the prototype for Rolling Thunder, created a negative precedent that condemned the pending air war.

Operation Rolling Thunder

President Johnson began Operation Rolling Thunder on 2 March 1965 in an attempt to convince the government of North Vietnam to abandon its support of the insurgency in the South. As envisioned, the bombing was not a strategic campaign, nor was it an interdiction effort. Instead, the bombing was intended as a signal to North Vietnam, demonstrating U.S. resolve as well as concern to not destroy the North and to limit civilian casualties. The campaign was marred by disputes between senior military leaders and the civilian administration from the outset. Military leaders advocated decisive strikes in order to isolate North Vietnam and to destroy its production capabilities and transportation systems. Instead, the Johnson administration continued to apply gradual force, using bombing halts followed by escalation in an effort to persuade North Vietnam to negotiate for peace with the United States and South Vietnam.

The administration believed gradualism to be a safer means of signaling than bombing every significant target at once. By managing the escalation, Johnson preserved control. This minimized the chance of direct confrontation with China, the Soviet Union, and allies that continued to trade with North Vietnam. Thus the targets with the highest probability of impacting the war also carried the risk of triggering direct confrontation with China and the Soviet Union, something to be avoided at all costs.

The Johnson administration insisted on unprecedented control of the air war, making tactical decisions and dictating aircraft types and numbers, the ordnance they carried, and even their flight profiles. This planning was chiefly done during the administration's infamous Tuesday luncheons. Through 1967 military leaders, including the chairman of the JCS, were not allowed to attend these meetings and were excluded from the target selection process. The lunch group limited targeting in terms of both geography and quality. Geographically, bombing was initially limited to targets south of the 18th parallel. It gradually moved north, a parallel each month, as North Vietnam failed to heed Washington's warnings. The value of targets gradually intensified as well, with specific targets hit in response to Communist attacks in the South.

Because the Tuesday lunch group had little idea of day-to-day combat realities over North Vietnam, campaign targeting and planning suffered. There was little military logic to the targeting process. McNamara acknowledged that "the decision to hit or not hit [a target] is a function of three primary elements: the value of the target, the risk of U.S. pilot loss, and the risk of widening the war, and it depends on the balance among those elements as to whether we should or should not hit."[10] Operationally, it meant that target lists issued by Washington did not include targets for which materials had been produced by tactical commanders. Other approved targets were included that had been rejected on scene. The lists of approved targets also included unknown targets that had been developed in Washington from photography and other sources not available in Southeast Asia.[11] Aircrews were given at most two weeks to destroy targets placed on the strike list before those targets were removed during the next meeting. According to Admiral Sharp, "Frequently we would make one or two strikes on a critical target, and then after it was hit (whether damaged or not) strike authorization would be retracted and permission to go back to that target would not be forthcoming for months, or maybe forever."[12] Monsoon weather prevented many targets from being struck, while at other times, targets remained on the list after they had been struck and destroyed. Serious delays were often experienced when tactical commanders asked for approval to strike targets because the JCS could not get an answer from the Tuesday lunch club. The process hobbled the air campaign from its initial stages to the bitter end.

Rolling Thunder execution was further hampered by poorly structured command-and-control arrangements driven more by political concerns and parochial interservice squabbling than tactical considerations. For example, the Seventh Air Force controlled its own aircraft and served as the Air Component Commander for MACV, Gen. William Westmoreland. The navy's Seventh Fleet air assets reported separately up their service chain to CINCPAC, Admiral Sharp. Coordination was next to impossible, and it created a situation in which five separate air wars were fought: one in South Vietnam, one in Cambodia, one in Laos, one to interdict supplies along the Ho Chi Minh Trail in southern Laos, and one in North Vietnam. Each air war had its own command-and-control arrangement and its own restrictions, including rules of engagement (ROE). MACV controlled all sorties in South Vietnam, while the ambassadors to Cambodia and Laos ran the air campaigns in their respective countries. The campaign against North Vietnam was controlled by CINCPAC. It proved maddening to all who flew and fought.

The campaign suffered from the administration's ambiguous goals and lack of coherent strategy. Throughout, Johnson and his staff remained divided over any goals, though they eventually became the following: (1) strategically deter North Vietnam from supporting the insurgency in South Vietnam; (2) raise the morale of military and political elites in South Vietnam; and (3) interdict North Vietnam's support of the Communist insurgency in the South. Early strikes in 1965 did not alter Hanoi's behavior, and the air campaign was viewed as a failure. Yet Johnson did not feel that he could back down without appearing weak on Communism. To stabilize the situation, ground troops became the quick and easy solution. Because the air war over North Vietnam and the ground war in South Vietnam were seen as antithetical, the air war was relegated to a secondary role, becoming a bargaining tool in exchange for negotiations. Johnson continually sought a middle ground, using policy options designed to result in the least international and domestic political cost. Fear of domestic repercussions pushed Johnson to continue using airpower, which offered results without risking additional lives, unlike the ground war. Thus interdiction, in the form of armed reconnaissance missions, became the means to achieve that end. Although he continually declined high-value targets that posed unacceptable risks, Johnson steadily increased interdiction sorties.

As a result, Rolling Thunder went through five distinct phases as interdiction efforts gained focus and intensity. During phase 1, from March to June 1965, a variety of targets were struck in failed attempts to deter North Vietnam. The air strikes, which were limited to targets below the 20th parallel to avoid heavy population centers, only hardened North Vietnamese resolve. More importantly, with Soviet and Chinese help, phase 1 led to the creation of the world's most complex and lethal air defense network.

Phase 2, from July 1965 to January 1966, became an interdiction campaign aimed at roads, bridges, boats, and railroads. At the urging of Admiral Sharp, the focus shifted from interdiction to petroleum products. Sharp realized the campaign was not achieving the desired results and believed that by focusing on energy resources, North Vietnam might be forced to negotiate for peace.[13]

Phase 3, from January to October 1966, focused on North Vietnam's petroleum, oil, and lubricant (POL) resources. Before this phase began, North Vietnam required only 32,000 tons of oil a year to supply its needs. By the time Rolling Thunder began targeting POL resources, North Vietnam had 60,000 tons of POL stocks in reserve. While the attacks destroyed an estimated 70 percent of the North Vietnamese supply, remaining stocks were dispersed throughout the country. These stocks proved more than adequate to meet North Vietnam's needs and did little to affect the war.[14]

Phase 4, from October 1966 to May 1967, concentrated the campaign's efforts on North Vietnam's industry and power-generating capabilities. For the first time, targets in Hanoi were struck, but, as with phase 3, these efforts failed to cripple a nonindustrialized country. Because North Vietnam's ports still remained off-limits, the strikes did not impede the country's ability to receive and distribute supplies destined for the insurgency in South Vietnam.[15]

Phase 5, the final phase, from May 1967 to October 1968, concentrated on isolating Hanoi from Haiphong and both cities from the remainder of the country. It continued the destruction of any remaining industrial infrastructure. At its height, U.S. aircraft averaged over thirteen thousand sorties a month, a threefold increase from phase 1. These missions encountered incredibly lethal air defenses. During any given month of 1967, North Vietnam fired over 25,000 tons of ammunition from ten thousand antiaircraft artillery (AAA) guns and hundreds of missiles from over twenty-five surface-to-air missile (SAM) battalions.[16] Growing frustration with the war and its rising cost in American lives ultimately led to Johnson's March 1968 decision to withdraw from the 1968 presidential election and halt all bombing north of the 19th parallel.

From March 1965 until November 1968, air force and navy aircraft flew hundreds of thousands of sorties over North Vietnam. American pilots dropped 864,000 tons of bombs on North Vietnam. It is worth noting that during the same time period, the United States dropped 2.2 million tons of bombs on South Vietnam, their supposed ally, and 2.1 million tons on Laos. Yet Rolling Thunder still failed to achieve any of its objectives. All of this effort came at great cost to the United States both in dollars spent and in lives lost. Between 1965 and 1968 air operations throughout Southeast Asia consumed 47 percent of all American war expenditures. In 1965 the CIA estimated that Rolling Thunder cost the United States $6.60 to render $1.00 worth of damage; one year later, it cost $9.60. It is estimated that the $600 million of damage inflicted by Rolling Thunder was dwarfed by the $6 billion it cost to replace all the aircraft lost during the campaign.[17]

The interdiction campaign failed to stem the flow of supplies to South Vietnam, and no peace agreement was signed. When Rolling Thunder began, farmers made up 80 percent of North Vietnam's laborers, and agriculture accounted for nearly half of the gross national product. Destroying industrial capability or oil supplies meant little to a nation that relied on bicycles for transportation and depended on water buffalo for farming. It was also inconsequential considering the amount of support given to North Vietnam by its Communist allies. As much as military leaders wanted to believe, Vietnam was not Germany in World War II and represented a poor choice for a bombing campaign. The Johnson administration never came to grips with these basic facts and wasted American lives, aircraft, and money on an air campaign that had little impact on the ability of North Vietnam to support the war in South Vietnam.

Rules of Engagement

The Johnson administration maintained its tight control by utilizing restrictive ROE. In theory, the ROE preserved control of the gradual approach, allowing Washington to ratchet up pressure on the government of North Vietnam, forcing it to bend and eventually break. In reality, the ROE minimized destruction to North Vietnam's most important targets while placing undue burden on military commanders and the men flying combat missions. The ROE required aviators to fly and fight in a manner contrary to common sense, training, and published doctrine. Washington's interference and senior military complicity in these rules at times defies explanation. The ROE quickly became the focal point of condemnation concerning conduct of the air war and have echoed in histories since.

The rules often changed with each weekly phase of Rolling Thunder, creating confusion for aviators flying missions. In addition, the rules varied in each route package, making it difficult for pilots to know the current restrictions and keep track in the heat of combat. Never mind that a completely different set of rules existed for missions flown over Laos. Yet pilots were still held accountable for anything they did that might escalate tensions with the Soviets and Chinese.

ROE did not authorize follow-up strikes. If a target was missed due to weather or if it was just partially damaged, the entire authorization process had to be repeated. Targets of opportunity were also disallowed, meaning that if the primary target and the alternate were obscured by weather, unexpended ordnance could not be used on another target.

This often resulted in carrier pilots jettisoning unexpended bombs in the water prior to returning to their ship.[18]

During interdiction efforts, restrictions limited the targets to be attacked along lines of communication such as roads, railways, and canals. Two types of targets were permitted, trucks and waterborne logistics craft (WBLC), and each came with its own special restrictions. Aviators were expected to differentiate military trucks from civilian trucks while flying thousands of feet in the air and often while evading hostile ground fire. They were permitted to strike trucks only when they were a safe distance from villages. Of course, the Vietnamese were aware of this restriction and routinely parked trucks in and around villages in order to take advantage of the modicum of protection. The restrictions associated with WBLCs, the name for any and all small ships (junks, ferries, barges, and even fishing vessels) were equally outrageous. Pilots were instructed that WBLCs presented a viable target only if they were motorized and traveling parallel to the coast within the international limit of 3 nautical miles, but not if they were transiting perpendicular to the coast. This restriction hampered aviators' efforts, as vessels could sail in international waters and dart into port to deliver supplies under the cover of weather or darkness, sometimes both, and only for short periods of time. That aviators were expected to make these distinctions is an example of the irrationality of the operation's rules.

Although the interdiction of supplies became the main focus of Rolling Thunder, the port facility of Haiphong remained off-limits. The presence of Soviet and Chinese ships and the potential reaction if they were struck were risks too great for Johnson and his advisors to take. Several NATO allies also continued to trade with North Vietnam, which only added to the sensitivities surrounding the port. The port at Cam Pha to the northwest of Haiphong included a significant Vietnamese coal depot, which remained off-limits as long as foreign ships were in the harbor. Of course, there wasn't a day when a foreign-flagged ship wasn't tied up at the pier, thus preventing any attack. Ships anchored offshore were also off-limits, even if visibly offloading munitions. Barges ferrying supplies to the piers were viable targets, but only once they were 600 meters from the ship.

Perhaps the most frustrating restrictions of the entire air war concerned the North Vietnamese defenses, specifically SAMs and MiGs.

The Johnson administration knew that Soviet and Eastern Bloc technicians were installing, training, and in some cases operating SAM sites. Secretary of Defense McNamara's concern about harming these advisors and the Soviet reaction led him to place the sites off-limits until they actually engaged American aircraft. At one point during the early stages of the air war, the assistant secretary of defense and McNamara's close confidant, John McNaughton, ridiculed a request to strike a SAM site under construction. "You don't think the North Vietnamese are going to use them!" he scoffed. "Putting them in is just a political ploy by the Russians to appease Hanoi." The administration's theory was that if the United States did not bomb the SAM sites, it would send a signal to the North Vietnamese, who, it was thought, would act in kind.[19] The consequences of this decision cost untold numbers of men and aircraft once American forces were finally given permission to destroy SAMs. Likewise, the fear of Chinese intervention led to prohibitions on MiG airfields through 1967. This allowed North Vietnamese fighter aircraft to operate freely, with little fear of repercussions.

Restrictions came at great cost to aviators and had major ramifications on the outcome of the war. Instead of demonstrating U.S. restraint, restrictions actually strengthened North Vietnamese resolve. They lessened the burden on North Vietnam's air defenses, allowing them to allocate and employ their defenses with great effect. The piecemeal targeting meant that each time a new set of targets was bombed, the North Vietnamese could expect similar targets to be attacked for the succeeding few weeks. This gave them the chance to concentrate their defenses on the predicted targets and routes, often with devastating results.[20] Each time the United States threatened to overwhelm North Vietnam's defenses, a bombing halt or some other self-imposed restriction invariably allowed the North to train, reequip, and overcome the Americans' hard-fought advantage. During each bombing halt, they redeployed AAA and SAMs to cover gaps exposed during the most recent raids. A Vietnamese history of the war states, "During the first three months of 1967 the enemy launched no large attacks against Hanoi and Haiphong. This was due in part to poor weather and in part to the restrictions of the American imperialist policy of escalation. In this situation the Air Defense Service directed forces in both cities to vigorously prepare for combat."[21] It was a defensive advantage that Hanoi exploited at every opportunity.

War on the Cheap and the Strategic Divide

While the United States was prepared for a potential nuclear showdown with the Soviet Union, it was unprepared for the sustained level of operations required to support the growing conflict in Vietnam. Operation Rolling Thunder began with a peacetime mindset stemming from President Johnson's attempts to limit American involvement and preserve his domestic agenda and his cherished Great Society programs. It ended up being fought using accounting and control measures introduced by Secretary McNamara, creating a state of mind that permeated all aspects of the war—from the government's budget process to the services themselves. As the war was fought on the cheap, shortages in personnel, ordnance, aircraft, and even aircraft carriers affected the operations of every service, including the navy. The largest and most unintended consequence of this parsimony is that it unnecessarily exposed American servicemen to greater threats both on the ground and in the air.

No one was better qualified to attempt to make Johnson's "guns and butter" policy work than Robert McNamara. During his tenure, McNamara introduced quantifiable accounting and control methods into his management of the Pentagon.[22] His ability to reel off statistics on any relevant subject astonished subordinates and often left stenographers struggling to keep up. McNamara kept close tabs on every facet of the sprawling Pentagon bureaucracy, using statistics and any other quantifiable data as a means of evaluating success. This included the use of expected sortie rates for each of the different types of aircraft then in service. Thus in his search for a measure to evaluate Rolling Thunder, McNamara chose sortie rates because of the lack of any other perceived criteria. In simplistic terms, the belief held that if the United States ratcheted up the pressure, flew enough sorties, and dropped enough ordnance, the North Vietnamese would mathematically be forced to quit. Coincidentally, this same thinking led to the use of "body counts" as a measure of success for the war in South Vietnam. Unfortunately, success or failure in war cannot be reduced to such simplistic terms, though this thought process dominated American policy throughout the war.[23]

Throughout, the navy and air force competed against each other over which service provided the most effective use of airpower. Though both services were committed to the use of airpower, animosity between the two services remained from the late 1940s, when the air force began efforts to wrest defense dollars for its large strategic bomber fleet at the cost of the navy's newest aircraft carrier. The navy spent large portions of its budget to build and develop aircraft carriers for what it believed was the best use of airpower. Neither the navy nor the air force could admit the failure of Rolling Thunder without having to acknowledge to a certain degree that their service's concept of airpower was based on a faulty premise.[24] Given that the navy was trying to obtain funding for its next generation of supercarriers, which were some of the most expensive and complex ships ever developed (not to mention completely new aircraft to fill their flight decks), this was an extremely bitter pill to swallow.[25] The navy stood to lose this funding, as it led to the question that if sea-based airpower could not succeed against North Vietnam, how could it be expected to succeed against the Soviet Union?

Funding concerns in conjunction with sortie counts resulted in aberrant thinking by service leadership. The reputation of each service became dependent on success as defined by sortie counts. Desire to impress exacerbated the normal interservice competition as each service strove to produce a higher number of sorties than the other. If McNamara's analysts could produce statistics that showed that one service was better than the other using the limited criterion of sortie rates, the apparently "inferior" service stood to lose in the next round of appropriations.[26] This was a fact not lost on either service.

When the sortie count was combined with restrictions imposed on aircrews by the ROE, a strategic divide developed between the pilots who were fighting the war and those directing it from thousands of miles away. This obsession with statistics rather than the real outcome of the bombing campaign was unfair, to say the least, to the men fighting. Service leaders forced tactical commanders to fly all the sorties allocated to them, even in marginal weather and when no real targets were available.[27] Ordnance shortages eventually produced a situation where six aircraft would be sent with only one bomb each, when one aircraft could carry six bombs, simply to keep up the sortie rate. Sorties became something that could be measured, assimilated by a computer, reduced to a mathematical formula, divided into dollar amounts, and analyzed for cost effectiveness—never mind actual combat effectiveness.[28] This obsession with numbers blinded senior leadership to the real goals of Rolling Thunder, as sorties were flown just for the sake of flying sorties, and bombs were dropped for similar reasons.

uss *Oriskany* and cvw-16

The strategic divide between Washington's failed strategy and the harsh realities faced by the men executing it is epitomized by the experiences of uss *Oriskany* (cva-34) and her embarked Carrier Air Wing 16 (cvw-16). At the end of World War II, aircraft carriers remained one of the primary instruments used to implement national policies and national security strategies, despite the growing reliance on nuclear weapons. *Oriskany* proved no different in this regard, using her aircraft to project power over land and sea. In Vietnam the "Mighty-O," or simply "O-Boat," as she was affectionately known, was one of the oldest carriers in the navy. Named after the costly Revolutionary War battle near Oriskany, New York, she was laid down in May 1944. Construction was rushed to ensure the carrier could participate in the end of World War II. With the end of the war, construction slowed and was eventually halted in 1947 as the navy and air force bickered over service roles and budgets. Design modifications were implemented, and *Oriskany* was eventually commissioned in September 1950.

Following multiple Far East deployments, including distinguished service in the Korean War, the carrier underwent refurbishment in San Francisco from 1957 to 1959. Originally built with a straight flight deck, *Oriskany*'s modifications gave her an angled flight deck, steam catapults, and many other improvements that permitted safer operation of new jet aircraft. These modernized carriers were known simply as 27c class carriers, in reference to the name of the modernization program: scb-27.

Oriskany's main battery, or primary weapon, was the embarked aircraft of cvw-16. Established in September 1960, Carrier Air Group 16 (cvg-16) was redesignated as cvw-16 during Secretary McNamara's early restructuring of the Defense Department. The air wing consisted of approximately seventy aircraft in nine squadrons and detachments. During Vietnam the air wing was comprised of two fighter squadrons flying f-8 Crusaders (vf-162 Hunters, vmf[aw]-212 Lancers, and later

VF-III Sundowners), two attack squadrons flying A-4 Skyhawks (VA-163 Saints and VA-164 Ghost Riders), one attack squadron flying A-1 Skyraiders (VA-152 Wild Aces), one heavy attack squadron flying A-3 Skywarriors (VAH-4 Four Runners), one photographic reconnaissance detachment flying RF-8 Crusaders (VFP-63 Eyes of the Fleet), one airborne early radar warning detachment flying E-2 Tracers (VAW-II Early Elevens), and a detachment of UH-2 Seasprite helicopters (HC-I Pacific Fleet Angels). The ship and air wing made one western Pacific deployment in 1962. They deployed again in August 1963, arriving in the South China Sea shortly before the coup d'état that resulted in Ngo Dinh Diem's death. As the situation in South Vietnam deteriorated, *Oriskany* returned home in March 1964. When the Tonkin Gulf incident propelled America into the conflict in Vietnam, *Oriskany* was still undergoing repairs in the Puget Sound Naval Shipyard. America's destiny in Vietnam had already been foretold before the ship was ready in 1965.

The original concept of Rolling Thunder called for air strikes that would eventually increase in force until the government of North Vietnam stopped supporting the insurgency in South Vietnam. Policy makers continually thought that the level of bombing needed to achieve this goal would soon be reached. When this plan didn't work, Johnson turned to interdiction, and the number of sorties and tonnage of bombs dropped expanded significantly each time. Politicians and military planners of the campaign never anticipated that Rolling Thunder would last for three and a half years, with thousands of tactical aircraft dropping hundreds of thousands of bombs. They also never anticipated the loss of over 850 aircraft over North Vietnam.[29] The campaign evolved through a series of reactions to North Vietnam's continued and increasingly conventional intervention in South Vietnam. Rolling Thunder never followed a carefully designed course or set strategy but simply developed out of a kind of impotent rage that American policy makers felt toward Hanoi's recalcitrance. Restrictions and growing North Vietnamese defenses virtually guaranteed that each mission resulted in casualties. The navy alone lost 382 aircraft over North Vietnam during the three-year campaign.[30] *Oriskany* and CVW-16 lost sixty-one aircraft during this time, accounting for nearly 20 percent of the navy's combat losses. Operational losses were nearly as high, and when combined, they account for over one hundred aircraft lost. This fact alone makes *Oriskany*'s and CVW-16's experience unique among the many squadrons and wings, both air force and navy, that flew during Rolling Thunder.

The significant losses experienced by CVW-16 while flying from *Oriskany* can be attributed to several factors. First and foremost was the strategic divide between those running the war and the pilots flying from Yankee Station. The restrictions imposed by both the Johnson administration and military leadership caused unnecessary losses and prolonged the war. Airpower could not be successfully used to send political signals to Hanoi, as North Vietnam construed the message differently from the way policy makers in Washington intended. North Vietnamese leaders saw that America lacked the determination to seriously threaten their support of the insurgency or the will to see the war through to the end. This led to North Vietnam's response, which was an escalation of the violence, which in turn led directly to higher casualties among American pilots as the Johnson administration replied in kind.

The second factor had to do with unfortunate timing, as *Oriskany*'s deployments coincided with each major escalation of Rolling Thunder. She arrived on Yankee Station as the summer monsoons began and the air war shifted into the next phase. In addition, the navy's shortage of aircraft carriers meant that there was little chance of altering the deployment dates in order to share the risk. In 1965 *Oriskany* arrived on station as Rolling Thunder began. In 1966 she arrived just as Rolling Thunder began targeting the North Vietnamese POL system. Following a disastrous fire in October 1966, there was inadequate time to train replacements before returning for the crescendo of 1967. As a result of the Stennis hearings, which publicly pitted McNamara against the military leadership, the restrictions were lifted, and *Oriskany*'s pilots paid a heavy price as they struck targets previously off-limits in Hanoi and Haiphong.

Finally, Air Wing 16 was aggressive. The men all realized the difference between America's goals and limited aims and the totality of their involvement. As the war continued to escalate, aviators found themselves fully committed. They responded in the only ways available to them—with courage and professionalism. Ironically, this led to further casualties as they pressed their attacks on North Vietnam in deference to Washington's limitations.

While *Oriskany*'s pilots never lost the will to fly and fight, their frustration steadily rose. As opposition to the war grew, the ROE became the focal point of this disenchantment. Men believed they had been hindered by the ROE and were then being unfairly criticized by their own leadership for failings that were not of their making.[31] It took extraordinary leadership, professionalism, and courage for these men to continue flying their missions. Moreover, the success or failure of airpower in Vietnam cannot be the measure of success of the men who flew and fought. The blame for Operation Rolling Thunder's failure falls squarely on the senior leadership of both the military and the politicians they advised. The pilots deserved much better than they got.

2

The Environment

IT IS NOT POSSIBLE to follow the air war as conducted by naval aviators without understanding the conditions under which they flew
and fought. As famed author and historian Stephen Ambrose noted
in his many works, war is dominated by factors that constantly dom-
inate the day-to-day life of those involved. They include the enemy,
the terrain, and the weather. The enemy included the North Vietnamese, as well as their Communist allies. While effects of poor weather
on operations are self-explanatory, the weather of the region wreaked
havoc on daily sortie counts and Washington's attempts to control
the air war. The terrain incorporated the operations area throughout
the Tonkin Gulf. Unfortunately for the aviators flying missions during
Rolling Thunder, these factors could and often did affect the daily routine during the air war over North Vietnam

North Vietnamese Defenses

Before further discussions on the air war, it is essential to discuss North
Vietnamese strategy and associated tactics. A reactive and thinking
adversary, the North Vietnamese continually adjusted both their strategy and tactics during the course of Rolling Thunder. They continually exploited U.S. mistakes and weaknesses, especially with regard
to the ROE. This adaptability, along with help from their Communist
partners, ensured their success.

First and foremost in this success was the overall North Vietnamese strategy. The central factor in Hanoi's strategic thought during the
war was the Vietnamese Communist Party's concept of *dau tranh*, or
"struggle." The concept was believed to be unique to the Vietnamese
because of their tradition of unity and patriotism. Over the centuries,
China, Japan, and France had all attempted, unsuccessfully, to exert control over Indochina. Out of this experience, the Vietnamese forged a

strong collective identity. The emerging conflict with the United States was seen as a continuation of more than two thousand years of foreign oppression. By using *dau tranh*, Vietnamese leaders generated support for the cause and reunification. A firm belief in the righteousness of the Vietnamese cause was furthered by the political development of their armed forces. The great success of *dau tranh* in its forty years of use against France, the United States, and, later, China was twofold: it clouded enemy perceptions and nullified North Vietnam's opponents' overwhelming military power. *Dau tranh* proved highly effective against the United States. It complicated the Johnson administration's strategy and caused great misconceptions in the United States about North Vietnamese goals and overall strategy, and it forced the United States to fight under unfavorable conditions.[1]

As Rolling Thunder began in 1965, American aviators fought an air defense system that had come into being only a few years earlier. Following the 1954 Geneva Agreement, the North Vietnamese leadership devoted very little support to their air force and air defenses. The fledgling Vietnamese People's Air Force (VPAF) had fewer than a hundred aircraft, none of them fighters, and only artillery guns for air defense. In 1963 the VPAF and Vietnamese Air Defense Force merged, creating a combined force, the Air Defense Forces—Vietnam People's Air Force. Unlike the Americans, who split the air campaign with bureaucratic controls, interservice rivalries, and global commitments, all aspects of North Vietnam's air defenses became unified under this command, following the concept of *dau tranh*.

The North Vietnamese defenses began to expand in response to U.S. efforts to collect information under OPLAN 34A. Initial growth focused on radar systems, in part because American efforts in 1964 focused on harassing coastal radars stations.[2] U.S. retaliatory strikes following the Gulf of Tonkin incident spurred a marked increase in Hanoi's air defenses. North Vietnam opposed the first U.S. air raids solely with World War II era AAA units that had been produced by the Soviet Union, China, and Czechoslovakia. These included 100 mm, 85 mm, and 57 mm cannons with limited fire control systems, 37 mm and 23 mm self-tracking guns, and, amazingly enough, several of the feared German 88 mm guns captured by the Soviets in the 1940s.[3] By February 1965 American intelligence estimated that almost a thousand antiaircraft guns were deployed in North Vietnam, manned by just five thousand personnel. More notable, however, was the arrival of the first VPAF fighter regiment. MiG-15 and MiG-17 fighters arrived at Phuc Yen airfield from bases in China on 6 August, the day after the retaliatory raids.

By the time President Johnson announced the end of Rolling Thunder, the North Vietnamese air defenses had evolved into a highly integrated network of SAMs, AAA, and fighters. These defenses were manned by about 110,000 personnel, of whom 90 percent were in the air surveillance, missile, and AAA units. U.S. intelligence estimates credited Hanoi with over 150 radar sites, almost 150 SAM sites, over 8,000 AAA guns of all calibers, and 105 MiGs.[4] As with any triad, this three-pronged approach proved to be a very capable system. Hanoi could call on any combination of resources to meet the threat, whether it be AAA, SAMS, or fighters. Controlling it all was an extensive radar network providing early warning to the entire air defense system. If any segment took too many losses, the other two segments stepped up their efforts, allowing the third time to reorganize and regroup. This highly organized system forced the United States to develop extensive countermeasures and intelligence-gathering systems that required continuous upgrades to neutralize the North Vietnamese advantage. In this tit-for-tat game, each side struggled to gain and maintain any tactical advantage, however fleeting it was.

Communist Partners

Communist support to North Vietnam was a key component of the North Vietnamese strategy. While many Communist governments supported the effort through either men, matériel, or money, the efforts by China and the Soviet Union were vital. The support given the North Vietnamese Air Defense Forces by the Soviet Union was the most significant. Both the United States and the Soviet Union fielded some of their best weapons in the skies of North Vietnam, making it significant to the global balance of power and far different from the war being conducted in South Vietnam. If an American unit defeated a North Vietnamese ground unit in the jungles of Vietnam, it had little bearing on whether or not that unit was capable of defeating a similar Soviet unit in Germany. But if American forces could operate freely in a Soviet SAM environment, there were serious repercussions for Soviet forces in Europe. Likewise, if North Vietnamese MiG-21s could shoot down the latest American fighters on a continual basis, it indicated how American aircraft might fare against the Soviets if war broke out.[5]

While the Soviets supplied the technology, the Chinese supplied manpower. Between 1965 and 1973 about 320,000 People's Liberation Army (PLA) troops, both technicians and soldiers, served in North Vietnam. Over five thousand Chinese were killed or wounded, almost all casualties from U.S. air strikes.[6] Chinese pilots downed at least nine American aircraft, while Chinese antiaircraft divisions took an additional, but unknown, toll. An additional eighty thousand troops labored to build and repair airfields, bridges, and other transportation routes.[7] These numbers are a key but often overlooked aspect. Their presence allowed Hanoi to free an equivalent number of its own men to expand the fighting in the South. Even though the United States intensified its interdiction campaign, the sheer quantity of laborers allowed North Vietnam to increase capacity and improve capability. By the end of 1967, the North Vietnamese transportation system had become less vulnerable to interdiction than prior to the initiation of Rolling Thunder.[8] The presence of these Chinese laborers also sent a clear signal to both North Vietnam and the United States concerning China's willingness to influence or intervene in the ongoing war to its south.

In 1964, as North Vietnam began efforts to improve its air defenses, it asked for assistance from the Soviet Union to create an antiaircraft missile force. By the end of January 1965, preparations were completed, and the first group of Soviet advisors was scheduled to fly to Vietnam to conduct reconnaissance. This plan never came to fruition due to China's Cultural Revolution, which caused a rift in Sino-Soviet relations before eventually resulting in clashes on Damanky Island in 1969. No Soviet shipments through China to North Vietnam were allowed. The Soviet plan of sending a brigade of twelve missile batteries, a radio-engineering battalion, and two regiments of MiGs was rejected by the Chinese, who insisted that they supply the manpower and training for Soviet equipment. The Soviet Union rejected this proposal.

The problem was resolved after a February 1965 visit to Hanoi by the Soviet leader, Alexey Kosygin. During Kosygin's visit, the first American strikes of Rolling Thunder occurred. The strikes could not have been timed better. Hanoi leadership used them to their full advantage, instantly requesting the Soviet Union's help in improving their air defenses with MiGs and SAMS. The Soviets promptly agreed, considering the aid project an emergency effort. Moscow began airlifting equipment, advisors, and, more importantly, Soviet air defense units. Chinese Foreign Minister Zhou Enlai followed the Soviets, visiting Hanoi in March. Because of the rivalry, Zhou told Ho Chi Minh that China opposed the Soviet aid program. Following Zhou Enlai's warning, Ho Chi Minh challenged Beijing to provide an alternative. The result was parallel Soviet and Chinese military aid to North Vietnam, with each vying to outdo the other in an effort to gain influence over its Communist partner. The North Vietnamese used *dau tranh* to manipulate both friend and foe alike, sometimes even against each other in order to further their goal of reunification. For the VPAF this meant Russian SAMS and MiG-21 fighters, as well as the Soviet technicians required to train Vietnamese forces. The Chinese supplied MiG-17s and MiG-19s, as well as their own forces. These exchanges in early 1965 created the basis for the North Vietnamese air defenses that the United States faced throughout Rolling Thunder.[9]

Antiaircraft Artillery

SAMS were instrumental to the increased effectiveness of North Vietnam's AAA defenses. While the number of aircraft lost to SAMS was never more than a small percentage of the overall totals, the mere presence of this new technology changed American tactics and caused greater losses. Once launched, SAMS disrupted American formations, driving aircraft to lower altitudes as they evaded missiles. At these lower altitudes, small arms and radar-controlled AAA took an excessive toll. Before SAMS were introduced, American aircraft could remain at altitude, above the effective range of even the largest guns.[10] American pilots became even more vulnerable to AAA as the North Vietnamese massed guns on an unprecedented scale. Large numbers of guns were placed in small areas such as critical installations and population centers. As Rolling Thunder escalated, North Vietnam continued to increase its numbers of early warning and fire control radars, which in turn increased the lethality of its AAA. While electronic warfare technology eventually degraded the ability of the SAMS, any time a SAM was launched, aircraft were forced to defend with maneuvers. These maneuvers came at a cost of airspeed and altitude, which resulted in increased losses from AAA.

Generally speaking, AAA came in two forms, radar guided and barrage fire. Early warning radars tracked flights coming from Laos or the Tonkin Gulf and before handing targets off to air defense sectors, where they would be engaged using SON-9 (NATO code name Fire Can) fire control radars, which calculated the trajectory of the aircraft and shot along the predicted flight path. But not all North Vietnamese guns were radar controlled. In fact, most were not—and they didn't need to be. Radar control came at the cost of mobility. It was much better to have a highly mobile force that could be moved to new sites easily. Barrage AAA was more commonly seen, and American tactics resulting from the ROE and the cumbersome targeting processes certainly helped in this regard. With barrage fire, gunners did not need to aim at the aircraft but simply fired into a predetermined block of airspace that aircraft flew through to reach their target. Often, weather and low ceilings further restricted the directions from which American aircraft attacked, making North Vietnamese barrage fire even more effective.

Surface-to-Air Missiles

With support from the new Soviet premier, Leonid Brezhnev, North Vietnam began receiving military aid and advisors as it built its air defenses. The aid included the s-75 Dvina (NATO code name SA-2 Guideline) SAM. First deployed to East Germany in 1959, the SA-2 had seen sporadic use since 1960. However, its first real test came in Vietnam. Designed to destroy high-altitude strategic bombers, it was used against smaller, highly maneuverable tactical fighters flying at low altitudes. The North Vietnamese had little choice, because although the Soviets had the s-125 Neva (SA-3 Goa), they were unwilling to supply North Vietnam with their most advanced SAM. One of the most important weapon systems of the Cold War, the SA-2 revolutionized modern air warfare. Its introduction to the skies of North Vietnam kicked off what came to be known as the "Wizard's War," which resulted in constant advances in electronic warfare, with each side battling to overcome the other's electronic weaponry.

North Vietnam activated its first SAM regiment on 7 January 1965. The regiment received the highest national priority; political officers searched the armed forces, universities, and technical schools of North Vietnam to find the best electricians, technicians, mechanics, and engineers to fill its ranks.[11] Vietnamese who had studied in the Soviet Union and knew Russian were the first ones selected to attend the training centers, followed by candidates with previous electrical and radio-engineering experience, as well as students. No one with less than eight years of education was permitted to attend.[12] Soviet doctrine required four months to train a missile regiment; however, this was shortened to two and a half months. Due to Chinese demands, the number of personnel was also dropped from seventy-five specialists to thirty-six. By May Vietnamese students had begun training on the actual systems, though this training was also cut short in order to deploy the missile systems to Hanoi and Haiphong. Rolling Thunder had begun in earnest, and the systems were desperately needed to help bolster AAA defenses and defend the two cities.

As agreed upon, the Soviets took the lead for missile air defense. They trained North Vietnamese crews in the Soviet Union while sending large numbers of air defense (Protivo Vozdushnaya Oborona Strany, or PVO-Strany) personnel to man ten training centers being formed in North Vietnam. These centers became the core of new SAM regiments. Missiles, launchers, and Soviet advisors from the Moscow and Bako PVO-Strany districts, headed by Gen. Maj. Grigoriy Belov, arrived in late April 1965 to begin training the Vietnamese. The first few Vietnamese SAM regiments were based around Soviet cadres; for example, the 274th Missile Regiment was based around the Soviet 260th SAM Regiment from Bryanks. Soviet officers commanded the regiment, its four launch batteries, and its associated technical battalion.[13]

It was not until 24 July 1965 that the first American loss to a SAM occurred. While reconnaissance flights had detected SAMS as early as April, there had been no electronic intelligence (ELINT) indicating they were operational until 23 July 1965. On that day, an air force RB-66 electronic warfare reconnaissance aircraft picked up signals from the missile guidance radar. The ROE in place at the time prevented U.S. aircraft from attacking the site before it became operational. The next day, the 236th Regiment, commanded by Colonel Tsygankov, shot down an air force F-4C and damaged three others during a strike on the Lang Chi munitions plant northwest of Hanoi. Because there had been insufficient time to train Vietnamese crews, Soviet personnel actually conducted the engagement. North Vietnamese crews finally conducted a full engagement on their own on 24 August 1965.[14]

By autumn, a second SAM regiment, the 238th Missile Regiment under Colonel Bazhenov, became operational. The two regiments fielded anywhere from six to twelve missile batteries, which constantly moved between thirty-two prepared sites. Due to the small number of AAA batteries, there was no way to establish an effective, mutually supporting defensive system. After each engagement, missile batteries moved to lessen the chance of destruction.

By February 1966 two more missile regiments had been fielded, the 261st, commanded by Colonel Zavadskiy, and the 274th, commanded by Colonel Fedorov. By 1967–68 Vietnamese officers had gradually taken over regimental command, with a Soviet officer delegated as a technical advisor, although some Soviet officers remained as battery commanders through 1969. Despite North Vietnamese successes with the SA-2, Soviet advisors and technicians continued to serve with North Vietnamese missile units at the battalion and regimental level for the remainder of the war.

Typical SA-2 batteries consisted of four to six missile launchers deployed around a circle. From overhead, crisscrossing supply roads looked like a Star of David, with the missiles at the ends—the telltale sign of the SA-2 layout per Soviet doctrine. At the center of the circle was the SNR-75 (NATO Code name Fan Song) radar needed to guide missiles, as well as communications vans supporting the battery. Most sites had their own early warning radar, a P-12 (NATO code name Spoon Rest). All sites were interconnected and capable of handing off targets to others nearby. Later in the war, P-35 (NATO code name Bar Lock) early warning radars added to this capability. These radars also did double duty, as the air picture they provided was then used to control intercepts of the emerging MiG forces. Because of the conspicuous Star of David pattern, each battery had additional sites that they rotated between. No less than three AAA regiments protected each battery or simulated position.[15] SAMs and AAA proved to be a deadly combination, something the Vietnamese and their Communist allies proved time and again. By June 1967 Hanoi was protected by the most lethal air defense network ever assembled. The 365th and 367th Air Defense Divisions had been brought into Hanoi to reinforce the 361st Division. The Air Defense Command had committed ten AAA regiments and five SAM regiments, totaling 60 percent of North Vietnam's available AAA batteries and 52 percent of its SAM battalions along with the entire VPAF to the defense of Hanoi.[16]

MiGs

The fighters flown by the VPAF provided the final critical link in the North Vietnamese Air Defenses. Because of their limited numbers and their pilots' limited abilities, MiGs were used sparingly. As pilot training continued and capabilities increased, MiGs tended to attack only when the outcome favored victory. Their focus remained intercepting American strike packages and forcing them to jettison their bombs prior to reaching the intended target. As Rolling Thunder progressed, the North Vietnamese fighter regiments became more critical in the integrated defensive network. As losses mounted within the AAA and SAM battalions, MiGs became more active in order to lessen the pressure. Conversely, when fighter regiments suffered setbacks and losses, the AAA and SAM battalions stepped up to fill the void.

The 921st Fighter Regiment arrived at Phuc Yen in August 1964 and was followed by the 923rd Fighter Regiment a year later at Kep. They would eventually be consolidated under the 371st Air Force Division in March 1967. In 1965 the 921st Fighter Regiment consisted of thirty-six MiG-15 and MiG-17 fighters flown into Vietnam from Mengtzu, China. Chinese pilots stayed at Phuc Yen as instructors into early 1965.[17] In December more MiGs arrived from China, bringing the total to fifty-three. The Chinese pilots served under the pretense of instructors, though they sometimes engaged in combat. Training fledgling Vietnamese pilots was a gargantuan task, because many of the men had never operated anything more advanced than a bicycle. To train these Vietnamese not only as pilots but as advanced tacticians in jet aircraft was no small feat. There were no tour-of-duty limitations for the Vietnamese pilots. Once they started flying, they flew combat missions until they were killed or they were promoted to training and administrative roles. While the Vietnamese pilots did not keep log books, it was not unusual for VPAF pilots to accumulate six hundred to seven hundred missions during the war.[18] The VPAF quickly grew from a poorly organized group of inadequately trained pilots flying antiquated Communist aircraft into a highly effective fighting force capable of holding its own over the skies of North Vietnam.

Chinese influence began to fade in mid-1965 as Soviet advisors assumed a bigger role. This coincided with the arrival of Soviet-supplied MiG-21s in July 1965. From that point on, the Soviets began intensive training of the Vietnamese ground-control intercept (GCI) network. Soviet pilots typically flew the target aircraft, teaching Vietnamese pilots how to perform the intercept. At the same time, the Vietnamese trained with their ground controllers, who were also being trained by the Soviet advisors. The total number of Soviets involved with training, including pilots, controllers, and advisors, never totaled more than thirty men at any given time, and they restricted their activities to training and performing acceptance test flights of the new MiG-21s. However, despite all this effort, Soviet pilots avoided actual combat.[19]

North Korea also sent pilots to help the North Vietnamese. Unlike the Soviets and Chinese, however, their sole purpose was to fight. The first contingent arrived on 20 September 1966 and eventually grew to thirty-four MiG-17 pilots. Initially deployed to Phuc Yen, the North Korean pilots deployed to Kep in April 1967 just in time to take part in some of the largest air battles of the war. Despite losses, they continued to participate in engagements throughout the remainder of Rolling Thunder, eventually withdrawing in early February 1969.

The VPAF used three different jet fighters throughout Rolling Thunder. These included the MiG-17, MiG-19, and MiG-21, all products of the famed Soviet aircraft manufacturer Mikoyan-Gurevich. The MiG-17, though antiquated by the start of the bombing campaign, remained the workhorse throughout the conflict. The MiG-19 was used in very limited numbers and was only supplied to the Vietnamese after 1968. The MiG-21, however, proved itself a deadly opponent upon its introduction in January 1966. It represented a colossal leap in capabilities for the VPAF, including air-to-air missiles. The MiG-21 could carry two Soviet K-13 (AA-2 Atoll) heat-seeking missiles. The AA-2 was reverse engineered from the U.S. AIM-9B Sidewinder. Besides the fact that it represented an espionage coup by the Soviets, the mere presence of the AA-2 in Vietnam forced a change in American tactics. Because of this capability, the bulk of the VPAF's air-to-air victories were made by pilots flying the MiG-21, which was at the time the best fighter produced by the Soviets.

Although North Vietnamese MiGs did engage navy strikes, air force missions were more frequently targeted. The reasons for this were two-fold. First, the proximity of aircraft carriers to the coast meant that navy aircraft spent less time en route to the target, denying the Air Defense Command sufficient time for the elaborate ground-controlled intercepts needed by MiG pilots. Second, the tactical formations flown by the navy, known as "Loose Deuce," proved relatively hard to counter. The air force's rigid formations were dictated by its electronic jamming pods, which made them easier prey for Vietnamese hit-and-run tactics, because if an aircraft broke formation, it lost its jammer protection and disrupted the overall protection of the flight.[20] These formations and the long distances flown by the air force from Thailand to North Vietnam meant the North Vietnamese had plenty of time to set up attacks in which MiG-21s attacked unseen from the rear and could usually escape before their presence was known.

The Weather

The uncertain and unpredictable nature of the Vietnamese weather was a factor that heavily favored the North Vietnamese and significantly improved their defensive capability. Precision weaponry such as GPS and laser-guided bombs that have dominated recent American conflicts did not exist during Rolling Thunder. In order to successfully bomb a target, the pilot had to see it. Any obscuration of the target or the route used to fly and navigate to the target could and often would result in the strike being canceled. During certain months of the year, the weather over North Vietnam posed severe limitations to air operations. During the winter, or the northeast monsoon, which starts in November and lasts until mid-May, the weather over North Vietnam and the Gulf of Tonkin is characterized by heavy clouds and large amounts of rainfall. Conditions are especially harsh when a weather phenomenon known as "crachin" occurs. Crachin is characterized by thick clouds and ceilings as low as 100 feet in combination with fog and persistent drizzle. Conversely, during the summer, or the southwest monsoon from May to October, the skies are generally clear and dry. This is the opposite of the monsoon seasons in South Vietnam and Laos. It is important, therefore, in any discussion of air operations over North Vietnam to keep in mind what weather period was involved.[21]

During the winter monsoon, cloud cover is usually low, about 6,000 feet, with solid overcast above. For a pilot to acquire the target in such weather, he had to descend through the cloud layer and fly between 4,000 and 6,000 feet, where he became increasingly vulnerable to ground fire. North Vietnamese gunners regularly knew the altitude of the cloud ceilings, so pilots were forced to fly even lower, into the effective range of small arms, to avoid being at a known altitude. The low ceilings also required the use of horizontal or low-angle bombing, which also brought aircraft closer to AAA. Finally, the low ceilings restricted the directions from which American aircraft could attack, making North Vietnamese barrage fire more effective. Under these conditions, strikes into North Vietnam would often be canceled, and the already strenuous task of landing aboard an aircraft carrier became a recipe for disaster.[22] Rear Adm. Dave Richardson, who commanded Carrier Task Force 77 (CTF-77) during 1966 and 1967, described how the weather affected the air war: "The nature of the weather in Vietnam was also a vital factor in the interdiction campaign that was never fully appreciated by Washington. With the centralized control of the war from afar, Washington could not keep in touch with the ever-changing weather which often required on-the-scene changes in target and weapon assignments."[23]

The weather's influence on operations cannot be understated. It was often responsible for hundreds of canceled or aborted missions; it delayed launch and recovery aboard the ship, which in turn delayed formation rendezvous; and it prevented aerial refueling or created difficulties for aircraft attempting to rendezvous for in-flight refueling. Poor weather forced aircraft to deviate from planned routes or planned targets, leaving pilots with the option of hitting their secondary target or aborting the mission. Quite simply, the weather was a large factor that played into every mission flown over North Vietnam and was not understood by the civilian leadership controlling the air war from thousands of miles away.

The Gulf of Tonkin

When examining the factors affecting the navy's air war, the geography of the northern Tonkin Gulf also deserves special consideration. The Communist Chinese island of Hainan dominates the Tonkin Gulf.

While launching planes in an already constrained area, the navy was required to honor the 3-mile international limit, further restraining the already crowded waters of the gulf. At 13,000 square miles, Hainan boasted numerous airfields, from which Chinese MiGs harassed and sometimes even attacked navy aircraft. Throughout the war, navy fighters flew combat air patrols (CAPs) to prevent not only North Vietnamese aircraft from attacking the fleet but also Chinese aircraft. These missions were a constant requirement for fighter squadrons whose pilots and maintenance personnel were being worn out by the pace of Rolling Thunder operations.

The Tonkin Gulf also had large amounts of seaborne traffic. Although CTF-77 usually operated more than 100 nautical miles from the coast, it was constantly surrounded by hundreds of small fishing boats and junks. Under the international law of the sea, these vessels often had the right-of-way. Therefore, it was not uncommon for a fishing trawler to cross the bow of an aircraft carrier engaged in flight operations, forcing it to alter course and cause a delay of critical launches and recoveries. The greatest danger, however, came from the early warning capabilities of these vessels. Most boats carried a radio, and within minutes of the navy launching aircraft, these boats would send Air Defense Command in Hanoi information about the number and types of aircraft bound for North Vietnam.[24] The Soviets excelled at this practice, and wherever the carrier went, a Soviet "trawler" was always within sight. Known as "tattletale ships," their ongoing mission was to relay the number and type of aircraft launched. As a reminder of Cold War tensions, the Soviets occasionally attempted to interrupt flight operations by crossing in front of the carrier, thereby forcing it off course. As this all happened in international waters, there was little that could be done to stop it.

Despite the early warning provided by Soviet and North Vietnamese vessels, the Tonkin Gulf did give the navy a tactical advantage not available to the air force. Because aircraft carriers could be positioned close to the shore, little to no aerial refueling was needed for large strikes over North Vietnam. There are several instances of captains sailing their aircraft carriers north, away from Yankee Station, in order to lessen the premission refueling requirements or to give fuel-critical aircraft a chance to make it home safely following harrowing missions. Additionally, the navy strikes could fly extremely low over the water, below radar coverage, and get to their target in a matter of minutes, limiting the time available for North Vietnamese defenses to react. Even when navy aircraft struck as far inland as Hanoi, the time from the coast to the target was much less than the time it took an air force strike group to arrive from Thailand via Laos.[25] This became more of a factor later in the campaign as the VPAF grew and trained, eventually allowing them to begin intercepting Rolling Thunder missions more frequently. Unlike the hostile terrain of North Vietnam and Laos, the gulf also provided a safe haven for crippled aircraft. The probability of a successful rescue increased dramatically if a pilot could just make it past the coastline, where rescues could be performed with much less opposition.

3

The Naval Air War

As the air war grew, the number of ships committed to the war put an unforeseen strain on the carrier fleet. Although the navy had over twenty aircraft carriers to cover its global commitments, not all were attack carriers suitable for operations in Rolling Thunder.[1] As a result, older 27C class carriers continued to operate throughout the war, even though they were at a distinct disadvantage compared to the new carriers with larger and more capable air wings. Initially, the war was fought by carriers from the Pacific fleet, but in mid-1965 Atlantic fleet carriers began participating in the war. The navy's only nuclear-powered aircraft carrier, USS *Enterprise* (CVAN-65), was transferred to the Pacific fleet in late 1965 to assist in the war effort. To further compensate for the shortage of carriers, the navy extended the duration of line periods for aircraft carriers on Yankee Station in the Tonkin Gulf beyond the normal three weeks and the length of their deployments beyond the six-month standard.[2] Carrier deployments during Rolling Thunder ranged from seven to ten months, though many went longer as the war grew. A carrier remained on the line from twenty-five to thirty-five days or longer before port calls in the Philippines, Hong Kong, or Japan.

Standard procedure called for a carrier to complete four line periods prior to returning stateside, although exceptions were common.[3] Training turnaround time between deployments, traditionally used for ship repairs, maintenance, and schools, was also reduced. The long deployments and limited time for refit caused even more problems, as the 27C class carriers either had reached the end of their functional lives or required a major overhaul. Major overhauls involved extended periods in a shipyard or dry dock for twelve to eighteen months, depending on the amount of work performed.[4] Any withdrawal of a carrier from combat caused follow-on effects throughout the navy. Thus the carrier fleet was gradually worn down, and 27C class carriers that should have been decommissioned continued to make cruises through the end of the war.[5] Accidents also affected the fleet. Three tragic fires on different carriers put ships out of action for prolonged periods. The disabling of carriers by fires increased the pressure on remaining ships and inadvertently amplified the degradation of the carrier fleet, a problem that continued to affect the fleet until the late seventies.[6]

Yankee Station

During Rolling Thunder, carriers operated from an area known as Yankee Station. From the outset, a minimum of two carriers operated from Yankee Station, plus one on Dixie Station, with one more on its way from the United States and one on its way home, for a total of five carriers at any given time. Of the two aircraft carriers on the line, each conducted flight operations for twelve hours and then stood down for twelve hours for maintenance. One carrier operated as the daytime carrier, while the other carrier operated as the night carrier. If carrier availability allowed three carriers on station, the schedule was designated Red, White, or Blue. One ship would fly from midnight to noon (Red), another from 0600 to 1800 (White), and the third from noon to midnight (Blue). This schedule had the advantage of allowing for double coverage during the daylight hours while still allowing for a twelve-hour stand-down. The schedule rotated every few weeks as carriers withdrew from the operating area for port calls or to replenish. Afterward, the schedule often flip-flopped, with carriers reversing their schedules.

Aircraft carriers conducted two types of flight operations: cyclic operations and Alpha strikes. During cyclic operations, anywhere from twenty-five to forty aircraft were launched every ninety minutes. After aircraft were launched, the carrier then recovered any airborne aircraft before preparing for the next launch. This sequence repeated itself throughout the day, with aircraft continually launching for and recovering from missions over Vietnam. When a target required a major strike, the aircraft carrier shifted operations to the Alpha strike. All available airplanes were launched in a single strike group to attack the specified target, which was likely in the vicinity of Hanoi or Haiphong. Alpha strikes interrupted cyclic operations for two hours as sailors loaded ordnance and prepared the flight deck for the upcoming strike. A carrier could launch two to three Alpha strikes a day, with cyclic operations conducted in between. It was a brutal schedule.

The missions flown during these operations cover a broad spectrum. They can be divided into several categories, including Alpha strikes, armed reconnaissance, and general support sorties. Alpha strikes included not only the attack missions but also Iron Hand missions to help suppress North Vietnamese defenses, flak (AAA) suppression missions, fighter combat air patrols (CAPS), and various support missions. Armed reconnaissance missions were flown both day and night to interdict North Vietnamese supplies. Support missions were the often mundane but vital missions that enabled the war over North Vietnam, including tanker sorties, electronic warfare, and early warning missions. Extremely high risk missions included photo reconnaissance missions and combat search and recovery (CSAR). Separate from all of these missions were close air support (CAS) missions flown "in-country," meaning South Vietnam, and Operation Steel Tiger, the covert bombing of Laos.

Alpha Strikes

Significant targets were listed in the "Alpha" section of the JCS master target list, used to select targets during the Tuesday luncheon; thus, missions against those targets became known as Alpha strikes. Alpha strikes were a major undertaking against heavily defended targets, although the size and scope varied. They could involve one or more carriers on Yankee Station or even be conducted in conjunction with air force aircraft. As one commanding officer noted, "Any mission in the North carried personal risks, but each Alpha strike took on a life of its own. The mere intonation of the words 'Alpha strike' sent shivers up my spine."[7]

Rolling Thunder was an attack pilot's war, and the responsibility of leading these missions fell upon a small cadre of men. Typically only the air wing commander, jet attack squadron commanding officers and executive officers, and a select few experienced senior officers in the attack squadrons were allowed to lead such strikes. The stress and workload were immense—mission success and survival of their fellow aviators depended on their ability to plan and lead the strikes.

While certain aspects of Alpha strikes were determined by the Johnson administration, each air wing's tactics evolved in an effort to be successful and survive to fight another day.

Armed Reconnaissance

Armed reconnaissance missions were the main focus of Rolling Thunder and were flown continually in an attempt to interdict the flow of supplies. These missions were flown both day and night with a minimum of two aircraft. Pilots sought specific types of targets as delineated in the current rules of engagement of each phase. One week it might be trucks or barges, the next week POL storage, transshipment points, and bridges. Time spent over North Vietnam varied with each mission and was dependent on the area to be covered and targets available—it could be as little as fifteen minutes or as much as ninety. Pilots avoided known AAA locations whenever possible, and in areas with no known defenses, they flew as low as possible in order to detect camouflaged trucks, trains, barges, and POL storage areas. Trying to spot targets hidden under trees while flying upward of 360 knots was a difficult task. It was not impossible, however, and after enough missions aviators became adept at spotting potential targets by finding tire tracks leading from roads to sidings or bridges and storage facilities hidden in the jungle.

While daytime armed reconnaissance sorties occasionally yielded positive results and offered a small respite from the gut-wrenching fear and adrenaline of Alpha strikes, nighttime armed reconnaissance missions were in a terrifying league of their own. Flights of two aircraft would fly in a preassigned sector, with their position lights out, with no ability to see each other or keep from hitting each other while searching for targets. Each aircraft carried a load of six MK 24 parachute flares, which would be dropped to illuminate any target found. If pilots were lucky enough to find and illuminate trucks or barges, they then had to attack under the dim light of the flares. The disorientation caused by such conditions often resulted in pilots flying into the ground. One squadron history openly questioned the value of these missions: "The effectiveness of the A-4E at night in locating and destroying targets of opportunity is a highly debatable subject.... In many cases it was the Air Wing pilots that were being harassed rather than the enemy."[8] When considering that these sorties were flown at night in heavily defended and often mountainous terrain, nighttime armed reconnaissance missions had limited success. Pilots then faced a nighttime carrier landing upon completing the mission. These missions caused immeasurable strain on pilots already worn down by the frenetic pace.

Iron Hand Missions

After SAMs became operational in 1965, the United States rushed to find and destroy them before they claimed more aircraft. On 12 August 1965 Admiral Sharp ordered Operation Iron Hand to destroy SAM batteries in North Vietnam. Thus Iron Hand became the name for American attempts to counter North Vietnamese SAMs. By 1966 these missions were centered around the AGM-45 Shrike, an antiradiation missile capable of homing in on North Vietnamese radar signals. These missions were mostly flown in support of Alpha strikes or any other mission in which a major SAM threat was recognized. They were considered some of the most terrifying and costliest missions flown throughout the war.[9]

The main problem affecting Iron Hand attrition rates was that naval aviators received little training in the mission. It was another mission to be mastered along with all the others already flown by attack pilots. Most air wings assigned the mission to one attack squadron in order to help familiarize pilots, but it meant the same pilots flew the deadly mission each time. For the most part, the training received by pilots involved listening to audio recordings of Fire Can and Fan Song radars in various states of activity and learning proper switch positions between missions.[10] Success depended on that training and actual combat on the wing of a senior pilot who may or may not have had more experience flying the Iron Hand mission. Simply put, it became a matter of on-the-job training in a high-stakes environment.

Typically flown by A-4 Skyhawks and a fighter escort, Iron Hand aircraft weaved ahead and above the strike group, listening for SAM radar signals on their APR-25. Once in the vicinity of the target, Iron Hand pilots then placed themselves between the SAMs and the strike. Orbiting between 8,000 and 10,000 feet and 8 to 10 miles from the SAM site, these aircraft were well inside the effective range of the SA-2 missiles they were hunting. For this reason, most squadrons kept a minimum amount of ordnance, usually a mix of Shrike and Zuni rockets, on the aircraft to increase their maneuverability.[11] While this tactic generated a higher SAM kill rate, it took nerves of steel, as the Shrike was slower than the SA-2. As one pilot related, "It was near suicidal to fire a Shrike at an SA-2 site that had missiles guiding on you because their missiles would get to you before your Shrike got to them."[12] Once it was fired, the detonation of the Shrike highlighted the position of the SAM site for follow-on attacks. However, SAM sites were always well defended by AAA, making attacks dicey at best.

North Vietnamese radar operators eventually became skilled enough to detect the launch of Shrike missiles from the Iron Hand aircraft. This allowed them time to shut down their radar while the Shrike was in the air, giving the missile nothing to home in on. American pilots did not necessarily consider this a bad thing, because if the radar was off, it was unable to cue either guns or missiles. The problem stemmed from the fact that the radar was not destroyed, allowing the operator to turn it back on after the Iron Hand aircraft had launched all their Shrikes. Iron Hand pilots eventually developed tactics whereupon they launched Zuni rockets first. The Vietnamese would see the missile and turn off their radars. Then, after the prescribed time, the radars came back on. While the radars were off, the pilot launched a Shrike, and the missile then homed in on the now-radiating radar. It was a cat-and-mouse game that required incredible bravery.

Flak Suppression

There was a wide range of opinion among air wings as to the use and viability of flak suppression. The suppression flight flew alongside the main strike force until they neared the target. At a prearranged point, they accelerated ahead to attack the defenses surrounding the target. By attacking the AAA sites first, American pilots forced North Vietnamese gunners to seek shelter when attack aircraft were most vulnerable: during their dive on the target, when pilots concentrated solely on the target and were unable to react to defensive fire.[13] The main benefit of this tactic came from the psychological boost it gave attack pilots, as flak suppressors were never able to completely suppress the Vietnamese AAA threat.

Although attack aircraft could be used for flak suppression, doing so meant less aircraft available to meet sortie requirements. As a result, fighters often became the primary aircraft used in this mission. This compounded the problem faced by older 27C class carriers and increased the risk they faced.[14] Air wings flying from larger carriers were comprised of newer airplanes capable of carrying greater amounts of ordnance. While some variants of the F-8 Crusader could carry ordnance from their wings, it was nowhere near the load carried by the Phantom, leaving air wings flying from the smaller carriers at a distinct disadvantage.

Fighter Missions: Air-to-Air Combat

Fighter squadrons flew a variety of support missions during Rolling Thunder, including escort missions for Iron Hand, photo recce missions, and combat air patrols (CAPs). Escort missions tended to be dangerous and terrifying solely because of the hazard each mission entailed: either dueling with SAMs as an Iron Hand escort or making high-speed passes over highly defended targets while escorting reconnaissance runs. Barrier CAP (BARCAP) missions were seen mostly as a nuisance and flown to prevent Communist aircraft from attacking the fleet. Whether or not the threat was real, the requirement strained already overtasked men and equipment. Target CAP (TARCAP) missions were used mainly during Alpha strikes in order to protect the attack aircraft in the vicinity of the target. Fighters established an orbit between the target and nearby MiG bases to guard against airborne MiGs.[15]

Fighters received a disproportionate amount of attention during Rolling Thunder. It stemmed from their surprisingly poor performance and less than stellar kill-to-loss ratio—all a result of the overreliance on technology and concentration on defending against nuclear war. The leap in aviation technology in the preceding decade, combined with advances in missiles and radars, resulted in aberrant thinking. Fighters developed for both the navy and air force during the period were designed to destroy hordes of Soviet bombers with long-range missiles before they reached the United States. This concentration on nuclear attack interception capabilities and an overreliance on technology meant that traditional fighter pilot skills atrophied.[16] This tremendous oversight came into focus over the skies of North Vietnam as pilots from both the air force and navy managed only a 2.5 to 1 kill ratio throughout the war. During World War II kill ratios were as high as 14 to 1.[17] The

United States could ill afford such an exchange rate, especially when considering the cost of such advanced aircraft and the cost it took to train the aviators compared to relatively cheaper Soviet aircraft.

Several factors contributed to the poor performance. Training for basic air-to-air combat took a backseat to long-range intercepts. Unfortunately, the ROE negated the advantage of any long-range missiles, forcing fighter crews to visually identify MiGs in case they accidentally engaged a civilian airliner or one of the International Control Commission (ICC) flights.[18] Once they identified the MiGs, fighter crews were wholly unprepared for the ensuing fight, which often hinged on completely unreliable missiles. It is no understatement to call the air-to-air missiles used during Rolling Thunder abject failures. The AIM-7 Sparrow suffered failure rates as high as 80 percent. A highly complex missile, its sensitive electronics could not stand up to the rigors of combat, from the heat and humidity of Southeast Asia, the high Gs of flight, and the rough handling aboard the aircraft carriers. Once engaged in aerial combat, the woes continued. As a radar-guided missile, the Sparrow depended on the launching fighter to illuminate its target. During a fight, crews often did not have the time needed to establish a radar lock. Once the missile was in the air, anything that degraded that lock, from ground clutter to maneuvering, made the missile miss. The AIM-9 Sidewinder was simpler and more reliable than the AIM-7; however, the Sidewinder still suffered a 56 percent failure rate. An infrared guided missile, it homed in on hot engine exhaust. Early variants suffered from an extremely small firing envelope and problems with the guidance. Pilots had no way of knowing if they were within the constantly changing employment envelope, or the area in which a missile could be successfully fired. Resembling a cone, the area constantly changed according to airspeed, altitude, and range to the target. In order for the earlier variants of the AIM-9 to guide, pilots had to position themselves almost directly behind the target aircraft, something that was nearly impossible during the extreme maneuvers of aerial combat. The guidance system also suffered problems, in that it could and often did guide toward the sun, clouds, or even the earth if one of these elements gave off greater infrared energy than the target. All of these failures compounded to drive down the kill-to-loss ratio to unacceptable levels.[19]

Perhaps the most important aspect of the poor showing is that it need not have happened at all. While the VPAF remained a threat, the existence of MiGs was really more of a nuisance. The bigger threat came from the lethal combination of SAMs and the massive quantity of AAA. However, the tight restrictions meant that Vietnamese airfields were off-limits, and the MiG threat, just like the SAMs, matured unmolested.

Electronic Warfare

The appearance of the SA-2 and its associated early warning network forced the United States out of its complacency with regard to electronic warfare. As North Vietnamese defenses grew, they became increasingly effective by using radars to control their AAA and SAMs. Both the American air force and the navy had airborne jamming aircraft that could jam early warning and fire control radars; however, these aircraft were few and far between. The navy and air force responded with crash programs to field new jamming platforms and self-protect jammers for tactical aircraft.

During Rolling Thunder, the navy depended on the aging A-1 Skyraider, specifically, the EA-1F, to fill its jamming needs. Only twenty-four aircraft existed, and they struggled to cover all of the navy's worldwide electronic warfare requirements.[20] Additionally, it was clear from the outset that the EA-1F was rapidly falling behind the threat due to its age and performance limitations. With vacuum tube technology and manually steered jammers, it was severely limited in both frequency coverage and power output, but it was the only aircraft capable of countering the growing threat. The EAK-3B Skywarrior and the EA-6B Prowler would eventually replace it, but not before Rolling Thunder ended.

Due to their vulnerability, EA-1s remained out over the Tonkin Gulf, which limited their effectiveness. The aircraft cruised at only 140 knots and had to be launched well in advance of any strike they were protecting. They usually operated in pairs, orbiting 5,000 feet above the North Vietnamese coastline. When an early warning radar was detected, the EA-1 pilots turned toward it and began jamming. As they reached the coast, pilots performed a Split-S, rolling inverted and diving in a manner similar to the bottom arc of an S. At the end of the maneuver, they began climbing outbound to begin the process anew.[21]

While EA-IS could degrade early warning and AAA fire control radars, they had insufficient power to counter the SAM threat. While the air force and navy both realized the need for self-protection capability, the navy acted first. In mid-1965 the navy began outfitting its aircraft with the APR-25 radar warning receiver (RWR) or radar homing and warning (RHAW) system. Coupled with the APR-26 launch warning receiver (LWR), which detected a power increase from the Fan Song radar upon SAM launch, these systems warned a pilot when he was being tracked and if a missile had been launched.[22]

If a pilot was alerted and saw the missile as it launched, he stood a chance. Evasive techniques were developed at China Lake that allowed pilots to perform last-ditch lifesaving maneuvers.[23] The SA-2's high speed and relatively small control surfaces meant that it could not match high-G turns performed by tactical aircraft. If the pilot spotted the launch, he could avoid the missile with a hard, descending turn into the missile, followed by a rapid pull-up and a high-G barrel roll around the missile. These maneuvers took nerves of steel and split-second timing. Time of flight for a SAM was somewhere around thirty seconds, though it seemed like a lifetime to the targeted pilot. If a pilot started his maneuvers too early, the missile had ample time to correct its course. If he started too late, the pilot had little chance of defeating the missile and its proximity fuze in the endgame.

A missile exploding anywhere within 300 feet usually caused catastrophic damage. Within 200 feet it was fatal. Of course, Soviet doctrine called for a second follow-on shot after the first. Most pilots, if they saw the first, usually never saw the second. Pilots initially believed that going low was the only way to avoid the SA-2. Of course, this had the unintentional effect of placing aircraft in small arms range, where even a farmer with a rusty rifle could theoretically bring down a plane with a well-aimed shot.

The combination of RWR gear and evasive maneuvers helped to an extent, but self-protect jammers were still needed. The air force adopted an external jamming pod, while the navy, limited by space availability on the carrier and unwilling to give up valuable weapons pylons that held bombs, went with jammers designed to fit inside the airframe. Under the aptly named Project Shoehorn, the navy mounted the ALQ-51 deception jammer in its tactical jet aircraft. Because the

ALQ-51 was small, it had relatively low power output. Rather than use excess power to jam radars, the ALQ-51 was a deception jammer that sent a false return signal to the SAM or AAA radar, the premise being that the confused radar operator would not be able to figure out which return signal to fire on.[24]

While Project Shoehorn was initially a success, it was not without its difficulties. Initial ALQ-51 reliability was poor, and for most of 1965 the navy had no self-protect jammer. Capt. Julian Lake oversaw the Shoehorn program at China Lake. Known as "Mr. EW," his knowledge was the driving force behind the program's success. He later noted the difficulties in teaching the importance of electronic warfare. Aviators lacked hands-on training, as equipment was sent to Yankee Station. This led to further issues, as the fleet couldn't use it, maintain it, or repair it properly. He explained: "When they were about to launch a plane they wouldn't send it if they couldn't start an engine, they wouldn't send it if the wings wouldn't spread, they wouldn't send it if the radio didn't work. We had to convince them not to send it if the EW equipment didn't work."[25] Lacking proper training, aircrew continually flew with their ALQ-51 gear in standby mode. Once they detected a missile site about to engage them, they would turn it on, lessening the effect of the system.[26] As the program came to fruition, the ALQ-51 began proving its worth. In 1966 the loss rate to SAMs eventually fell to one plane per fifty missiles fired, compared to one plane per ten missiles with no ALQ-51.[27]

The tit-for-tat game continued as each side sought to counter the other's technological advantage and electronic warfare finally came of age. On several occasions, North Vietnamese defenses were overwhelmed by American electronic warfare. However, North Vietnamese leaders attributed each defeat to internal ideological weaknesses and mistakes, not American superiority in firepower and technology. North Vietnamese leaders knew that if they ever allowed themselves and their subordinates to blame their problems on U.S. material and technological superiority, defeatism would spread through the ranks like wildfire.[28] Faith in the ultimate success of their cause became a matter of dogma, and political officers stood by, ready to reeducate any who faltered.

Tankers

Aerial refueling was one of the least glamorous but extremely vital missions flown during the war. While early jets were faster than their propeller-driven counterparts, they burned fuel at higher rates and often did not have the range for longer strikes. These shortcomings were alleviated by aerial tanking. By trailing a refueling hose and drogue, a tanker could transfer thousands of pounds of fuel per minute to other aircraft. While A-4 Skyhawks were capable of performing the tanking mission using a refueling pod known as a buddy store, it meant less attack aircraft for the daily sortie requirements. The tanker mission thus fell upon the A-3 Skywarrior. Known as the Whale, it first flew in 1952 and was intended for use as the navy's heavy bomber. The introduction of ballistic missile submarines ended its role as a nuclear bomber, and it was relegated to a tanker or conventional bomber. It was the largest aircraft operating on the carrier, which limited it to small numbers. The A-3 did fly some bombing missions over both North and South Vietnam, but the growing threat prevented practical use, and it proved more valuable as an airborne tanker. The Skywarrior not only extended the range of a strike force but also saved returning aircraft that were short on fuel. KA-3 detachments were responsible for countless "saves," that is, saving jet aircraft critically low on fuel and unable to make it back to the ship. There are numerous instances of Whales flying into North Vietnam to help save aircraft providing cover for downed pilots or to save planes leaking fuel from battle damage. Such missions, while not routine, were all in a day's work.

Early Warning

The Grumman E-1B Tracer provided airborne early warning (AEW) for the navy. A radial engine propeller aircraft introduced during the mid-1950s, the E-1B Tracer was already being replaced by Grumman's E-2A Hawkeye when Rolling Thunder began. The Tracer soldiered on for the duration of the war while slowly being replaced on the larger aircraft carriers. As with all the newer aircraft coming on line, the Hawkeye had greater capability but was too large to operate from the 27C class carriers. Typical AEW missions provided radar coverage, including MiG warnings, as their air wings flew missions over Vietnam. Tracers operated from a standoff position over the Gulf of Tonkin, where the crew could spot North Vietnamese MiGs as they launched to intercept strikes. At the completion of its mission, the aircraft flew to Da Nang to refuel before launching on another mission. After this second mission, the Tracer recovered aboard the carrier. This arrangement provided excellent radar coverage and at the same time freed up much-needed deck space, which was always at a premium on the smaller carriers. Without the rather large E-1B on the flight deck, it was much easier to respot aircraft and position them for the next launch.

Photo Reconnaissance: Operation Blue Tree

Throughout Rolling Thunder and indeed the entire air war in Vietnam, the only constant was the need for aerial reconnaissance. The ROE required that any Alpha strike target had to be photographed on the same day, immediately before the strike and immediately afterward. Regardless of restrictions, weather, or bombing halts, photographs were still required. In an era before easily accessible satellite imagery, each service had its own photo community to collect intelligence badly needed by the entire chain of command, all the way up to the president and his advisors. It was necessary to know how effective a bombing raid had been: Was the target destroyed, or would it need to be attacked again? If a bridge had been previously destroyed, had the North Vietnamese repaired it or erected a bypass? If there was a bombing halt in place, were the North Vietnamese violating the supposed agreements?

Known as Operation Blue Tree, photo reconnaissance missions were some of the most dangerous and terrifying missions of the war. The way in which targets were released piecemeal allowed the North Vietnamese to build their defenses in anticipation of the next round of bombings. If a reconnaissance aircraft passed over a bridge, it was likely to be attacked that same day, and the Vietnamese would be alerted. Conversely, once a target was bombed, the poststrike photography had to be accomplished. After the raid, North Vietnamese gunners were always in a heightened state of alert, waiting for the expected overflight. This usually occurred anywhere from five to fifteen minutes after the strike, which was enough time for dust and debris to settle and enable good pictures. It also meant that recce pilots always received a hostile reception. Officers writing the daily flight schedule in fighter squadrons often received much verbal abuse when they scheduled fellow officers for photo-escort missions. No one really wanted to trail the photo-birds, which were faster, were unarmed, had more gas, and always flew over hot areas, which the fighter escort was obliged to follow. Because of the dangerous nature of these missions, photo-pilots became some of the most decorated aviators of the war out of all the services. This glory came at a high cost, as they suffered extremely high losses. Of the eighty-seven RF-8s built, nineteen were lost in combat over North Vietnam.

Combat Search and Rescue

At the start of the Vietnam War, neither the navy nor the air force had any real combat search and Rescue (CSAR) helicopter or capabilities. Early attempts were marred by inexperience, lack of training, and improper equipment and tactics, leaving aviators shot down over North Vietnam with little hope of recovery. Initially, the only helicopter available to the navy was the UH-2 Seasprite. While an excellent helicopter for search and rescue operations near the carrier, it did not have the lift capability, range, weaponry, or armor plating required for CSAR. By late 1965 the SH-3A Sea King began arriving and was quickly adapted for CSAR missions. With a greater range and payload, it could carry extra weaponry and armor without sacrificing any capabilities. At the same time, the first Seasprites modified for CSAR began arriving in the Tonkin Gulf. The modifications added ceramic armor and door guns and removed anything not essential to CSAR from the aircraft. Individual squadrons and their detachments literally wrote the book on CSAR procedures as they went along.[29]

In the summer of 1966 the navy established northern and southern search and rescue zones in the Gulf of Tonkin. The northern CSAR task force was named Clementine One; its southern counterpart was Clementine Two. A destroyer was positioned at each station to provide forward staging for helicopters. Another four similarly armed and armored Sea Kings were based aboard one of the nearby carriers as the primary rescue helicopters. During Alpha strikes, one or two CSAR helicopters orbited over the destroyers, enabling a rapid response to any downed airman.

Though these changes made an immediate impact, the navy still relied on the air force for many of the most difficult overland rescue attempts. It became apparent that a dedicated CSAR squadron was required. Despite the best efforts of the helicopter crews, the lack of training, specialized equipment, and knowledge continued to hinder operations. As squadrons rotated back to the United States, much of their hard-won experience went with them. New squadrons were then thrown into the fire with no training and nothing more than a quick turnover between select members of the squadron they relieved.[30] Even the small detachments suffered the same woes. By 1966 HC-1 had detachments on ships throughout the Pacific, each conducting continuous combat operations. With operations in Vietnam continually growing, keeping track of each detachment proved insurmountable. The navy's bureaucracy finally caught up with the realities in September 1967 when it established HC-7 as the primary CSAR squadron for operations in the Tonkin Gulf. Though established late in Rolling Thunder, HC-7 continued with its CSAR mission through the end of the war. By the end of America's involvement in Southeast Asia, the squadron had successfully recovered 150 aviators from the Tonkin Gulf and North Vietnam.[31]

Close Air Support: The In-Country War

As the ground war in South Vietnam expanded rapidly, it became the main focus of American efforts. While the Seventh Fleet supported the ground war with countless sorties, these efforts often took a backseat to Rolling Thunder. This mismatch of priorities stemmed directly from the complicated command relationships and interservice rivalry as each service sought to gain control of air assets. As bad as the command-and-control structure was for the air war over North Vietnam, it was even worse over South Vietnam. Each service had its own aircraft, and attempts by any service to control the others, no matter how well intended, led to even more parochialism.

During the early stages of Rolling Thunder, carriers began each line period on Dixie Station, where they flew close air support (CAS) missions in support of the expanding American ground forces. These "in-country" missions were considered a warmup prior to arrival on Yankee Station. Flying missions over South Vietnam allowed aviators and ship's personnel to reach certain levels of proficiency in a relatively benign environment prior to flying up north. As a result, these missions could be uncoordinated and ungainly, as everyone learned. While local air assets knew the lay of the land and could coordinate their efforts, this was simply not the case for a carrier that spent one week maximum on Dixie Station prior to departing. Their priority was to gain levels of proficiency that would enable them to survive in the skies of North Vietnam.

Not only were the navy's CAS missions a method for on-the-job training, they were also secondary to the all-important numbers game. While flying from Dixie Station, every aircraft that could carry ordnance flew CAS missions. This allowed a carrier to maximize its sorties. In order to launch the maximum number of flights, the carrier's hour and a half cycle times took precedence over the target, let alone the actual results of those sorties. If a flight launched and could not make it to the target and back within its scheduled time, it would be ordered to drop its ordnance in the sea and make its scheduled landing time. Even worse, to maintain high sortie counts during the bomb shortage, carriers often launched four plane flights with one bomb each—four sorties and four bombs, when one sortie could have carried all four bombs.[32] For the most part, however, aircraft were able to contact their airborne controller, known as "Hillsboro" or "Cricket," and be handed over to any available forward air control (FAC) aircraft to direct their bombing. The FAC then passed a preliminary bomb damage assessment (BDA), usually given in percentage of the target covered or number of structures damaged or destroyed. When ground commanders began to use body counts as a measure of success, killed by air (KBA) counts became yet another metric used to calculate success.

Laos: Barrel Roll and Steel Tiger

Separate from Rolling Thunder missions, additional sorties were flown in support of Operations Barrel Roll and Steel Tiger, the covert bombing of Laos. These missions were flown as frequently as Alpha strikes and involved similar amounts of planning and support. Because of their covert nature, both operations had their own ROE. These included a special circuitous route of flight, requiring pilots to fly over South

Vietnam prior to entering Laos instead of a direct flight over North Vietnam. The biggest impact of these operations and their requisite missions was that they never allowed the aircraft carriers and carrier air wings a chance to stand down. While the North Vietnamese used each bombing halt to their advantage, flight operations continued over Laos in a threat environment containing large quantities of AAA. The pace of operations thus continued to take its toll in men, planes, parts, and other assets while North Vietnam rested and rearmed in preparation for the resumption of Rolling Thunder.

The Culture of Naval Aviation

The navy pilots who flew and fought during Rolling Thunder were part of a distinct fraternity that consisted of older and highly educated volunteer officers. This differed dramatically from the experience of the American ground forces, whose frontline combat units consisted mainly of conscripts with no professional commitments to the military. As volunteers, these naval officers were often more patriotic and promilitary than soldiers drafted into service against their will.[33] Once in the navy, these pilots quickly adopted a careerist attitude toward the war, in that they had a vested interest in the institutional success of naval aviation, regardless of the politics of the war. Many believed it their professional obligation to fight the war to the best of their abilities while working hard to enhance the reputation of naval aviation. The ultimate litmus test for these men, therefore, was to fly in combat. Most of them had flown and trained too long and hard, enduring constant danger, to simply give up and not go to war. For a naval aviator, not flying in combat was tantamount to failure.[34]

After a 1967 carrier visit, famed author Tom Wolfe described this mindset in his portrayal of naval aviators flying over North Vietnam for *Esquire*:

> The idea is to put your hide on the line and then to have the moxie, the reflexes, and the experience, the coolness to pull it back in the last yawning moment—and then be able to go out again the next day and the next day and every next day and do it all over again—and, in its best expression, to be able to do it in some higher calling in some action that means something to thousands, to a nation. At

the Apex in military flying has always been the business of flying fighter planes in combat.[35]

The key ethos developed by Wolfe eventually became known as the "right stuff" and the basis for his book and subsequent movie bearing the same title. As Wolfe noted, naval aviators of the era embodied the right stuff. They were cocky, aggressive, and proud. Many lived by the adage that they "would rather die than look bad."[36] While this devil-may-care, "kick-the-tires-and-light-the fires" attitude may seem egotistical, it was a mentality that belied a sense of invulnerability. It allowed pilots to continue flying in the high-threat environment they faced day after day. Leading this group of highly competitive, type A personalities required someone of the same ilk but who had reached "the Apex," as Wolfe described it.

As Rolling Thunder evolved and North Vietnam's defenses matured, human motivation became more and more important. Quality leadership quickly became the most important factor affecting an aviator's chances of survival. Because the air war over North Vietnam tended to illuminate the difference between the courageous and the timid, this leadership was not dependent on rank but rather on fighting spirit and combat experience. While every pilot had the basic skills, not everyone was up to the task of flying and leading missions "over the beach" into Hanoi and Haiphong. How leaders motivated these professionals and volunteers to fly and face these defenses day in and day out, sometimes two or three times a day, is of paramount importance. A pilot's experience in Vietnam was different from the ground war in that it was fought alone in the cockpit of each aircraft, and as one pilot recalled, "Everyone knew that the moment he went feet dry, he was over a death pit that would lash out with flak, missiles and MiGs, the sole purpose of which was trying to kill you."[37] Every man had to continually muster the strength and courage to face the enemy on his own.

The stress of combat and frequent cruises took an immeasurable toll on the officers and enlisted personnel of the Pacific Fleet. Prior to the war, both the navy and air force produced just enough pilots to fly the aircraft in their inventory, but once combat began in earnest, both services were hard-pressed to train pilots to fill cockpits as squadrons rotated in and out of Southeast Asia. By 1966 the navy faced severe personnel problems, especially with pilots and aircrews. The navy did not limit the number of combat missions an aviator could fly over North Vietnam. Since a typical tour of duty in a squadron aboard the carrier could last three years, it was normal to make two or three cruises to the Tonkin Gulf during that time.[38] Depending on the operational tempo, naval aviators could fly well in excess of one hundred missions during a single deployment, and they could still reasonably expect to be sent back during follow-on assignments. Of course, the air force policy caused its own set of problems. The air force directed pilots to fly one hundred missions over North Vietnam before a tour of duty ended. It also required that no one would serve twice until everyone had served once. As a result, many who had never flown a tactical aircraft or even knew the tactical mission, including many who had not flown for years, were suddenly rushed through several months of refresher training and sent to Southeast Asia. Quite often, on account of their rank, these men found themselves in combat leadership roles for which they were vastly unqualified. By the fall of 1966 it was not unusual for a naval aviator to fly two missions over North Vietnam in a twelve-hour period. On average, naval aviators flew sixteen to twenty-two combat missions per month, with some pilots going as high as twenty-eight.[39] In 1967 the situation became so serious that the navy implemented a policy that aviators could have only two combat cruises in fourteen months. While this improved the situation somewhat, it still meant that in fourteen months a naval aviator would deploy to Vietnam twice, fly nearly two hundred missions over North Vietnam, and then be called upon to repeat the same hectic pace again during follow-up tours of duty.[40]

In an attempt to increase the number of carrier-qualified pilots, the navy instituted programs to speed replacement aviators through training. Slots in carrier aviation were opened up to "must pumps"—pilots identified as having the potential to meet accelerated training requirements. These men were pumped through training as fast as possible to be available as attrition replacements. Those not needed immediately were held as ready replacements and kept 100 percent ready, including carrier landing qualifications. Usually, it was not a long wait. Must pumps were usually held at the Replacement Air Group (RAG) as instructors until needed. There was always a group of senior officers who had been selected to command squadrons waiting in the must pump line, as squadron leadership suffered extremely high attrition rates during Rolling Thunder.[41]

Though the navy did try to train more pilots, the high standards necessary for carrier aviation made it difficult to increase the number of pilots quickly. No matter how badly the navy needed new aviators, each pilot had to be able to land aboard the ship. A pilot was not considered fully qualified until he had performed the requisite number of landings. Maintaining the qualification required a pilot to have made a landing within a certain time period, usually a week; if he did not make a landing, the qualification would expire. Frankly, no matter how good the aviator was, if he couldn't land his airplane on the same ship he'd launched from, he did the navy no good. Because of the extra training required for an aviator to land on a carrier, the navy's training system was slow to respond to the urgent need for replacements.[42]

Because of their continued exposure to combat in the skies over North Vietnam, naval aviators who did survive became highly experienced. Regrettably, pilots with little experience and some men who had transitioned to jets after having flown helicopters or multiengine propeller aircraft quickly became cannon fodder in the heavily defended skies over North Vietnam.[43] Pilots who did survive the high loss rate were forced to fly even more combat sorties as the supply of new aviators diminished. The result was that the same cadre of pilots flew the missions over North Vietnam—and bore the brunt of the losses. This combination of extensive combat losses with little hope of relief and the war's increasing unpopularity quickly began to cause morale problems within naval aviation.

The stress dominated daily life, even if men would never admit it. Lt. Frank Elkins, an attack pilot in VA-164, one of the two Skyhawk squadrons aboard *Oriskany*, described this issue throughout his journal, which he faithfully kept until his death. By the midpoint of its 1966 deployment, his squadron had already lost four of its nineteen pilots. Elkins described searching for courage as he prepared to launch for yet another nighttime armed-reconnaissance mission:

> During the brief in Air Intelligence you know you're going and you listen carefully. Then back in the ready room, you begin to dread

it and you go on briefing though, even though you're beginning to look for a way out, to hope that you're really not going out, that the spare will be launched in your place, that you'll be late starting, that you'll have no radio, or a bad ALQ, or something—anything—that'll give you a decent, honorable out of that particular night hop. After the brief, waiting to suit up and man aircraft, you really dread it most then. A cup of coffee and another nervous call to the head, and you're told to man your aircraft for the 03:00 launch.

Up on the flight deck, you start looking for something wrong; you go all the way around the aircraft, looking for that little gem that'll be reason enough to your conscience and your comrades to refuse to go out. And it doesn't come. You never give up though, first the damned radio works, and the damned ALQ works, and the damned Tacan [Tactical Airways Navigation, a navigation device] works.[44]

Failures of courage did happen, though they were not unique to Vietnam, nor were they rampant.[45] In order to remove himself from the fighting, a man could feign sickness for a few days or find a deficiency while performing the preflight inspection that prevented him from flying on that particular mission. To permanently remove himself from combat, all an aviator had to do was turn in his wings. Surprisingly, the men who turned in their wings were actually appreciated by pilots who continued to fly. No one wanted to go over the beach with someone whose heart wasn't in his work. It was thought to be much better to fess up and make room for somebody with "tiger blood" in his veins.[46]

How, then, did senior leaders motivate men to continue flying? In such an environment, air wing and squadron leadership struggled as well. These men felt the same emotions as their junior pilots but had to maintain the facade of the gung-ho aviator. Squadron commanders and flight leaders had to fly every rugged mission lest they be found wanting. Great leaders flew these missions and motivated the junior pilots, making them feel as if they too could fly, fight, and survive. These leaders developed a reputation among the junior officers for teaching their wingmen the skills necessary to survive, taking care of them in dangerous situations, and getting the job done. These leaders were making tough decisions under extremely trying circumstances when there was often no real solution to the issues they faced. As Rolling Thunder continued, senior officers found themselves at the vanguard, leading tougher and more costly missions with their junior pilots.[47] Because of this, these officers suffered high casualties throughout the air war. Flying over North Vietnam was dangerous enough, but being a senior officer was downright deadly.

The numbers reveal the real story. Nearly sixty air wing commanders, squadron commanders, and executive officers were lost during Rolling Thunder.[48] These men led from the front and paid the ultimate price. Those who weren't killed continued to lead men while imprisoned by the North Vietnamese. All told, *Oriskany* lost nine of these men, either killed, wounded, or as prisoners of war (POWs), during Rolling Thunder.

Their sense of professionalism drove most men, but the quality of leadership was often the decisive factor that motivated aviators during difficult times. There was no question about senior leaders treating junior officers as equals. They were not. Senior leaders were experienced tactical carrier aviators, and the junior officers were neophytes in the air war. But these junior aviators were going to be wingmen for the senior leaders during an extremely dangerous combat tour, and the senior officers wanted to be certain junior pilots had all the information necessary to be the best wingmen possible. Whether or not their skills and courage would rise to the task remained to be seen, but they would not lack tactical knowledge. If the information helped junior pilots to survive, that was simply a dividend.[49]

Part 2

1965

As the first people out there in 1965, we had no one to tell us what to expect. The turnover procedures hadn't really been developed, the rules of engagement were literally incomplete, and we'd get ROE message changes every day. It was really quite chaotic. There were beaucoup international orange flight suits, which are great for spotting people on the ground and exactly what we didn't want. If anything stands out in that early period, it's how well we did for being so ill-prepared, and by ill-prepared I don't mean in the training, but in the knowledge of what kind of training we should have.

—Wynn Foster, VA-163, quoted in Jeffrey L. Levinson,
Alpha Strike Vietnam

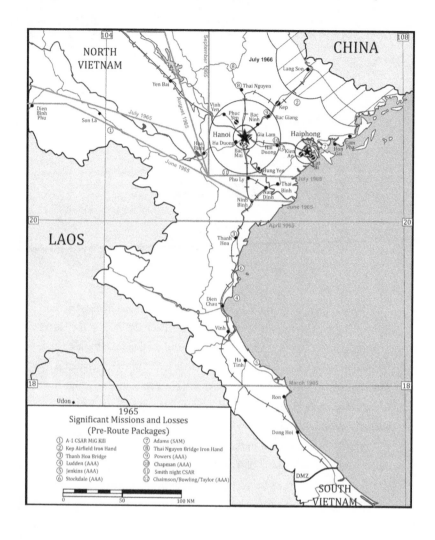

MAP 4. Significant missions flown and losses incurred by USS *Oriskany* in 1965. Created by the author.

4

Gradual Beginnings

THE YEAR 1965 WAS a portent of the most tumultuous period in modern American history. It began with President Johnson calling for the creation of his Great Society, whose major goals included the elimination of poverty and racial injustice. It was not to be. Although Johnson viewed the landslide Democratic victories of 1964 as validation of his policies, domestic turmoil and the fight against Communism, especially in Vietnam, derailed his vision.

Politically, Johnson's involvement in Vietnam seemed logical. Fearing the specter of Communist hegemony, his administration had to act. The lack of any coherent strategy doomed it to failure, however. On 13 February 1965 President Johnson approved the inauguration of what was to become Operation Rolling Thunder. The initial raid was to be against the Quang Khe naval base and Vu Con barracks on 20 February. The targets were all in the southern part of North Vietnam and relatively minor. Due to political unrest in Saigon, Ambassador Maxwell Taylor canceled the raids. One of the initial political restrictions required South Vietnamese participation in the strikes, something they could not do while faced with the likelihood of another coup. It seemed the situation in Vietnam was spiraling rapidly out of control, though in fact the country had seen continuous turmoil for months. Since the bloody coup of Diem in 1963, the Republic of South Vietnam had gone through seven presidents.

Rolling Thunder finally began on 2 March with a strike by U.S. Air Force and South Vietnamese Air Force aircraft. These first strikes reverberated around the world, drawing criticism from both free and Communist capitals. Despite this, the United States was about to rapidly expand its role. On the same day that African Americans were beaten for attempting to march from Selma to Montgomery, elements of the Ninth Marine Expeditionary Brigade landed at Da Nang. They landed not as part of an overall troop buildup but to protect the Da Nang air base, from which American aircraft were operating. After an almost two week-delay, further strikes were finally authorized, this time with the aircraft carriers of CTF-77 participating. Under the semblance of restraint, these deliberate responses were designed to prevent an all-out aerial assault that would result in open conflict with the Soviets or the Chinese, which could lead to the possible use of nuclear weapons. Politically, these token efforts under the guise of limited and deliberate responses may have made sense, but the restrictions and insignificance of the early Rolling Thunder targets dismayed military command-ers executing the orders. In early April Johnson expanded the mis-sion of the marines at Da Nang from passive air base defense to active patrolling. The Americanization of the war had begun, and by year's end two hundred thousand American servicemen would be in Vietnam. It was under these circumstances that *Oriskany* set sail on 5 April 1965.

Onboard *Oriskany*, her men knew they were sailing into harm's way, though they knew little else. Other than a perceived need to staunch the spread of Communism—to save the Southeast Asian dominoes from tumbling—the United States' involvement had not been truly defined. Nevertheless, President Johnson and his advisors had crossed a critical threshold by deciding to commit American forces to fight in Vietnam. They did so on the predication of a much larger commit-ment, even though they had neither declared war nor informed the American public.[1] Indeed, Robert McNamara admitted years later that all the errors in Vietnam had been committed by the spring of 1965; after that, there seemed no way out.[2] Over time, the goal of maintain-ing U.S. credibility would quietly surpass the supposed objective of a free and independent South Vietnam. Once blood had been spilled, however, it would be impossible to withdraw with any credibility intact. This mindset resulted in increased bombing without any clearly defined objectives. Leadership became fixated on the means rather than the ends. Casualties steadily mounted, and the futility of it all would eventually cause the American public to lose faith.[3] This lack of strat-egy had tremendous implications for *Oriskany* as she sailed for war.

Jim Stockdale

In the rank structure aboard the navy's aircraft carriers in the 1960s, the commander, air group (CAG) was subordinate to the captain of the ship. Though the air wing was the carrier's main battery to project power ashore, air wing commanders could find themselves answering to people who knew little about combat—or had little idea of the tactical realities of the air war over North Vietnam, whether they were out-of-touch ship captains or staff officers trying to drum up numbers for Pentagon briefings. With the exaggerated emphasis that was placed on sorties, the promotion of the captain of an aircraft carrier to admiral often depended on how many sorties his ship produced.[4] As the officer primarily responsible for what the sorties actually accomplished during day-to-day tactical operations over North Vietnam, the position of CAG became one of the most revered and sought-after leadership positions in naval aviation. Those selected as CAGs were typically above-average pilots with superior performance throughout their career. They had successfully completed a tour as the commander of a fighter or attack squadron and made the cut above their peers. The competition has always been extremely harsh: since the position was created in the 1920s, fewer than a thousand men have held this coveted job.[5] Selection as CAG was seen as the culmination of nearly twenty years of preparation and training, making that man the acknowledged leader in a profession that was very unforgiving of error.[6]

Cdr. James Bond Stockdale was the archetypical air wing commander. He commanded CVW-16 during the 1965 cruise and set the stage for the air wing's accomplishments during Rolling Thunder. A native of Abingdon, Illinois, Jim Stockdale graduated from the United States Naval Academy in 1947. By 1954 he'd been accepted into the Navy Test Pilot School alongside future astronaut John Glenn. Before he became the commanding officer of VF-51, a fighter squadron on USS *Ticonderoga* (CVA-14), Stockdale earned his master's degree from Stanford University and was on the fast track. Stockdale took command of CVW-16 in April 1965, just as *Oriskany* departed for Southeast Asia. Stockdale had a wealth of experience concerning operations in Vietnam, since his squadron had already been on station in the Tonkin Gulf. He had also been airborne as the on-scene commander during the Tonkin Gulf incident and knew that there had been no second North Vietnamese attack in August 1964. Stockdale also took part in several of the initial reprisal raids. These experiences made him uniquely suited for command of *Oriskany*'s air wing as she departed for her first Vietnam War cruise.

A large part of Stockdale's success can be attributed to his relationship with *Oriskany*'s captain, Bart Connolly III. Connolly commanded PT-115 alongside John F. Kennedy's PT-109 in the Solomon Islands during World War II. He was awarded the Navy Cross before eventually becoming a naval aviator in 1947. Connolly assumed command of *Oriskany* in March 1965, immediately making an impact with his leadership style. Connolly gave the CAG authority to run his air wing as he saw fit, something seldom seen on other aircraft carriers. Administratively, this meant that CAG Stockdale had the authority to sign for and release all messages that dealt with air wing matters. Instead of waiting for approval from the captain of the ship, CAG Stockdale decided whether a downed pilot was missing in action (MIA) or killed in action (KIA) and sent the appropriate message from the ship to Washington.[7] Operationally, CAG Stockdale was given complete authority over his air wing, though he often consulted with Captain Connolly on matters that he felt could put the captain in jeopardy. According to Stockdale, "Captain Bart Connolly, skipper of the *Oriskany* and a living jewel in the combat environment, was very tolerant of my ever-more-flagrant rule-bending in my attempt to maintain tactical autonomy for the sake of effectiveness and safety. Bart watched me like a hawk, and as long as I met his standards, all the pilots aboard—those regularly assigned to my air group and the many that were being sent out from shore bases to temporarily reinforce us—were mine to work with as I saw fit."[8] It was a working relationship that set the tone for how Carrier Air Wing 16 and *Oriskany* operated for the next two years.

As *Oriskany* sailed from Hawaiian waters to the Philippines, the leadership of both Stockdale and Connolly became more focused. Despite the lack of clear strategy from above, these men knew that in a short time their pilots would be flying combat, and they had little use for peacetime thinking. Captain Connolly gave pilots time to fly despite a restrictive schedule. He realized that if pilots didn't fly during the voyage, their skills would atrophy, with potentially dangerous results once they were flying over Vietnam. CAG Stockdale spent time in VA-164's ready room, talking with squadron pilots about their role in what was already recognized as a war of limited aim.[9] Adm. U. S. Grant Sharp described one impromptu meeting in his 1978 memoir, *Strategy for Defeat: Vietnam in Retrospect*. CAG Stockdale did not make a two-hour speech, nor was the entire wing present, as has often been reported. It was simply the CAG leading his men by providing insight during a twenty- to thirty-minute pep talk:

> I think I owe you in addition a straight from the shoulder discussion of pilots' mental attitudes and orientation in "limited war" circumstances. . . . I want to level with you right now, so you can think it over here in mid-Pacific and not kid yourself into imagining "stark realizations" in the Gulf of Tonkin. Once you go "feet dry" over the beach, there can be nothing limited about your commitment. "Limited war" means to us that our target list has limits, our ordnance loadout has limits, our rules of engagement have limits, but that does *not* mean that there is anything "limited" about our personal obligations as fighting men to carry out assigned missions with all we've got. If you think it is possible for a man, in the heat of battle, to apply something less than total *personal* commitment—equated perhaps to your idea of the proportion of *national* potential being applied, you are wrong. It's contrary to human nature. So also is the idea I was alarmed to find suggested to me by a military friend in a letter recently: that the prisoner of war's Code of Conduct is some sort of "total war" document. You can't go half way on that either. The Code of Conduct was not written for "total wars" or "limited wars," it was written for all wars, and let it be understood that it applies with full force to this Air Wing—in *this* war.
>
> What I am saying is that national commitment and personal commitment are two different things. . . . We are all at a fork in the road this week. Think it over. If you find yourself rationalizing about moving your bomb release altitude up a thousand feet from where your strike leader briefs it, or adding a few hundred pounds fuel to your over target bingo because "the Navy needs you for greater things," or you must save the airplane for some "great war" of the future, you're in the wrong outfit. . . . Let us all face our prospects squarely. We've got to be prepared to obey the rules and contribute without reservation. If political or religious conviction helps you do this, so much the better, but you're still going to be expected to press on with or without these comforting thoughts, simply because this uniform commits us to a military ethic—the ethic of personal pride

and excellence that alone has supported some of the greatest fighting men in history. Don't require Hollywood answers to "What are we fighting for?" We're here to fight because it's in the interest of the United States that we do so. This may not be the most dramatic way to explain it, but it has the advantage of being absolutely correct.[10]

Stockdale gave this forewarning in April 1965, before the Americanization of the war began in earnest, and yet he knew enough about Vietnam and the salient issues, including America's limited commitment, to know that the war would eventually cause great debate among Americans. His caution to the pilots of VA-164 before they entered combat showed that he had a greater understanding of the realities facing them and the United States than many of his superiors, including the politicians and military leadership running the war from Washington.

In the six months he led Air Wing 16, CAG Stockdale had a profound effect on the air wing that lasted throughout their time onboard *Oriskany*. Stockdale's drive and personal commitment obliged him to fly frequently, often two missions per day in addition to his daily duties as CAG. He recalled, "High-spirited pilots are more effective pilots and safer pilots. And they like to see their boss in the cockpit. I gave all major strike briefings myself and always flew in these missions, but not always as strike leader; as often as not, I would give strike lead to a squadron commander and I would fly back in the pack. Every one of my 120 pilots knew my voice, however, and knew that I maintained override authority over any airborne action taken or order given."[11]

His style of leadership was seen as almost superhuman and caused many of the officers in the air wing to emulate him. Lt. (junior grade) Rick Adams, a Crusader pilot in VF-162, remembered, "Stockdale used to walk around the flight deck when we were manning airplanes and look for an airplane with a good bomb load on it. He would find one and say to the pilot, 'You,' motioning him to get out. Then he would strap in and away he would go. The man had *cojones* as big as bowling balls."[12] Cdr. Wynn Foster, the executive officer of VA-163, had a closer affiliation with Stockdale and described him more succinctly: "Although he was generally quiet and low key, there never was any doubt about who was in charge of the air wing. Jim never was heavy handed or meddlesome in the affairs of the several squadrons, but he always knew what was going on. He allowed skippers free rein in running their outfits while masterfully molding their efforts into the highly effective main battery of the uss *Oriskany*."[13] CAG Stockdale's leadership affected even the most junior sailors on the ship. His full name was James Bond Stockdale, and he used the popularity of Ian Fleming's James Bond novels to his advantage, taking "double-oh-seven" as his personal radio call sign. *Oriskany*'s crew loved it and painted 007 on airplanes, tow tractors, starter jeeps, forklifts, and crash cranes.[14] Jim Stockdale left an indelible mark on his air wing. Put simply, he was the right man in the right place at the right time.

Beach Boys

The flight deck on an aircraft carrier at sea is one of the most hazardous places to work. The advent of jet aircraft made it even more so. Sailors contended not only with spinning propellers capable of hacking a man to pieces in a split second but also with jet engines. A jet could suck a man down an intake, or its exhaust could blow unsuspecting men anywhere—into other propellers or intakes or even overboard the ship. Men had to be constantly alert lest they fall victim. In carrier squadrons the men who worked on the flight deck and prepared aircraft for upcoming missions were members of the Line Division, commonly known as the Line Shack. Upon checking into a squadron, junior sailors were usually assigned there not only to perform basic grunt work but to be exposed to the flight deck. Under the close supervision of a chief petty officer, these young sailors learned the skills needed to keep them safe while at the same time learning their trade. It was on-the-job training in an extremely deadly environment, and it usually led to a sense of camaraderie that existed nowhere else. This sense of camaraderie was personified in VA-164's Line Shack, led by Aviation Machinist Mate 1st Class Vernon Beach. They became known throughout the ship and air wing as "the Beach Boys" in honor not only of their leader but also of the extremely popular rock band of the time.

On 5 May, as *Oriskany* steamed through the South China Sea, her men experienced the deadly nature of carrier operations. During late afternoon operations, an F-8 Crusader taxied into position for launch. Following the signals of a flight deck director, the Crusader's pilot added power to make a sharp turn. The sudden increase of the turning fighter's exhaust caught five flight deck crewmen off guard, swept them off their feet, and blew them toward the edge of the flight deck. One man managed to grab onto a nearby aircraft's landing gear as he tumbled by. Another grabbed an aircraft's tie-down chain and hung on for dear life. Two others managed to grab hold of the scupper along the deck edge and slow themselves enough to drop into the safety net outboard of the flight deck. The fifth man, Tom Prezorski, wasn't as fortunate as the others. He was lifted completely off his feet and blown clear of the flight deck.[15] He fell six stories into the ocean, and the impact knocked him unconscious. *Oriskany*'s plane guard helicopter was overhead immediately. Prezorski was scooped from the water and returned to the flight deck, where medical personnel met the helicopter and began to apply emergency resuscitation to no avail. Airman Tom Prezorski, nineteen years old, from Brooklyn, New York, had become the *Oriskany*'s first casualty of the Vietnam War.[16]

Dixie Station and Disaster at Bien Hoa

During the fall of 1964 and spring of 1965, as the war continued to escalate, the air force began deploying squadrons of tactical aircraft to bases throughout Southeast Asia. Bien Hoa air base near Saigon was just one of the many bases from which the air force flew in-country missions. The base supported a variety of aircraft flying daily missions over South Vietnam, Cambodia, and Laos. Bien Hoa was also a training base for Vietnamese pilots and was often used as a divert field for carrier-based aircraft operating off the coast. At the request of MACV, which ran the ground war in South Vietnam, the navy began stationing aircraft carriers off the coast of South Vietnam to complement the air force's tactical aircraft flying CAS missions in South Vietnam. In May 1965 this became formally known as Dixie Station, and *Oriskany* became the first aircraft carrier to conduct operations from there, although the experience would be marred by a disastrous accident at Bien Hoa.

Sunday, 16 May 1965, was by all accounts a quiet day for the in-country war. *Oriskany* had just finished a week of Dixie Station operations and was preparing to sail north for the resumption of Rolling Thunder following the first bombing pause. Maj. Robert Bell, an air force pilot flying on an exchange tour with VF-162, had launched on a CAS mission over South Vietnam. During the course of the flight, he was unable to drop one of his bombs. Rather than bring the hung bomb back to the *Oriskany*, he diverted to Bien Hoa air base to have the bomb downloaded before returning to the ship. Upon landing, his Crusader was parked adjacent to several rows of B-57 Canberra bombers. Although Bell had gone into base operations to file the requisite paperwork, he had forgotten some in his cockpit. As he walked back to his aircraft to retrieve the papers, a bomb on a B-57 taxiing out of the parking area exploded. Nearby aircraft were parked wingtip to wingtip, and each had been serviced with fuel and ordnance in preparation for the day's missions. Flaming debris, bombs, and ordnance hurtled into these aircraft, causing a chain reaction of explosions that turned the whole tarmac into a raging inferno. For the next two days and nights, ordnance continued to cook off on the flight line. On Monday evening, ten 500-pound bombs still remained on the ramp. These bombs had become extremely unstable from the intense heat. Compounding the danger, the bombs were equipped with delayed fuzes and antidisturbance devices. On Tuesday, explosive ordnance disposal (EOD) teams successfully detonated the remaining bombs, and by early Wednesday morning, the parking ramp was finally declared safe. The devastation was complete. Twenty-seven men, including Bell, were killed, and 105 were wounded in the inferno. Huge craters 20 feet across and 6 feet deep pockmarked the area. Debris was scattered everywhere. On top of Bell's F-8, ten B-57s and fifteen South Vietnamese Air Force A-1s were destroyed. More than thirty helicopters and A-1s were also damaged by the flying debris. Five 50,000-gallon fuel tanks full of jet fuel went up in smoke.[17]

Although the air base opened for operations on Wednesday, 19 May, it took another week before the air force could replace the aircraft lost in the disaster. Surviving B-57s were transferred to Tan Son Nhut and continued to fly sorties on a reduced scale until new airplanes could be flown in from the United States. As a result of the disaster, the air force began an emergency program for revetment construction. Civil engineering teams deployed to Vietnam to commence construction at major air bases. After it was discovered that a number of men lost their lives in collapsed bunkers, hardened structures were also built to provide additional protection for personnel. The accident, arguably one of the worst of the war, had cost dearly in human lives and property. It was a tremendous setback to the budding American efforts. In the meantime, as the only carrier on Dixie Station, *Oriskany* remained off the coast of South Vietnam for an additional nine days to cover the lost sorties.

In the early days of the war, day-to-day operations around the ship proved more costly than actual combat. On 25 May *Oriskany* lost its second aircraft during normal operations. A VAH-4 A-3B Skywarrior was launching on a routine tanker flight when the catapult ripped the nose landing gear out of the aircraft. An earlier wheels-up landing in 1962 had damaged the Skywarrior's catapult attachment points, and when the heavily laden aircraft launched, the hook finally broke. The aircraft had enough momentum from the failed catapult shot to go careening off the bow but not enough speed to fly. As the Whale crashed into the sea, *Oriskany* took evasive action so the ship wouldn't run over the doomed aircraft. The crew struggled to escape the sinking aircraft in part because the normal three-man crew was flying with a guest, and both the pilot, Lt. Cdr. Richard Walls, and his bombardier/navigator (b/n), Lt. (junior grade) Jerry Adams, suffered broken legs in the impact. Lt. (junior grade) Ignatius Signorelli and Lt. (junior grade) Frank Tunic were unhurt. Underscoring the dangers of carrier aviation, Tunic was a non-aviation-rated officer who just happened to be along for the flight as the whole incident unfolded around him. Though he suffered from a compound fracture in one of his legs, Walls assisted Tunic out of the sinking airplane, even helping him inflate his life vest. Oriskany's UH-2A helicopter picked up Walls, Adams, and Tunic, while the plane guard destroyer, USS Boyd (DD-544), rescued Signorelli.[18] Frank Tunic and the rest of the crew were lucky to have survived. With less than three weeks on the line, *Oriskany* had lost two airplanes and two men in operational accidents. *Oriskany* closed out her first line period by finally sailing north to Yankee Station, launching several strikes in support of Rolling Thunder 16. Worsening weather from Typhoon Babe precluded operations over North Vietnam, and on 31 May, USS *Bon Homme Richard* (CVA-31) relieved her on Yankee Station. Though *Oriskany* had a rough first line period, flying over North Vietnam would eventually prove even deadlier.

Skyraiders for Air America

The war was still young in June 1965, and while they were prepared for nuclear conflict, the services were simply unprepared for the conventional fighting, and the peacetime supply system lagged behind emerging needs. For example, the only flight suits in the supply system were orange or khaki, neither of which was suitable for combat missions over the jungles of Southeast Asia. Aviators scrambled to buy green dye while *Oriskany* was in port at Subic Bay so that they would not have to wear orange flight suits during missions over North Vietnam. As Wynn Foster commented, "In peacetime its high visibility was an advantage during search and rescue. But in combat it was a distinct disadvantage, crying 'Hey, here I am!' to a converging enemy force should a pilot have to bail out into a green jungle."[19] Throughout Rolling Thunder, men purchased custom flight suits made in the Philippines or wore camouflage utilities altered to wear as flight suits. While the utilities' fire retardant capabilities were certainly less than those of the issue flight suits, being able to blend into the jungle far outweighed any concerns of that nature. Period photographs readily illustrate this fact, as *Oriskany*'s aviators look like they just walked off the set of the TV show *M*A*S*H*.[20]

Politics and interservice rivalries combined to make operations anything but routine. Following a short port call in Subic Bay, *Oriskany* returned to Dixie Station for a week of CAS missions. Missions flown by the air force over both North and South Vietnam came under the overall control of MACV. Saigon detailed the specifics of each mission in daily frag orders. Navy missions in South Vietnam and Laos were also subject to these controls. Confusing the issue, however, was the fact that the admiral in charge of CTF-77 and Yankee Station operations (who, incidentally, reported directly to CINCPACFLT, not MACV) controlled navy missions over North Vietnam. It was not a good command structure, and it was an even worse working relationship. Chaos reigned. In an effort to stop the confusion, the Rolling Thunder Coordination Committee (RTCC) was established. Under the auspices of the RTCC, policies and procedures for assigning the weekly Rolling Thunder programs were changed daily. In reality, these efforts only added another maddening level of bureaucracy to the daily existence of aircrew flying missions.[21] Unexpected last-minute mission substitutions, modifications, and cancellations were the norm. It meant that normal sixteen-hour working days were often extended into exhausting twenty-hour days as missions were added, planned, and then often cancelled.

Rolling Thunder programs 16 through 21 continued the weekly cycle of authorization from Washington. They included the gradual northward trend of strikes. Significantly, they finally allowed for the restrike of fixed targets and armed reconnaissance missions. On June 18 *Oriskany* joined USS *Coral Sea* (CVA-43) on Yankee Station, and Rolling Thunder began to interdict roads, bridges, and railways feeding supplies to South Vietnam. These raids had the dubious distinction of introducing *Oriskany*'s aviators to the increasing AAA now protecting key bridges and transportation nodes. AAA was already a significant issue and getting worse as hundreds of Soviet and Chinese guns arrived each month. The growing North Vietnamese defenses, coupled with the aforementioned lack of coordination, began to impact morale. In mid-1965 pilots flying from Yankee Station might fly once a day with little perceived impact, while pilots flying over South Vietnam could fly several missions a day with the added benefit of knowing they were supporting U.S. servicemen on the ground. According to Cdr. Harry Jenkins, the commanding officer of VA-163, "The war up North was very controlled. Down South, you were assigned a FAC, and wherever he placed you, that's where you'd go. Up North, the routes were picked for us and the targets did not extend beyond the highway. We ran the roads looking for trucks and if there was nothing, dumped our ordnance on a place called Tiger Island."[22]

As the pace of Rolling Thunder picked up, losses began to mount. It became obvious very quickly just how unprepared the military was, especially with regard to CSAR. Both the navy and air force struggled to cobble together any rescue capability. In the interim, both forces relied on Air America to help recover downed aviators. Air America was the name given to the CIA's secretive passenger and cargo airline, which supplied and supported covert operations and counterinsurgency efforts throughout Southeast Asia. Despite limited numbers of both helicopters and pilots, Air America performed the preponderance of rescues during the early months of Rolling Thunder. In fact, between June and July 1965, Air America rescued twenty-one aviators, while the air force rescue services picked up five.[23] It was an ad hoc task Air America pilots were not prepared for nor trained to accomplish. They made it happen, however, as leaving downed airmen to an unknown fate in Vietnam and Laos was not an option.

Concurrent with Air America's sudden thrust into the CSAR business, VPAF MiGs became an active part of the North Vietnamese defenses. After several air force aircraft were lost, all strikes became wary of the new threat. On 17 June, the day before *Oriskany* arrived back on Yankee Station, F-4 Phantoms from VF-21 on USS *Midway* (CVA-41) officially shot down the first MiGs of the war.[24] Three days later, CAG Stockdale led a large strike against the Moc Chau army barracks, taking the air wing deep into North Vietnam, as the target was over 50 miles west of Hanoi. It also took them relatively close to Phuc Yen, the primary VPAF MiG base. Stockdale's strike encountered no MiGs, perhaps because they had been vectored to intercept an unrelated air force strike against army barracks at Son La. During the Son La strike, an F-4C piloted by Capt. Anthony Kari and Capt. Curtiss Briggs from the Forty-Fifth Tactical Fighter Squadron (TFS) had been shot down.

The downed crew's squadron mates established themselves overhead, beginning one of the more storied rescues of the war. Captain Kari was captured immediately, while Captain Briggs was able to evade. A division of VA-25 A-1 Skyraiders from *Midway* diverted from their armed reconnaissance mission and proceeded to reinforce the on-station rescue combat air patrol (RESCAP). VA-152 on *Oriskany* was standing CSAR alert and launched a division consisting of Lt. Charles Mullaney, Lt. R. A. Price, Lt. Jack Smith, Lt. Gordon Wileen, Lt. Bud Edson, and Lt. (junior grade) Ed Davis to assist with the CSAR. As the *Midway* A-1s went feet dry and began their 150-mile transit, they were easy prey for MiGs. At this early stage of the war, there was very little coordinated radar coverage of Vietnam; however, on this day, USS *Ernest Small* (DDR-838) was on station. About 80 miles from the shoot down, both flights of Skyraiders heard the "Skylark Red" call from Texaco (Skylark Red was the daily code word for MiGs, and Texaco was *Ernest Small*'s call sign). In a highly unlikely scenario, *Midway*'s Skyraiders engaged two MiG-17s and eventually shot one down. With even more MiGs being vectored toward the *Oriskany* and *Midway* aircraft, the Skyraiders were unable to reach the distant rescue scene. According to Lt. Gordon Wileen,

Jack and I saw it all as we were evading just above the treetops. Since all of us had punched off our tanks, we didn't have enough fuel left to make it back to the ship, so we joined up with a USAF C-118 transport in near darkness and flew his wing into Udorn Air Base, where we landed 3.7 hours after leaving the ship.

We were ecstatic over the MiG kill, and the USAF guys at Udorn celebrated with us. They took us into the nearby town to a clean little hotel and we drank ourselves to sleep with Singha beer. Next morning the Seventh Air Force commandeered all six of us and teamed us up with Air America crews hunting for downed airmen. We flew two 4.5–6.0 hour missions each day until we were released back to US Navy control on 23 June. While at Udorn, an A-3 from *Oriskany* brought Jack Smith and me $20.00 and a toiletries kit. We had to pay for some fine meals in the Air America compound, and it was worth every cent.[25]

What happened during the actual rescue of Captain Briggs was overshadowed by the ostensible David versus Goliath MiG engagement. Two Air America UH-34s flew into North Vietnam from their bases in Laos. At the presumed survivor location, both helicopters were engaged by extremely heavy North Vietnamese 37 mm and 57 mm AAA in the vicinity of the just-bombed army barracks. On board the lead helicopter was Colonel Thong, an ethnic Lao who had been helping the CIA fight the Communist Pathet Lao and North Vietnamese in Laos. He had volunteered for the emergency mission in order to help guide the helicopters through uncharted and unfamiliar territory. Thong was killed by machine gun fire, and the crew of his helicopter limped back to Laos. The second helicopter, flown by Dick Casterlin, was also severely damaged. As both helicopters returned to Laos, they left Briggs behind to evade through the night. Casterlin and his crew made an emergency landing at a secret airfield in Laos, where they spent a wet night in their severely holed helicopter. The next day, two new UH-34s were flown in, and another rescue was attempted. To the crew's amazement, Briggs had become disoriented during the night and had actually trekked several miles back toward the army barracks. With North Vietnamese soldiers searching in close proximity, Casterlin and his crew brought their helicopter to a hover over the marshy area Briggs was hiding in and lowered the rescue hoist. Some twenty-six hours after being shot down, Briggs was dragged along the ground before finally being hoisted onboard. The crew flew to a remote Air America field where local Hmong villagers gave Briggs a crossbow before continuing on to the Air America compound at Udorn.[26]

As a result of this rescue, the military began implementing procedures to improve its CSAR capabilities. The Skyraider became critical to this improvement. Because the air force didn't have an aircraft with such firepower and loiter time, it kept VA-152 Skyraiders in Thailand. Eventually, the air force procured the navy's old Skyraiders as navy attack squadrons transitioned to newer aircraft. In the meantime, however, the absence of six A-1s left CVW-16 unable to cover their own sortie requirements. Only after CAG Stockdale intervened was the issue resolved, and the pilots and planes returned to *Oriskany*. According to Jim Stockdale,

> One unusual event that took place during my CAG tour was the Air Force kept borrowing our A-1s to augment their search and rescue forces in trying to find and rescue shot down pilots in western Vietnam. At times, half or more of our A-1s were "TDY [temporary duty] to Udorn." Our A-1 skipper was getting upset over half his forces being out of his control, and he had a point.
>
> The guy in charge of SAR forces over in Udorn had been a recent National War College classmate of the admiral and, at the admiral's suggestion, Capt Connolly and I arranged for me to be launched to Udorn in a "Spad" [nickname for the A-1 Skyraider] just after midnight when night carrier operations were over. It was just daylight when I got there and at the Officers' Mess breakfast, I found the brigadier general in charge, explained Admiral Cousins' concern about the situation, and he freed up the planes—provided they would do a little SAR up and around Dien Bien Phu on the way home. I joined them on that trip, and we got back to the *Oriskany* about noon.[27]

This impromptu arrangement provides a good example of how the military struggled to meet the growing commitments of 1965. More U.S. forces arrived daily, yet there was little strategic guidance, other than restrictions coming from Washington. Unfortunately, the situation would not improve, as the war proved to be all consuming. There would be no grand strategy, hence the inability of achieving desired ends through the most efficient use of available means. The initial rationale of Rolling Thunder was to coerce Hanoi into suspending its support of the revolution in the south. But because North Vietnam was an agricultural nation—and subsistence agriculture at that—the bombing would never have the devastating economic effect presumed by planners who envisioned a strategic bombing campaign similar to that carried out against Nazi Germany. Furthermore, as aviators were about to discover, the Soviet Union and China gave North Vietnam a blank check. Manpower and the latest in Communist weaponry flooded into North Vietnam, and its partners rapidly replaced whatever the United States bombers destroyed. Compounding the lack of American strategy were the continued instability and incessant coups that plagued South Vietnam. In June Nguyen Van Thieu became president, while Nguyen Cao Ky became prime minister. While these men appeared to have calmed the volatility, any American strategy was doomed without a viable government in South Vietnam.

The bombing continued to inch northward, and on 30 June *Oriskany* and *Coral Sea* took part in a joint strike on the airfield at Vinh. Previous strikes against Vinh encountered heavy flak and cost several aircraft. The forty-seven-plane strike received moderate AAA and managed to destroy part of the runway. While no aircraft were lost over the target, *Oriskany*'s air wing still lost several aircraft during the day. Upon returning from the strike, Capt. Ross Chaimson of VMF(AW)-212 could not lower the nose gear of his Crusader. Rather than risk a landing aboard the ship, he diverted to Da Nang, where he landed, albeit with serious damage to the aircraft. *Oriskany* lost another aircraft while launching on an unrelated mission. Lt. Cdr. Eric Schade's Skyraider crashed into the water when his engine failed following his catapult shot. He escaped the sinking plane and was picked up by USS *Perkins* (DD-877). *Perkins* returned him to *Oriskany* in exchange for 35 gallons of ice cream.[28] Flying from the aircraft carrier continued to be more hazardous than combat in the skies over Vietnam, though that would soon change.

On the afternoon of 2 July, the air wing struck a POL storage facility at Nam Dinh, roughly 40 miles south of Hanoi—the closest any strikes had come to the capital. The restrictions remained very tight, and due to the weekly Rolling Thunder programs, this particular target had just been struck, albeit with mixed results. This second effort, led by VA-163's Cdr. Harry Jenkins, destroyed the majority of the facility, with thick black smoke rising past 20,000 feet. The strike encountered the heaviest AAA to date, though only one aircraft sustained damage. As *Oriskany* wrapped up operations on Yankee Station, Lt. Hank McWhorter, an RF-8 pilot with the VFP-63 detachment, managed to photograph crates of SA-2 SAMs stacked on the docks of Haiphong—an ominous development, to be sure. Though the air wing spent the remainder of the line period flying in-country missions, they would face this new threat the next time they ventured north.

During Dixie Station operations, Lt. Cdr. Bill Smith of VA-163 suggested that the ship invite some of the FAC pilots they had been working with out to the ship. The idea was acted upon immediately, and soon six air force pilots came out to the ship for a three-day visit. It was a huge success, as both sides discussed capabilities and limitations unique to carrier operations, as well as ongoing ground operations.[29] Of course, the air force pilots reciprocated, and the air wing sent several pilots to fly with them. VA-152's Lt. Cdr. Paul Merchant even found himself on the ground patrolling with army Rangers and gaining far more insight into ground combat than he bargained for. The exchange was an eye-opening experience for all involved, earning front-page status in the Pacific edition of the *Stars and Stripes* under the headline "Spotter Lauds Navy Pilots."[30]

On 18 July *Oriskany* wrapped up operations on Dixie Station and set sail for Yokosuka, Japan, and a well-deserved port call. The day was marred, however, by the ship's fourth operational loss and third fatality of the cruise. An A-4 Skyhawk from VA-163 suffered engine failure during its catapult shot. The airplane crashed into the water just ahead of the ship, killing Lt. Malcolm Art Avore instantly. The event put the air wing in a somber mood for the voyage and upcoming port call in Japan.

On 28 July, as *Oriskany*'s crew enjoyed liberty in port in Yokosuka, Japan, President Johnson shocked the nation by announcing his decision to commit even more troops to the conflict in Vietnam. By sending, in his words, "the flower of the nation's youth to battle," he raised the troop numbers in Vietnam from 75,000 to 125,000 men, with additional numbers sent as requested. He also doubled the monthly draft call from 17,000 to 35,000 men per month to meet the growing war needs. He did so without the concurrence of the Joint Chiefs of Staff, without mobilizing the reserves, and without asking Congress for additional funding authorization. Blinded by his desire to pass the Great Society legislative programs, President Johnson found it impossible to balance the demands of war with those of his Great Society. In the next week, he signed landmark bills, including the Social Security Act and Voting Rights Act, into law. Unfortunately, there was to be no Great Society equivalent in foreign policy because there was no perceived latitude or flexibility with regard to Communism. By using rhetoric equating any opposition to his policies to the abandonment of America's soldiers on the front lines, Johnson quickly found himself in an untenable situation. If he denied Gen. William Westmoreland's requests for more troops, the same rhetoric would be used against him, and his Great Society would be in peril. Thus, with no real strategy on how to proceed in Vietnam, the Johnson administration forged ahead, and the country was committed.

5

The War Heats Up

FOLLOWING HER ARRIVAL IN Yokosuka on 24 July, *Oriskany* underwent a two-week refit before getting under way on 5 August to return to the war zone. Aircraft had flown off to various air bases throughout Japan to have inspections and repair work done—items that could not be accomplished during the hectic line periods. The NIPPI Repair Facility in Japan proved its worth as the war grew. The facility began performing depot-level repair work on naval aircraft in the 1950s, and as losses mounted, the ability to repair badly damaged aircraft without having to return them stateside helped immensely.

As the ship left Japanese waters, *Oriskany*'s airplanes flew out to meet her. While sailing past Taiwan, aircraft from the *Oriskany* took part in mock raids against Taiwan. With Cold War tensions still simmering from the first and second Taiwan Straits crises in the 1950s, these raids were a chance to help train Chinese Nationalist forces against the Communists. This period proved to be the calm before the storm. As *Oriskany* arrived on Yankee Station, it entered a virtual hornet's nest. From this point forward, all flights over North Vietnam noted a marked increase not only in the amount of AAA but in its accuracy. AAA sites surrounded any area of importance, and flak traps began appearing. While *Oriskany* had been in port, the North Vietnamese had successfully shot down their first aircraft with a SAM. The air war had changed.

SAM Hunting and the Dragon's Jaw

Oriskany's line period started roughly. On 11 August, as the Watts riots erupted in Los Angeles, VA-152 lost a Skyraider. Lt. (junior grade) Lawrence Mailhes disappeared during a nighttime RESCAP mission. Later that morning, the air wing launched raids against army barracks at Son La and Thau Chau. CAG Stockdale was hit over the target. AAA blew a large hole in the wing of his Skyhawk, though he managed to nurse the crippled aircraft back to the carrier. *Oriskany* spent the next two days down south on Dixie Station and missed what became known as Black Friday. The night *Oriskany* sailed south, *Midway* lost the navy's first aircraft to a SAM. After frequently asking Washington for permission to strike the SAMs before they became operational, the go-ahead was finally granted. The problem now became trying to find the sites. The North Vietnamese and their Soviet advisors had plenty of lead time to build multiple prepared sites, allowing SAMs to shoot and immediately move. Under the code name of Iron Hand, the cat-and-mouse game of destroying SAM sites began. On Friday, 13 August, *Midway* and *Coral Sea* launched seventy-six sorties, with disastrous results. Airplanes from each ship flew around North Vietnam looking for SAM sites to bomb. In forty-five minutes, five aircraft and three pilots were lost to AAA. Another seven aircraft were severely damaged, but no SAMs were discovered. Through November, both the air force and navy attempted twelve more large-scale Iron Hand strikes, with four or five smaller scale strikes per week. All failed, though none suffered the disastrous outcome of that first mission.[1]

The repercussions were significant. Without an overarching strategy, other than graduated pressure, the American effort was doomed. Policy makers found themselves being inexorably sucked into greater involvement. Instead of destroying the SAMs before they became a threat, aircraft were being lost, with their pilots killed or captured, to something they knew was in the offing. Dealing with the SAM threat now meant even more forces for the war. It also meant untold sums of money, as extra sorties were allocated and technologies developed to deal with the threat.

Oriskany rejoined the other two carriers on Yankee Station on 14 August, taking the midnight to noon schedule. Several strikes against barracks were attempted, but weather interfered. The morning of 17 August was a rare clear day, and the air wing made their first strike against the famed Thanh Hoa bridge. Certain targets developed a mythical status, and the famed Thanh Hoa, or Dragon's Jaw, bridge, spanning the Song Ma River south of Hanoi, was perhaps the best known. Originally built by the French, it had been destroyed and eventually rebuilt by the Communists. In fact, it had been overbuilt, with massive concrete abutments and a single span resting on a large concrete pier.

THE WAR HEATS UP

It was ringed by several SAM sites and hundreds of AAA positions. The bridge quickly became symbolic of the Americans' frustrations with the air war. Almost nine hundred sorties were eventually flown against the bridge to no effect. In time, aviators on Yankee Station developed a running joke: the world was composed of two spring-loaded hemispheres, hinged somewhere under the Atlantic and held together by the Thanh Hoa bridge. If the bridge was severed, the world would fly apart, flinging humanity into space.[2]

Many strikes had already tried and failed to bring down the bridge, and this strike was no different. Weather continued to deteriorate throughout the gulf, and flight operations ceased due to Tropical Storm Nadine. During this lull, Lt. Col. Ed Rutty, the executive officer of VMF(AW)-212, approached CAG Stockdale with an innovative idea. Instead of losing an American airplane a week trying to drop the bridge with relatively small bombs, Rutty proposed using F-8 Crusaders to drop 2,000-pound Mk 84 bombs. Rutty had already figured out how to load, arm, and drop the ordnance from an aircraft that was not designed to carry it. Rutty asked Stockdale for permission to fly test missions with the large bombs.[3]

What Stockdale in turn proposed to Captain Connolly had never been attempted. The Crusaders were too heavy to catapult with such a heavy bomb load and a full load of fuel. The unorthodox answer was to launch them with one-third of their fuel, then refuel the Crusaders once they were airborne. Getting approval through official navy channels would have taken months and ran the risk of being turned down outright. Stockdale recalled, "In other words, what I wanted would stick the captain's neck out a mile. What actually happened was that I kept him abreast of the 'test project' we ran as we tried these procedures out on a series of hops off the ship. Once we agreed it was practical, he said to go with it. Without mentioning it, we both agreed to let Washington go to hell."[4] Not many carrier captains would have been willing to give their ship's air wing the latitude to attempt such a risky procedure. But on *Oriskany*, Captain Connolly realized that this new tactic might help save the lives of pilots and was willing to let CAG Stockdale and his pilots try. As the weather lifted, two more days of strikes against the Dragon's Jaw followed before the tactics were finalized. The next air wing strike against the bridge would be the test. Unfortunately, SAM hunting remained the priority, and Stockdale never got to see the results when the Thanh Hoa bridge reappeared on the target list.

Photo reconnaissance missions discovered a suspected SAM site under construction near Kep, a MiG base nearly 30 miles northeast of Hanoi. The air wing received permission to bomb if they found the target and then only if it was indeed a SAM site being built. Because of the bombing restrictions, it was the closest any strike had come to Hanoi, and the mission came with plenty of restrictions. The air wing planned a strike for 23 August, a task made herculean because planning was based on limited intelligence data, as well as the fact that pilots were using French survey charts from 1950.[5] Large portions of North Vietnam at that point were still uncharted, which made meeting the restrictions imposed nearly impossible. The strike consisted of twenty-four Skyhawks in three waves of eight. Cdr. Harry Jenkins led the first wave, with Cdr. Jack Shaw following to hit whatever they found, if anything. Cdr. Wynn Foster led the third and final wave, which was to be held in reserve until the site was found. For reasons unknown, Foster's wave of eight Skyhawks plus four Crusader escorts launched, even though the first two waves found nothing significant. They proceeded on their hair-raising ingress, flying 360 knots at less than 100 feet in uncharted territory. Navigation at that altitude proved difficult, and Foster, with help from junior wingmen, eventually found the target: construction equipment atop a small hillock in dense jungle.

The North Vietnamese defenses had been alerted by the previous two waves, and by the time Foster's group arrived they were ready. The ground fire was so intense that pilots could hear the gunfire and explosions in their cockpits, despite the roar of their jet engines. Of the eight Skyhawks, five received significant damage. Lt. (junior grade) Charlie Stender took the worst hit. His plane was hit by a 57 mm round that went through his intake. It knocked off the generator, went through the engine, and came out the other side. Because they were so low, the shell didn't have time to arm and thus didn't explode. By retarding his throttles to limit the strain on his vibrating engine, Stender flew his burning plane all the way back to the *Oriskany*. When he landed, his plane was so hot that nobody could touch it.[6] The plane had been so badly damaged that it needed to be craned off in Cubi Point for repairs. Lt. (junior grade) Ken Kreutzman was unlucky enough to be the last man over the target and was also hit badly. Streaming fuel through multiple holes, he would not have made it back to the ship had the pilot of an A-3 tanker not saved him by flying over Haiphong Harbor for a very timely rendezvous. The tanker pilot flew back to the *Oriskany*, transferring life-saving fuel in small increments. Kreutzman unplugged from the tanker astern the ship and made a rather anticlimactic landing. Though sieved, his aircraft would be repaired on the ship. Lt. (junior grade) John Shore was plain lucky. A 57 mm round hit on the edge of his right intake and traveled through the fuselage just inches behind the cockpit. Again due to the extreme low altitude, the round didn't have time to arm.[7]

The Kep mission was a watershed moment for *Oriskany* aviators. Just like the pilots of *Midway* and *Coral Sea* on Black Friday, *Oriskany*'s pilots were finding out just how deadly the skies over North Vietnam had become. The combination of SAMs and concentrated AAA had changed the air war, with shock waves rippling all the way up the chain of command to the JCS and the president's advisors. Conspicuously absent were the MiGs. Since July, VPAF MiGs had retreated to bases in China to regroup and refine their GCI tactics after the losses over the summer. It would take time and even more losses before American pilots began to change their tactics. For now, however, the SAM threat was still new and so terrifying that all flights continued to fly at low altitudes, despite growing losses to AAA. Meanwhile, life in the United States continued as if nothing had changed. Ever the politician, Johnson continued to downplay the growing commitment in Vietnam to ensure his domestic agenda succeeded. Along with his Great Society, the space race was on, and the country was captivated. In a crucial step toward putting men on the moon, Gordo Cooper and Pete Conrad had just launched America's longest space flight in Gemini V. Even the new manned space program had a strategy to achieve defined goals, but there continued to be no strategy in Vietnam.

Losses Mount: Jim Stockdale

Strikes continued unabated through the rest of August. AAA continued to grow more concentrated with each passing day. The air wing lost three planes to AAA in three days, with two pilots killed and one captured. Tropical Storm Polly granted them a reprieve, and the ship sailed south to support in-country operations. *Oriskany* was back on Yankee Station by 4 September, when two senior aviators relearned a very valuable, albeit costly, lesson concerning attacking AAA sites. Lt. Col. Charles Ludden, the commanding officer of VMF(AW)-212, spotted a gun emplacement on Cape Falaise while returning from a BAR-CAP flight. As Ludden rolled in to strafe the site, he encountered heavy fire and took hits in the nose, wing, and cockpit area. Ludden received serious shrapnel wounds in his face, arms, and leg that rendered him momentarily unconscious. Small fragments penetrated the visor of his helmet and lodged in his left eyeball and the orbital area of his right eye. That Ludden actually had his visor down probably saved both him and his aircraft. He regained consciousness with the airplane streaking toward the ground and pulled the airplane out of its uncontrolled dive at extreme low altitude. Ludden was able to fly back to the *Oriskany*, though his plane had to be craned off at Cubi Point: he had pulled so many Gs to keep from crashing that he had actually overstressed the Crusader and bent the airframe.[8] Because of his injuries, Ludden was grounded throughout the remainder of that line period.

Two days later, Cdr. Harry Jenkins had a similar experience. He had just led a strike against the barracks at Ha Tinh. He recalled the mission for Jeffery Levinson's *Alpha Strike Vietnam*:

> The plan worked well, a good mission, and I was assessing the damage in the air and noticed there were a couple of flak sites sitting up on a hill, not doing anything. So I called my wingman and said let's make a strafing pass at those flak sites; we'll see if those guys have any hair on their balls.
>
> The wingman went in, laying it on one site, and all of a sudden a guy at another site opened up on me. I hadn't seen him, and a shell blew the canopy off, went in forward of the instrument panel, exploded and blew out all my instruments.
>
> I limped back to the ship and had to tell the squadron Wynn was right—don't duel with a flak site. It was a hard lesson and expensive. The airplane was ruined; the shell hit right on the reinforced area of the canopy, which deflected the round forward of the instrument panel. I went down and laid a broom handle up the hole the

crease had made, and had it [the shell] not deflected, it would have gone right through my headrest. I wasn't hurt, but the next day I was putting on my G-suit and noticed there was a hole in the pocket. I reached inside and found shrapnel had penetrated my G-suit, but hadn't reached the inner lining.[9]

Some lessons come slowly during wartime, and others must be relearned from constant training using lessons learned from previous wars. That two experienced senior aviators in the air wing were hit doing the same thing was a good lesson for the rest of the pilots. While both were lucky, their near misses served to demonstrate just how capable the North Vietnamese defenses had become.

Normal armed reconnaissance missions usually offered little hope of hitting meaningful targets. Aircraft would fly low, trying to avoid AAA while looking for supplies moving south. As the air campaign grew, so too did the number of sorties attempting to interdict supplies. But instead of stemming the flow of supplies before they reached Haiphong, pilots had to wait until the supplies had been received and unloaded for transshipment south before attempting to stop the flow, hence the oft-quoted phrase of bombing "a suspected truck park." On 8 September VA-163's Lt. Cdr. Bill Smith and Lt. (junior grade) Charlie Stender actually found an eighteen-truck convoy. The North Vietnamese had gambled on being able to move the trucks under the cover of the poor weather. It was the kind of target that every aviator dreamed of as they launched on these missions: undefended trucks sitting in the open during the daytime. Smith broadcast to everyone airborne in the vicinity, "We've got a real turkey shoot here," and they were quickly joined by four other aircraft to help finish off the hapless convoy.[10] The mission was a huge success but in reality did very little to stem the flow of supplies. When compared to the efforts required, the real benefit was the morale boost for pilots risking their lives in the vain effort of armed reconnaissance, especially those missions flown at night under the light of parachute flares.

On 9 September the air wing received a crushing blow. On their last day on the line, they were to strike the Thanh Hoa bridge. It would be a maximum effort, with thirty-two bomb-laden Skyhawks and Corsairs. Cdr. Harry Jenkins would lead twelve planes, followed by Lt. Cdr.

Jack Shaw with another twelve. Lt. Col. Ed Rutty would lead eight Crusaders in what was to be the true test of the plan he had pitched to CAG Stockdale in August. Weather did not cooperate, however, and all planes were held on deck awaiting a weather report. They eventually got the go-ahead and launched. As the strike formed up, the pilot of the weather reconnaissance amended his original report, noting the deteriorating weather. Stockdale split up the strike, directing all planes toward their secondary targets. He and Cdr. Wynn Foster then proceeded to a railway siding along the coast, attempting to sneak in under the weather. Stockdale was hit as he came off target. The 57 mm guns were so close that he could hear them firing.

In an instant, Jim Stockdale went from flying and being the master of his own destiny to ejecting from his crippled Skyhawk and into captivity. He came down in the middle of the village of Tin Gia and was immediately captured. Foster didn't even have time to complete a turn overhead before a crowd of villagers set upon Stockdale and dragged him out of sight. It all happened so quickly that Foster didn't know if Stockdale was alive or dead. In fact, Jim Stockdale was taken into captivity and spent the next seven and a half years as a POW. However, at this stage of the war, little was known about the fate of men held captive by the North Vietnamese, and even less was made public. It was a conscious decision by the Johnson administration in an attempt to quell dissent.

Jim Stockdale's loss profoundly affected the air wing, and a deep pall settled over the *Oriskany*. Cdr. Wynn Foster described the mood felt throughout the ship upon his return: "We all lost a lot on the ninth of September, a grim day for Air Wing 16, and a terrible one for me."[11] Concerning the effect Stockdale's loss had on the air wing, Foster continued, "The loss of CAG shook the air wing emotionally; it just shattered us all. The man was dearly loved."[12] Stockdale's absence was immediately felt throughout the ship and air wing, though their loss ultimately became the POW's gain. Despite his absence, Jim Stockdale's legacy continued to influence *Oriskany* and her air wing for the rest of Rolling Thunder. Air wing commanders who followed him were often unfairly judged against the standard that Stockdale had set. As the air war grew in intensity, it became a standard that grew increasingly hard to meet.

By prior agreement, Lieutenant Colonel Ludden became the CAG. Stockdale had discussed this at length with Captain Connolly. Even though Ludden was a marine, they both decided on him, as he was the most senior following Stockdale. For the first time since World War II, a marine commanded a navy carrier air wing. It was a momentous decision, and it would be over forty years until another marine commanded a carrier air wing.[13]

Underway Replenishment

Oriskany departed Yankee Station for Subic Bay in the Philippines the next day. It was a changed ship from the one that had arrived on the line a month prior. The losses of the last two weeks, capped off with CAG Stockdale's loss, made for a somber mood. En route to the Philippines and eventually Hong Kong, ordnance had to be off-loaded so that it could be transferred to the next carrier arriving on station. In order to fly over one hundred sorties every day, the *Oriskany* and every other carrier in the Tonkin Gulf required tremendous logistical support. The transfer of supplies to aircraft carriers at sea was accomplished via underway replenishment (UNREP). The navy's ability to replenish at sea, pioneered during World War II, was one of the most remarkable accomplishments of the war in Vietnam. The navy honed its skills to an art form during Vietnam. Virtually all of the products transferred, from fuel, ammunition, food, and spare parts to toiletries, came directly from the United States. There was virtually no transshipment through ports in the Far East. Although carriers went into Subic Bay after almost every line period, this was mainly for ship repairs, the off-loading of battle-damaged aircraft, and crew rest and relaxation. Over 99 percent of all other logistical support was delivered to the carriers from logistical support ships during UNREPS at sea.[14]

The supply ships responsible for providing Seventh Fleet carriers with stores were loaded out in U.S. ports. Ammunition ships would take on ammunition at the ammunition depot in Concord, California, and then set sail for the Tonkin Gulf. They would transfer ammunition to the carriers several times a day for up to a month. Once their stores were getting low, it would join up with another ammunition ship in the gulf whose ammunition stocks were also depleted. The two ships would then consolidate. The ship that had been in the Seventh Fleet the longest would transfer its remaining cargo to the other ammunition ship and then return to the United States to repeat the cycle. Oil tankers and general cargo ships conducted similar product consolidations as they rotated in and out of the Seventh Fleet. The oilers carried both aviation fuel and ship's fuel. Although most of the fuel came from the United States, fuel was also available from U.S. stocks at storage sites across the Pacific. Singapore was one such example: fuel would be delivered by commercial tankers and then downloaded by oilers for quick delivery to the Tonkin Gulf. A prime example of the efficiency of this system is that throughout the war, general cargo ships delivered fresh fruits and vegetables to the carriers directly out of the port of Oakland from California farms.[15]

Despite the apparent cost, there were many added benefits to this supply system. Efficiency was significantly improved. Instead of having to move these supplies through a port in the Philippines to a depot, then move them from the depot to a port again, having the carrier spend three or four days of premium in-port time loading ammunition or fuel, the ships never left the line. Each carrier replenished every twenty-four hours from at least one of the various supply ships. By continually replenishing, carriers did not wait for their fuel bunkers or magazines to become low. Carriers were kept topped off so that they always had enough fuel and ammunition for ten days' worth of flight operations. That way, if logistical support was interrupted or another crisis emerged, such as the 1968 USS *Pueblo* incident, carriers could be sent immediately without taking time to load out.[16] However, the carriers still needed a port call in Cubi Point at the end of every line period in order to off-load combat-damaged aircraft so they could be repaired at depot-level maintenance facilities. Such repairs were extremely vital to the overall logistics of the air war, and without that ability, a carrier's hangar deck would have been crammed full of unflyable airplanes.

While the carrier was transferring fuel, ammunition, or other supplies aboard, work throughout the ship continued unabated. The maintenance and movement of aircraft around the flight deck and hangar deck was a twenty-four-hour-a-day operation. The aircraft were continuously spotted for launch and recovery as the cycles repeated. After flight operations ceased for the day, the aircraft would be moved to various locations for repairs and maintenance. Combat-damaged aircraft were usually stored in the forward end of the hangar deck. Flight operations lasted twelve hours, then sailors used the balance of the day to maintain, repair, and get aircraft ready for the next day's missions and at the same time move ammunition out of the magazines to the flight deck and load the weapons on the aircraft. This in itself was no easy task, considering the number of bombs that required assembly, fuzing, loading, and then a complete check to ensure that they would go off only when and where they were supposed to.[17] For the aircraft carriers operating in the Gulf of Tonkin, this tempo of operations—twelve hours of flying, six to eight hours to replenish, and six hours getting ready for the next day—continued without letup for the entire thirty days the ship remained on the line.

Throughout naval aviation, there exists a good-natured rivalry between commands. It exists at all levels, from squadrons up through ships and embarked air wings. Thus, with UNREPS occurring daily to meet sortie counts, this same rivalry extended down to which ship replenished the fastest. Because everything needed to be quantified in McNamara's number-driven Defense Department, even transfer rates were tracked. As *Oriskany* departed the line in September, her crew set a new Seventh Fleet record while transferring ammo to USS *Pyro* (AE-24). Obviously, the crew had become quite proficient: *Oriskany* would eventually do 216 underway replenishments during the 1965 cruise, an often-overlooked but vital aspect to the war.[18]

6

The Bridge Campaign

ORISKANY'S FOURTH LINE PERIOD started much like the third. By this point, operations on Yankee Station had begun to take on a deadly routine: no real aim to Rolling Thunder despite losses and new restrictions being constantly imposed from on high. From the start, the Johnson administration imposed a 30-mile restricted area around Hanoi and a 10-mile restricted area around Haiphong. The administration also imposed a similar 25- to 30-mile-wide buffer zone along the North Vietnamese border with China, with similar restrictions. In September, worried that any violation could lead to even greater restrictions, service leadership changed these restrictions into prohibitions. Attacks on targets within populated areas were to be avoided at all costs. Prohibited areas of 10 and 4 miles were placed within the restricted areas of Hanoi and Haiphong, respectively. Targets within those areas required specific White House authorization. There was no restrike authority for targets within prohibited areas. Such actions served only to further disenfranchise the pilots risking their lives. The men realized quickly that the administration and military leadership had no idea of the operational realities the men faced. While the JCS added their own restrictions, they pushed McNamara to expand the air war, but their recommendations were vetoed by the administration as being too risky.[1] Thus, the only increase in Rolling Thunder while *Oriskany* was in port was in the quantity and quality of the North Vietnamese defenses.

The unknown status of aviators shot down over North Vietnam also proved to be a source of great consternation. Aviators had no way of knowing if their friends were dead or alive or if they'd even survived being shot down. The men simply vanished. CAG made an educated guess before deciding their status: KIA or MIA. It was a gut-wrenching decision with far-reaching consequences, especially for the wives and children. If a man was declared dead, his widow could perhaps move on with her life. If he was not, she was stuck in purgatory, with no help offered by the U.S. government and certainly not by the North Vietnamese. That the United States and North Vietnam did not have diplomatic relations compounded the problem. There was simply no way to ascertain an aviator's fate. As *Oriskany* returned to the Gulf of Tonkin, the North Vietnamese published snippets of a letter they purportedly sent to the International Red Cross. They claimed that since there was no formal state of war, U.S. pilots shot down over the North were not prisoners of war and would be treated as war criminals. It was an omen of what awaited men should they be shot down, and it did little to help morale.

In late September, as *Oriskany* sailed for Subic Bay, the First Cavalry Division (Airmobile) arrived in An Khe, South Vietnam. As the first elements of the dramatic troop increase announced in July, their arrival had far-reaching implications as U.S. ground forces rapidly began offensive operations. *Oriskany* arrived on Yankee Station on 30 September and immediately commenced flying. For the next five days the air wing flew mostly armed reconnaissance missions, slowly getting back in the saddle after almost three weeks of not flying. Cdr. Bob Spruit arrived on 4 October, relieving Lt. Col. Charles Ludden as CAG. The arrival of this veteran A-4 pilot was welcomed by the attack squadrons, because his experience helped relieve the pressure on the small cadre of men leading missions.

The air wing's first day of strikes for the line period was 5 October. In the attempt to stem the flow of supplies south, destruction of bridges became one of the main efforts. The air wing planned and launched two strikes against a small railroad bridge near Kep. The strikes weren't successful, as the bridge was left standing despite several hits. The day also marked the air wing's first loss to SAMs. The commanding officer of VF-162, Cdr. Dick Bellinger, and his wingman, Lt. (junior grade) Rick Adams, flew BARCAP during the strikes. Aggressive fighter pilots often pushed their orbits closer to land in the hopes of tangling with MiGs during these mind-numbing missions. Bellinger and Adams were no different, and their CAP point put them in close proximity to Haiphong. While crossing the coast at 30,000 feet, Bellinger noticed two SAMs launch and begin tracking his and Adams's flight. He radioed a warning to Adams, who never heard it and thus never took evasive action. One missile exploded just behind Adams's Crusader, causing severe damage to his aircraft. With the recent North Vietnamese announcement of war criminals fresh on his mind, Adams stayed with his burning plane. Better to take his chances with a burning plane that was still flying than to risk the fate that awaited him on the ground. With Bellinger coaching him, Adams flew his Crusader 40 miles out to sea. At one point, Adams nearly ejected before thinking better of it. Eventually, the burning Crusader exploded, and he pulled the ejection handle. As Adams came down in the water, Bellinger set up an orbit over Adams, flying so low that Adams could see into Bellinger's cockpit.[2] An SH-3 helicopter from the *Midway* eventually picked Adams up and delivered him to USS *Galveston* (CLG-3) on the northern SAR station. While there, he was treated for second-degree burns on his hands. Before Adams's eventual transfer back to *Oriskany*, word of his coolness under pressure and decision to fly a burning plane out to sea and relative safety spread around the entire fleet and quickly led to his legendary status.

The bridge campaign continued. On 7 October Lt. Col. Ed Ruddy planned and led a joint air force and navy strike on a bridge near Vu Chau, a small hamlet along the Song Thuong near Kep airfield. Because the target was near the Chinese border, the raid received plenty of scrutiny from the Johnson administration and the senior military leadership, all of whom were concerned about the potential to violate the restricted areas. The mission finally gave Ruddy the opportunity to prove the value of the idea he'd pitched to Stockdale in August. Planes from the *Coral Sea* had bombed the bridge the previous day; however, it was still standing. That day's strike had also seen the first VPAF MiGs since the summer. An F-4B from VF-151 claimed to destroy a MiG-17, though in reality the crew had just damaged it.[3] The *Oriskany* strike was a success. Capt. Ross Chaimson and Capt. John Dolan achieved direct hits on the bridge with their 2,000-pound bombs, dropping the north span and twisting the remainder off the abutments. A concurrent strike by air force F-105s destroyed rail tracks and approaches to the bridge to the point that follow-on strikes could be diverted to other targets. The mission's success provided fleeting hope that Rolling Thunder could succeed within the imposed constraints.

While aviators continued bombing bridges, civil unrest at home began. The seeds of dissent sown during the civil rights movement began to coalesce, with U.S. involvement in Vietnam as the focal point. As involvement grew in Vietnam, so too did the outrage on campuses. Student movements began as early as March with protests organized by the Vietnam Day Committee in Berkeley. The Berkeley movement called for the International Day of Protest on 15 October, resulting in the biggest demonstrations to date, with one hundred thousand people protesting across the country and Europe. The antiwar sentiments continued to grow, crystallizing around the debate caused by the bombing.

The bridge campaign continued as interdiction efforts began to focus on the northeast railway between Hanoi and China. In one of the largest Alpha strikes yet, air force fighters joined planes from USS *Independence* (CVA-62) and *Oriskany* to hit the Bac Can rail bridge and Thai Nguyen highway bridge on 17 October. Due to their close proximity to China, the raids once again resulted in severe scrutiny. Because of the targets' close proximity to a known SAM site, the raids were accompanied by a group of Iron Hand aircraft authorized to strike the site. The strikes were a success, although they did not come without cost. Both bridges were destroyed. Five Iron Hand aircraft from the *Independence* found the SAM site and destroyed transporters, launchers, and guidance vans. Explosions caused one SAM to ignite and snake around the area, causing even more destruction.[4] This marked the first success of the Iron Hand mission since its inception more than two months earlier.

The strike packages were not as fortunate. Though *Oriskany* lost no planes, six were severely damaged by the ferocious AAA. The *Independence* air wing took the worst losses, losing three F-4B Phantoms to the intense AAA. Six men were lost: Lt. Roderick Mayer and Lt. (junior grade) Robert Wheat, Ens. Ralph Gaither and Lt. (junior grade) Rodney Allen, as well as Lt. Cdr. Stanley Olmstead and Lt. (junior grade) Porter Halyburton. With three crews down in North Vietnam, a rescue was attempted. Four Skyraiders from *Oriskany* flew to the scene. They met heavy resistance, including the first SAMs launched at Skyraiders, and the attempt failed. VA-152 couldn't even get close enough to determine the fate of the downed men. Only Olmstead and Halyburton were declared dead, while the others were simply missing. Olmstead and Halyburton's Phantom had been hit and crashed into a ridge. It happened so quickly that no radio calls were made, and no one saw an ejection. Other aircraft flew over the wreckage and determined there was no possibility of survival. In reality, however, Halyburton *had* survived. Though his wife and family were notified of his death, it took a year and a half before the U.S. government discovered the truth.[5]

Despite their lack of losses to North Vietnamese defenses during the day's strike, *Oriskany* still managed to lose a Crusader due to weather. As the monsoon season began, the weather began hindering flight operations throughout the gulf. In spite of extremely poor weather and a pitching deck in rough seas, the BARCAP was still a requirement. Capt. Ross Chaimson was unlucky enough to be flying during the proverbial dark and stormy night. He struggled to land and on his second attempt crashed into the ship's pitching flight deck. Chaimson miraculously managed to get airborne again before losing control of the airplane. He ejected and was picked up by *Oriskany*'s SH-2. It was a very rough day on Yankee Station, and at this rate, losses could not be sustained without severely impacting the rest of the navy.

Weather prohibited further strikes, and *Oriskany* closed the line period with a limited number of sorties, mostly armed reconnaissance and BARCAP. As she left the line, it was a repeat of the September process: transit to Subic Bay to off-load severely damaged aircraft and then on to Hong Kong for a well-deserved break.

The SAM Threat and Dick Powers

As *Oriskany* commenced her fifth and last line period of the deployment, destroying North Vietnamese bridges remained the priority. With unfettered access to supplies from Haiphong, the defenses continued to grow. Pilots now saw SAMs on every mission. With only marginally effective equipment for detecting and locating SAM sites, pilots' tactics improved, albeit slowly. Small numbers of preproduction AGM-45 Shrike missiles showed great potential, but there were insufficient quantities. By September the few remaining were ordered to be held in reserve until production began.[6] In August the air force began its Wild Weasel program, named after the notorious animal that goes into its prey's den to kill it. The air force took specially trained electronic warfare officers (EWOS) and paired them with fighter pilots in modified F-100 Super Sabres.[7] Their job became hunting and killing SAM sites. The crews would not arrive until late November, however, and in the interim both services continued to collaborate in an attempt to suppress the SAM threat.

The largest Alpha strike to date was scheduled for 31 October. In another collaborative effort, aircraft from *Oriskany* and *Independence* joined air force fighters for a sixty-five-plane strike against the Bac Giang bridge near Kep. Once again, the presence of SAM sites near the bridge forced aviators to come up with unique solutions to the problem. *Oriskany* fielded a division of Skyhawks from VA-163 to perform Iron Hand, with authorization to attack any SAM encountered. If no SAM site was found, pilots were instructed to bomb the bridge.[8]

The air force also fielded eight F-105s from Takhli, Royal Thai Air Base (RTAB) for Iron Hand. Because the air force had not yet equipped their aircraft with APR-25s, they had no hope of finding the SAM sites. The day before the mission, *Oriskany* sent two A-4s to Takhli to act as pathfinders for the F-105s. VA-164's executive officer, Cdr. Paul Engel, and Lt. Cdr. Dick Powers flew to Thailand. Engel blew a tire upon landing, leaving Powers to lead the mission. If all went as planned, Powers would find a SAM site using his APR-25 receivers and lead F-105s from 334 and 562 TFS in to bomb it. Powers and the F-105s launched on the mission, and after refueling, they headed north. At their planned descent point, a solid overcast blocked the route. Powers continued regardless, leading the eight Thunderchiefs through the clouds. Finally below the weather, they raced toward the target, which was surrounded by hills on each side and weather above. Powers succeeded in leading the flight through 600 miles of uncharted, cloudy, mountainous terrain, managing to arrive at the target precisely at the prebriefed time to support the strikes by *Oriskany* and *Independence*. One SAM site was quickly destroyed by the *Oriskany*'s Iron Hand package, which homed in on the gigantic smoke trails left by several SAM launches.

As they arrived in the target area, Powers transmitted to his flight, "I've got 'em on my nose, starting my run." As he did so, more SAMs launched off his right wing. He split the F-105 flights to attack the multiple sites. Powers delivered his Snake Eye bombs from 150 feet as the F-105s popped up to medium altitude to begin their dive-bomb deliveries. Thunderchief pilots watched in horror as withering ground fire tore through Powers's A-4. Gary Barnhill remembered the moment:

My turn. I lit the burner and popped up to about 7500 feet, Powers' emergency locater beacon screeching in my headset. As the nose came up, I clearly remember saying aloud to myself, "Oh Crap, I don't want to do this."

During that brief dive bomb run, which seemed an eternity, there was a sharp knocking sound, like a fist on a door—it was enemy ground fire hitting the plane.... The anti-aircraft hits caused multiple red and yellow emergency lights to blink incessantly. I transmitted my intention to get to the water off Haiphong before ejecting. Radio chatter was understandably chaotic. Each Thud pilot was individually living his own hell, jinking violently to get away from the unrelenting ground fire.

Alone and doing 810 knots on the deck (that's right, Buddy, 810 knots!) I slowly overtook a Navy F-8 Crusader as if passing a car on the freeway. We exchanged gentle pathetic waves as if to say: "Oh, Hi there, don't know you, but hope you're having a nice day?" I swear it was the most surreal moment of my life.[9]

With his aircraft on fire, Powers attempted to climb. He made it to 200 feet before ejecting. Although he was seen waving to his wingman, and his SAR beeper was briefly heard, attempts to contact him via radio failed. Powers was never seen or heard from again. He never arrived in a POW camp, and American prisoners never saw him or heard of his name being listed among their fellow prisoners. In 2014 declassified intelligence documents revealed that North Vietnamese soldiers immediately took Lt. Cdr. Dick Powers prisoner. Chinese troops engaged in road construction nearby overpowered his captors and summarily executed him.[10]

The raid on the bridge was considered a success. Despite the fierce defenses, Cdr. Harry Jenkins led planes from both carriers to destroy the bridge. The Iron Hand aircraft successfully destroyed four SAM sites.[11] Previous to this mission, most raids experienced one or two SAM launches. During this raid, however, airplanes dodged nearly twenty SAMs—the profound effect of the Communists' ability to supply North Vietnam.[12] Besides Powers's loss, AAA severely damaged seven *Oriskany* aircraft, including one F-8 that had to be craned off the ship in San Diego at the end of the cruise. The air force fared little better. Gary

Barnhill eventually made it back to Thailand. His F-105 was so badly damaged that it required over 4,000 man hours to prepare it for ferry elsewhere for more extensive repairs.[13]

The air force had been so impressed by Powers's skill and tenacity that the men who flew the mission pleaded with their leadership to award him the Air Force Cross. They made their point, and the paperwork was submitted, although the award was eventually changed to the Navy Cross. No matter the service or the award, the posthumous award did little to ease the pain of Powers's loss.

Hai Duong Bridge and Night CSAR

With losses continuing at a steady rate, the ability of CSAR forces to rescue downed airmen in North Vietnam and the Tonkin Gulf became of utmost importance. The need to save fellow airmen from an unknown and possibly terrible fate only added to the sense of urgency, no matter the cost in men and equipment. The day after Powers's loss, VA-152's Lt. Gordon Wileen and Lt. (junior grade) Eldon Boose provided RES-CAP for one of the most daring rescues thus far. AAA hit Capt. Norman Huggins's RF-101 during a photo reconnaissance mission near Haiphong. Huggins managed to fly out over the harbor before ejecting. He came down near a small island and swam ashore but promptly changed his mind after villagers on the island began shooting at him. As Huggins swam away from the shore, he found himself in a pistol duel with several villagers who swam after him. With Wileen and Boose strafing nearby junks, an HU-16 Albatross amphibious aircraft landed on the water to rescue Huggins. With the downed pilot finally onboard, the Albatross took off and flew to Da Nang.[14] The successful CSAR was the first recovery that far north, though it proved more important to morale than to the war effort. If a pilot was in trouble, he stood a chance and might be saved if he could make it to the relative safety of the gulf.

Early November saw a marked increase in the number of Alpha strikes. Weather permitting, pilots on the *Oriskany* flew, on average, two Alpha strikes a day. The defenses they encountered grew exponentially, and it was not uncommon for more than 50 percent of aircraft on each strike to receive combat damage.[15] Cdr. Harry Jenkins led another Alpha strike on 5 November, bombing the Hai Duong highway and railroad bridge, located in the Red River valley between Hanoi and Haiphong. The strike consisted of eight Skyhawks and eight Crusaders loaded with 2,000-pound bombs. On the way to the target, the aircraft met little resistance, but as they began their bomb runs, AAA suddenly became heavy and accurate. VMF(AW)-212's Capt. Harlan Chapman's Crusader was hit by 57 mm fire during his dive. With his aircraft tumbling out of control, he ejected. Reconnaissance photos showed him descending in his parachute; however, because of the target's location, no rescue was possible, and he was captured immediately. Another five of *Oriskany*'s aircraft suffered some degree of damage. Iron Hand aircraft destroyed a SAM site being built and partially occupied; however, the bridge was still standing, necessitating another strike. The air wing's next attempt to bomb Hai Duong would have disastrous results with larger implications for the U.S. involvement in Vietnam.

The night of 6–7 November bore witness to the superhuman efforts required of the CSAR forces. Lt. Col. George McCleary, the commanding officer of the 357th TFS at Korat, RTAB, had been shot down on 5 November, and severe weather prevented any attempt at rescue. The next day, rescue forces attempted to find him and paid heavily. Losses began with two A-IES and one CH-3C and grew steadily worse. The CH-3, one of two specially modified rescue helicopters in Southeast Asia, was flying at 3,000 feet to stay away from small arms fire when the crew started taking AAA fire. With the helicopter on fire, the crew actually bailed out (all aircrew on Jolly Green rescue helicopters carried parachutes as part of their survival equipment). Three of the crew parachuted into a village and were captured. The flight engineer, S.Sgt. Berkely Naugle, forgot to unhook his gunner's harness, which prevented him from parachuting to safety. In reality, it saved him. As he struggled to release himself from the burning helicopter, it separated him from the rest of his crew. When he finally freed himself, he came down unnoticed. While the rest of his crew was captured, Naugle came down on a karst ridge roughly 20 miles southwest of Hanoi. In the Gulf of Tonkin, Lt. Cdr. Vernon Frank and his crew from HS-2 were the airborne CSAR alert in their SH-3 Sea King, call sign Nimble 57. Vernon and his crew overheard the radio chatter and volunteered for the rescue. As Vernon and his crew of four headed into North Vietnam, the remaining two A-IE escorts from the downed Jolly Green met them to provide escort. As they approached the wreckage of the CH-3, one of the A-IEs called that he was hit and then vanished into a cloud. With nighttime rapidly approaching, Nimble 57 could not accept any delay due to their low fuel state. The flight searched in vain to find the missing A-IE until Nimble 57 was forced to return to *Independence* to refuel.

Onboard *Oriskany*, the executive officer of VA-152, Cdr. Gordon Smith, had just finished debriefing an armed reconnaissance mission when he was notified of the ongoing crisis. He asked to be launched but was denied due to impending nightfall (no rescue had ever been attempted at night). The chance of any survivors making it through the night was not good, so Smith pressed his case to Adm. Ralph Cousins's staff. He was eventually given permission to launch along with Lt. Garry Gottscholk. While Nimble 57 refueled, the two Skyraiders arrived overhead Staff Sergeant Naugle.

As it grew dark, ascertaining Naugle's position became even more difficult. Unbeknownst to Smith and Gottscholk, Naugle was in a niche on the ridge that blocked any transmission of his survival radio except in one direction. Three 37 mm AAA sites located nearby made the task even more dangerous, though in the darkness they had been unable to hit the searching aircraft. Before Smith could bring in a helicopter, they had to know Naugle's exact position. According to Smith,

> I wanted to get a helicopter in there, but we certainly needed a better location first. I tried to make voice contact on [Naugle's] survival radio, but to no avail. We could hear him try to transmit, but all we were receiving was a "rasping" noise. Apparently, he could hear us but we couldn't hear him. I asked him if he had a flashlight. Nothing in response.
>
> I asked him several other things—I don't remember what—and finally I mentioned a cigarette lighter. I told him that I was going to make a run on where I thought he was, and when I came close, he was to light the lighter. I did, and he did, and there he was off to our left.[16]

With Nimble 57 returning for the rescue, Smith had to figure out exactly how he was going to guide the helicopter to Naugle in the darkness. With Gottscholk directing from above, Smith flew over Naugle's position, flashing his lights as he flew over Naugle. With the correct location, they could now guide the helicopter. In Nimble 57, Lt. Cdr. Vernon Frank was worried whether he'd spot the survivor, to which Smith replied, "He's the one with the cigarette lighter."[17]

The nighttime rescue went exceedingly well. Smith and Gottscholk turned on their lights to draw fire away from Nimble 57. At some point, Smith became disoriented down low and actually flew into a tree! It scared the hell out of him, but they continued suppressing AAA sites. With Naugle safely aboard Nimble 57, Frank flew for the gulf. It was a small victory, because there were still five men on the ground, including the original survivor, Lt. Col. George McCleary. Smith and Gottscholk then picked up a second emergency beacon after Naugle's rescue. With Naugle's radio now off, they could home in on this new position. The multiple emergency beacons, all transmitting on the same frequency, had been one of the reasons why Smith had been unable to pinpoint Naugle earlier in the evening. Smith and Gottscholk had been airborne for nearly five hours now, and their fuel state was critical. Smith began coordinating another rescue and, for their relief, hoping they could rescue the next survivor at daybreak. Smith continued:

> At that point I figured that if we left within the next few minutes, we had barely enough fuel to get back to the ship. I concluded that Gary had a bit more than I did because I'd wasted a lot tooling around making runs. Nevertheless, it was clear that both of us were in trouble. I advised the ship that, if necessary, I'd remain on scene until I could affect a visual hand off, and if I didn't have enough fuel I'd ditch in Brandon Bay.
>
> Suddenly, Adm Ralph Cousins came on the horn, identified himself and directed that I head home NOW. I responded that he was cutting out, that I was transmitting blind, and that I intended to wait for relief.[18]

Two F-4 Phantoms eventually arrived to relieve the Skyraiders. Smith quickly grew frustrated with them. In the darkness, the Phantom crews proved reluctant to fly low enough to spot the survivor. It didn't help that AAA sites were still active, their tracers illuminating the darkness. CSAR was the realm of Spad drivers, and their expertise could not be matched.

With Gottscholk already returning to the *Oriskany*, Smith began the harrowing flight back, resigned to ditching. As Smith crossed the coast, he was surprised to find the *Oriskany* 40 miles closer than he'd expected. As he descended through the weather, he spotted the ship just 7 miles ahead. Smith recalled, "The LSO came up on the radio and told me that we wouldn't change frequencies, and to call the ball. I came back with '507 Ball. State Zero.' His calm response was 'Roger Ball, Roger Zero.' I landed without any fuss."[19] Gordon Smith landed with no fuel—his engine was literally running on fumes. He then headed into the ship to brief Admiral Cousins on the night's CSAR. With the debrief complete, Smith grabbed Lt. Gordon Wileen as his next wingman, as well as Lt. Cdr. Paul Merchant and Lt. F. Howe, to brief the next RESCAP. Smith insisted on going, as he was now intimately familiar with the area.

Even though *Oriskany* was operating on the noon to midnight schedule, her flight deck crew respotted the deck and launched the four Skyraiders in the predawn darkness. The flight escorted Nimble 62, another HS-2 Sea King, flown by Lt. (junior grade) Terry Campbell and Lt. (junior grade) Mel Howell. In the early morning, clouds had settled into the valleys, though as the day broke they began to dissipate. Smith commenced searching beneath the clouds for any possible avenue of approach for the helicopter. Unfortunately, during the early morning hours, the North Vietnamese had brought in several more 37 mm guns. Now, in addition to waiting for the weather to improve, the Americans needed to suppress the new guns before attempting any rescue. As Smith climbed back above the clouds, he realized Nimble 62 had drifted out of position. Just as he began to key his microphone to tell them of the danger, AAA hit the helicopter. As was becoming all too common, the crew could hear the guns shooting at them. Howell even asked his crew what they were shooting at, to which they responded that they weren't shooting but taking hits.[20]

The helicopter staggered from the volume of hits, and the rescue quickly came apart. Howell dove the helicopter into nearby clouds to escape further punishment. As it popped back out, the helicopter streamed fuel. Neither pilot could see due to the fuel vapor inside the cockpit. Then it caught fire. Fortunately, crewmen Merle Huseth and John Cully were standing ready with fire extinguishers. They quickly put the fire out, but the helicopter had lost prodigious amounts of fuel. Then Wileen called to say that he'd been hit.

Smith faced the difficult choice of escorting the stricken Sea King or his wingman, Wileen. He chose the helicopter and ordered his wingman to head for the water. Nimble 62 initially headed for the water as well; however, they only had 1,000 pounds of fuel left and were losing 200 pounds a minute. They wouldn't make it. Smith instructed Nimble 62 to fly southeast, away from the water. He later recalled:

> Of course he thought I'd gone completely insane, but we finally talked it out. Besides, I told him to "Trust me"—and he did.
>
> About thirty-five miles ahead was a 5500 foot hill, which I think is the tallest point in North Vietnam. The top is barren, and it is extremely remote. I'd often thought that if I ever found myself on the ground in that region, that's where I'd want to be. I figured that it would take days for the bad guys to get there. As the countryside got more remote, the helicopter was losing fuel at a faster rate than we previously thought, and it was going to be very tight.[21]

As the helicopter came to a hover over the mountain, the pilots began questioning Smith's choice. The mountain had a clear top with a cliff on one side and thick jungle on the other. The clear area had recently been logged and was covered with stumps, leaving the pilot little choice but to set the helicopter down on the stumps. Then the motors died from fuel starvation. When Smith radioed to tell them he'd have another helicopter there to pick them up within the hour, the response was, "We trusted you so far, didn't we?"

The drama continued with the rescue of Nimble 62. A single-engine Sea Sprite from USS *Richmond K. Turner* (CG-20) approached the crash site. The SH-2 hoisted John Cully aboard but was unable to hover at altitude. With only one engine, the combination of weight and altitude proved too great. The pilot made one more effort and succeeded in snatching Merle Huseth with the jungle hoist. The helicopter literally fell off the mountain, gaining speed to generate lift out of the hover, with Huseth dangling beneath the helicopter as they flew down the mountain. The Sea Sprite made one more pass, with the crew waving good-bye to Campbell and Howell, both of whom were rescued by a Jolly Green CH-3 a short while later. After stopping at several landing zones in Laos, the pilots eventually made it to Thailand via Air America before they met *Independence* at Cubi Point. A-1s eventually destroyed their helicopter so that it could not be salvaged from its remote mountaintop location.[22]

Lt. Gordon Wileen's Skyraider suffered a complete hydraulic failure. The bottom side of his aircraft was full of holes, and he couldn't extend his landing gear. Rather than ditch his aircraft alongside *Oriskany*, Wileen opted for a gear-up landing at Da Nang. Smith had already landed at Da Nang and witnessed Wileen's landing:

> I sorely wanted to see what we could do to go back and get that poor bastard we'd left in that Karst eighteen miles from Hanoi. It was clear though that we'd never get approval to mount another effort under the circumstances.
>
> Besides, I was getting tired, and it was showing. I hadn't had any sleep in the last thirty hours, and I'd been airborne for more than fifteen of the last twenty-two. The adrenaline rush was gone and I was having a sinking spell. . . . I watched him come in and everything was perfect—a real professional job. After giving "Gordie" a hug and downing four cups of coffee, I returned to the ship. Another day in the Tonkin Gulf.[23]

Smith clearly understated the formidable effort he and the CSAR forces put forth. In a twenty-two-hour period, he had been airborne for seventeen hours and twelve minutes. Both he and Wileen received Silver Stars for their efforts during the two rescues. Two more A-1Es were seriously damaged before the search was finally called off. When it was all over, rescue forces had lost two A-1s, two valuable rescue helicopters, and a total of five airmen. An additional four A-1s had been severely damaged. The rescue attempts during the previous two days were a testament to the dedication of the CSAR forces. Their willingness to make sacrifices so that downed airmen might live greatly improved pilot morale at a time when many were beginning to question the rationale behind Rolling Thunder.

It would take years for *Oriskany*'s role in the rescue to be fully told. Resigned to ditching following the night rescue, Smith surprisingly found the ship much closer than he expected. Captain Connolly listened to the rescue unfold over the radios, and once he realized that Smith likely couldn't make it back, he acted. According to Smith, "He cleared the bridge of all personnel except for himself and the officer of the deck, Lt(jg) Bruce Bell, and headed west in violation of all the rules. He wanted no witnesses and he swore Bell to secrecy. There is no question that without Connolly's aggressive action I would not have made it back that night."[24] Connolly's actions spoke volumes. Not many men would have risked their ship and career by sailing far west of Yankee Station and into shoal waters to save a man under the cover of darkness. But Connolly did, thus cementing himself in the hearts of *Oriskany's* men. It was, after all, just another day in the Tonkin Gulf.

While the rescue saga had been unfolding, *Oriskany* launched yet another strike. The previous day, reconnaissance drones had found two occupied SAM sites near Nam Dinh. Led by VA-164's executive officer, Cdr. Jack Shaw, the Iron Hand strike successfully destroyed one site, but it also lost one aircraft. Aircraft from *Independence* received orders to conduct a follow-on strike to destroy the remaining SAM site, which they did. VA-163's Lt. Cdr. Charlie Wack had been the *Oriskany's* sole loss. He had been hit before reaching Nam Dinh, declaring that he "hadn't hauled those bombs all the way just to jettison them a few seconds short of the target." He continued with his bomb run and helped to destroy the site. Coming off the target, his engine developed severe vibrations. He barely made it out to the gulf before his wingman reported flames burning through the fuselage. Wack waited until his flight controls quit working before he finally ejected 15 miles offshore. He spent a mere seventeen minutes in the water before being picked up by an HU-16 piloted by Capt. Joe Kirby. Upon landing in Da Nang, Wack became somewhat of a celebrity, as no naval aviator had been rescued and brought to Da Nang. Air force personnel, from flight surgeons to colonels, as well as the crew that rescued him, plied Charlie Wack with drinks. When the COD showed up to ferry him back the next day, Wack felt so bad that he quipped, "I sure hope I don't get shot down again. I couldn't stand the hangover!"[25]

The Iron Hand missions had a devastating effect on North Vietnamese missile crews. The attacks hit the 236th Missile Regiment, destroying two of the regiment's four missile battalions and the regimental technical support battalion responsible for assembling and transport-

THE BRIDGE CAMPAIGN

ing missiles to the regiment.[26] Though the attacks took the 236th Missile Regiment out of action for some time, the psychological effect was even more profound. Unlike most North Vietnamese soldiers, missile crews consisted of educated urban youth unfamiliar with the strain of war and trained more on technical matters than in combat and political ideology. As Iron Hand efforts gained momentum, such attacks could make entire missile units waver, afraid to fire a missile for fear the launch would expose them to attack by American aircraft.[27]

By mid-November the end of the line period loomed, thus signaling the end of the eight-month cruise. *Oriskany's* pilots began to secretly believe that they might actually survive to the end. Pilots averaged one hundred missions or more over North Vietnam. They were exhausted, and it began to show. Complacency became an issue as pilots grew numb to the dangers they faced on a daily basis. By 10 November poor weather covered the entire Tonkin Gulf. With the arrival of monsoon season, the air wing only managed two days of combat over the next week. This taxed men's already frayed nerves as mission upon mission was canceled. The two days they did manage to fly proved extremely costly.

On 13 November Cdr. Harry Jenkins and Lt. (junior grade) Vance Schufeldt launched in their Skyhawks for an armed reconnaissance mission near Dong Hoi. As it was one of Schufeldt's first missions over North Vietnam, Jenkins selected a quiet area with little activity and very few defenses. The river crossing they intended to bomb appeared unnavigable, so they decided to bomb a road junction south of Dong Hoi. Jenkins recalled:

> On the day I was shot down, if that had been one of my earlier missions, there is no way that gunner would have gotten me. I'd just seen so much flak, and had been hit several times. I was just tired, I guess, and not thinking. . . .
>
> On the way to the junction, about ten miles from the coast, I passed a clump of trees where it looked like a lot of traffic had driven, very easily a truck park. Schufeldt orbited and I went down very low, maybe ten or twelve feet off the ground, looking under the trees. Nothing was around, and I wasn't going particularly fast because it was a quiet area.

Pulling off and heading toward the coast, I heard a gun start firing. I looked back and could see these two streams of tracers from a 37mm, a twin mount, almost dead astern from me. If this had been on one of my first flights—and I've thought of this moment a thousand times—I would have turned hard left because the gunner tracking me would have overshot. But there was a little broken overcast at about 4,000 feet and my intent was to just pop up into the overcast, figuring he'd lay off. So I pulled up, but I wasn't going fast enough to really pull up hard; and with the easiest shot in the world, just a dead astern-on shot, he hit me. The first round, I think, must have been directly in what we call the hell hole area, just aft and under the seat where the control junctions, electrical busses and all are. My controls were immediately disconnected, the stick wouldn't do a thing, just like a noodle.[28]

The Vietnamese captured Jenkins almost immediately. His fellow pilots didn't know that, however, and spent some time looking for him. Before they quit, four A-1s from VA-152 were severely damaged. Just like Wileen's a week prior, Lt. Douglas Clarke's A-1 took extensive hits underneath the wing, and he too landed gear up in Da Nang. Cdr. Albert Knutson, the commanding officer of VA-152, took control of the RESCAP. His Skyraider ended up with twenty-six holes in it.[29] There were no more quiet areas in North Vietnam, and losses were becoming difficult to sustain. In the two weeks since the line period began, five aircraft had been shot down. Twenty-seven had been damaged, some severely enough that they needed to be craned off for further repair. It would get worse before the ship left the line. The losses being incurred during Rolling Thunder and the costly battles now being fought by the new ground forces combined to shake civilian leadership. They had perhaps the greatest impact on Robert McNamara, altering his belief in the war that he helped orchestrate.

Ia Drang and Disaster at Hai Duong Bridge

After its arrival in September, the First Cavalry Division had begun conducting offensive operations in the central highlands of South Vietnam. A major battle had been brewing ever since. As monsoon rains ended in the mountains of Pleiku province, three regiments of the

People's Army of Vietnam (PAVN), more commonly known as North Vietnamese Army (NVA), planned to lay siege to the American Special Forces camp at Plei Me. The siege was a ruse. The NVA planned to draw the helicopter-borne soldiers of the First Cavalry into the jungle in order to engage them and see how well they fought. It took a month of costly operations before both sides eventually met in the battle of the Ia Drang valley.

The ensuing battle raged from 14 to 18 November and consisted of multiple bloody engagements at different helicopter landing zones (LZS). The cost was staggering. In just four days at LZ Albany and LZ X-Ray, 234 American soldiers were killed, with an additional 240 wounded. Both sides claimed victory that day. The North Vietnamese believed they could survive the ferocious firepower of American artillery and airpower if they could only get close enough to prevent its use. The Americans came away believing in a strategy of attrition. If they just killed enough North Vietnamese soldiers, then maybe North Vietnam would cease supporting the insurgency. From this point forward, body counts became the tool by which the United States measured progress.[30]

While the First Cavalry Division fought for survival in the Ia Drang valley, *Oriskany* received an equally crushing blow. Because of their failure to previously destroy the bridge at Hai Duong, the target remained a priority. With targets released every two weeks, the bridge remained on top of the list until the next one came out. The North Vietnamese knew this and prepared their defenses accordingly.

The next strike was scheduled for 17 November and involved over forty aircraft from *Oriskany* and USS *Bon Homme Richard* (CVA-31). The strike went poorly from the start, proving extremely costly in both lives and aircraft. Heavy AAA began from the moment the aircraft crossed the coast and never subsided. VMF(AW)-212's Capt. Ross Chaimson was the first loss when 37 mm AAA hit his Crusader during the ingress. The hit destroyed his electrical system. Unable to drop his bombs, unable to talk to anyone, and with no way of navigating, he flew back toward the gulf. With no electrical system, he also had no way of transferring fuel, and his engine eventually quit due to fuel starvation. Fortunately, he was near *Bon Homme Richard* when it occurred, and he ejected safely. Chaimson was quickly rescued by a Seasprite from the carrier.

Over the target, AAA hit Lt. Cdr. Roy Bowling's Skyhawk. A 37 mm round neatly severed the horizontal stabilizer from his A-4 with catastrophic results. The entire strike group was escaping the area at low altitude, and without a stabilizer, Bowling's Skyhawk became aerodynamically unstable and plunged into the ground. Lt. Larry Spear was flying behind Bowling when it happened and thought he had seen a parachute. A quick turn overhead revealed nothing, though Spear called for RESCAP. Unfortunately, Bowling had been shot down in a heavily defended area west of Haiphong, between the port city and Hanoi.

Over the Tonkin Gulf, the CSAR alert proceeded to the crash scene. Lt. Cdr. Eric Schade and the air wing operations officer, Lt. Cdr. Jesse Taylor, arrived overhead amid intense AAA. They could see the wreckage and a parachute, but the AAA was too heavy for a rescue. Then both Skyraiders were hit. Schade managed to make it back to the *Oriskany*. Taylor did not. Schade's badly damaged aircraft was barely flyable, resulting in a hard landing that destroyed the wing spar. His aircraft was written off. Taylor's A-1 caught fire before he reached the coast, and though he tried to ditch at sea, the plane crashed in coastal marshes close to the shore southwest of Haiphong. Jesse Taylor was killed in the crash, and though a helicopter crew attempted to recover the body, they were driven off by intense ground fire.

Taylor's loss was especially painful. He had enlisted in the navy during the Second World War and had sailed with VB-11 aboard the USS *Hornet* (CV-12) in 1944. Following the war, he joined the naval reserves and became a naval aviator during the Korean War. In September Taylor had been selected for commander but had not yet been promoted. He had just taken over duties as the air wing operations officer from Cdr. Paul Engel. The job of air wing operations officer was seen as a stepping stone toward eventual selection as the commanding officer of a squadron—something Engel accomplished when he departed to become the executive officer of VA-164. A fighter pilot by trade, Taylor volunteered to take the mission in order to familiarize himself with the many different aircraft flown within the air wing. It was an unnecessary but calculated risk. The navy posthumously awarded him the Navy Cross and eventually named the USS *Jesse J. Taylor* (FFG-50) in his honor.

The raid failed to destroy the bridge. Although the approaches were cratered and some boxcars were destroyed, the bridge still stood. Another strike was required, and the defenses would be even greater. Similar to the ongoing battle in Ia Drang, the cost was staggering. The *Oriskany* lost three aircraft to AAA, with another six heavily damaged, two of which would be stricken from inventory. The mission cost over half the airplanes assigned to hit the bridge. The *Bon Homme Richard* fared better, with two A-4s damaged and one F-8 lost. Cdr. Robert Chew, the commanding officer of VF-194, managed to fly his crippled Crusader out over the gulf before ejecting. To add insult to injury, *Oriskany* lost a fourth aircraft that night. Once again, the BARCAP had been launched despite poor weather, and 1st Lt. Gary Piel crashed his Crusader into the ship while trying to get aboard. The ensuing fireball flung wreckage across the flight deck and injured many sailors.[31] Losses of this magnitude should have garnered headlines back in the United States, but they were overshadowed by the ongoing battle in the Ia Drang. American involvement in Vietnam suddenly exploded into an open-ended and massive commitment of American men, money, and matériel to a war that Defense Secretary McNamara began suspecting would be difficult if not impossible to win.

The country was not prepared for the war it was now in. In the wake of Ia Drang, the first telegrams to shatter the lives of the innocent began arriving. The war was new, and the casualties to date had been so few that the military did not yet have casualty-notification teams. Later in the war these teams would personally deliver the bad news and stay to comfort a young widow or elderly parents.[32] Even the navy's leadership struggled to realize the magnitude of American involvement. Wynn Foster remembered the period wryly:

> Near the end of the 1965 cruise, I'd lost my CAG, my skipper, my operations officer. I was really down in the dumps for about two weeks and trying to act like a new, fresh caught, recently promoted CO.
>
> I sat down to read message traffic and there's a message exhorting the hell out of everybody for not having made their contributions to Navy Relief. To have gone through two combat missions that day and then read that sort of thing—it was hard to imagine people whose mental set was still that way.[33]

Everyone, including the military, was taken totally by surprise by the magnitude of the casualties that burst on the scene during those four days in November.

The war had grown beyond what President Johnson and his advisors had ever imagined in early 1965. But all was not lost—not yet. For most civilian and military leadership running the war, the evidence of a tougher enemy just underlined the need to roll up their sleeves and get on with the job: send in more troops and weaponry till Hanoi caved.[34] But attitudes began changing, especially among the aviators cheating death several times a day. Wynn Foster noted the change among VA-163: "As a squadron, we went out ready to win the war and came back quite a different crew of people, a lot more mature and maybe with a little bit of cynicism. Out went a bunch of Jack Armstrong, All-American Boys going to win this war. By December of 1965, all of us realized it was not a winnable war. It was obvious to us, and obvious to everybody flying over there, we couldn't hit the North Vietnamese where it hurt."[35]

The men realized the absurdity as sortie production became an end in itself. Pilots were well aware of this dichotomy and mocked it in an attempt to mask their growing frustration with the war. Again according to Foster, "At naval air stations back in the States, posters prominently reminded pilots and other aviation personnel, 'Of all our operations, SAFETY is paramount!' In Ready Room Five, the flight-scheduling officer Larry DeSha, after working hours to juggle the availability of the pilots against a frequently amended daily mission plan, posted his own notice: 'Of all our operations, GETTIN' THEM SORTIES OUT is paramount!'"[36]

The shift in attitudes was apparent elsewhere in the air wing. Prior to the 1965 cruise, VF-162's Lt. Bud Flagg had written to Charles Schulz, asking for permission to use a Snoopy caricature on their airplanes. Schulz, a World War II veteran, readily agreed. In a nod to the nose art that adorned aircraft in the Second World War, VF-162 painted emblems of Snoopy riding a Sidewinder missile on the tails of their Crusaders. The use of such an influential and hugely popular cartoon character spoke to the naïveté of many in the early days of Vietnam.

Such notions changed after November 1965. Most Americans still backed the war, though dissent grew steadily. In early November, Nor-

THE BRIDGE CAMPAIGN

man Morrison, a Quaker activist, immolated himself at the Pentagon to protest the war. At the end of November, Coretta Scott King, among others, spoke at an antiwar rally of about thirty thousand in Washington DC in the single largest demonstration to date. On that same day, President Johnson announced the significant escalation of U.S. involvement in Vietnam, from 120,000 to 400,000 troops, with the option for another 200,000 on top of that. American involvement in Vietnam now began to poison everything from international relations to domestic politics. It even began to threaten Johnson's Great Society. In a bid to save his domestic agenda and disguise the true cost of the war, Johnson would fight the war on the cheap, against the advice of all advisors, both political and military. There would be no mobilization of reserve units, no declaration of a state of emergency to permit the military to extend the enlistments of its best-trained and most experienced men. Instead, the war would be fed by stripping units throughout Europe and the United States of men and equipment, while a river of new draftees flowed in to do the shooting and dying.[37]

Oriskany's involvement in Vietnam during 1965 came to an uneventful close on 26 November as she departed Yankee Station for Subic Bay. As she continued across the Pacific, a divided Johnson administration deliberated yet another bombing pause. The recent uptick in losses both in the air and on the ground, with little improvement to the situation, led McNamara to summarize his views in a memorandum to President Johnson on 30 November: "It is my belief that there should be a three or four week pause in the program of bombing the North before we either greatly increase our troop deployment to Vietnam or intensify our strikes against the North. The reasons for this belief are, first, we must lay a foundation in the minds of the American public and in world opinion for such an enlarged phase of the war, and second, we should give North Vietnam a face-saving chance to stop the aggression."[38]

It is worth noting that military leadership was not involved in the decision. In fact, Adm. U. S. Grant Sharp was not privy until President Johnson announced it during the Christmas truce. The "hard-line" pause, as it became known, was doomed to failure. Both the North Vietnamese and the United States used the pause to their seeming advantage. Just as McNamara intended, President Johnson used the pause to show the American public that he was serious about peace before announcing the even greater escalations that had already been planned. The North Vietnamese viewed the supposed peace initiative for what it was: a thinly veiled excuse for further escalation. They used the period to strengthen their defenses under the continued goal of winning the war and achieving national unity under Communist control.[39] The pause had major implications. It exposed a rift among the president's advisors. It created an even bigger rift, if not an outright chasm, in civil-military relations. Moreover, for the men who eventually resumed the bombing, it meant even more casualties as they faced North Vietnamese defenses, which had had thirty-seven days to resupply and fortify. In 1966 the American air campaign would be met with even fiercer resistance, resulting in even greater casualties.

Part 3

1966

Experience was the key to survival. The first combat cruise involved a
matter of getting used to combat, seeing and feeling what it's really like.
Next time back, you built on that experience, really the big kid on
the block instead of the new guy.

—Denis Weichman, VA-164, quoted in Jeffrey L. Levinson,
Alpha Strike Vietnam

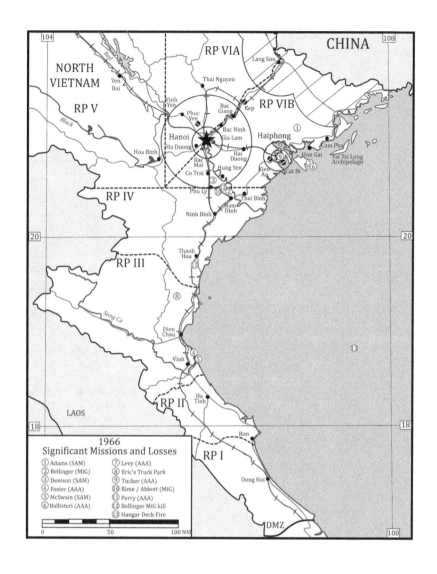

MAP 5. Significant missions flown and losses incurred by USS *Oriskany* in 1966. Created by the author.

7

The POL Campaign

As 1966 BEGAN, FALSE hopes for peace with Hanoi drove officials in Washington to continue the hard-line pause through January. In 1965 American bombing severely disrupted the North Vietnamese economy, costing incalculable lives, yet the North Vietnamese had no desire to discuss peace. When air operations finally began again on 31 January, they increased only to the extent that weather allowed. Unfortunately, pilots faced even more restrictions than had been imposed in 1965. No strikes were authorized in the restricted areas. Armed reconnaissance missions were only allowed south of the 21st parallel, and no Iron Hand missions were allowed to counter the increasing number of SAMs. Instead of expanding the air campaign, the JCS viewed these restrictions as a step backward that took another two months to reverse. In the interim, they argued unsuccessfully for authorization to strike North Vietnamese POL facilities and to close North Vietnamese ports. It took months of haggling before consent was given to target POL, but the act of mining was deemed too dangerous by an administration fearful of Soviet or Chinese intervention. The expansion grew steadily as the weather improved, with sortie totals eventually expanding to almost eight thousand a month by March.

The expansion of the air war eventually caused serious problems, as the United States was ill prepared for the war in Vietnam. Despite the harsh demands of combat over the previous eleven months, the military and the American economy continued operating at a peacetime tempo. Consequently, severe shortages began hampering the war effort. Because President Johnson did not want to jeopardize his Great Society programs, he resisted mobilizing the American economy for war, despite advice to the contrary. This resulted in runaway inflation, which took years to eventually overcome.

Upon *Oriskany*'s return to the United States in December 1965, the crew immediately began preparing for its imminent return to Vietnam. The ship spent the holidays in "cold iron," during which the boilers on a steam-powered ship are completely shut down in order to perform major maintenance. With the bombing pause still in effect, maintenance was completed and the boilers were relit as training began in earnest. The ship and air wing would have little more than five months before departing once more for Yankee Station. The training period and the 1966 cruise would be marked by severe shortages of men, equipment, and the ordnance needed to meet the daily demands of Rolling Thunder.

In particular, personnel shortages wreaked havoc as *Oriskany* prepared for combat. The large turnover of men placed a heavy burden on training during the short period between deployments. The navy's Bureau of Personnel implemented a policy of keeping 50 percent of combat-experienced pilots in their squadrons, while new pilots reported earlier in the training period. These efforts improved problems in pilot training; however, the loss of highly trained sailors continued unabated. Most significantly, the loss of men in technologically advanced avionics and ordnance fields posed considerable problems. The increased sophistication of weapons systems in electronic warfare compounded the shortages, and at best the number of skilled technicians was barely sufficient to meet daily flight schedules.[1] Peacetime manpower plus the need for career-enhancing moves for officers may have looked good on paper but in reality placed an undue burden on squadron leadership tasked with training their men to survive in combat. Upon arrival in the Tonkin Gulf, squadrons found the peacetime supply system unresponsive to wartime realities. Often there weren't enough parts to fix aircraft damaged in combat. When combined with insufficient peacetime personnel levels, the potential for accidental losses greatly increased.[2] Fully manned, a squadron struggled to meet daily sortie requirements, but with 80 percent and less, squadrons fought just to keep aircraft flyable. In addition to performing all the daily maintenance required to keep complex jet aircraft flying, sailors needed to fix scores of aircraft damaged in combat. Furthermore, whenever a squadron lost an aircraft and received a replacement, full inspections were required before that airplane could fly, adding to the workload. When coupled with the pressure to fly all sorties allocated, it is not difficult to imagine the pressure induced and the potential for mishap due to these shortages.

That American carriers were at the end of a long supply chain further compounded the situation, as losses far exceeded prewar estimates. By mid-1966 the loss rate for the A-4 Skyhawk was catching up with the navy's planned procurement rate and budget. At the time, Skyhawk losses averaged six per month. Peacetime Department of Defense procurement contracts provided for only ten Skyhawks a month to both the navy and the Marine Corps in both the Atlantic and Pacific fleets.[3] Depleting stateside and Atlantic fleet commands of their aircraft provided short-term relief. This process often included aircrew, equipment, and even ordnance until production rates increased. Long-term relief only came about as aircraft like the Skyhawk and Crusader were phased out by newer and more capable aircraft such as the A-6 Intruder, A-7 Corsair, and F-4 Phantom.

Shortages even affected the supply of uniforms. The lack of camouflaged flight suits continued to pose problems. Aviators could buy custom-made fatigues or attempt to dye their orange flight suits a less conspicuous color. Even sailors lacked the basic equipment required to work on the flight deck. In some cases, squadrons sent their sailors' boots to cobblers, as there were no replacements available when the soles were worn through by the nonskid coating of the flight deck.[4]

Perhaps the best-known shortage to beset Rolling Thunder was an insufficient amount of ordnance. The massive amounts of bombs being dropped on Laos, South Vietnam, and North Vietnam created a shortage by early 1966. Production of conventional "iron bombs" had virtually ceased as the military concentrated on nuclear weapons and more advanced ordnance such as the AGM-12 Bullpup, AGM-45 Shrike, and AGM-62 Walleye. Stockpiles of modern ordnance vanished, while surplus supplies of World War II and Korean era bombs dwindled. Military commanders in South Vietnam reported that the ordnance shortfall created an "emergency situation" that forced them to cancel planned strike sorties. By mid-1966 there were inadequate inventories of thirteen different types of ordnance. In April 1966 newspapers across the United States began reporting that the Pentagon had repurchased, for $21.00 apiece, 5,570 bombs that had been sold to West Germany for scrap at $1.70 each. Later the Defense Department admitted that in order to supply the war in Vietnam, the United States had repurchased eighteen thousand bombs sold to various nations. Throughout this period, Secretary McNamara denied the shortage. At one point, McNamara responded to media questions: "All this baloney about lack of bomb production is completely misleading."[5]

In an effort to solve the ordnance shortage, the Johnson administration offered two solutions. President Johnson assigned "the highest national priority" to several types of munitions, including 250-pound, 500-pound, and 750-pound bombs, while Secretary McNamara ordered Adm. U. S. Grant Sharp to make tentative sortie allocations for the remainder of 1966. Each service was given ordnance-loading limits for planned sorties. The JCS consistently argued for full loading of aircraft to ensure some degree of success during strike missions. McNamara asserted that large ordnance loads were not warranted simply because aircraft could carry them.[6] The pressure to maintain sortie rates with insufficient amounts of ordnance caused considerable concern among the men who were expected to risk their lives carrying less than optimal bomb loads. The shortage of bombs resulted in aircraft being sent on missions to high-risk areas with one or two bombs instead of their full load. In the interim, shortfalls were met by using surplus ordnance left over from World War II. Using twenty-plus-year-old ammunition posed serious hazards and further exposed men to unnecessary risk.[7] Not only was the ordnance unstable, leading to such tragedies as the fire on USS *Forrestal* (CVA-59), but large percentages of these bombs were duds. As a result, aviators were lost while bombing the same target time and again, often with dubious effects. Even today, the mere mention of the bomb shortage among veterans evokes a strong reaction. It serves as a stark reminder of just how badly mismanaged Rolling Thunder actually was.

While politicians and military leadership bickered over Rolling Thunder, *Oriskany*'s men continued to prepare for her return to Vietnam. The turnover of personnel continued, including the ship's captain. On March 11 Capt. John H. Iarrobino relieved Capt. Bart Connolly III as the commanding officer. Iarrobino had unique family ties to the ship, as his older brother Charles Iarrobino commanded her four years earlier.[8] It would be a fast-paced learning period for the new captain, with little room for error as he prepared himself and his ship for combat. On 26 May, a little over five months after returning home, *Oriskany* got under way for her second deployment to Vietnam. After a brief transit to the Hawaiian Islands, *Oriskany* conducted a three-day operational readiness inspection (ORI) to certify the crew's preparedness for combat. Aviators wryly noted the standard grades given at the conclusion of the inspection, meaning that they would continue with their deployment to Vietnam—as if there was any other choice. The need for carriers meant they would have sailed for Vietnam regardless. While in Hawaii, senior leadership within the air wing received briefings from Sharp's staff, updating them on the status of Rolling Thunder. All were disappointed, as the heavy-handed restrictions continued unabated, although many of the restrictions imposed earlier in the year had been lifted by this time. It seemed little had changed since *Oriskany*'s departure at the end of November.

One significant change, however, was to the route package system. In 1965 the air force and the navy struggled to conduct joint operations, competing for resources and targets. In December the RTCC attempted to organize the confusing command-and-control structure to alleviate the problems. They split North Vietnam into six distinct areas, which became known as Route Packages I–VI. The term "Route Package" was quickly shortened to RP, or simply "Pack." In April 1966 Admiral Sharp ordered further changes, with Route Package VI being divided into two sections. Now responsibility for strikes in each area was permanently assigned to Task Force 77 or Seventh Air Force. The air force assumed Route Packages I, V, and VIA, while the navy took II, III, IV, and VIB. Because RPs VIA and VIB contained targets in Hanoi and Haiphong, respectively, they were the most heavily defended. The lines, drawn so precisely at CINCPAC, worked only for planning purposes. In reality, during missions, both air force and navy crews crossed them at will. No matter how much better or well intentioned the new system was, the route package concept was indicative of the central failure of Rolling Thunder: the lack of one person directing the air war. As a result, interservice rivalry worsened, with both services bickering over sorties flown, bombs dropped, and which RP was tougher. At times it seemed the common goal was not fighting alongside fellow countrymen in order to defeat a common foe but rather outperforming the other service. It led to a disunity of effort that took on almost mythical proportions as the war grew.[9]

Dixie Station: A Prelude

Oriskany arrived on Dixie Station on 30 June, thirty-seven days after departing San Diego and, more importantly, just seven months after leaving Vietnam in 1965. In 1966 carriers began each line period on Dixie Station prior to moving north. Accordingly, air wing pilots spent their first eight days focused on in-country missions. For veterans of 1965, the war was already old hat. For newcomers, it proved to be a case of on-the-job training. Under the navy's efforts to rotate aviators, Lt. Cdr. Dick Schaffert transferred from an East Coast Crusader squadron and joined the Sundowners in early 1966. Although the Nebraska native was an experienced aviator, Schaffert was considered a new guy because he had not yet experienced combat. Schaffert explained this baptism by fire and these early operations from Dixie Station: "My first mission on 30 June was napalm, and that was the first time in my then 2,928 flight hours as a Navy Fighter Pilot I had carried any real live air-to-ground ordnance other than 20-mm. I was a Lt Cdr flight leader and one of the most experienced in VF-111, but I knew I was not properly trained for what I was about to do."[10]

This lack of experience often resulted in colorful moments as air wings commenced operations. Schaffert continued:

> There was no meaningful coordination between our air wing and the locals during our Dixie ops. When I dared to later ask someone who would know about that, the answer was that Dixie was meant to be a training exercise for our ordnance loading crews. Heaven knows, we needed that. I diverted into Bien Hoa with hung napalm. There I discovered that the safety pins in the wing pylon that were supposed to be pulled on the catapult were still in.
>
> On one of the first missions south of Saigon in the maze of canals and rivers that was the Mekong, Childplay [*Oriskany*'s radio call sign] Strike handed off my flight of four F-8Es with a total of

eight napalms to an airborne FAC. The haze was bad below 10,000 ft. and it took about ten minutes to find him. When we finally had a tally-ho, we descended into the haze and he led us toward a target described as a small peninsula covered with heavy vegetation.

There were several such "small peninsulas" jutting out into a wide river and I requested some smoke to better mark the target. The FAC advised he'd rather not do that because his chances of survival depended on the VC believing he hadn't seen them. When I asked where the friendlies were, he said our radio channel was not secure and he couldn't disclose their position. I asked if we could make a low pass over the peninsula I had in mind, to double check if I had the right one. Again, the FAC said that was not a good idea— the VC he was after would scatter and those that didn't would be ready to shoot at us.

To me, that was a whole lot of negatives, and very few positives. But we set our switches to deliver the requested one napalm each, lined up our run from west to east, fanned out into a finger-four formation, and earned our flight pay. Jinking and looking back, the napalm looked even more horrible than John Wayne's. Then, I was shocked and horrified to hear the FAC say, "Nice drop, Old Nick, now let's try the next peninsula to the north." Had I just dropped on the wrong target? I didn't ask. I really didn't want to know. We lined it up again and delivered our remaining napalm.

The visibility was three miles or less and we dropped the napalm somewhere below 500 feet. As we pulled off the target, we were suddenly in the midst of many helicopters. Four Crusaders at 400 knots amongst at least ten helicopters! We didn't have a mid-air only because God was protecting fools, drunks, and pilots (both fighter and helicopter types). From the radio conversation that followed, it was obvious FAC didn't know those guys were going to be in the area. He was as surprised, and paralyzed, as we were.[11]

Lt. Freeman Marcy, also a Crusader pilot in VF-111, had similar recollections of these early missions: "The other planes in these flights also dropped a lot of duds. The bombs we were dropping were surplus World War Two and obviously the fuzes were bad. This was particularly disgusting because to drop we came in right over the tree tops, down into small arms fire, where a 25 dollar rifle could bring down a million dollar airplane and fully trained pilot."[12]

On 8 July USS *Intrepid* (CVA-11) relieved *Oriskany* on Dixie Station; *Oriskany* then proceeded north to relieve USS *Hancock* (CVA-19). As she steamed north, an event happened that sent shockwaves throughout the tight-knit air wing. Cdr. Al Williams, the new Sundowner executive officer, turned in his wings. Lt. Cdr. Bob Pearl was one of those closest to the event and described the effect on VF-111:

> Our executive officer was a fine aviator. We had just been through an ORI in Hawaii and VF-111 got very high marks in a large part due to his flying and gunnery skills. Subsequently, O-boat was sent to Dixie Station for about 4 days to cut our teeth in combat after we arrived in the Gulf of Tonkin. . . . Then we headed north. That afternoon in my stateroom I got a call from my skipper, Cdr Cook, asking if I would be willing to be his XO. I was stunned to say the least but of course agreed and asked him what had happened. Turns out we had a quick all officers meeting (AOM) in the ready room shortly thereafter where the XO explained that he was turning in his wings and why.
>
> He knew, I'm sure better than anyone, the timing was critical and that we had a full ready room of junior officers that needed his leadership. Turns out that it was his feeling that "leadership in combat" was the one thing he didn't feel he could provide because of a fixation he had developed (head in the cockpit) from a previous aircraft incident earlier in his career. [Williams had ejected from an F-8A, and memories of the accident caused him to focus on his instruments instead of looking outside the cockpit, a deadly habit in combat.] He had once tried to give up his wings in the RAG but had been convinced not to. One can argue that it took a huge individual to make that decision at that critical juncture. Others will have different views. One thing I can say is that we had a magnificent bunch of officers in VF-111. They took it in stride and performed extremely well in combat in spite of the leadership void. To this day they are all very close. I stepped up as XO for a short period until Cdr Rasmussen arrived from the states then I reverted to Maintenance Officer.[13]

Williams was transferred immediately. Unfortunately, as he was being flown off the ship in a transport aircraft, his seat came unbolted, and he was severely injured during the catapult shot. The aircraft turned around and landed back aboard *Oriskany*, where he spent several hours in surgery. In the years since, many variations of the story have circulated. Most accounts are unfounded and miss the true lesson—that it indeed took tremendous amounts of fortitude to make such a decision. As the events of 1967 eventually proved, having sound leadership was critical to survival. Even though Williams's resignation was a momentary setback, VF-III was well served by the turn of events. Cdr. Bob Rasmussen proved to be very capable, and his leadership helped pull the Sundowners through the dark months ahead.

The Bridge at Co Trai

As *Oriskany* steamed north, she joined USS *Constellation* (CVA-64) as Rolling Thunder 50, the campaign against North Vietnam's POL system, reached its peak. In March the JCS proposed strikes against the entire POL system and major industrial centers in northeastern Vietnam. For the first time since Rolling Thunder's inception, McNamara actually sided with the JCS and recommended seven of their nine proposed targets. Planning began between Seventh Air Force and Seventh Fleet for strikes against the POL system in late April 1966.[14] Though the strikes were planned for late April, McNamara's concern that only approved targets would be hit, without collateral damage to third-country shipping or civilians, delayed them. After two months of consultation and analysis, McNamara finally ordered the attacks. The order came with heavy restrictions to avoid shipping in Haiphong and to minimize civilian casualties.[15]

The strikes were scheduled for 23 June, but the impending raids were leaked to the media. Newspaper stories written by *Wall Street Journal* correspondent Philip Geyelin appeared throughout the United States, revealing that North Vietnam's POL system was going to be struck soon and giving vital details.[16] After postponing the raids for yet another week, the POL system was finally struck on 29 June 1966, more than a year after Rolling Thunder had begun. The attacks came too late, because during that time the North Vietnamese had been able to disperse their POL stocks and build up defenses around POL facilities. As expected, the POL campaign triggered intense domestic and foreign debate concerning the expansion. The Soviets and Chinese vowed to send even more aid to the Hanoi regime.

Despite the leaks, the escalation stunned the North Vietnamese and evoked a strong response. On 1 July North Vietnamese torpedo boats launched attacks against the guided missile frigate USS *Coontz* (DLG-8) and destroyer USS *Rogers* (DD-876). The attacking boats were spotted by aircraft from the *Constellation*, which destroyed them with help from the *Hancock*. On 6 July North Vietnamese officials turned to their newest propaganda weapon, American POWs. Insisting that the Americans were common criminals, the North Vietnamese paraded fifty-two POWs through the streets of Hanoi. However, instead of undermining the U.S. war effort, as was hoped, the event became a public relations nightmare. Frenzied crowds lining the streets of Hanoi almost killed several POWs, as well as their guards. The event highlighted Hanoi's suspected mistreatment of POWs and revolted the free world. The escalation of the POL campaign in July resulted in the largest number of SAMs fired to date, as well as a dramatic increase in MiG activity by the VPAF. Because of the increased activity by both sides, July became the deadliest month yet for American airmen, with forty-three aircraft lost.

On 8 July McNamara and several aides arrived in Honolulu to attend a conference with military commanders. The report given by Admiral Sharp was sobering. Despite significant efforts and tremendous casualties on both sides, Hanoi was not willing to negotiate and had actually increased its level of support in South Vietnam. Despite recommendations for more troops and increased sorties, McNamara balked. He acquiesced to a partial increase in sorties, and the next day Rolling Thunder 50 became Rolling Thunder 51. Several bridges were added to the target list, though POL continued to be the primary focus. Admiral Sharp also asked for permission to strike airfields to deal with the growing MiG threat, a request that was denied. More importantly, armed reconnaissance was now permitted throughout North Vietnam except for the restricted areas around Hanoi and Haiphong and the buffer zone along the Chinese border. This expansion of the air war had grave consequences for *Oriskany* and her aviators. Under Rolling Thunder 51, the number of sorties flown over North Vietnam increased to ten thousand per month, *2.5 times the number of sorties flown during the same period a year prior.* At the same time, the North

Vietnamese defenses grew daily: Hanoi's antiaircraft gun inventory had risen from about 849 to 4,200, or an average of about 205 guns per month.[17] The dramatic increase in sorties, coupled with good weather and the mounting North Vietnamese defenses, meant that Air Wing 16 was walking into the proverbial hornets' nest.

It did not take long for *Oriskany* to get stung. On 12 July the ship launched her third Alpha strike in as many days—a strike against the Dong Nam fuel storage area 20 miles northeast of Haiphong. A-4s from both VA-163 and VA-164 bombed two large POL tanks with good results, while an Iron Hand flight destroyed a SAM site in the vicinity.

During the strike, the air wing suffered its first loss of 1966. After being shot down and rescued the previous October, Lt. (junior grade) Rick Adams became something of a lucky charm among the pilots of VF-162 due to the tale of his coolness under fire. Adams was flying the TARCAP when multiple SAMs forced the entire strike to evade, losing precious altitude in the process. Eventually, his flight ended up low enough that Adams took hits in his tailpipe, which quickly caught fire.

Once again Adams turned his burning Crusader for the safety of the gulf. He cleared one ridge line before the plane began an uncontrollable death roll to the right. Adams's wingman on this flight was Lt. Cdr. Butch Verich, who called for Adams to eject. A terse exchange followed, with Adams finally commenting, cool as ice, "Sorry about that. See you next year!" before he ejected.[18] He had really meant to say, "See you in ten years." Adams landed in rugged jungle near a village less than 20 miles from Hanoi and the plethora of defenses surrounding the city. Any rescue attempt was certain to be hotly contested.

Fortunately, Verich followed Adams's chute and marked his location, thus giving the CSAR forces the information they needed to attempt a rescue so far inland.[19] A flight of four VA-152 Skyraiders orbited nearby as the RESCAP, and Cdr. Gordon Smith, VA-152's commanding officer, left two Skyraiders with the rescue helicopter while he and his wingman flew ahead to begin the rescue. Verich and Lt. Dick Wyman talked the Skyraiders onto Adams's location. Smith took control of the rescue and called for the CSAR helicopter, a Sea King from HS-6.

Lt. Cdr. Eric Schade and his wingman, Lt. Jack Feldhaus, escorted the helicopter toward Adams, making repeated runs on several gun positions in order to draw fire away from the helicopter. Despite hits to Schade's Skyraider, they suppressed AAA long enough for Lt. Bill Waechter's Sea King to reach the surreal scene: Adams's bright parachute draped atop the jungle canopy, close to the wreckage of his F-8, which stuck out of the mountain with a smoking tailpipe. The jungle foliage was dense enough that the wreckage never actually reached the ground. While the helicopter hovered overhead its crew lowered a jungle penetrator (essentially a heavy weight with folding seats capable of being lowered through the dense jungle foliage) and pulled Adams to safety. As Adams arrived in the cabin of the SH-3, ground fire erupted. Waechter was on his first mission over North Vietnam. "Is it always this rough?" he asked, not knowing that this was Adams's second shoot-down in less than nine months.[20] Less than four hours later, Adams was back aboard the *Oriskany*. The rest of the strike had landed much earlier, and they all crowded around him to welcome him home. After his first shoot down, fellow squadron members, each carrying mock missiles and guns, lined up to greet him as he walked their gauntlet. Now they hollered, "No one gets shot down twice!" As the war ground on, they would be proven wrong on more than one occasion.

As the only aviator to have been shot down and rescued twice, Rick Adams gained even more notoriety. *Time* magazine ran an article covering his exploits in its 29 July 1966 edition. In the article, Adams mused over the events: "The carrier isn't much, but it beats being paraded around Hanoi with a rope around your neck."[21] The navy declared that after ejecting twice, Adams could not fly over North Vietnam anymore. He was transferred back to the United States, where he became a member of the navy's aerial demonstration team, the Blue Angels.

In an attempt to counter the increased VPAF MiG activity during July, the navy took steps to improve radar coverage of the airspace over North Vietnam. Its goal was to provide timely intelligence and warning of airborne threats to American aircraft. The navy had taken small steps toward this goal in April 1965, deploying destroyers far into the northern limits of the gulf. In July 1966 CTF-77 established a Positive Identification Radar Advisory Zone (PIRAZ) that covered eastern North Vietnam and the gulf. Typically a guided missile frigate or cruiser, the PIRAZ ship—immortalized by its call sign, Red Crown—used its advanced air surveillance radar and communication gear to track and identify all aircraft within the zone. Red Crown monitored incoming and outgoing strikes to warn them of airborne MiGs and vectored aircraft that were low on fuel to nearby airborne tankers. The creation of the PIRAZ, coupled with the air force's deployment of EC-121 "College Eye" Airborne Command and Control, helped compensate for the enormous advantage enjoyed by VPAF pilots flying under their own radar control. The main PIRAZ ship, stationed only 25–30 miles from the mouth of the Red River, was supported by two destroyers, one to the north and one to the south. These became the northern and southern SAR destroyers, whose mission was not only to protect Red Crown but to act as a staging base for CSAR operations.

As part of Rolling Thunder 51, the bridge at Co Trai, the Uong Bi thermal power plant, and the Hanoi-to-Haiphong highway were authorized as new targets. They were well inside the restricted areas and only struck when authorized. As one of the main river crossings south of Hanoi, the Co Trai bridge was heavily defended. On 13 July it was attacked for the second time in two days. During this second strike, F-4 Phantoms from *Constellation* managed to shoot down a 923rd FR MiG-17.

The next day it would be *Oriskany*'s turn to tangle with MiGs; however, the outcome would not be as fortuitous. Cdr. Dick Bellinger, the Hunters' (VF-162) boisterous commanding officer, attempted new escort tactics that backfired badly and resulted in him being shot down by MiGs in the vicinity of Co Trai. Bellinger and the other pilots of CVW-16 noticed a pattern to the defenses during Rolling Thunder 50 and 51. MiGs repeatedly intercepted the last Alpha strike of the day, using GCI and the poor visibility normally encountered in the later afternoon to their advantage.[22]

On 14 July Cdr. Wynn Foster led the last Alpha strike of the day, a strike against the Red River storage facilities at Nam Dinh. Simultaneous with *Oriskany*'s strike, Air Wing 14 from USS *Ranger* (CVA-61) attacked the Phu Ly bridges that had been missed but damaged by Air Wing 16 four days earlier. Foster coordinated with Cdr. Fred Palmer, Air Wing 14's CAG, to ensure that both strike groups launched at the same time. CVW-14 would enter and exit their Phu Ly targets on a north-to-south heading, while CVW-16 proceeded feet-dry 40 miles farther up the coast and track toward Hanoi. It was hoped that the simultaneous approaches would appear on North Vietnamese radar scopes as a massive two-pronged strike on Hanoi and elicit a response from North Vietnamese MiGs.[23] Bellinger took the idea a step further and developed a plan to deploy a flight of F-8s ahead of the afternoon Alpha strike. He reasoned that North Vietnamese GCI controllers would vector MiGs against the F-8s, believing them to be an unescorted flight of bombers.

VF-162 launched four Crusaders on 14 July to serve as the deceptive MiG CAP. Bellinger launched with Lt. Cdr. Chuck Tinker and Lt. Dick Wyman. The fourth aircraft returned to *Oriskany* due to damage sustained during the catapult launch. The Alpha strike followed three minutes behind Bellinger's flight and remained at 20,000 feet to make the impression that Hanoi could indeed be the target.

As the Alpha strike went feet-dry, it turned south toward Nam Dinh, and Bellinger's flight continued westward to simulate a strike on the Co Trai bridge. The North Vietnamese took the bait. The three Crusaders were at 3,000 feet over broken cloud layers when they heard a MiG warning from the air wing's E-1B Tracer. Shortly after, Wyman, on Bellinger's left wing, sighted two 923rd FR MiGs below, the MiGs passing aft of the flight going from right to left. Wyman called out the MiGs, and the fight was on.

Both Wyman and Bellinger immediately lit their afterburners to accelerate and then broke left and down, trying to spot the MiGs. Upon hearing Wyman's call, Tinker jerked his head to look around and unintentionally disconnected the cord connecting his radio to his helmet. Unable to hear the ensuing radio calls, Tinker was out of position for a left turn. He broke right, intending to reverse and join back up with Wyman and Bellinger.

VF-162's engagement was off to a bad start, and so was the rest of the strike. After going feet-dry, the strike package flew inland for 10 miles before turning south toward Nam Dinh and beginning a rapid descent from 20,000 feet. As *Oriskany*'s strike approached the target, Foster looked down and was appalled to see four Skyhawks from *Ranger* fly directly over Nam Dinh at roof-top level. The *Ranger*'s Skyhawks were 30 degrees and 10 miles off course as they raced back to *Ranger* following their own strike. According to Foster, "So much for surprise. The Nam Dinh gunners were wide awake for our arrival, and all prior speculation about a possible North Vietnamese ammunition shortage was dispelled a few seconds later."[24]

As Foster and his strike dodged AAA over Nam Dinh, the odds continued against VF-162. Bellinger and Wyman searched frantically for the MiGs and nearly collided with them. According to Wyman, "I dove down through the clouds expecting the MiGs to be going in the direction I initially saw them. Radar must have been turning them as we dove. I was looking to the left and almost ran into the first MiG."[25]

While separated, Tinker saw a MiG-17 streak by, its guns firing. The MiG broke away without hitting any Crusaders and was not seen again. Tinker then spotted a second MiG coming up through clouds to his right, its pilot attempting to maneuver into a position behind Wyman. As this was happening, both Wyman and Bellinger engaged a third MiG-17. Wyman pulled lead on the MiG, attempting a shot with the Crusader's 20 mm cannons. Wyman was about to shoot when Tinker flew through the engagement, passing in front of his MiG. The MiG pilot also spotted Tinker, reversed his turn, and commenced tracking him. Unable to hear his radio, Tinker now had a MiG-17 behind him, with both Wyman and Bellinger behind the MiG, screaming alerts at Tinker. All four aircraft were in a tight left turn when another MiG joined the fight.

Now there were five aircraft doing level turns between a layer of clouds and the ground. Wyman eventually squeezed off some shots at one of the MiGs, but he only had one working cannon—the rest had jammed under the heavy Gs. Noting that his hits in the wing had no effect, Wyman then fired a Sidewinder. Because Wyman fired outside the effective envelope of the missile, it missed. Bellinger then pulled into position to attempt a shot on Wyman's MiG. As he pulled up, the remaining MiG, piloted by Ngo Duc Mai, cut across the circle and blasted Bellinger in the right wing, tail, and lower fuselage.[26]

Still unable to hear any of the radio calls, Tinker saw Bellinger get hit. At the same time, he finally noticed the MiG on his tail. Tinker dove for the ground in afterburner and headed for the safety of the gulf. As the MiG broke away from Tinker, Wyman fired his second Sidewinder. The missile appeared to guide but then failed to explode as it passed behind the MiG. With no more missiles, Wyman could only watch as the two MiGs joined up and headed home. Wyman turned to find Bellinger and escort him back to *Oriskany*.

Foster's strike was successful despite the lack of surprise. Every Sky-hawk dropped its ordnance along the long, narrow waterfront in Nam Dinh, destroying the storage buildings with 24 tons of bombs. VA-164's Iron Hand division had encountered no SAMs in the area and instead employed as flak suppression. In less than three minutes, the attack was over, with all of the *Oriskany*'s airplanes safe and headed for the gulf.

All of them but Bellinger's. Cannon hits from the MiG-17 destroyed his hydraulic system and caused his port spoiler to stick in the full-up position. Without hydraulics, Bellinger couldn't raise the Crusader's wing and thus could not land onboard *Oriskany*. Bellinger flew toward Da Nang, trailing a stream of fuel. His fuel worries were compounded by the discovery that he couldn't refuel from airborne tankers because the refueling probe wouldn't extend. An initial vector given to Bellinger by *Oriskany* meant that he had a chance of making Da Nang. Unfor-tunately, they were wrong—once the heading was updated, Bellinger realized he would not make it. Just 16 miles from Da Nang, Bellinger's fuel-starved Crusader finally quit, and he ejected. Wyman barely had enough fuel to remain overhead while he contacted the rescue forces at Da Nang. As Bellinger landed in the water, two Vietnamese junks began heading for him. Wyman made several low passes to dissuade them before an air force HH-43 Huskie helicopter from Da Nang res-cued Bellinger. Bellinger was tired, wet, and mad as hell at the unex-pected turn of events. In typical fighter pilot fashion, both Wyman and Bellinger spent the night drinking at the Da Nang officers club before returning to *Oriskany* the following day.

As was his style, Bellinger remained upbeat about his narrow escape. He didn't hold a grudge, nor did he blame others for the turn of events. Later, he chided Wynn Foster, claiming that Foster's mission planning had been so precise that it included having the lead fighter shot down.[27] During Rolling Thunder, most fighter pilots considered themselves lucky if they even saw MiGs during their tour, let alone tangle with them. Bellinger, however, vowed he would get a MiG, and by October, he would have his revenge.

By mid-July, ordnance shortages began impacting operations through-out the Gulf of Tonkin. The shortages affected not only bombs but also valuable air-to-air missiles. *Oriskany* suffered from a shortage of AIM-9 Sidewinders and launch rails, which meant that F-8s could only carry two Sidewinders, not four. A new version of the Sidewinder, the AIM-9D, was available, but on a limited basis. The AIM-9D had a much wider look-angle, meaning it could detect the heat of an enemy aircraft at a much greater angle, and a pilot could fire it without getting directly behind the enemy's tail. However, due to shortages of both missiles and rails, *Oriskany* F-8s began flying with just one AIM-9B and one AIM-9D, if it was available. The missile shortage would eventually got so bad that by August, helicopters ferried the few available missiles from carrier to carrier, depending upon who needed them the most.[28]

Starting on 15 July, Typhoon Mamie began hampering air operations in the gulf. Flights over North Vietnam ceased as ships scurried out of the Category II typhoon's path. By 19 July the weather had improved enough to resume Rolling Thunder, and it was *Oriskany*'s turn to revisit the Co Trai bridge. The air wing mustered a maximum effort, launching thirty-seven airplanes carrying 25 tons of ordnance. Led by CAG Bob Spruit, the crews launched and rendezvoused overhead, with Crusaders and Skyhawks refueling from airborne tankers. Once the entire strike package topped off their fuel tanks, they pressed into North Vietnam. As the strike crossed the coast, they turned toward Co Trai. However, Spruit had difficulty spotting the bridge. In the wake of the recent typhoon, scattered clouds covered the target area. The clouds, coupled with the usual haze, made it tough to spot the target. Breaking radio silence, Spruit asked if any of the pilots had acquired the target. Lt. Frank Elkins of VA-164 responded that he had the target visually and that the rest of the aircraft should follow him as he began the attack run.

As predicted, the North Vietnamese response was fierce. As Lt. Frank Elkins wrote in his diary, "For twenty-three minutes there was flak, bullets, and everything that they could throw at us. I damn near blacked myself out dodging some of that garbage. At the target, our visibility was greatly reduced by flying steel."[29] At least thirteen SAMs were launched at them. Coming off the target, Elkins looked up to his left and saw an F-8 flying home. At the same time, he noted a SAM launch in his mirror. After making a quick call noting the SAM launch over the radio, Elkins began to evade. While Elkins evaded down among the karsts, he looked up in time to watch the SAM hit Lt. Terry Denison's F-8. The missile struck the intake of his Crusader, destroying the aircraft immediately. The strike package flew toward the gulf as Cdr. Charles A. Lindbergh "Cal" Swanson, VF-162's executive officer and the Crusader flight lead, tried to raise Denison on the radio. It was a grim and somber Hunter ready room after the strike returned to *Oriskany*. The Hunters had just lost their third airplane in a week, with their first fatality. As with the losses experienced over bridges at Hai Duong and Thanh Hoa, the bridge at Co Trai began to take on a sort of mythical status.

The Legend of Captain Hook

On 23 July the air wing returned to the Dong Nam POL storage facility where Rick Adams had been shot down eleven days prior. Sixteen aircraft flew a hair-raising low-level flight through mountains and thunderstorms to destroy several large POL storage tanks. As they escaped toward the gulf secondary explosions and oily black smoke rose thousands of feet in the air. VF-111's Lt. Cdr. Foster Teague and Lt. Freeman Marcy spotted a MiG and attempted to give chase, only to fly through a well-laid flak trap. Other than being terrified, the pair was unscathed and wisely turned for the water and safety.

Events that same morning produced one of naval aviation's greatest legends to come out of Vietnam. Cdr. Wynn Foster's tale is one of courage and determination under duress, along with a will to survive when the odds were decidedly against him. Foster led a pair of Skyhawks to attack POL facilities at Vinh, a known AAA hot spot that was usually to be avoided at all costs. Foster performed a very thorough brief for his new wingman, Lt. (junior grade) Tom Spitzer, who had joined the squadron a few days earlier after traveling halfway around the world to meet *Oriskany*. Foster and Spitzer launched at 0750 and climbed overhead the ship. Once joined, the two Skyhawks departed at 0810 and proceeded toward the coast. As the flight crossed feet-dry, the section started its descent, quickly running into barrage AAA off to their right. Foster later wrote,

> I called the flak to my wingman's attention, and told him to keep jinking. A few seconds later I heard a loud "bang" followed by a "whoosh" and I felt a stinging sensation in my right elbow. I realized I had been hit and looked down at my right arm. The arm was

missing from the elbow down and half my right forearm was lying on the starboard console."

During the first few seconds I had a hard time convincing myself that most of my right arm was missing, but when I tried to move the stick, I was convinced. I took the stick with my left hand and started to head the aircraft back out to sea. I radioed my wingman that I had been hit, then broadcast "Mayday," giving my side number and general position. I told my wingman to keep jinking and to get clear of the area. My airspeed was dropping so I eased the nose down and tried to hold about 220 knots.[30]

Taking stock of his situation, Foster estimated at least a 57 mm shell had blown out most of the canopy, and his cockpit was a mess, with shrapnel, flesh, and blood splattered over the windscreen and instrument panel. Foster attempted to make a couple of radio calls to Tom Spitzer to see if he was okay, but the noise was too great.[31]

Bleeding profusely, Foster debated flying back to *Oriskany* but thought better of it. Instead, he opted to fly toward the nearest SAR destroyer, stationed roughly 30 miles from where the flight had gone feet-dry. The decision likely saved Foster's life. As it turned out, USS *Reeves* (DLG-24) was the only ship north of Yankee Station with a doctor onboard. Heading for the ship, Foster descended through 2,500 feet. He had previously been flying on only 70 percent of the damaged Skyhawk's power: "Things had been pretty confusing, and it was the first time I had looked at the RPM since getting hit. I advanced the throttle and the RPM began to build up. The engine seemed to be working properly and I climbed back to 4,000 feet."[32] He and Spitzer contacted *Reeves* to inform them they were approaching and that he would require immediate medical attention. Beginning to feel weak, Foster knew he would have to eject and inflate his flotation gear, which made up part of his survival equipment, before he passed out. Passing through 3,000 feet and a small undercast layer, Foster saw the ship turn and head toward him.

With shock setting in, Foster began experiencing tunnel vision. He was only 3 miles from *Reeves* when he reached up and pulled the ejection handle with his left hand: "The next thing I knew I was tumbling or spinning. I heard a sequence of several snaps and pops, then felt the bladders toss me out of the seat. Shortly thereafter the chute opened and I seemingly was suspended in midair. . . . I looked around. The view was beautiful—Blue Ocean, white clouds above, and the destroyer steaming below. The war seemed a million miles away."[33]

Foster landed roughly half a mile from the destroyer, and the ship already had a whaleboat in the water. Bobbing back to the surface, Foster managed to disconnect himself from his parachute so that it wouldn't drag him beneath the surface. Once the whaleboat came alongside, numerous hands reached out to pull him into the boat. Up to that point Foster had felt little pain, but the ejection combined with immersion in saltwater made the pain unbearable. A corpsman in the whaleboat gave him one injection, which he never felt:

> The pain was severe, so I asked the sailor holding my head to break out the morphine Syrettes I carried in my left sleeve pocket. He said he had never given morphine so I mumbled step by step instructions. I told him to unscrew the plastic cap and throw it away, push the wire plunger all the way into the Syrette, then pull it out and throw it away.
>
> The sailor was obviously shook because he pulled out the plunger and threw the Syrette over the side. We went through the whole thing again with the second Syrette, this time successfully, and the sailor got the morphine into my arm. I thought I was going to pass out so I told the sailor to remember to tell the doctor that I had been given morphine.[34]

Once onboard *Reeves*, Foster received initial medical treatment and was then prepped for transfer back to *Oriskany*. In his drug-induced haze, Foster mistakenly thought he was being transferred to *Ranger* and yelled at the doctor that he wanted to be returned to *Oriskany*, not *Ranger*. Injuries notwithstanding, pride in one's ship took priority! Foster made one more request as four sailors carried his stretcher down the passageway. Foster stopped them by grabbing hold of the nearest solid object, announcing that he was not leaving without his beloved blue flight boots. The boots had been a prank from the junior officers of VA-163. While he was temporarily off *Oriskany* seeking medical attention for an ulcer, Foster's junior officers had taken his flight boots and dyed them blue. Their squadron color was blue, and the good-hearted prank was in deference to his efforts in refurbishing the squadron ready room on the ship, which was now resplendent in blue. With reassurances from the doctor, Foster relaxed and was flown back to *Oriskany*.[35]

Back aboard *Oriskany*, tales of Wynn Foster's saga flew throughout the air wing and other ships on the line. It also gave the aviators something else to think about. While each loss affected the men, losses in the air war typically meant that a pilot had been killed or captured and that he would not return to the ship. The nature of Foster's wound terrified the pilots in the air wing who were unaccustomed to such events. Frank Elkins described the effects of Foster's loss in his journal:

Falcon's [Foster's] accident has given everyone a different twist in their bowels, a different fear. It's easier in some ways to see someone blown to bits instantly than to see a man lose an arm. I've always said it's easier to die for an ideal than to live for it. Dying takes only a moment's courage, while life is a battle against day-by-day eroding and grinding forces. To stand up to life and to hold to high standards sincerely is a more difficult price than an instant death. It's easier to go out in a glorious flaming surrender to death in favor of some cause than it is to boldly, drudgingly, daily stand up to be counted on the side of that you value most.[36]

Foster's loss also typified the demoralizing effect the loss of a senior officer could have on a junior pilot. Tom Spitzer had just joined the Saints (VA-163) and was on his first combat mission over North Vietnam. Though Foster was gravely wounded, one of his main concerns while he lay in *Oriskany*'s sick bay was the impact on Tom Spitzer: "With the squadron for only a week, Tom had had a traumatic introduction to combat as an eyewitness to his skipper's getting shot out of the sky. I was concerned that Tom might somehow think that my getting shot down was his fault."[37]

Wynn Foster remained onboard *Oriskany* for another week. His condition was still quite serious. The wound was left open and treated only to stop the bleeding and prepare for surgery to be performed off the ship. Both the flight surgeon, Lt. Dan Lestage, and the ship's surgeon, Dr. Dick Donahue, had done what they could, but Foster's condition required proper medical facilities not available onboard. Medical evacuation to the Philippines was warranted; however, it was unknown if Foster could survive the stress of the catapult shot required to get him off the ship. *Oriskany* was scheduled to depart Yankee Station in a week, and the doctors decided that he should remain onboard the ship until it pulled into Cubi Point in the Philippines.

There were other reasons for delaying Foster's departure. He had taken command the previous November when Cdr. Harry Jenkins was shot down. At 0800 he was the executive officer, and by 0900 Foster found himself in command. The war ground on, and the change-of-command ceremony he and Jenkins had planned never happened. In a service steeped in ceremony and tradition, the change-of-command ceremony is a time-honored tradition. Now it was all happening again. CAG Spruit intervened on Foster's behalf, taking his case to Capt. John Iarrobino. It was simply the right thing to do. Now Foster would remain in command for another week, and as *Oriskany* pulled into port there could be an official change-of-command ceremony.

On 23 July heavy weather began to hinder air operations. The next day, Tropical Storm Ora was upgraded to a typhoon as it plowed into the gulf. Attacks on POL targets continued despite the heavy thunderstorms. However, on 25 July most of the day's sorties were canceled due to the high sea states and even poorer weather. Both *Oriskany* and *Ranger* evaded the storm, although they still launched a limited number of sorties—mainly BARCAP and the tanker support required for those missions. While the ship evaded the storm, aviators used the down time as a chance for much-needed stress relief. Attack squadron pilots were summoned to Ready Room 5 for an impromptu medical brief. The brief was, in reality, a secret opportunity for everyone to drink lemonade fortified with 190 proof medicinal alcohol. Drinking aboard U.S. Navy ships had been done away with during the Prohibition era, but senior leadership looked the other way during Vietnam. As long as things didn't get too out of hand, drinking was seen as a chance for pilots to blow off a little steam after the tremendous stress of flying missions over North Vietnam. Most aviators never drank during days when flight operations were in progress, but if there was guaranteed down time, such as when transiting from one area to another, out came the stash. While it was not condoned, the higher-ups knew about it, and when one of the stateroom parties got a little boisterous,

rules would come down from the bridge that no more than four officers were allowed to gather for the stateroom "meetings." On this occasion, due to the weather, everyone from the CAG down to the ensigns
took part in the partying.

Subic Bay and Liberty

As the weather cleared, the end of the line period loomed, yet missions continued for the next two days. Before departing the line, VA-152
took part in the dramatic rescue of a downed F-105 pilot, Capt. James
Mitchell. Shot down near Dong Hoi, Mitchell would have been captured without the cover provided by the Skyraiders.[38] On 28 July VA-
164 lost their first Skyhawk when Ens. George McSwain disappeared
during an Iron Hand mission against a SAM site at the mouth of the
Song Ca River near Vinh. The flight lead detected a SAM site radiating
and closed for a Shrike missile attack. McSwain saw multiple missiles
launch from different sites and called, "Missiles away," to the flight of
three A-4s. He called again, "Keep it turning and hit the deck."[39] The
flight managed to evade six missiles from multiple sites, but the other
two pilots never saw McSwain get hit, so no rescue was attempted—he
had simply vanished.

The next day, *Constellation* relieved *Oriskany*, which duly departed
for a port call in Subic Bay. For the aviators, their first line period was
over. Unfortunately, carrier aviation is a dangerous business, and the
transit was marred by one more loss. The Ghost Riders suffered their
second loss in as many days when a new replacement, Lt. (junior
grade) Donovan Ewoldt was killed during a night proficiency flight.
Cdr. Paul Engel wanted to give Ewoldt more flight time before they
returned to combat. Engel later recalled the incident: "This was a very
sad accident in my time as the skipper of VA-164. . . . Lt Cdr Yost led
Ewoldt out of Cubi to accomplish the refreshment. It was reported
to me that weather forced the lead to descend. Ewoldt was no doubt
focused on the lead and flew into the water. The very thing that was
my worry materialized!"[40]

On Saturday morning, 30 July, *Oriskany* moored at Cubi Point's carrier pier. The crew, from the lowest seaman to the senior officers, eagerly
anticipated liberty. Sailors lived in compartments that held upward
of sixty men in tight, confined spaces. Bunks were stacked four high,

with all the sailor's worldly possessions stowed in lockers seemingly right out of a high school locker room. Sailors lined up to brush their teeth, shave, and even shower. Lines for eating, if sailors were given time to eat during flight operations, were even worse. Therefore, liberty ashore was *very* important to them. To say that the men eagerly anticipated a little female companionship and a drink away from the confines of the ship is no understatement.

Before members of VA-163 could go ashore, however, there was one last task to complete. At 1000 Cdr. Wynn Foster and Cdr. Ron Caldwell performed their change-of-command ceremony. During the ceremony, Foster received the Silver Star and a Purple Heart for his traumatic mission. He also received the Distinguished Flying Cross for leading an Alpha strike against a POL facility a few days before his life-changing flight. After the ceremony and tearful good-byes to all the members of VA-163 and Captain Iarrobino, Wynn Foster left the ship. Refusing to leave the ship via a gurney, he instead walked down the ship's brow, albeit with the assistance of doctors Lestage and Donahue. Wynn Foster faced a long period of recuperation and therapy, fighting the navy's bureaucracy to remain on active duty. The navy eventually approved his request, and Foster retired in 1972 as a captain.

The escalation of the air war resulted in higher attrition rates. While on the line, aviators found themselves living what has been described as "the tyranny of the present." The past and the future did not concern them. It could not. Their concern was day-to-day survival.[41] Time was measured by days spent on the line and how long it had been since the last port visit. As carriers came off Yankee Station for ports of call and periods of rest and recreation (R&R), pilots and the hardworking sailors had a chance to decompress. Favorite ports of call included Singapore, Hong Kong, and the much-beloved Subic Bay in the Philippines.

Stories abound of the indulgences to be had in the Philippine Islands, or the P.I. to those who had experienced them. Sailors especially loved Subic mostly because of the attractions of Olongapo City, located just outside the main gates to Subic. For ridiculously low prices, a sailor could have all the booze he wanted and satisfy any carnal urges a young mind could imagine. Po City quickly became legendary among sailors of Seventh Fleet and Task Force 77.[42]

While aviators enjoyed the P.I. as well, most of their debauchery was contained within the confines of Naval Air Station (NAS) Cubi Point. Subic Bay was a large and sprawling naval base split between the surface navy and the aviators of Cubi Point. On the Subic side of the bay was the port facility, which was not frequented by aviators. The Subic Bay officers club was typical of the period, with proper dress and etiquette being required, along with the autocratic policies of the surface navy. NAS Cubi Point and its officers club might as well have been on a different planet. The war in Vietnam had created an atmosphere in which "work hard, play harder" antics became de rigueur. As long as aviators stayed on their side of the base, the crazy behavior that occurred within "the zoo" was allowed to continue.[43]

While the Cubi officers club was not quite the *Star Wars* cantina, it was a rough and rowdy tavern. There were fistfights. There were food fights. There was broken furniture. There were aviators passed out behind the bar. The large plate-glass windows that overlooked the serene setting of Subic were often shattered by bottles of San Miguel beer. The bar often did not close until the last person left. Any damage was paid for, and the club kept going. It was not unusual to see men climbing in the exposed rafters like monkeys and setting fire to the dangling crepe-paper streamers while seeing who could let them burn the longest without torching the club. One of the favorite drinking games involved drunken attempts to emulate carrier landings.[44] The practice often ended in disaster, as most men crashed on the floor in a broken mess. It was all done to fruitlessly divert young aviators from the stresses they faced and quickly became part of the culture. An aviator could get toilet-hugging drunk and forget the stress of flying missions up north. The days would be spent recovering, either golfing or lounging poolside at the club before repeating the entire process again.[45]

As long as the war continued, Subic Bay remained a favorite of the sailors and aviators of CTF-77. Lewd behavior was permitted, as it was generally acknowledged that the men needed a way to blow off steam. More to the point, what choice did the authority figures have? The worst punishment they could mete out was to make pilots fly more missions over the beach, and they were already doing that at record-setting levels. The men were needed for the war effort, and anything that allowed them to decompress and recharge before the next line period and even more combat was acceptable.

8

The Battle Increases

As THE POL CAMPAIGN continued into August, most, if not all, of the existing large above-ground POL storage facilities were destroyed. North Vietnam expended considerable effort on dispersing remaining POL stockpiles throughout the country. Though inefficient, this proved more than enough to meet North Vietnam's small needs. The focus of effort shifted as pilots attempted to find and target smaller underground tanks and 55-gallon fuel drums scattered alongside roads. Carriers were no longer afforded the luxury of a warmup period on Dixie Station prior to moving north. The new routine consisted of three carriers on Yankee Station, with the newly arrived carrier performing several days of armed reconnaissance in lower route packages as pilots looked for POL storage sites.

As the air war intensified, each side began a series of measures and countermeasures in a desperate attempt to gain the advantage. The introduction of SAMs gave the Vietnamese an initial advantage; however, the SA-2 was vulnerable to electronic countermeasures (ECM) at key nodes in its "kill chain"—the sequence of events necessary, from initial radar detection to missile launch, for the SAM to destroy an aircraft. In the late summer of 1966, both the navy and air force began attacking the various nodes of this chain in an attempt to defeat the SAM threat. SAM regiments began operations by acquiring an aircraft with early warning radars, which then handed the target over to the SAM battery's Fan Song search radar. Jamming or otherwise disrupting the acquisition or tracking radars interrupted the kill chain. When the Fan Song began tracking an aircraft, it emitted a very distinct radar signal that could be picked up by the aircraft's RWR gear. Evasive maneuvers could often break the Fan Song's automatic tracking, and by the time an operator reacquired the fighter forty five seconds later, the aircraft could be out of range. This phase was the most critical, because with ample warning a pilot could evade a missile. Once pilots became accustomed to the systems, aural alerts provided by the RWR gear, coupled with evasive maneuvers and self-protection jammers, often defeated the SAM.

These new electronic warfare countermeasures considerably degraded the SA-2's performance and greatly alarmed the North Vietnamese. Soviet PVO-Strany specialists estimated that it took one to two missiles per kill in 1965 but three to four in 1966. However, since Soviet and Vietnamese kill claims were about seven times higher than actual losses, the figures were probably closer to ten missiles in 1965 and twenty-five missiles per kill in 1966.[1] As the war ground on through the late summer and fall, the U.S. countermeasures became so effective that the North Vietnamese were forced to place a greater emphasis on the VPAF. By committing the still immature VPAF, North Vietnam eventually lost half of its MiGs during early 1967's infamous air battles.

Oriskany began combat operations on 7 August in her deadliest month yet. Unfortunately, operational accidents continued to be as lethal as flying over North Vietnam. During the last week of August, *Oriskany* lost more airplanes in operational accidents than in actual combat. At times, it seemed that luck was the only difference between life and death. One incident on 7 August is a case in point. Lt. Cdr. Dick Schaffert was loaded with two Mk 83s for a mission when he got a bad catapult shot. In the seconds between Schaffert's salute and the catapult officer's launch signal, the holdback fitting broke before the catapult fired. Without tension, the bridle fell off his airplane in the split second before the catapult fired. The catapult flung the launch bridle ahead of the ship as Schaffert roared down the bow in afterburner. Schaffert attributed his ability to stop his Crusader on the oil-soaked flight deck just feet short of the bow to divine intervention. With his airplane in seemingly good shape, he unbelievably taxied back for another launch. Schaffert explained what happened next: "The Air Boss asked if I wanted to try it again, and with probably 25-liters of adrenalin in a 5-liter blood stream, I replied in the affirmative. Thankfully, a 19-year-old 'final checker' noticed a trail of hydraulic fluid as I was again lining up on the cat. It led to a split in the nose strut from bridle damage, which would have certainly failed on the next cat shot."[2]

In August the bomb shortage began to seriously hamper the POL campaign. Aboard *Oriskany*, this meant that Crusader squadrons, which normally used 1,000-pound Mk 83 bombs for flak suppression, were reduced to using 2.75-inch Zuni rockets. With its smaller warhead, this rocket did little to deter Vietnamese gunners. There were further consequences as old AN-M 60 series high-drag bombs came out of storage. The AN-M 65 1,000-pound bomb looked like a garbage can and was about as aerodynamic. The increased drag reduced the diminutive Skyhawk's speed by 40 knots at a minimum.[3] In a world where speed equaled life, this put pilots at even greater risk. Despite the influx of these older munitions, the fleet still lacked sufficient quantities. After mid-August, *Oriskany*'s attack squadrons often flew with less than full bomb loads, while the fighter squadrons continued to be short of Sidewinder missiles.[4]

POL and Dual Rescues at Hon Gai

As part of the POL campaign, pilots hunted the coastal waterways in an attempt to interdict supplies being ferried south. The entire Vietnamese coast, from Haiphong to the Chinese border, was a formidable area that included notable hot spots such as the naval base at Hon Gai and port facilities at Cam Pha. The region is dominated by Cat Ba and Cai Bo Islands, as well as the Fai Tsi Long Archipelago. The archipelago forms an inland waterway bounded by hundreds of small islands that provided shelter for barges, coastal freighters, and small craft plying the waters. To protect this vital flow of supplies, virtually every island was fortified with coastal artillery and AAA.

On 11 August *Oriskany* struck the few remaining POL facilities in the northern route packages. Later that day, Lt. (junior grade) Cody Balisteri of VF-111 was shot down during an armed reconnaissance mission. Roughly 10 miles south of Hon Gai, Balisteri was hit by AAA from one of the many islands. As he turned south to escape, his Crusader took more hits. Balisteri barely made it out of Ha Long Bay before numerous caution lights illuminated and his F-8 began vibrating badly. His Crusader began an uncontrollable roll to the right, and he ejected, landing at the base of a 400-foot cliff on the Île de l'Union in Ha Long Bay. A Sea King from HS-6 launched from USS *Chicago* (CG-11) to attempt a rescue. Lt. Cdr. Don Nichols and Lt. (junior grade) Rick Grant flew their helicopter toward the area, carefully picking their way through the islands of the archipelago. They eventually spotted Balisteri on a small beach at the base of the cliff. Balisteri had lost his raft upon landing and was rather reluctant to brave the pounding surf. Due to the proximity of the cliffs, the helicopter could not get close enough, so the rescue swimmer, Aviation Antisubmarine Warfare Technician 3rd Class Gary Smith, jumped into the water and swam a raft to Balisteri. Both men then paddled far enough away from the cliff to be picked up. It was at this moment that the helicopter's other crewman, Aviation Structural Mechanic 2nd Class Royce Roberts, discovered that the rescue hoist had failed. Nichols opted to attempt a capability unique to the Sea King and its boat hull–shaped fuselage. He made a dangerous water landing to allow both men to swim over to the helicopter. Fortunately, there was no North Vietnamese fire, and the rescue was successful.[5] Nichols received the Distinguished Flying Cross for the daring rescue, while his crew members each received an Air Medal. Despite his luck that day, Cody Balisteri perished during the *Oriskany*'s disastrous fire (see chapter 9 for more details about this fire).

Two days later, the Sundowners lost another Crusader in the same area. Armed reconnaissance missions continued in earnest as pilots searched for POL supplies. During a nighttime mission south of Hon Gai, eight *Oriskany* aircraft discovered a dozen fuel barges among the islands—an exceedingly rare occurrence, given the circumstances. Led by VA-163's Lt. Cdr. William Smith, they succeeded in destroying eight barges and left the remainder on fire. In the dim light of the burning barges, Smith observed a PT boat attempting to flee the area. Despite heavy AAA, Smith sank it with a direct hit. As he exited the area, Smith spotted another PT boat in a well-camouflaged position.[6] As his flight had no ordnance remaining, Smith called the nearby RESCAP for assistance.

VA-152's commander, Gordon Smith and his wingman, Lt. (junior grade) Bud Watson, responded. After a pass to verify the boat's location, Smith sank it with Zuni rockets. Another six aircraft arrived, and the air wing continued to attack the remaining barges throughout the early morning. By daybreak, the air wing had sunk eleven barges and two PT boats and had destroyed two AAA sites. Unfortunately, Lt. Cdr. Norman Levy was hit by 37 mm fire as he pulled up from his second attack run. Levy's Crusader rapidly lost its hydraulics, and the nose of the aircraft pitched up. Unable to control the Crusader, Levy ejected 5 miles south of Hon Gai and only half a mile from Dao Cat Ba, one of the largest islands in Haiphong Harbor.

As the rescue began, Lt. Cdr. Jim Harmon and Lt. (junior grade) Pete Selkey of VA-152 escorted another HS-6 Sea King through the heavily defended islands. Among the crew of the Sea King were Lt. (junior grade) Rick Grant and Petty Officer Gary Smith, who helped rescue Cody Balisteri from the same area two days prior. Due to the excellent route provided by Harmon, the helicopter flown by Grant and Lt. Cdr. George Tarrico arrived over Levy and picked him up without a shot fired.[7] The helicopter delivered Levy to the SAR destroyer, USS *Towers* (DLG-9), where he received a quick medical check prior to returning to *Oriskany*. Sadly, like his squadron mate rescued days earlier, Norman Levy also perished in the October fire (see chapter 9).

Gentleman Andre and Eric's Truck Park

The need for photo reconnaissance became critical during the POL campaign. Photo specialists spent countless hours poring over thousands of photos, looking for evidence of new or previously undiscovered POL storage sites. On 17 August Lt. Andre Coltrin, an RF-8 pilot with VFP-63, was tasked with an extremely hazardous photo reconnaissance mission to photograph POL facilities near Kep airfield northeast of Hanoi. Escorting "Gentleman Andre," as he was known within the air wing, was Capt. Wilfred Abbott, an air force fighter pilot assigned to VF-111. With Coltrin leading, the flight threaded its way through the mountains north of Haiphong and then headed west to Hanoi and Kep. Flying as low as 100 feet and as fast as 675 knots, the flight was literally so low that North Vietnamese gunners were firing down on the plane from nearby ridgelines as it roared past.[8] When his photos were developed, sailors studying the film could see clothes hung out to dry on clotheslines.[9]

After a successful pass over the intended target, Coltrin led the flight back toward the safety of the gulf. As the flight fought their way eastward, they were again under intense North Vietnamese fire. Coltrin's RF-8 shuddered from 37 mm and 57 mm AAA bracketing his aircraft. With his fuel and hydraulic gauges dropping to zero, Coltrin notified Abbott that he was in trouble. Unsure of the condition of his airplane, Coltrin climbed to a safer altitude to assess the situation and to allow Abbott to check his aircraft for damage. His RF-8 was still flying, though Coltrin didn't know if he had enough fuel to make it back. Fortunately, an alert A-4 tanker pilot was waiting for him just off the coast. Despite not having an airspeed indicator to assist in his rendezvous, Coltrin spotted the Skyhawk and received enough fuel to recover on *Oriskany*. Postflight maintenance inspections revealed that one piece of shrapnel had missed the fuel manifold by mere inches, while other pieces had damaged his airspeed and angle-of-attack indicators. Lt. Andre Coltrin received the Distinguished Flying Cross for this mission, one of three he received during the war.

The three-day period from 18 to 21 August resulted in some of the more notable moments of the 1966 cruise. On 18 August Lt. Cdr. Eric Schade and Lt. Jerry Garvey of VA-152 were flying an armed reconnaissance mission between Route 1A and Route 15 just west of Cape Bang when Schade noticed some tracks leading into a wooded area. Leaving his wingman up high, Schade dove down and discovered several trucks hidden among the trees. Schade fired several Zuni rockets and was rewarded with large secondary explosions. Every rocket and strafing run by Schade and Garvey added to the inferno. As thick black smoke climbed high into the air, the pair flew their Skyraiders down low for one last check, revealing ten destroyed trucks amid the fires and secondary explosions.[10] In terms of the POL campaign, they had hit the proverbial jackpot. Schade called for assistance, and they were relieved by four more Skyraiders from VA-152. When these aircraft left, smoke from burning trucks and POL drums had climbed almost 7,000 feet. Two days later, poststrike photography showed a large forested area that had been completely burned and was still smoldering. Total damage was estimated at twenty-two trucks and three hundred to eight hundred barrels of POL stocks destroyed. It remained as a huge brown burnt-out section of jungle. Known as "Eric's Truck Park," it became a common landmark for aviators flying from Yankee Station.

Three days later, VA-152 enjoyed another similar success. Anxious to repeat Eric Schade's performance, Cdr. Gordon Smith spent time scrutinizing reconnaissance photos for areas he believed to be truck parks. After launching from *Oriskany*, Smith and his wingman arrived over one suspected area. Heavy barrage fire confirmed Smith's notion, and he discovered ten camouflaged trucks hiding in the heavy jungle. Smith's and his wingman's attacks were rewarded with numerous secondary explosions and thick black smoke from burning oil. After using all their ordnance, Smith broadcast for any aircraft to join the melee. When all was said and done, twenty-two trucks were confirmed destroyed, and large quantities of POL supplies were left burning. The success of these missions resulted in congratulatory messages from Rear Adm. Dave Richardson.[11] Unfortunately, these achievements were becoming rare for the old propeller-driven Skyraiders. Though heavily armored, A-1s lacked the speed of jets, and the skies soon proved too deadly for continued operations.

The Terrible Ts: "Come Now, or Don't Bother!"

Lt. Cdr. Foster "Tooter" Teague of VF-111 and Lt. Cdr. Tom Tucker, the VFP-63 detachment officer-in-charge (OINC), were well known among the pilots in the air wing. The pair got along famously and quickly became known as the "Terrible Ts" for their antics while on liberty. On 31 August Tucker drew the unenviable task of photographing shipping within Haiphong Harbor. Teague volunteered to be Tucker's wingman for the flight, a mission that produced some of the most dramatic images of the war. Because his mission was to fly directly over one of the most heavily defended targets in North Vietnam, Tucker planned his route to maximize his odds of survival should he be hit. Tucker planned to go feet-dry first before turning around and making a high-speed pass, heading east from the shore toward the sea. That way, if he was hit while getting the low-altitude photos of the shipping in the harbor, he would already be headed out to sea and relative safety.[12] That was the plan, anyway.

With Teague escorting him during their 600-knot photo run, Tucker ran the gauntlet of North Vietnamese defenses in the harbor. Everything from 85 mm and 37 mm AAA to 12.7 mm machine guns reached out to knock his Crusader from the sky. Eventually, a burst of 37 mm AAA hit Tucker's aircraft. He lost control and ejected as he passed 1,500 feet. Tucker's plan was a good one. He made it feet-wet, but not quite far enough. Tucker parachuted into the secondary shipping channel of Haiphong Harbor, between the coast and Dao Dinh Vu, and was immediately in trouble. He landed in the water not far from a Soviet freighter tied up to the quay wall. The Soviet crew began to lower a life boat, while sampans and sailboats got under way from the shore. Tooter Teague made multiple strafing runs to dissuade the Soviets and force the remaining boats out of the area.

At this moment, Cdr. Bob Vermilya and his copilot, Ens. Bill Runyon, and crewmen, Aviation Antisubmarine Warfare Operator Chief Petty Officer Tom Grisham and Aviation Machinist Mate 2nd Class Jerry Dunford, were flying as the on-call CSAR helicopter at the north SAR station. Vermilya was the commanding officer of HS-6 on USS *Kearsarge* (CVS-33). Five days earlier, his crew rescued two air force pilots who ejected from their stricken F-4C. Now, as they completed their second refueling of their flight, the crew heard Teague's desperate radio calls.

As Tucker began the fight of his life, Teague began to muster any and all forces available for the immediate CSAR attempt. Vermilya heard these calls and flew toward Haiphong. However, without approval from "harbor master," the shipboard SAR commander in the Tonkin Gulf, Vermilya couldn't proceed. Vermilya notified Teague he was waiting for permission and RESCAP. Teague's response was a chilling "Come now, or don't bother!"[13]

Vermilya and Runyon responded by pushing the nose of their helicopter over, flying toward the harbor as fast as they could go. As their Sea King approached the mouth of the harbor, still 6 miles from the shipping channel, the crew looked up to see two SAMs streak overhead toward Teague. AAA, machine guns, and mortar fire began zeroing in on the helicopter. At the same time, a flight of four VA-152 Skyraiders led by Lt. Cdr. William Smith and Lt. Jack Feldhaus heard Teague's radio transmission; they gathered their wingmen and proceeded to Haiphong at maximum speed. Before they arrived, Smith began coordinating with Teague, an airborne KA-3 tanker, and the SAR destroyer, whom he informed that a rescue was indeed possible. Smith told the tanker pilot to orbit overhead the destroyer for future in-flight refueling as needed. Orbiting over the harbor, Smith quickly spotted Tucker, who by this time had climbed into his raft in a frantic attempt to put some distance between himself and the ships in the harbor.

That Tucker had landed in quite possibly the worst location possible did not deter Teague or Smith's flight of Skyraiders. The aircraft were in range of many coastal AAA batteries and ships' AAA, and they were less than 5 miles from Cat Bi airfield. They also happened to be orbiting near three known SAM sites. Smith's flight continued to orbit overhead Tucker, while Teague began making strafing passes at junks along the helicopter's route of flight.

In his furtive efforts to paddle away, Tucker noticed that the nearby guns seemed to be holding their fire. Even with Smith and Feldhaus orbiting overhead, plus a new division of *Oriskany* Skyhawks, the guns remained strangely quiet. This all changed as the helicopter drew near. Previously, Vermilya had been flying at 3,000 feet, supposedly below the minimum altitude of the SAMs and still above the effective range of small arms. After watching the two SAMs pass overhead, Vermilya quickly changed his mind, dropping to wave-top height. Big Mother, as the large and ungainly Sea Kings were affectionately known, threaded her way through the harbor. Vermilya kept the helicopter so low that he believed some of the gun batteries on the shore actually held their fire so as to not hit ships in the harbor. No matter how badly the Vietnamese wanted to bring down a rescue helicopter, it would not do to damage a ship owned by one of their Communist allies.[14]

It seemed to take an eternity for Big Mother to cross the 6 miles between the outer harbor and the shipping channel. As the Sea King neared Tucker, Smith began providing course corrections to the helicopter. Meanwhile, the remaining Skyraiders and the division of Skyhawks began to strafe and bomb the guns along the harbor.

Amid the confusion, while dodging shell splashes, shipping, and smaller junks, Big Mother managed to fly right by Tucker. Even though Tucker used a signal flare, it was only Chief Grisham who spotted the red smoke and alerted the pilots. Vermilya hauled the helicopter around to the right, coming to a hover right above Tucker's raft. The maneuver caused a good deal of consternation with both Grisham and Dunford, who had been firing their guns at boats in the water. Only their quick reflexes kept them from shooting the helicopter's rotor blades as Vermilya reefed the aircraft into its turn. Vermilya had been in a hover only seconds when he heard Chief Grisham call over the intercom, "We've got him." When the cable and rescue sling hit the water, Tucker grabbed it on his first try. Before Tucker could even be lifted into the cabin, Vermilya nosed Big Mother over to run the same gauntlet through the shipping channel and the 6 miles of harbor before reaching the gulf.[15] When Tucker reached the relative safety of Big Mother, he chided both Grisham and Dunford for not firing their guns. Moving to Grisham's station, he helped feed belts of ammunition as the chief began returning fire. Tucker was furious that he had been shot at while in his chute and yelled to Grisham that he wanted to stay and fight.[16]

The whole rescue effort was caught on film, producing one of the most iconic images of the Vietnam War. Photographer's Mate 2nd Class Mike Delamore, a Seventh Fleet photographer, had hopped aboard Big Mother as she launched for the CSAR flight. He hoped to get some footage of a rescue mission over North Vietnam. He got his wish, shooting rolls of film while Grisham and Dunford manned their weapons and hoisted Tucker out of the water. Delamore's photos garnered worldwide attention and were used in newspapers and countless publications following the war.

As Vermilya cleared the outer limits of Haiphong Harbor, Smith and his division of Skyraiders departed the area, their mission complete. Despite being under continuous fire for over twenty minutes, the lumbering Sea King was untouched. USS *Towers* (DLG-9) was on SAR duty and steamed to close the fight. She was on station just outside the harbor and just outside the range of gun batteries on the shore. Vermilya and his crew successfully transferred a soggy but happy Tucker to the ship and returned to orbit around *Towers*, their time as the CSAR helicopter for the day not yet complete. Tucker was flown back to *Oriskany* later that day. For their part in rescuing Tucker, Teague and Vermilya were each awarded the Silver Star, while Runyon was awarded the Distinguished Flying Cross. Both Grisham and Dunford received Air Medals.

While Tucker's successful rescue did wonders for the morale of men flying daily missions over North Vietnam, in reality it was just another day in what had become a meat grinder. The air war had evolved into an all-out bloody battle, with each side trading continuous blows. By the end of August, it was obvious to military leadership that the POL campaign had failed. McNamara thought otherwise, and the emphasis on POL continued, with large numbers of aircraft being sent after small, dispersed POL sites. It didn't help that restrictions remained in place. The CIA estimated that out of 66,000 tons of POL stocks remaining, up to 17,000 remained in off-limits areas. Reconnaissance photographs showed city streets lined with 55-gallon barrels that couldn't be touched. In September two Communist ships docked in Haiphong and offloaded another 20,000 tons of fuel, adding to the task of interdiction. The POL campaign continued, despite recommendations from CINCPAC, the JCS, the DIA, and the CIA.[17]

PIRAZ Failure

As American ECM against SAM and AAA radars became more effective, VPAF MiG activity increased. The second line period saw a marked growth in the tenacity and aggression displayed by MiG pilots. Communist pilots worked closely with GCI units at Phuc Yen and Bac Mai, demonstrating their ability to sneak up on strike packages virtually undetected. The VPAF quickly realized the importance of concentrating on bombers, forcing them to jettison their loads, versus tangling with American fighters. As a result of this increased MiG activity, the PIRAZ system became an essential element of U.S. operations over North Vietnam.

During the last two weeks of August, MiGs continually intercepted strikes. On 16 August VA-163's Lt. Cdr. William Smith and Lt. (junior grade) Peter Munro were jumped by MiG-17s as they attacked a train. Both Smith and Munro evaded the MiGs while calling for support from available fighters. CVW-16 encountered MiGs on one other occasion, while other air wings had their own MiG encounters. These engagements were uneventful until MiGs finally drew blood on 5 September.[18] On that fateful Monday, *Oriskany* launched a late-afternoon mission to destroy a train discovered between Nam Dinh and Phu Ly. VF-111 provided four Crusaders for the TARCAP, led by Lieutenant Commander Teague.

With no tanker support available, Teague planned to break up the TARCAP. Teague's section would go over the beach first, and upon reaching bingo fuel, they would call the second section of Capt. Wilfred Abbott and Lt. Randy Rime, waiting just offshore. During the mission, things went according to plan until Teague called bingo fuel. As Abbott and Rime relieved Teague's section, things began to unravel. Rime didn't know it, but his radio had failed. At the same time, poor weather and heavy clouds made it difficult for Rime to fly Loose Deuce. He often found himself flying in trail just to keep sight of Abbott.

The Skyhawks struck the railroad cars and headed for the gulf. Abbott and Rime continued to orbit in the target area, waiting for the A-4s to call feet-wet when they were hit. Vietnamese CGI controllers successfully vectored two MiG-17s from the 923rd FR onto the Crusaders. The section was on its last turn when Abbott spotted the MiGs behind them. Abbott called for a right break as the MiGs began firing their cannons. Rime was hit first and was immediately in trouble. Rime had taken 23 -mm hits in the cockpit. Miraculously, the 23 mm shell never exploded, sparing his life. Nevertheless, he was severely cut by glass as his canopy exploded around him. Rime was also streaming fuel. Several 37 mm hits destroyed both leading-edge wing droops and punctured his wing fuel tanks. They also destroyed his radio and the emergency air system used to raise the Crusader's wing in the event of hydraulic failure, leaving Rime in dire straits.[19]

When the MiGs plastered Rime, Abbott pitched up to cover him, attempting a nose-high, high-G reversal. It was a calculated risk—the maneuver would put him directly in front of the MiGs but traveling perpendicular to them. Abbott had hoped the Vietnamese wouldn't be able to handle a high-deflection shot, arguably the most difficult aerial gunnery skill to master. Unfortunately for him, they could.

The Vietnamese pilot almost opened fire too late but managed to get enough rounds into Abbott's Crusader to completely destroy it. At least one round hit Abbott's cockpit. His canopy was shattered, his instrument panel was a mess, and the control stick went limp. Somehow, his helmet disappeared, along with the upper ejection handle and face curtain to his ejection seat. Abbott ejected in a steep nose-down attitude, breaking his right leg in the process. He was quickly captured by the Vietnamese and spent the next seven years as a POW.[20]

Rime was lucky to have survived, but he wasn't out of the woods just yet. His crippled F-8 was the last airplane to make it back for *Oriskany*'s next recovery. He was down to just 700 pounds of fuel, which was enough for one landing attempt. He couldn't raise the Crusader's wing, which meant dangerously fast landing approach speeds. Because he didn't have a radio, *Oriskany*'s flight deck crew wasn't notified of his situation and thus didn't have time to rig the barricade, a gigantic nylon net that literally caught damaged aircraft in midair. He had one chance at landing and that was it. Rime made his approach using left and right rudder to see over the nose of the Crusader. As he crossed the ramp, Rime saw wave-off lights. Normally Rime would have obeyed these signals at any cost, but he continued—he had no choice. Rime remembers saying to himself, "I don't care if the Captain himself is walking across the deck, I'm landing."[21] He landed and caught the number 4 arresting wire. His plane was so damaged, the approach so fast, that when his Crusader hit *Oriskany*'s flight deck the right axle broke, and the tire went careening down the flight deck. His Crusader had less than 300 pounds of fuel left. Once out of the cockpit, Rime was taken to ship's medical, where shards of canopy glass were removed from his arms. With his wounds cleaned, he was given a sedative before being sent off to get some sleep.

Abbott's and Rime's misfortunes on 5 September can be directly attributed to a breakdown in the new PIRAZ system. After Rime made it back, *Oriskany* checked with the controllers responsible for monitoring Vietnamese radio nets and tracking the MiGs. It became apparent that the two MiGs had made a previous pass and missed the Crusaders in the clouds. The MiG's GCI controllers then vectored them around for another pass. The second one was successful. Rime was summoned to the bridge, where Capt. Iarrobino showed him charts compiled by the northern SAR destroyer. It showed the exact flight path taken by the MiGs, from takeoff at Phuc Yen to their first missed pass and eventual interception and then landing. Iarrobino wanted to know what warnings had been passed to the flight, but Rime had never heard anything.[22]

Believably, the Vietnamese claimed two Crusaders that day. One of the Vietnamese pilots was none other than Nguyen Van Bay. Van Bay was on his way to becoming one of a handful of Vietnamese aces of the war. If Nguyen Van Bay had pressed his advantage, VF-III quite probably would have lost both airplanes that day. It is also rather telling the positive effect the PIRAZ system had on the air war over North Vietnam in the short period since its inception and, conversely, how fast the balance could tip toward the North Vietnamese in its absence. By December, MiG activity had become so great that all U.S. strikes in and around Hanoi and Haiphong were met by MiGs. By year's end, MiG attacks forced approximately 20 percent of all strikes into Route

Package VI to jettison their loads before reaching the target. In all reality, this number would probably have been greater had the PIRAZ not been implemented.

SS *August Moon* Rescue

At the end of the second line period, *Oriskany* sailed for Subic Bay. Prior to leaving the line, her crew transferred ordnance and other critical supplies to waiting supply ships. On 6 September, nearly a year after setting the previous transfer record, *Oriskany* set another transfer record with USS *Mount Katmai* (AE-16). As evidence to the growing war, crews from both ships transferred 406.5 tons of ammunition in fifty-six minutes, almost four times the amount of their prior record.[23] Following a five-day port call in Subic Bay, *Oriskany* sailed for Hong Kong and further liberty on 15 September. While sailing north, *Oriskany* took part in the rescue of fellow seafarers and suffered from one of the most bizarre events of their 1966 cruise.

That same morning, the ore carrier SS *August Moon* ran aground and was wrecked on the submerged Pratas Reef. Managed by the Eastern Sun shipping company in Hong Kong, the converted tanker had seen extensive convoy duty in the North Atlantic during World War II. She had been sailing from Calcutta, India, to Yokohama, Japan, with 13,600 tons of iron ore when she ran aground at 0230. The crew immediately began sending a distress signal, "Breaking up in swell.... Urgently require assistance to take off crew. Too rough to lower ship's boats."[24] The message was received in Hong Kong and Manila and by ships throughout the area. Under international maritime law, with deep roots in customary and humanitarian principles, it is the duty of any vessel in the area to render assistance. *Tokyo Maru*, a Japanese freighter, was the first ship to respond; however, heavy seas prevented her from lowering life boats to rescue the endangered crew. *Oriskany* and the Royal Navy frigate HMS *Loch Fada* soon arrived to assist. At 0530 *Oriskany* began launching aircraft to surveil the reef. Skyraiders reported that the crew was still safe but confirmed reports that swells were pounding the ship up against the rocks. Beginning at noon, three helicopters from *Oriskany* began rescuing the stranded crewmen.

The dramatic rescue of the *August Moon*'s forty-six-man crew was made even more dangerous by the huge green waves pounding the ore carrier. Eventually, a 60-foot wave claimed one of *Oriskany*'s helicopters as well. As Lt. Cdr. Dale Barck and Ens. Daniel Kern hovered their Seasprite over the stern of the *August Moon*, Petty Officer 2nd Class William Thoday prepared to haul crew members to safety. The helicopter was abruptly drenched with spray from an enormous wave. The sudden intake of water doused the helicopter's turbine engines, and it immediately stopped flying. Barck later recalled, "She went down and sank in two seconds." None of the crew recalled how they escaped the sinking helicopter, though Barck thought, "It must have been the surging water which washed us out of the helicopter." Uninjured, the crew bobbed in their lifejackets through the heavy swells until another helicopter came to their rescue after being alerted by *Loch Fada*.[25] Sadly, Daniel Kern perished in the tragic fire in October.

By 1615 all of *August Moon*'s crew members had been rescued. *August Moon* eventually broke in two and sank as *Oriskany* and her crew enjoyed liberty in Hong Kong. While in port, the shipping company presented a silver cup to Captain Iarrobino for *Oriskany*'s role in the rescue. During the ceremony, the Eastern Sun's managing director, James Lu, described the rescue operation as "one of the most heroic ones he has ever heard."[26] On 23 September, with their respite from the war over, *Oriskany* left Hong Kong for the Tonkin Gulf and her third line period.

SAM Hunting: Lt. Cdr. Dick Perry and Lady Jessie

The story of Lt. Cdr. Dick Perry is the quintessential story of Carrier Air Wing 16. It is also a sad one. Perry, a native of Carlin, Nevada, joined VA-164 in January 1966 and immediately became the lifeblood of the Ghost Riders. An effective leader and one of the squadron's senior pilots, he knew how to mentor junior pilots, instilling confidence while teaching them the skills needed to survive over Vietnam.[27] Perry also introduced a very important person to the air wing, one who would become a key supporter of the aviators: Lady Jessie. To Nevada, she was known as Jessie Beck, or "the Gambling Grandmother of Reno." An astute businesswoman, Jessie started out as a cashier and roulette dealer. She quickly rose to the top at Harold's Club. During the 1950s, Jessie and her husband, Fred Beck, ran the Keno game at Harold's Club in Reno. A major historical figure in Nevada, she was the first woman to own a major Nevada casino—the Riverside Hotel and Casino.[28] It was at Harold's that she became acquainted with Dick Perry, then attending the University of Nevada Reno and working part-time dealing cards at the casino. Perry essentially became an adopted son to the Becks, and though he graduated and moved on to flight school, they kept in continuous contact. When Perry joined VA-164, Jessie was still sending him care packages. She contacted all the Bell Telephone operators in Nevada and had them start sending gifts as well. Soon these care packages began spilling over to the other aviators in the air wing. Jessie Beck spent untold thousands of dollars and hours sending packages to servicemen in Vietnam. In 1968 the Department of Defense presented her the Award of Merit. It is the highest honor that can be given a civilian.[29]

Dick Perry's pride in Lady Jessie's affection was readily apparent to all. As the squadrons prepared for deployment to Vietnam, they spent several weeks at NAS Fallon, Nevada, dropping bombs on the adjacent ranges. Perry arranged for a squadron party in nearby Reno, the first of many hosted by Lady Jessie. Jessie brought the entire squadron to her hotel, including the wives, and paid everyone's bill. Word traveled fast among the tight-knit group of aviators, and soon they all had a chance to sample the famous Jessie Beck hospitality. In a gesture to Jessie and her kindness, Dick Perry had the words "Lady Jessie" painted underneath the cockpit of his Skyhawk.[30]

By the time *Oriskany* returned to the Tonkin Gulf for her third line period, Perry and his squadron mates in VA-164 were in the forefront of the battle to suppress North Vietnamese defenses. During 21–27 September, strikes near Thanh Hoa destroyed five SAM sites.[31] Such attacks forced the Vietnamese to frequently move launchers and radars lest they be found and destroyed. The North Vietnamese had on average 5.6 prepared sites for every launcher available, and the SA-2 success rate was falling.[32] When SAMs first appeared in 1965, they had a success rate of 5.7 percent. A year later, ECM advances and persistent Iron Hand strikes had lowered that number to just 3.1 percent.[33] It was mainly the perseverance of men flying Iron Hand missions that kept the SA-2 kill rate so low. Terrifying though it was, the SA-2 never downed the numbers of aircraft that AAA did.

One Iron Hand mission on 28 September illustrates the dangers involved. That afternoon, Perry had completed briefing his wingman for a two-plane armed reconnaissance mission when they were notified of a newly discovered SAM site. Perry's flight was combined with another section, and the men hastily briefed for an attack on the SAM site just south of the famous Thanh Hoa bridge. The flight of Skyhawks approached the SAM site at sunset, giving the Vietnamese gunners an easy target in the waning light. They encountered extremely heavy and accurate 37 mm and 57 mm AAA. Despite the opposition, Perry found the SAM site and rolled in to attack it. Just as he commenced his dive, Perry's Skyhawk was hit in the nose by a 37 mm shell. Perry's cockpit immediately filled with smoke. The blast penetrated the firewall of his cockpit, hitting Perry's leg with enough force that his leg then hit his chest—no small feat in the cramped Skyhawk cockpit. Chunks of shrapnel tore through his boot into his foot. A large segment of the nose, including the entire radome, was blown off. Debris struck the vertical stabilizer, and some debris was ingested by the engine, causing all indications of an impending failure. Despite all this, Perry pressed home his attack and succeeded in hitting the SAM site along with the others.

As he came off target, Perry was on his own. Darkness and haze near the coast precluded joining his wingman. As he flew toward the gulf, Perry surveyed the damage. He jettisoned his empty bomb racks and drop tank to lighten the load on his struggling aircraft. All his navigation aids were destroyed, including his radio and IFF. The angle-of-attack indicator, critical for landing back aboard the ship, was destroyed. The airspeed indicator would not indicate below 150 knots, and his engine was running rough. He was on his own, nursing his crippled Skyhawk back to the Tonkin Gulf in the dark. Using dead reckoning, Perry flew 120 miles out to sea before he spotted the lights of a cargo ship. He continued searching until he found a destroyer and eventually *Constellation*. Knowing that he still had enough fuel, Perry continued on, searching for *Oriskany*. When his search came up empty, Perry returned to *Constellation* and slowed his aircraft down to see if he could land it. After determining that he could, Perry made continuous low passes over *Constellation* until they got the message and readied the flight deck to bring him aboard. All told, it took almost ten minutes before *Constellation* was ready and he landed safely. It took almost another hour for word of his exploits and safe recovery to be passed back to *Oriskany*.[34] For the other members of the flight, he had simply vanished. No one had seen him get hit, and no one knew that he had been able to pull out and head back to the gulf. He was just unaccounted for.[35] That Perry had survived a direct hit by AAA was a minor miracle. That he had flown his crippled airplane 120 miles out to sea in order to make an emergency landing in the dark on an unfamiliar ship was extraordinary.

The next day, *Oriskany*'s aircraft destroyed yet another SAM site when an alert photo interpreter discovered an occupied site just south of Vinh Son. His discovery was quickly reported, and an immediate strike was authorized, planned, and launched. The total time from the initial discovery until the first attack was only three hours and fifty minutes. Follow-on flights and reconnaissance photographs confirmed its destruction. After destroying two SAM sites in two days, *Oriskany* had made a small dent in Vietnam's air defenses. As a result, the air wing received a congratulatory message from the carrier division commander, giving them the "Prize for SAM Busting" for the line period.[36] The following week, the Soviet newspaper *Krasnaya Zuezda* reported that PVO-Strany experts had come under fire during recent U.S. raids against North Vietnamese SAM sites. Until this point, both the Soviets and the Chinese had denied they had personnel in North Vietnam, though U.S. officials had long suspected otherwise. This was the first public acknowledgment that the Soviets had trained North Vietnamese missile crews and were observing them in action. The risk of a wider war suddenly seemed quite possible. By this time, China was undergoing its Cultural Revolution, and the Johnson administration became increasingly concerned that China might enter the war. The incident served to strengthen McNamara's resolve concerning his tight control of Rolling Thunder.

Man Overboard!

The pilots flying daily missions over North Vietnam were not the only ones facing extreme danger. *Oriskany*'s sailors and squadron maintenance men working on the flight deck did so at great risk to life and limb. While working on the flight deck of an aircraft carrier may not have been as dangerous as that of an infantryman fighting in the jungles, the job still took its toll. A sailor faced many hazards while working on the flight deck. The job required constant vigilance. It became more dangerous at night, when visual cues disappeared. With aircraft taxiing about the flight deck, launching from catapults, and making arrested landings, danger lurked everywhere. For the sailors working upward of sixteen hours day on the flight deck, exhaustion was the only constant, yet they still needed to keep their wits about them.

Oriskany lost several men to accidents during the previous line periods. In one instance, a VF-162 Crusader suffered a hard landing following a combat mission. The landing gear snapped off, causing a flash fire as hydraulic fluid sprayed from broken hydraulic lines. Although the fire was put out in less than ten minutes, two sailors were injured. Chief Petty Officer James LeBlanc was scalped by debris flung by the aircraft, and a young sailor, Richard Morrell, was blown over the side. Morrell suffered little more than scrapes and was quickly rescued by the plane guard helicopter. LeBlanc underwent surgery in the sickbay before recovering.[37] In the predawn hours of 23 August, Lt. Cdr. George Farris, the VAH-4 detachment OINC, and his young bombardier/navigator (B/N), Lt. (junior grade) Ignatius Signorelli, had an accident while attempting to land following a night airborne tanker mission. Farris was making his third pass after two missed attempts. With a low fuel state he came in high and fast. When Farris realized he was going to miss again he dove for the deck. Because of the Skywarrior's size and weight, along with the excess speed from the dive for the flight deck, *Oriskany*'s arresting gear failed under the stress of the arrested landing. What happened next was the predictable and catastrophic result. As the plane's tail hook grabbed the number 4 arresting gear wire, it snapped. In most instances, the aircraft will have lost enough airspeed that it cannot fly away. Miraculously, Ferris had enough airspeed to get airborne again and was diverted to Da Nang for the evening. After the cross-deck pendant parted, it flayed itself across the flight deck like a gigantic scythe. If it had been daytime, flight deck personnel might have had a chance to see it and escape the onslaught. Because it happened at night, the wire cut through anything and everything on the flight deck without warning. Lt. (junior grade) Raymond Sheenan lost his right leg, while Aviation Ordnanceman 1st Class James Johnston lost both his legs in the accident.[38] The flight deck was a very dangerous place indeed.

On 2 October Aviation Structural Mechanic 3rd Class Larry Harrison, a young mechanic from VF-162, almost became another victim of operations on the flight deck. Harrison had been checking a hydraulic leak when jet exhaust blew him over the side. Fortunately for him, an HS-6 Sea King happened to be on a logistics flight when it happened. The pilots of Indian Gal 65, Lt. (junior grade) Gale Prickett and Lt. (junior grade) Dick Lynas, made the pickup in what was for them a routine logistics flight. They were orbiting nearby, waiting for a clear deck, when they heard the "man overboard" call on the radio. The crew watched as *Oriskany*'s Seasprite flew down the wake while the plane guard destroyer crews searched the water. After watching the proceedings for several minutes, the crew of Indian Gal 65 flew three miles down the wake and slowly flew back toward *Oriskany*, eventually finding Harrison. As they flew back to the ship, they received permission to land. According to Lynas, "The sailor had been puking up seawater all over the back, but the medics hauled him off without a stretcher. The flight deck director gave us a 'hold' signal and we waited for a minute or two until some officer came running out of the island and handed us a brown paper bag." The bag contained four *Oriskany* cigarette lighters and ashtrays for each of the crew members—their reward for saving a life. After their rescue of Harrison, the crew continued on with their logistics mission before heading back to *Kearsarge*. Harrison spent the night in sickbay before returning to work on the flight deck. Operations onboard *Oriskany* continued unabated. It was, after all, just another day in the Gulf of Tonkin.[39]

Phu Ly: Belly Gets His MiG

On 1 October *Oriskany* launched a major twenty-plane strike against the Phu Ly railroad complex. Led by Lt. Cdr. Denis Weichman of VA-164, the strike evaded multiple SAMs as the pilots went feet-dry before encountering heavy concentrations of AAA in the target area. The strike destroyed two bridges and left the rail complex in flames. Despite this, the air wing would return in a week. According to the current regulations, a target would be authorized and remain on the strike list despite results, remaining until the Tuesday lunch club met again to select new targets. As a result, targets such as the Phu Ly complex would be bombed and bombed again, while the Vietnamese moved every available piece of AAA and SAMs into the area. What began with a single strike by *Oriskany* eventually evolved into a major strike with aircraft from the carriers *Intrepid*, *Coral Sea*, and *Oriskany* on 9 October. This strike would be heavily opposed.

Cdr. Ron Caldwell led *Oriskany*'s part of the strike. To help mitigate the stiffening Vietnamese defenses, he chose a new route of flight around known AAA concentrations that had built up over the previous strikes. The different flight path also allowed *Oriskany*'s airplanes to avoid the heavy weather that degraded other strikes. Even with effective flak suppression, Vietnamese defenses in Phu Ly proved ferocious. The strike was a success, however. *Intrepid*'s Skyhawks knocked down more spans of the Phu Ly bridge, while transshipment areas and rail yards were destroyed by aircraft from *Coral Sea* and *Oriskany*.[40] Two MiGs were also shot down, including a MiG-21—a first for the navy. At this point in the war, only four MiG-21s had been shot down, and the aircraft held almost mythical qualities. That it had been brought down by Cdr. Dick Bellinger made the victory even sweeter. Unfazed by his earlier shootdown, Bellinger remained anxious to try out new tactics against the MiGs. Bellinger and his wingman, Lt. Lee Prost, provided the TARCAP for *Intrepid*'s twenty-four Skyhawks. Bellinger planned to orbit at very low altitudes to the northwest of Phu Ly as the bombers hit the rail complex. The TARCAP would be controlled by the PIRAZ ship USS *King* (DLG-10). Bellinger also coordinated to have an E-1B Tracer from *Oriskany*'s VAW-11 detachment orbit just off the coast to provide another layer of control.[41]

The TARCAP was in their orbit when radar controllers onboard *King* called MiGs closing on *Intrepid*'s Skyhawks. Bellinger and Prost proceeded toward Phu Ly at low altitude. *King*'s controllers vectored Bellinger to a position beneath a MiG-21 about to attack an Iron Hand Skyhawk at 9,000 feet. Bellinger started climbing in afterburner, simultaneously making calls for the remaining F-8s to join the fight. Bellinger and Prost made it within a mile before being spotted. The MiG pilot rolled inverted, diving down low. Both Bellinger and Prost followed. Bellinger got a tone indicating his AIM-9 Sidewinder had locked on. He fired an AIM-9B first and quickly followed up with an AIM-9D. The first missile blew off the MiG's right wing as the second exploded alongside. The MiG pilot ejected from his disintegrating aircraft as

Bellinger roared by. Bellinger barely pulled out from his 60-degree dive, skimming treetops as he and Prost turned toward the gulf. The pair flew back to *Oriskany*, where they were met with a rousing celebration of sailors and squadron mates on the flight deck.

Less than an hour after Bellinger's success, another MiG was shot down as it attacked a flight of four A-1 Skyraiders. The A-1s from *Intrepid* were participating in the rescue of an F-4 crew from *Coral Sea* that had been shot down during the strikes on Phu Ly. As with Bellinger, the aviators had been given ample warning by an E-2A Hawkeye from *Coral Sea*.[42] That a World War II vintage prop aircraft had downed a much faster VPAF MiG was big news—so big, in fact, that it trumped Bellinger's MiG kill. Headlines blared, "Skyraider Downs MiG over North."[43] Not that it mattered. For *Oriskany*, VF-162, and, most importantly, Bellinger, his victory was sweet revenge.

Following his MiG kill, Bellinger was summoned to Saigon. The navy was anxious to spread the story of Bellinger's success, and the best way to do it was for him to appear at the official daily press briefings, known as the "Five O'Clock Follies." During these briefings military officials provided news releases and verbal accounts of battlefield and air activity to reporters. The "Follies" became infamous for its upbeat scenarios about the war. It was arranged for Bellinger to catch a ride in a Skywarrior to Tan Son Nhut, the sprawling air base in Saigon. Bellinger's pilot for the flight, Lt. Cdr. Tom Maxwell, recalled the trip:

> In 1966, following a routine daylight tanking mission, I trapped aboard *Oriskany*. Since we were normally last to trap, we were backed into the slot just aft of the island. I was taxied up forward and parked next to the island. I was told on tactical frequency that I was going to be hot refueled [refueled with the engines still running] and transport a VIP passenger to Saigon. My B/N, John Milward, was to deplane the aircraft. After John had left the aircraft I turned and saw Commander Bellinger climbing up the chute and get into the right B/N seat. Once he plugged his headset in it was obvious that he had received several medicinal brandies before boarding. Following refueling they attempted to taxi me to the number 1 cat[apult]. I did not move, since Commander Bellinger was not strapped in. When I told the commander to strap in he asked if I was planning

on crashing, and I answered hopefully not. So with a not too happy air boss, at me not moving, I taxied out with the reluctant commander, still not strapped in. Once airborne I proceeded overhead to pass my extra gas to the airborne tanker. My OINC, Lt. Cdr. Bill Laurentis, was the pilot. Unfortunately, the drogue controls were at the B/N's console, so I explained to Commander Bellinger how to put out the drogue and turn on the fuel. Looking through the periscope, every time Bill attempted to plug the basket, the commander would pull the drogue in. As you can imagine, my OINC was not a happy camper. I switched to tactical and explained to Bill what was going on. We finally completed tanking and headed for Saigon.

En route to Saigon, Belly said that he had never flown the A-3 and wanted me to change seats with him. Not willing to do this, he said he would not protest if I would agree to do a Victory roll over the field as we made our approach over the field at Saigon. Approaching the break at the field, I did an aileron roll and broke to land. As I taxied off the runway I was asked to hold on a taxi way while a blue vehicle came screaming out to the aircraft. We opened the hatch, and shortly I had one irate air force colonel in my cockpit. I turned the situation over to my right-seater, and he was able to calm the colonel.[44]

A VIP car took Maxwell and Bellinger to the studio, where Bellinger described his victory over the MiG-21. Due to a shortage of tankers, *Oriskany* needed the A-3 back as soon as possible, so Maxwell left Bellinger behind and returned to the ship. Several days later, another A-3 flew back and picked up Bellinger.

The same day Bellinger shot down the MiG, Secretary McNamara arrived in Vietnam. As part of his tour of the war zone, McNamara spent time onboard *Oriskany*. While there, he toured the ship and witnessed aviators flying missions over North Vietnam. He also presented Bellinger with a Silver Star for shooting down the MiG. A problem arose, however, when Bellinger didn't show up for the evening meal in the wardroom, where the presentation would take place. His wingman, Lee Prost, found Bellinger in his stateroom, still quite drunk from his time in Saigon. McNamara didn't appreciate waiting around for a navy commander who hadn't shaved for a couple days and smelled pretty bad.[45] Dick Bellinger was a polarizing individual who was either loved or hated, sometimes both; however, there was often no difference between the two.

Secretary McNamara's visit highlighted the growing divide in the Johnson administration. While the POL campaign was the turning point in McNamara's support for the air war, the Jason Report and McNamara's visit to the *Oriskany* solidified his position as the main critic of the air war. On 29 August 1966 a committee of scientists from the Jason Division of the Institute for Defense Analysis submitted what became known as the Jason Report. Their report, which evaluated the results of the Rolling Thunder campaign, began:

> As of July 1966 the U.S. bombing of North Vietnam (NVN) had had no measurable direct effect on Hanoi's ability to mount and support military operations in the South at the current level. Although the political constraints seem clearly to have reduced the effectiveness of the bombing program, its limited effect on Hanoi's ability to provide such support cannot be explained solely on that basis. The countermeasures introduced by Hanoi effectively reduced the impact of U.S. bombing. More fundamentally, however, North Vietnam has basically a subsistence agricultural economy that presents a difficult and unrewarding target system for air attack.[46]

Armed with the report, which calculated that only 5 percent of Hanoi's fuel supply was used by trucks to move supplies south, McNamara became convinced that the air war had been unproductive and that the war was not winnable, though he kept pressing for a greater American commitment and more sorties.[47] During his time aboard *Oriskany*, one of the first questions McNamara asked Captain Iarrobino concerned the number of sorties pilots flew per day. When Iarrobino answered that his pilots flew two missions a day, McNamara immediately became critical, wanting to know why pilots were not averaging only one and one-half sorties a day, as his guidelines stated. Iarrobino's response that there were too few pilots for too many missions did not please the numbers-driven secretary. Iarrobino could have also told McNamara about the severe shortage of sailors affecting operations aboard *Oriskany* but instead chose not to press the situation, as Secretary McNamara was already obviously agitated by the disconnect.[48]

Secretary McNamara's visit produced another telling, if not humorous, story. Just prior to McNamara's visit, a *Peanuts* cartoon strip depicting Snoopy as the World War I flying ace circulated throughout the ship. Dick Schaffert later recalled:

> Snoopy was low on ammunition but was scheduled to fly against the Red Baron. That intrepid beagle predicted he would defeat the World War One Ace, even though he was down to one last bullet. When questioned by Charlie Brown as to how he could possibly expect to win with only one bullet, Snoopy replied "It's a silver bullet!"
>
> SecDef McNamara was aboard the Oriskany the day after that comic strip made the rounds. He would sit in on an Alpha Strike briefing, and then monitor the action on strike common frequency. We two-dozen pilots were called to attention when SecDef and the Admirals entered the briefing room. The front row of seats had been reserved for the dignitaries. Before McNamara sat down, we saw him bend over and pick up a piece of paper from the seat of his chair. We aviators at attention in the next row could see the color rising in his face as he looked at it. He stuffed the paper in his note book and the mission briefing proceeded. Scuttlebutt later confirmed it was the silver-bullet comic strip.[49]

Attitudes to the war were changing both at home and in Vietnam. This simple act of rebellion proved that pilots didn't always appreciate risking their lives. Though they did so as professionals, they certainly made their feelings known. McNamara returned to Washington, where he briefed the president, faulting the services for their overly optimistic estimates of what unrestricted POL strikes could accomplish but not mentioning that the strikes were *never unrestricted*. At the same time, McNamara shamelessly paid lip-service to the very same issue, saying, "Any limitation on the bombing of Vietnam would cause serious psychological problems among the men who are risking their lives to help achieve our political objectives."[50]

Simultaneously, McNamara did his best to quiet the growing anti-war movement with the advent of Project 100,000. Envisioned as part of the War on Poverty, it was a sociological experiment gone awry. Due to the immense number of births in the years following World War II, the country had more than enough men to fight in Vietnam.

McNamara and his staff could have raised draft standards and still met the quotas. Instead, they lowered the standards to include men who would previously have failed medical or mental standards in order to avert the political bombshell of dropping student deferments or calling up the reserves. Whether Project 100,000 was purposely calculated to spare the elite and middle class and thus keep the "silent majority" from turning against the war, as some have theorized, remains a matter of speculation.[51] But that was the end result, as the country was torn asunder by violence over the next two years. It was a policy with disastrous consequences for the military and the nation as a whole.

9

Fire!

As always, the onset of the fall monsoon curtailed strikes against the North. September's daily rate of four hundred plus sorties, the highest recorded in 1966, fell off in October and remained low for the remainder of the year. Reduced operations did not, however, lessen the danger. During the first three and a half weeks of October, *Oriskany* launched strikes against ammunition dumps, rail lines, and bypasses. In this period, the air wing lost four planes in combat and two to operational loss, with four fatalities. Unfortunately, VA-152 bore the brunt, suffering three of those fatalities. Lt. (junior grade) James Beene was lost at sea after he flew into the water during a dark night laced with thunderstorms. A search of the area proved futile, yielding only an oil slick on the surface of the ocean that marked his watery grave. Beene had cheated death earlier in the cruise. On the night of 25 August, he ditched his Skyraider immediately in front of *Oriskany* following a malfunction during the catapult launch. The ship nearly ran him over before he was plucked from the ocean. In less than a week, VA-152 lost both Lt. Jack Feldhaus and Ens. Darwin Thomas to AAA. The loss of Feldhaus had been particularly troubling, as he had been a courageous leader in the cockpit and the ready room, and his loss was felt by all. The skies over North Vietnam had become very dangerous for the Skyraiders.

Oriskany had been initially scheduled to leave the line on 15 October, but unforeseen circumstances caused an extension. USS *Franklin D. Roosevelt* (CVA-42) needed emergency repairs on one of her screwed propellers. The only suitable port capable of performing the work was in Yokosuka, Japan, so *Oriskany* remained until she was repaired. With *Roosevelt* finally back on Yankee Station, *Oriskany* was scheduled to head for Hong Kong on 27 October. The ship had been on the line for over a month, and the crew was tired. Only a few days stood between them and a well-deserved respite. Unfortunately, those days were frustrated by the monsoon season, which was in full swing. Heavy cloud cover and low ceilings frequently hampered flight operations. Rain further hindered the already limited visibility. On 23 October poor weather canceled flight operations throughout the gulf. Instead of a reprieve, it meant more work as men downloaded ordnance from airplanes and returned it to the ship's magazines. The next day was spent conducting a day-long UNREP before the crew commenced midnight-to-noon flight operations. Once again, inclement weather canceled flight operations, and the crew went through the same process of downloading and storing ordnance.

The evening of 25 October proved to be a repeat of the previous two nights. Airplanes were loaded and fueled in preparation for flight operations on 26 October. Though the weather remained uncooperative, aviators briefed and waited for the word to launch. Midnight came and went with no word as they waited in their ready rooms. Finally, at 0130 operations were suspended until 0730. At 0630 a weather reconnaissance flight from *Constellation* would launch and report if daytime flights could proceed. New orders were relayed throughout the ship, from the flight deck to ready rooms and ordnance-handling stations. Pilots went to bed in a vain attempt to catch some precious sleep. And for the third time in four days, ordnancemen began the arduous task of downloading ordnance so that it could be properly stowed, included dozens of Mk 24 parachute flares loaded on Skyhawks and Skyraiders. The flares, critical for nighttime armed reconnaissance missions, were not used during daytime. As sailors downloaded the flares, they placed them on skids (wheeled dollies used to move ordnance about the flight deck) before sending them to the hangar deck for off-loading and storage.

The job of stowing the 117 downloaded flares fell upon twenty-year-old seaman apprentice John Gervais, who, three years earlier, had dropped out of high school and joined the Naval Reserves. A year later, he volunteered for active duty as the war in Vietnam heated up. During the previous cruise in 1965, he worked in the confines of the ship's magazines. By 1966, despite his lack of apparent motivation for promotion (he was still at the lowest rank possible), he was considered an old hand, mostly due to his time onboard and experience working with ordnance below decks. Because of this, he was given special tasks, such as the unsupervised handling and stowing of the Mk 24 flares, despite having no formal training with them. Insufficient manning compounded the problem. The Gunnery (G) Division to which Gervais was assigned only had seven of the ten men it rated.[1] As a result, Gervais found himself working alone as he stored the 25-pound flares. At the 0600 shift change, Gervais was told to stop working and leave the remaining flares for the oncoming day shift.

The unfinished task of stowing the roughly seventy remaining flares fell upon two junior airmen, eighteen-year-old George James and seventeen-year-old James Sider. Despite being untrained in the correct safety procedures for the Mk 24 flare, these two unsupervised sailors began stowing the flares. The compartment used to stow flares was at the forward edge of the hangar deck, while the seven skids full of flares extended aft into the hangar bay. As the airmen unloaded each skid, the distance to the locker increased. Angered at the prospect of having to stow unused flares for the third morning in four days and in an effort to save time doing a job they felt should have been done by the night shift, James and Sider began passing the 25-pound flares to each other using an underhand toss. On one of these tosses, a lanyard used to ignite the flare caught on the hatch and ignited the 2-million-candlepower magnesium flare. Sider panicked, threw the burning flare in the locker containing some 650 flares, closed the hatch, and turned to run away. James was already gone. Sider then ran into the hangar bay shouting, "Fire!"

The resultant fire was immediately out of control. An alert petty officer, Henry Brooks, standing a safety watch in the hangar, ordered sailors to start throwing the remaining skids over the side. He then called the bridge to inform them of the fire. At the same time Brooks called, the men on the bridge noticed the heavy smoke billowing from the starboard side of the ship. Knowing full well the gravity of the situation, they sprang into action. In the excitement of the moment, however, the quartermaster on watch announced over the ship's public address circuit (the IMC), "This is a drill. Fire, fire, fire." Realizing his mistake, he corrected himself: "This is NO drill. This is NO drill. Fire, fire in the hangar bay, starboard side forward, frame forty-two."[2]

By the time the announcements were made at 0725, almost seven minutes had elapsed. Lt. Cdr. Mel Berg, *Oriskany*'s damage control assistant, was finishing breakfast when the call came. The excitement evident in the man's voice made him hurry to Damage Control Central. Once there, men on watch told him that they had a fire in compartment A-107-M. Berg knew immediately that this fire would be bad. A for "Alpha" meant that the fire was in the forward part of the ship, and "107" indicated that it was on the starboard side of the hangar deck. But M for "Mike" meant magazine, which in turn meant ordnance and probably lots of it.[3]

In those decisive minutes, sailors reacted immediately without waiting for direction from the bridge, seizing the initiative and beginning efforts to save their ship. They fought fires while trying to save their fellow shipmates. They performed a thousand acts of courage that will never be recorded. Above all, they did their duty. Men dragged fire hoses toward the burning locker. Other men fought desperately to roll four nearby Skyhawks to the far end of the hangar deck. Three airplanes were loaded with bombs, and the fourth was a tanker with an additional 300 gallons of jet fuel.[4] Firefighters watched in helpless horror as the steel bulkheads of the flare locker started ballooning under the 4,500-degree fire. An intense overpressure rapidly built up inside the compartment. The loosely secured hatch of compartment A-107-M blew open with the intensity of a blowtorch. The resultant explosion sent rockets of flame, toxic fumes, and thick, acrid smoke throughout the forward passageways and the forward elevator pit and aft into the hangar bay. Men manning hoses on the hangar deck were knocked down, their unmanned hoses snaking about wildly.

Responding to the fire call, *Oriskany*'s executive officer, Cdr. Francis Brown, hurried to the hangar bay. He arrived on scene immediately following the first explosion, and what he saw terrified him. Though it took him some time to find a working phone, he called the bridge to tell them the fire was out of control and recommended that they go to general quarters. Captain Iarrobino then ordered the ship to general quarters. The rapid gonging of the alarm made many men realize just how critical the situation had become. Men on the hangar deck never heard the alarm, however, as a second explosion tore through the hangar. Automatic sprinkler systems only made a bad situation worse, as the extremely high temperature of the fire instantly vaporized the deluge of water into flammable hydrogen. Combined with the gaseous products of combustion (nitrogen, carbon dioxide, and nitrous dioxide), the mixture proved deadly. The second explosion was much more violent than the first, with gouts of flame reaching back into Hangar Bay Two. As the wall of flames tore through the forward part of the ship, particles of magnesium were carried along and immediately began burning whatever they came in contact with. Whatever oxygen was left in the forward staterooms was immediately snuffed out. Following the second explosion, two helicopters in Hangar Bay One began to burn. By now, heavy smoke had reduced visibility to zero.

At 0735 a third explosion tore through the hangar bay. This explosion occurred when a liquid oxygen (LOX) cart caught fire. Liquid oxygen was used to fill oxygen bottles on the airplanes, enabling pilots to breathe while flying at altitude. The resulting explosion from the highly volatile servicing cart added more carnage to the hangar bay and effectively sealed off the forward part of the ship because the explosion occurred on the port side of the hangar bay. Besides the two burning helicopters, a Skyhawk caught fire, and the 20 mm ammunition from its cannons began to cook off, exploding from the heat. Throughout it all, young sailors worked feverishly to jettison bombs over the side lest they detonate and cause catastrophic damage. In a valiant effort, firefighters trained their hoses on those bombs that had yet to be pitched. Many bombs became so hot that their paint began to crackle and blister, while wisps of smoke emanated from the open fuze holes. There were countless stories of heroism as young men rolled, carried, and dragged bombs to a spot where they could be thrown overboard. In one instance, Airman Enrico Massagli literally picked up two 500-pound bombs, one after another, and, with adrenaline pumping, tossed them over the side.[5]

The smoke was so thick and choking that it caused two men to fall overboard. Lt. Cdr. John Fisher, the hangar deck division officer, was attempting to get to his general quarters station. Blinded by the dense smoke, he tripped and fell overboard through the starboard elevator opening. Aviation Ordnanceman 3rd Class Rolly Foster had been helping move ordnance when the second explosion occurred. After being knocked to the deck, he was stunned and disoriented. Stumbling about in the smoke only worsened his confusion. Foster dropped to his knees and began to crawl away from the smoke and heat, but, unknowingly, he crawled out the same elevator opening. Both men were rescued by helicopters and delivered to nearby destroyers.[6]

On the bridge, Captain Iarrobino led his ship through the ensuing chaos. He ordered changes of course in response to requests relayed from the executive officer on the hangar deck. By placing the wind on alternating sides, Iarrobino attempted to clear away smoke and improve firefighting efforts on the hangar deck. At one point the ship momentarily lost control of steering, as electrical power was secured to prevent electrical fires from adding to the inferno. Firefighters slowly gained control of the fire, though the flares in A-107-M still burned out of control. The intense heat of the fire warped bulkheads in the vicinity of the magazine and buckled the hangar bay overhead. In Damage Control Central, Lt. Cdr. Mel Berg flooded the ship's magazines at 0847. Several decks below the fire, temperatures in magazines had risen to dangerous levels—better to flood them than risk losing the ship.

Two hours after Airman James Sider tossed the flare in the compartment, it seemed that the fires were under control. Then a fourth explosion wracked the hangar deck. Several 55-gallon drums of paint stored in the forward elevator pit burst into flames. For the fourth time, flames and heavy, noxious smoke filled the hangar deck and berthing compartments forward of the hangar deck. The crews battled on. By 1000 damage control teams reported all fires under control, though the ship was by no means out of the woods. At 1009 the remaining electrical-power system failed, leaving the ship on emergency power. Firefighting efforts literally pumped thousands of gallons of seawater into the ship. While much of it poured over the side, a great deal of it drained below decks, threatening the stability of the ship.[7] There was not much more damage *Oriskany* could sustain without succumbing.

Captain Iarrobino wisely kept the crew at general quarters, with the ship buttoned up. Throughout the day, flash fires continued, hindering efforts to locate survivors and retrieve the remains of those who had perished. By 1500, with the fires out, it was finally deemed safe enough to release the crew from their general quarters stations. Explosive-ordnance disposal teams then began the task of cautiously inspecting and clearing compartment A-107-M of any remaining flares. They found that 650 Mk 24 flares had burned, leaving nothing but ash in their place. Strangely, four flares survived the fire: two were partially burned, while the other two managed to survive the fire still packed inside their wooden shipping crates.[8]

With the fire finally out, *Oriskany*'s men set about the task of repairing their gravely wounded ship. As they cleaned up the aftermath, the shock of what they had experienced settled upon them. Three Skyhawks were damaged. One Skyhawk and two helicopters were completely destroyed. Forty-four men had perished. Twenty-four pilots from the air wing, including the new air wing commander, had died. Because flight operations had been canceled the night before, most pilots used the respite to catch up on sleep in staterooms immediately forward of the hangar bay. Forced air ventilation systems pumped noxious fumes and smoke into these staterooms. A great majority of the casualties died from asphyxiation in their rooms or in the passageways immediately outside, unable to escape the holocaust. The fire decimated the pilot ranks of the air wing. Living spaces forward of the fire were uninhabitable. Catapults used to launch aircraft, as well as the forward elevator, were rendered inoperable, making flight operations impossible. Due to the extensive damage and large loss of life, *Oriskany* was taken off the line.

On 28 October she sailed for Subic Bay. Upon arrival in the Philippines, crewmen stood in silent mourning as colors flew at half mast in honor of her dead. An honor guard of Marines stood at "present arms" as the flag-draped coffins bearing the victims of the fire were taken from the ship to a waiting Flying Tiger Line Boeing 707 for transportation to the United States. The surviving pilots of the air wing escorted the bodies home, where they were met by crowds of antiwar protesters as they landed at San Diego's Lindberg Field. *Oriskany* remained in Subic Bay for another week of repair work before sailing for California. While en route, one of the victims, Lt. Cdr. Omar Ford, was buried at sea during a solemn ceremony. The ship arrived in California on 16 November 1966. It was a somber homecoming.

The Survivors

Over the ensuing years, much has been written concerning the tragedy that occurred on the morning of 26 October. A full recounting of the courage, skill, and devotion to duty shown by all hands in response to the fire can never be fully told and is far beyond the scope of this book. However, a broad synopsis of the tragedy is appropriate. The following stories are a few of the many.

Cdr. Ron Caldwell and Cdr. Dick Bellinger lived adjacent to each other, one deck above and just slightly forward of compartment A-107-M. A fortuitous phone call from the VA-163 duty officer woke Caldwell minutes before the fire started. As he sat pondering whether or not to go back to sleep or get up and have breakfast, he heard the IMC calls. The panicked voice, plus the location given for the fire, jolted him awake, and he threw on his flight suit. He was in such a hurry that he just grabbed his boots and left the stateroom. As he walked out the door, he was hit by a blast of hot air that stopped him in his tracks. As he turned to make his way forward, he stopped and pounded his boots on Bellinger's wall to tell him of the fire. He made it halfway to the forecastle before the lights failed. In the dark, he fought to overcome panic in the heat and smoke. He gradually made his way forward and stumbled onto the forecastle. Caldwell eventually made his way up the flight deck and back to VA-163's ready room.[9]

Caldwell's pounding woke Bellinger, who stumbled out of bed. As he opened his door to see who pounded on his wall, he was met by a blast of intense heat. Bellinger slammed the door closed, now fully awake. He was fortunate in that his stateroom contained a porthole. Originally, it had been open to the outside and a weather deck, but during the course of the ship's history, the weather deck had been enclosed, and the porthole now led to an enclosed passageway. With his stateroom cut off by the fire, the porthole became Bellinger's only option. He made one escape attempt, but he couldn't fit through the 14-inch opening. With smoke and heat making his situation untenable, he was quickly running out of time. Bellinger did the only thing he could do. He hastily stripped and used the sink in his room to lubricate himself with soap and water before squeezing his 205-pound frame through the porthole.[10] His hips caught on the small porthole, but Bellinger was able to reach up and grab a heavy cable to pull himself through. The heat of the deck burned his feet as he ran naked but alive toward the forecastle and eventual safety.

VF-111's Lt. Cdr. Dick Schaffert and Lt. Cdr. Norm Levy shared a stateroom on the 01 level. Both men had been scheduled for early morning flights, which had been canceled. The squadron duty officer called Levy at 0700 after only three hours of sleep to wake him for the Alert-Five (as part of their duty, fighter squadrons stood various alerts, in this case sitting in the cockpit of an F-8 waiting to launch in less than five minutes should an incoming threat be detected). Schaffert volunteered to take the alert to allow his roommate some more precious sleep. Schaffert finished shaving and was walking back to their stateroom when he heard the announcements over the IMC. Smelling smoke, he glanced behind him and noticed smoke roiling toward him. Schaffert ran back to their stateroom and turned on the lights. He shouted, "Norm, this is no drill. Let's get the hell out of here!" Schaffert then ran down the passageway around the elevator pit, banging on the metal wall and shouting, "It's no drill. We're on fire! We're on fire!" He rounded the last corner of the passageway as the first explosion rocked the ship. The blast blew him out of the passageway and onto the hangar deck.[11] It was the last time Dick Schaffert saw his roommate. Levy died trying to escape their stateroom. His body was discovered next to the oxygen breathing apparatus (OBA) locker near their room.

VA-152's Cdr. Gordon Smith was not scheduled to fly the previous night but stayed up until flight operations were canceled. Intending to sleep in, he inexplicably woke early, at 0715. As he dressed, he smelled smoke. A short time later, he heard the fire calls. He grabbed his shirt and opened his door to be met by clouds of smoke. Smith started running down the starboard 01-level passageway, pounding on stateroom doors and waking men as he went. As he made his way to the port side, he cut through the junior officer stateroom and instructed the men to make their way forward.[12] On the forecastle, Smith and his new entourage were met by two sailors. Smith told them to close the door to limit smoke in the forecastle but to be ready in case more men escaped. He then went back to alert more men. He had only taken a few steps aft when he heard the first explosion. Smith turned and ran back to the forecastle, where the alert sailors heard him yelling. They opened the door for him and barely managed to close it before the inferno arrived. They were not a moment too soon, as angry flames licked through gaps around the door frame.[13]

Smith then shepherded the roughly fifty men up toward the flight deck, where he met Lt. Cdr. Jim Harmon, the operations officer for

VA-152. After a quick discussion, the two decided to return to the fore-castle. There, they teamed up with the two young sailors Smith had met previously. The four armed themselves with OBAS and began to search for survivors. With one of the sailors manning a fire hose to spray the other three, the team made their way down a trunk (a watertight shaft connecting two or more levels of the ship) to the main deck on the starboard side. They were met by heavy smoke and extreme heat. Crawling on their hands and knees, they tried to make their way aft. The heat quickly became so intense that water from the hose began flashing into steam, causing the team to abandon their efforts and return to the forecastle.

On the forecastle, the team decided to make another attempt, this time on the port side. Outfitted with fresh OBAs, Smith and Harmon made their way to the second deck. Though the heat was not as intense, they could not see due to the smoke. Crawling around, they began to check staterooms, though they quickly became disoriented in the dark-ness. The pair eventually crawled into a head, where in his disorien-tation Smith stuck his hand in a toilet. Their battle lanterns provided just enough light for Smith to recognize their location. Smith had been trying to find his executive officer, Cdr. John Nussbaumer, who lived in a nearby stateroom. Now confident of their location, he led them to the stateroom, where they found Nussbaumer's body. Smith hoisted the body on his shoulders and began to carry him toward the forecastle. Unfortunately, his OBA ran out, and he had to give the body to Harmon. Lacking any air, Smith collapsed at the bottom of the trunk, where the alert sailors pulled him up to the forecastle while Harmon carried the body behind. After a few moments of relatively fresh air Smith came to. As other men carried the lifeless Nussbau-mer to the flight deck, Smith and Harmon took gulps of fresh oxy-gen from a bottle, promptly causing them to cough up black mucus. Refreshed, they headed below, eventually making a total of six trips. Each time one of them felt like quitting, the other would say, "Well, ready to go again?" and off they went, back down into the smoke and fire.[14] In all, they recovered another three victims before being forced to quit by doctors.[15]

VA-163's Lt. Cdr. Marv Reynolds and Lt. Cdr. John Miles shared a stateroom just forward of the flare locker. Miles woke early to prepare for his flight with Cdr. Rodney Carter, the new CAG. His departure disturbed Reynolds, who woke shortly thereafter. As Reynolds shaved, he heard the IMC calls and men running. He opened his door to investigate and noticed men running by just as the fireball from the first explosion roared by. He slammed the door closed, but flames still made their way through the gaps and louvered vents around the door. Reynolds used his towel to stem the smoke as decorations in their stateroom began to catch fire in the intense heat. As with Bellinger's stateroom, their room also had a porthole. Fate intervened as Reynolds struggled to open it. Several days earlier, he and Miles had borrowed a specialized wrench to open the porthole in order to throw empty liquor bottles overboard, and they had failed to return it. That forgetful act saved his life as he grabbed the wrench and began to loosen the nuts holding the porthole closed. Before he got it open, however, Reynolds blacked out. He eventually came to and realized he had somehow opened the porthole and was lying there breathing fresh air.[16] Then he realized that all the clothes had been burned off his body. In desperation, he reached over and turned on the sink to soak a blanket and cover his exposed body from the flames. He found a mismatched pair of shoes and contemplated walking out when the second explosion occurred. The heat grew even worse, causing paint on the walls of his stateroom to catch fire. In a last stand, he soaked his mattress and pulled it around him for shelter as he gulped fresh air from the porthole.

As Reynolds struggled to survive, Boatswain's Mate 1st Class Noel Hartford appeared to be everywhere, doing everything. When the alarm sounded, he ran forward on the flight deck, taxied two aircraft off elevator number 2, and then ran the elevator down to the hangar so that aircraft could be moved from the burning hangar to the flight deck. Next, Hartford directed a firefighting party to the forecastle and instructed the sailors on the use of OBAS. As he made his way back to the flight deck, Hartford was alerted to Reynolds's plight. An alert helicopter crewman had noticed Reynolds waving from the porthole as they hovered nearby. They notified the ship, and soon Hartford leaned over the side to call to Reynolds. "Hey, what are you doing?" he yelled. "Right now, I'm burning up," Reynolds yelled back.[17] Hartford disappeared, to return a few moments later with a fire hose. Hartford swung the fire hose back and forth until Reynolds could snag it. Reynolds then attempted to spray his room. He quickly realized his mistake as the intense heat caused the water to flash into steam. He abandoned that plan and turned the hose on himself and the mattress. Hartford then lowered an OBA and two battle lanterns to Reynolds. Reynolds made five attempts to escape, and each time, he was driven back to the relative safety of his stateroom. Finally, on his sixth attempt, Reynolds made his way to the forecastle and safety. Reynolds was extremely lucky—fourteen men died in the immediate area surrounding his stateroom.[18]

Hartford continued to help. After helping Petty Officer Billy Coleman wet down the liquid oxygen compartment, Hartford helped with bomb and ordnance removal near the blazing flare locker. In the words of one officer, "It was amazing to see one man doing so much in so many places."[19]

At 0725 Lt. John Bentley, a pilot from the VAW-13 detachment, called his roommate, VAH-4's Lt. (junior grade) Ignatius Signorelli, to wake him and warn him of the fire. Half asleep, Signorelli stumbled about, slowly putting on clothes before leaving their stateroom. As he turned to walk aft down the passageway, a blast of heat hit him. Signorelli turned and ran, passing Reynolds's room just as Reynolds opened his door. Signorelli continued running down the athwartship passageway and headed back aft, but before he could make it to the last door to the hangar, the 0728 explosion caught him. Signorelli ducked into a nearby head and was knocked down by Lt. Cdr. Dave Yost of VA-164, who jumped in after him as the explosion roared by.[20]

Signorelli and Yost were wetting their T-shirts to use as masks in a vain attempt to stop the smoke when they were joined by Cdr. Rodney Carter and Lt. (junior grade) Dewey Alexander. Both men were badly burned, and Signorelli's last memory before he drifted into unconsciousness was of the men pleading to the Almighty. Sometime after 0800, a rescue party fought past the burning helicopters and LOX cart to make their way into the port-side passageway. In the head, they found Yost unconscious but alive. The rescue party carried him aft, past the raging inferno, to safety. Once clear of the fire they were able to resuscitate Yost before heading back for the other three victims. One by one, the lifeless bodies of Carter, Alexander, and Signorelli were carried aft to a casualty collection station. There, each man was reported as a fatality to Damage Control Central. Miraculously, after lying in the temporary morgue for several minutes, Signorelli began hacking up black mucus. A startled sailor summoned a corpsman, who applied resuscitation and saved Ignatius Signorelli. He was placed on a stretcher and taken to the sickbay. Signorelli survived but recalled little of the experience.[21]

The miraculous story of Cdr. Charles A. Lindbergh "Cal" Swanson, the executive officer of VF-162, and thirteen other men is one of the more extraordinary tales of the fire. The announcements over the IMC woke most, and a group of five men, including Lt. Cdr. Foster Teague, stumbled out of their rooms on the second deck, forward of the elevator. The men remained calm, as smoke had not yet made its way down to them. A quick survey of possible exits showed heavy smoke through view-ports in the hatches, while bulkheads were quickly becoming hot to the touch. With their only escape routes blocked, the officers searched for any exit from their dilemma. When the smoke became intolerable, the only option was to enter a watertight trunk that extended straight down from the second deck to the seventh deck and provided access to voids in the ship's hull. It was not the place in which one would normally seek refuge on a ship in peril, as there could be no escape.

The small group continued to grow as men joined them. Four more officers were roused from their staterooms nearby. Two sailors, David Cox and Jerry Robinson, were driven down from their general quarters stations one deck above. They had been going from stateroom to stateroom waking men before being driven away by the smoke and flames. Cdr. Harry Juntilla and Lt. (junior grade) Larry Ross stumbled down from the main deck as well, though both were severely burned by the 0728 explosion. Juntilla was so badly burned that he had gone into shock and tumbled down a ladder, injuring himself further. As Jerry Robinson reached out to stop the delirious man from stumbling away, Juntilla's skin simply sloughed off in Robinson's hands. Juntilla said to him, "Sailor, I'm dying."[22]

Swanson faced the unenviable decision to lead the men into the trunk and seal the hatch behind them. They gingerly lowered the burned men down and climbed in. A ladder ran down the side, with small platforms jutting out from each level. Ross lost his footing and tumbled off the ladder, knocking himself unconscious as he landed on a small platform. The survivors tried to comfort the two severely injured men as best they could while distributing themselves on the different platforms to lessen the demands on the limited air supply. They were cut off, isolated in the darkness of the trunk and unsure of the fire's severity.

As the senior man, Swanson was concerned with their predicament. No one knew the group had taken refuge in the trunk; thus, no rescue would be forthcoming. Their air was running out, and the men were beginning to show signs of hypoxia. From somewhere, someone produced an OBA, and Teague was chosen to see if they could escape. He didn't make it far in the black smoke and was driven back to the trunk, as flames still blocked their exits.

For nearly two hours, time stood still in the dark trunk. Swanson faced the no-win decision: stay and die of asphyxiation, or venture out and potentially suffer the same fate or worse. He ordered David Cox to don the OBA and venture out. Cox was gone just a few moments before he returned with a rescue party that had made its way to the second deck. The men began the grim chore of lifting Juntilla out of the trunk, a nearly impossible task, as his skin kept coming off. Once through the hatch, they put him in a litter and began to carry him out. They immediately hit a tight turn in the smoke-filled passageways that took several minutes to negotiate with the stretcher. Once outside, Swanson turned and headed back to the trunk, where he grabbed Ross and instructed the others to follow. Swanson led them through the choking smoke and darkness and past the tight corner. They stumbled into the fresh air. Once outside, Swanson was startled to realize that no one had followed him, so he headed back again, this time equipped with OBAs and two sailors carrying a stretcher.

Swanson found the men in the trunk, where they'd retreated after losing him in the smoke. One man had passed out, and he was quickly loaded onto the stretcher. Somehow in the confusion, the stretcher party ended up in front of the human chain and stopped progress as they negotiated the tight turn in the smoke. Swanson helped them with the stretcher, and the group eventually made their way to safety, only to find that just one man had followed them out. The rest had retreated again, so Swanson went back *for a third time*. Determined not to leave anyone behind, Swanson led the chain through the smoke.

Once again, they were held up at the same corner by stretcher-bearers struggling to carry a victim of the fire. Swanson yelled for them to make way for the living and proceeded to bring the last of the survivors to safety.[23] Twelve men survived the harrowing ordeal. Juntilla passed away several days later, the last victim of the fire.

Among the many acts of heroism, the efforts of Lt. (junior grade) Jay Meadows stand alone. Meadows, a Crusader pilot in VF-III, was in the cockpit of his aircraft waiting for the 0730 launch to start when the fire occurred. He shut down the engine and proceeded toward the fire, where he discovered that two squadron mates were trapped in their third-deck stateroom.[24] Very few, if any, pilots had ever seen an OBA before the fire, and Meadows improvised to overcome this deficiency. He was seen running across the flight deck with an emergency oxygen bottle from an airplane and his oxygen mask from his flight gear. He put on his mask, plugged in the emergency bottle, and climbed down into the smoke.[25] With a sailor following him, Meadows made his way to the third deck, where intense heat and dense smoke stopped them. After several attempts, they were compelled to abandon their efforts.

Meadows then joined a rescue team made up of two repairmen on the forecastle. Finally equipped with an OBA, he lowered himself through a trunk into the dense smoke and heat in the main-deck stateroom area. Unable to see because of the dense smoke, Meadows dropped to the deck and felt his way through the passageways to a head, where he stumbled upon VA-163's Lt. Cdr. Clem Morisette in a shower stall. Morisette was unconscious but still alive. Meadows dragged his fellow pilot from the head and turned him over to the other men in his party so that they could evacuate him. However, they were unable to carry him up the ladder to the forecastle. Meadows had the two sailors help him put Morisette on his shoulders and then carried him up the narrow trunk's vertical ladder to a waiting stretcher. From the forecastle, Lt. (junior grade) Vance Schufeldt and Lt. (junior grade) Peter Munro carried Morisette to the flight deck, where corpsmen began artificial respiration in an attempt to revive him. It proved futile, however; he had already died from smoke inhalation.[26]

Through it all, Meadows's goal was the rescue of his squadron mates, Cody Balisteri and William McWilliams III. He returned to the third deck in another attempt to reach them. Once again, flames and smoke thwarted his attempts. He returned to the main-deck state-rooms to search for victims of the fire. After seeing that larger rescue parties had gained access from the hangar bay he returned to the second deck in a last effort to locate his squadron mates trapped below. Waist-deep seawater now precluded entry to the third deck, so Meadows searched the second-deck staterooms, discovering another body. Meadows remained on the scene until access to the third deck finally became possible. By then, time had run out on the trapped men, and Meadows could only help remove their bodies. Five men had perished: Balisteri and McWilliams plus their two roommates, Ens. Daniel Kern and Lt. (junior grade) Gerald Siebe, along with Lt. John Francis in the neighboring stateroom. While carrying the last of the casualties to the flight deck, Meadows was finally overcome by smoke inhalation and exhaustion and had to be removed himself. For his efforts during the fire, Meadows was one of thirteen men awarded the Navy and Marine Corps Medal.[27]

Even as Meadows performed his heroics, his actual roommates struggled to escape the fire. Meadows lived in a large junior officer stateroom with several other officers, including Lt. (junior grade) Ralph Bisz and Lt. (junior grade) Tom Spitzer. Both men were close friends, having previously gone through flight school together prior to joining VA-163. Bisz was woken by the fire call and woke Spitzer. Hand in hand like children, the two men left the stateroom, with Bisz in the lead.[28] Bisz turned aft toward the hangar bay as smoke rapidly filled the passageway. Then the lights went out. In the confusion, Spitzer's hand slipped, and then Bisz walked into a bulkhead. Stunned and disoriented, Bisz then bumped into someone in the darkness. Desperate to escape and unable to breathe in the choking smoke, Bisz started running. Although he didn't know it at the time, Bisz was actually retracing his steps, which took him forward, away from the fire and toward the safety of the forecastle. As he was about to give up, incapable of holding his breath any longer, he saw the darkness give way. With his lungs screaming, Bisz made a last-ditch lunge and stumbled into the light of the forecastle.

Tom Spitzer's body was discovered in the passageway just outside their stateroom, near the bulkhead Bisz had walked into. Next to him lay the body of Lt. (junior grade) James Brewer. Though he would be killed by a SAM in 1967, Ralph Bisz spent the next nine months suffering from extreme survivor's guilt. Bisz could not be swayed from his belief that he'd bumped into Tom Spitzer after walking into the bulkhead. He remained convinced that he could have saved his friend if he'd not been so desperate to escape.[29] The capriciousness of the day's events made the tragedy that much more difficult to bear. Throughout the fire, it seemed the fickle finger of fate decided who lived and who died. Death came randomly. Some men burned, while others nearby survived unscathed. The survivors were left reeling, struggling to cope while continuing to fight as the air war escalated in 1967.

For the men who survived the holocaust, the experience was tragic. Captain Iarrobino attempted to sum it up, addressing the crew over the IMC as they sailed for Subic Bay:

> As terrible as this tragedy is, it could have been much worse. If it hadn't been for the courageous and daring actions of many of you, our casualty toll would have been much higher and damage to the ship and aircraft would have been much more extensive.
>
> There are many reports that I have heard, and I know I haven't heard them all, which describe officers and men risking their lives together to save shipmates, jettison bombs over the side, remove aircraft from Hangar bay No. 1 and to battle the fire in the hangar and the forward part of the ship under the most adverse conditions.
>
> To all these men—to all who assisted in any way to bring the fire under control, to all who cared for the casualties and to all the repair parties who did such a magnificent job—I want to express my sincere thanks and admiration. Watching you react to this crisis . . . made me even more proud than I was before to be a shipmate of yours.[30]

But perhaps the valor was best described by one seasoned chief petty officer: "Those crazy rock-'n'-roll jitterbuggers, they saved this ship today. Getting into that fire and pushing those bombs over the side and volunteering for rescue parties—those kids were everywhere doing everything."[31]

Postscriptum

The hangar deck fire resulted from several factors. First, in 1966 the navy in general was still conducting the war with peacetime manning requirements. The Gunnery Division onboard *Oriskany* was manned with only seven sailors in what should have been a ten-man division. This shortage of personnel led directly to the untrained and unsupervised Airman Sider and Airman James mishandling ordnance. Second, the hectic pace of operations during Rolling Thunder meant that the undermanned crew onboard *Oriskany* was pushed to their limits. There was no respite from operations. Four months prior to the accident, Lt. Frank Elkins wrote, "Night operations were cancelled after I wrote last night. A good thing. People are really getting worn down, particularly the ordnance crews who load tons and tons of ordnance on the aircraft, reconfigure for different kinds of weapons, fix discrepancies on the ordnance gear, and catch naps as best they can, behind the island, on aircraft wings, or under the gun mounts."[32]

Finally, *Oriskany* was one of the oldest carriers then operating. The pace and type of operations meant that there was no suitable place to store the new Mk 24 flares. Instead of being stored in the ship's magazines like other ordnance, the flares were stored in an empty compartment forward of the hangar bay. All these factors combined to make shortcuts and mishandling inevitable—it was just a matter of time before accidents occurred as the undermanned and overworked crew struggled to meet the daily sortie requirements demanded of them. In fact, the fire onboard *Oriskany* was the first of three major aircraft carrier fires involving similar circumstances with similar results. Due to the dynamic wartime requirements, the navy had no firefighting materials, no equipment, and no techniques available to extinguish the new magnesium flares should they begin burning. The carrier's automatic sprinkler systems only made a bad situation worse, as the extremely high temperature of the fire instantly vaporized water into flammable hydrogen.

The fire and loss of life created many challenges and further strained the carrier fleet. *Oriskany*'s early departure from the Tonkin Gulf complicated scheduling for the remaining carriers and increased the operational tempo of an already overtasked navy. The navy rushed to repair *Oriskany* at Hunters Point Naval Shipyard in San Francisco Bay, as it desperately needed her. Unlike the other carriers that experienced fires, she would not get a reprieve.[33] The biggest challenge facing *Oriskany* during the coming months would be the loss of combat-experienced personnel and the gaping holes left in the wake of the fire. Every squadron in the air wing lost personnel, including the CAG, commanding officers, and executive officers. The loss of life was a blow to morale and certainly to the core leadership of the air wing. With pilot ranks devastated, squadrons received fresh pilots with minimum amounts of training prior to departing again in 1967. But without combat-experienced leadership, the survivors would be hard-pressed to train the new arrivals and pass on enough knowledge before *Oriskany* returned to Vietnam. It was a situation that would have grave consequences during the next year.

FIG. 1. Capt. Bart Connolly presents CAG Stockdale with a Distinguished Flying Cross in August 1965. While Stockdale set a leadership standard that few could emulate, his success was due in part to Captain Connolly. Together, they set a standard for cooperation between the ship and air wing that few could meet. NH Series, USN 1114972, National Archives, Naval History and Heritage Command, Washington DC.

FIG. 2. Explosions rock the air base at Bien Hoa, 16 May 1965. Maj. Bruce Bell, an air force pilot on an exchange tour with VF-162, had just landed and was killed along with twenty-seven men in one of the worst accidents of the war. Wikipedia Commons, U.S. Air Force.

FIG. 3. Lt. (junior grade) Rick "Bulb" Adams onboard the USS *Galveston* (CLG-3) after being rescued on 5 October 1965. Hit by a SAM, Adams flew his burning Crusader 40 miles out to the Tonkin Gulf before ejecting. USS *Galveston* 1965 cruise book, p. 86, U.S. Navy.

FIG. 4. Lt. Cdr. Richard Powers (*left*) and Lt. Bernard Marks (*kneeling*) in front of the Cubi Point Bachelor Officer Quarters (BOQ) during a port call in 1965. Powers was killed while leading an Iron Hand mission on 31 October 1965. Courtesy Jim Abbitt.

FIG. 5. Plane captain Larry Neff stands in front of VA-163's CAG aircraft. Note "007" beneath the cockpit—CAG James Bond Stockdale used the popularity of Ian Fleming's novels and the new movies to his advantage. Courtesy Bill Tomko.

FIG. 6. The same VA-163 CAG aircraft later in October 1965, after Jim Stockdale's loss. Note the number of missions and CAG Bob Spruit's name. Courtesy Jim Palmer.

FIG. 7. An RF-8G Crusader during an Operation Blue Tree mission, July 1966. The need for pre- and poststrike intelligence meant that photo-reconnaissance missions were always highly dangerous. USN Series, USN 1116640, National Archives, Naval History and Heritage Command, Washington DC.

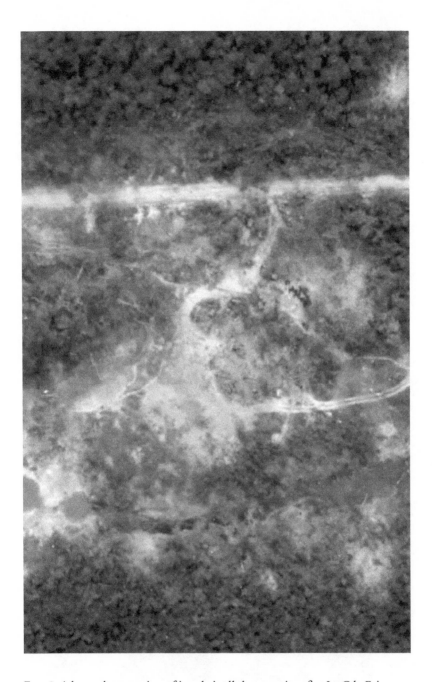

Fig. 8. A burned-out section of jungle is all that remains after Lt. Cdr. Eric Schade and Lt. Jerry Garvey found a truck park on 18 August 1966. Naval aviators called it "Eric's truck park," and it became a geographical reference point during missions. U.S. Navy, author's collection.

FIG. 9. (*opposite top*) Lt. Cdr. Tom Tucker is hauled aboard an SH-3 Sea King from HS-6. Shot down in Haiphong Harbor, Tucker was saved in one of the most daring rescues of the war. This widely circulated photograph was taken by Photographer's Mate Mike Delamore, who hopped aboard the helicopter prior to the mission. NH Series, USN 1126615, National Archives, Naval History and Heritage Command, Washington DC.

FIG. 10. (*opposite bottom*) Lt. Cdr. Tom Tucker chastises Chief Tom Grisham because he wants them to stay and fight. He later helped feed belts of ammunition to Grisham as the helicopter fought its way out of Haiphong. U.S. Navy.

FIG. 11. (*above*) Lt. Cdr. Dick Perry stands in front of his badly damaged Skyhawk aboard USS *Constellation*, September 1966. AAA destroyed his radio and navigational aids, as well as the instruments he needed to land aboard the carrier. Flying alone in the dark, he managed to land on the first carrier he found. Courtesy Steve Perry.

FIG. 12. Secretary McNamara presents Cdr. Dick Bellinger with a Silver Star for downing a MiG-21 earlier in October 1966. Bellinger almost missed the presentation, as he was still inebriated after several days in Saigon. USS *Oriskany* 1966 cruise book, p. 176, U.S. Navy.

FIG. 13. (*opposite top*) Secretary McNamara and Chairman Wheeler listen to a briefing aboard *Oriskany* on 12 October 1966. Moments earlier, an anonymous aviator placed on McNamara's chair a *Peanuts* cartoon making light of the ordnance shortage. NH Series, USN 1118318, National Archives, Naval History and Heritage Command, Washington DC.

FIG. 14. (*opposite bottom*) Cdr. Paul Engel, the commanding officer of VA-164, dons an OBA during the fire. The stress of having lost many of his men is readily apparent on his face. 1996.488.197.008, Robert Lawson Collection, National Museum of Naval Aviation.

FIG. 15. (*opposite top*) Sailors drape hoses down to their shipmates battling the inferno in the hangar bay as others push ordnance away from the area. Note the damaged Skyhawks, including one whose ejection seat fired from the intense heat. These planes were moved from the hangar bay to prevent further catastrophe. Courtesy Tailhook Association.

FIG. 16. (*opposite bottom*) A fire-damaged stateroom. Most of the men who perished were asphyxiated by toxic fumes as they slept following canceled night operations. 1996.488.197.017, Robert Lawson Collection, National Museum of Naval Aviation.

FIG. 17. (*above*) Flag-draped remains of the victims are off-loaded at Cubi Point in a solemn ceremony. The air wing pilots who survived escorted the remains back to Lindbergh Field in San Diego, while *Oriskany* sailed to Hunters Point Naval Shipyard in San Francisco for repairs. 1996.488.197.013, Robert Lawson Collection, National Museum of Naval Aviation.

FIG. 18. An Iron Hand A-4 Skyhawk from VA-164 proceeds feet-dry over North Vietnam. Note the mixed load of Zuni rockets and Shrike missiles used for dueling with SAM sites. By 1967 the number of aircraft needed to suppress Vietnamese defenses sometimes outnumbered the aircraft tasked with destroying the target. Courtesy Dick Schaffert.

FIG. 19. (*opposite top*) VA-164 Skyhawks refuel VF-III Crusaders prior to escorting an Iron Hand mission over North Vietnam. The closest Crusader (AH 106) was flown by Lt. Cdr. Dick Schaffert during his epic duel against six MiGs in December 1967. Courtesy Tailhook Association.

FIG. 20. (*opposite bottom*) The burning USS *Forrestal* as seen from *Oriskany*'s bridge, 29 July 1967. With fresh memories of their own holocaust, *Oriskany*'s crew raced to *Forrestal*'s assistance, providing firefighting supplies and medical support to the stricken carrier. NH Series, USN 1125490, National Archives, Naval History and Heritage Command, Washington DC.

FIG. 21. Pilots of VA-164, resplendent in orange socks, pose for a publicity photo in October 1967. The Burlington Company sent twenty-five socks in their squadron colors as an act of goodwill, and this photo was sent in return to show their appreciation. Courtesy Bill Span.

FIG. 22. (*opposite top*) Tuesday luncheon, 10 October 1967. (*Left to right*) George Christian, Walt Rostow, Robert McNamara, Tom Johnson, Richard Helms, Dean Rusk, President Johnson. The next week they approved strikes on Phuc Yen. LBJ Library photo by Yaichi Okamoto.

FIG. 23. (*opposite bottom*) The first bombs explode on Phuc Yen, North Vietnam's primary MiG base. The base remained off-limits for over two years before being authorized by President Johnson. Aircraft from *Oriskany*, combined with aircraft from *Coral Sea* and air force fighter wings in Thailand, struck the base during massive joint raids in October 1967. National Museum of the U.S. Air Force, photo 090810-F-12340-011.

FIG. 24. (*opposite top*) Bombs from *Oriskany*'s aircraft strike a hangar at Phuc Yen. This photo is one of several taken by Lt. (junior grade) Vance Schufeldt as he orbited overhead the embattled airfield. *Oriskany*'s aircraft evaded thirty-six SAMS in less than six minutes, and for the second time in two days Schufeldt's Skyhawk was damaged by AAA. Courtesy Dick Schaffert.

FIG. 25. (*opposite bottom*) Bombs impact the Hanoi thermal power plant, 26 October 1967. Seconds later, Lt. Cdr. John McCain ejected from his Skyhawk, landing in Truc Bach Lake, in the center of this photo. The future senator and presidential candidate spent the next five and a half years as a POW in Hanoi. Courtesy Dick Schaffert.

FIG. 26. (*above*) Lt. Ed Van Orden's F-8 Crusader sits on the bow following a bad catapult shot. Thinking his aircraft was going off the flight deck, the young Texan ejected and was killed when his parachute snagged on the side of the ship. Courtesy Dick Schaffert.

FIG. 27. A MiG-17, the last of six MiGs outfought by Lt. Cdr. Dick Schaffert as he escorted Lt. (junior grade) Chuck Nelson during an Iron Hand mission in December 1967. When the tables turned, Nelson began snapping photos of the MiG as it attempted to escape *Oriskany*'s Crusaders. It was shot down moments later by Lt. Dick Wyman. Courtesy Dick Schaffert.

Part 4

1967

This . . . cruise was really a high point of the war, and we lost an awful lot of people. Air Wing 16 became known as "Bloody 16." . . . CAG-16 was doing what had been done and worked in the past, but it didn't work in 1967. We followed the same tactics so often the North Vietnamese were setting up for it, they knew what to expect. Eventually CAG picked up on a little diversity, helped by suggestions like "CAG, we're not flying with you anymore."

—Denis Weichman, VA-164, quoted in Jeffrey L. Levinson, *Alpha Strike Vietnam*

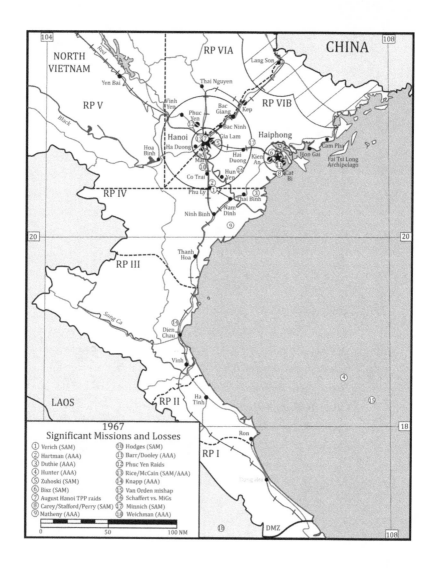

MAP 6. Significant missions flown and losses incurred by USS *Oriskany* in 1967.
Created by the author.

10

Long, Hot Summer

IN JANUARY 1967 ADM. U. S. Grant Sharp reviewed what had been accomplished during the previous two years of Rolling Thunder. In communications with Washington, he wrote, "Unless something was done, within a very short time the growing enemy air defense system will make air operations in the Hanoi-Haiphong region too costly for the type of targets we are not permitted to hit." Sharp recognized four alternatives: first, to accept losses without a commensurate return in targets destroyed; second, to expand the target list; third, to attack the enemy's air defense system, including the MiG bases and aircraft on the ground; or fourth, to abandon the air war over the Red River Delta.[1] His words proved stunningly prophetic as the Johnson administration attempted each alternative over the next year. By all accounts, the air war in early 1967 appeared to be repeating the same failures, though it soon grew beyond anything President Johnson and his advisors could have ever imagined. By autumn, the air war had erupted into a massive effort, releasing an impotent rage at the seeming unwillingness of North Vietnam to negotiate.

Unknown to the men fighting, however, was "Marigold," the codename given to top secret peace negotiations. Despite pressure from China to continue fighting, North Vietnam *was willing to negotiate*.[2] The peace process began in late 1966, with Polish diplomats authorized to broker a peace arrangement on behalf of their Communist allies. The talks quickly gained momentum, though they were eventually derailed by President Johnson's and McNamara's continued attempts to seek the political middle ground. Even as Johnson sought to extricate the country from the morass, he continued to expand the war in an attempt to appear tough on Communism. Despite repeated warnings from the Poles and Johnson's national security team, the president authorized attacks in December that ended any chance for negotiations. In February 1967 the *Washington Post* revealed the top secret initiative. Once the negotiations became public, they were angrily denied as the American public sought answers from their government. Recently declassified American and Communist archives show that the Johnson administration never understood that a favorable deal could be brokered. Because of this missed opportunity, direct talks between the United States and North Vietnam did not occur until May 1968. In the interim, the war spiraled out of control, and American casualties continued.

With no end to the fighting in sight, pilots sought creative ways to deal with the increasing North Vietnamese defenses. Throughout the fall, MiG activity continued to increase as electronic warfare suppressed the North Vietnamese SAM and AAA systems. VPAF MiGs regularly intercepted F-105 missions, forcing them to jettison their bombs well short of the target as pilots defended against them. On 2 January the Eighth Fighter Wing in Thailand launched a large mission to destroy MiGs. Conceived and led by the legendary Col. Robin Olds, Operation Bolo was a complex ruse using F-4 Phantoms flying the mission profile usually flown by F-105s. Olds's pilots used F-105 call signs and mounted QRC-160 self-protect jammers normally carried by the F-105 to complete the deception. Bolo was a huge success—seven MiGs were shot down without a single loss in an epic air battle.[3] The loss forced the VPAF to ground their MiGs for several months as they devised new tactics.

In late February, Rolling Thunder 54 began. In all, sixteen targets deemed vital to the North Vietnamese industry were added to the target list, including the Thai Nguyen steel works, the Haiphong cement works, and several power stations. Estuaries and inland waterways up to the 20th parallel became candidates for mining. Despite the limitations imposed on the mining, the Joint Chiefs viewed mining positively. Long advocated by the military, mining remained taboo in Washington due to fears that mining Haiphong might result in outright war with China. As the weather began clearing in March, strikes grew in frequency. As expected, the North Vietnamese defenses became increasingly deadly. In March EB-66 jammers began escorting Rolling Thunder missions. The EB-66 offensively jammed many radars, as opposed to the QRC-160 and ALQ-51, which defensively jammed single-fire control radars. In the words of one air force history, this marked the first

LONG, HOT SUMMER

attempt "to attack the entire enemy electronic defense system, not just a part of it."[4] Despite the success, pilots believed that success could only be achieved by destroying the SAM sites, not suppressing them electronically. It led to the paradox of exposing even more aircraft to the defenses in the hope of suppressing them.

In response to the effective suppression of the early warning radars and SAMs, MiGs once again entered the fray. Though they downed few aircraft, MiGs consistently forced strike packages to jettison their bombs. Aviators often watched in frustration as MiGs taxied for takeoff, knowing they were prohibited from attacking them while at the same time knowing the same MiGs would soon be attacking. McNamara denied continuous requests to strike the MiG bases, dismissing the threat by noting that they were only credited with ten shootdowns. Attacking the MiG bases was deemed too dangerous. McNamara believed such attacks might force VPAF MiGs to flee to China and could result in outright Chinese intervention.[5] The Johnson administration's fear of war with China trumped all reason, and the airfields remained off-limits.

In late March, while repairs on *Oriskany* continued at a rapid pace, the weather over North Vietnam finally improved enough to increase the pace of Rolling Thunder. The increase came with a cost, however; the North Vietnamese took full advantage of the lull caused by weather and American restrictions, working feverishly to build more airfields and strengthen its defenses. In early April the North Vietnamese downed the five hundredth U.S. aircraft since the opening stages of the air war in February 1965. Even Secretary McNamara realized that something needed to be done to counter the increasingly lethal MiG-SAM-AAA trifecta. On 23 April the execute order for Rolling Thunder 55 was received from the White House. Though limited in scope, it marked a major escalation in the air war. For the first time, select targets within the 10-mile circle around Hanoi were authorized, though the order limited strike packages to eight airplanes or less. McNamara approved strikes on MiG airfields, but, true to form, he limited them in scope. Rather than permitting attacks on all six MiG bases or at least those bases posing the greatest threat, the administration deliberately selected Kep and Hoa Lac, two bases with the least number of MiGs. Unfortunately, three major MiG bases (Phuc Yen, Kien An, and Cat Bi) remained off-limits, thus providing a sanctuary. The following week, Rolling Thunder 56 added another ten targets to the JCS target list. As the weather improved, the tempo accelerated, and maximum efforts against all approved targets became authorized. Over nine thousand sorties were being flown each month, nearly triple the amount from 1965. Carriers on Yankee Station began launching several Alpha strikes a day as the United States sought to isolate Hanoi and Haiphong from the rest of North Vietnam. The North Vietnamese were ready. In the months following Operation Bolo, the VPAF learned to coordinate their MiG and SAM forces, allowing both to operate simultaneously. There would be no more "MiG days" and "SAM days." From this point forward, every strike encountered heavy SAMS, AAA, and MiGs. In April 425 SAMS were fired at U.S. aircraft, and in May the number topped 500.[6] The pace and subsequent losses would be shocking once *Oriskany* returned to Yankee Station.

The detrimental effects of the fire on the men of CVW-16 and *Oriskany* cannot be understated. The massive increase of Rolling Thunder in the spring of 1967 exacerbated the already critical shortfalls faced by the navy, and the fire could not have happened at a more inopportune time. As a result of the fire, the navy was short an aircraft carrier, leaving it little choice but to hastily repair *Oriskany* and return her to Vietnam as soon as possible. For the first time since the dark days of the Solomons campaign in early World War II, when the damaged USS *Enterprise* (CV-6) was hurriedly repaired and pressed back into service, *Oriskany* did the same. Yankee Station was by no means the Iron Bottom Sound, but the rush was the same. Repairs were completed at Hunters Point Naval Shipyard on 23 March, leaving little more than two months for the ship and air wing to train together before departing. It led to a changed air wing and ship dynamic that came as Rolling Thunder reached its high point. The consequences would be disastrous.

Although the official investigation cleared him of any wrongdoing, Captain Iarrobino's career was finished. The navy stuck with the old adage that held the captain ultimately responsible for the fate of his ship. Iarrobino received a Letter of Reprimand, which he successfully fought and had removed from his record. However, the navy issued a nonpunitive Letter of Instruction in its place. In the highly competitive rank structure of the navy, the Letter of Instruction, coupled with the fact that the fire occurred under his watch, eliminated any possible promotion to admiral. Iarrobino eventually retired from the navy in 1972. Capt. Billy Holder assumed command of *Oriskany* and began the unenviable task of repairing the fire-ravaged ship and preparing her traumatized crew. A career naval aviator, Holder earned his wings in December 1942, although he spent the war stateside as an instructor. Rising through the ranks, he commanded an attack squadron and eventually CVW-2. He was intimately familiar with the crisis in Vietnam, having already served three tours in the region, and the upcoming deployment would mark his fourth. Holder possessed a different leadership style, and many aviators chafed at the change. Both Captains Connolly and Iarrobino had developed close relationships with the air wing, and aviators felt that Holder isolated himself on the bridge, limiting his interaction to CAG and the occasional squadron commander. Gone were the days of friendly ready room visits by the captain. They had been replaced by a contentious relationship between the ship and her air wing. The friction was palpable, and at times it seemed as if the captain himself delighted in running drills and chipping paint in the few off-hours pilots had to rest in between missions. To be fair, however, much work remained to complete repairs on the ship, and the drills were intended to train the crew should the unthinkable happen again. Simply put, Captain Holder had been thrust in a tough position with little time to prepare his ship and crew before returning to Vietnam.

The fire left gaping holes in the ranks of CVW-16. The loss of so many senior aviators and combat-experienced pilots proved deadly in 1967. VA-164 experienced a 75 percent turnover rate among sailors and 50 percent among pilots from ranks already thinned by the fire.[7] Other squadrons experienced similar turnover. The returning veterans faced a herculean task to prepare themselves and inexperienced replacements for combat. That *Oriskany* remained unavailable during repairs further compounded the problem. Though some training occurred at NAS Fallon and MCAS Yuma, real training simply could not happen until *Oriskany* was repaired. Once she was ready for sea, they were given just four weeks to train together prior to departing for Vietnam—a shockingly short amount of time considering the pace of operations and defenses awaiting them.

After CAG Carter perished in the fire, the air wing also received new leadership under Cdr. Burton Shepherd. CAG Shepherd realized the overwhelming task he faced and set about to ensure he had the right people to help the air wing succeed. One of his first steps was to keep his air wing operations officer, Lt. Cdr. Elmore "Buck" Sheeley. Due to transfer, Sheeley was talked into extending with the promise that he'd be given command of a squadron of his own if he stayed to help.[8] Sheeley became a core member of a team of men that included *Oriskany*'s assistant strike operations officer, Lt. Cdr. Lew Chatham; VA-164's Lt. Cdr. Bob Arnold and Lt. Cdr. Denis Weichman; and VA-163's Lt. Cdr. Dean Cramer and Lt. Cdr. Jim Busey. Together, these men became the cooperative brains that held the air wing together during 1967 as everything else seemed to come apart. These men waited impatiently for the Pentagon's last-minute instructions and then instantaneously put together a workable plan.[9] To be certain, strong personalities dominated as the air wing regrouped. The senior officers were bound together by the requirements laid upon *Oriskany*. Even though they competed against each other for performance reports and promotions, they remained professional when it came to leading missions. The department heads (senior lieutenant commanders), by nature of their duties, were in fierce competition within the squadrons and between the squadrons. For the most part, junior officers were along for the ride, fighting for survival and, unsurprisingly, drawn toward the natural leaders—those men who were most capable in the cockpit, independent of their rank. The cohesion experienced during the previous cruises had been all but shattered by the fire and personnel transfers. Rebuilding that cohesion would be one of the key problems faced by CAG Shepherd as Rolling Thunder reached its deadly climax.

A fine naval officer and capable naval aviator, CAG Shepherd also found himself thrust into an impossible position. He was dedicated and he cared for his aviators, continually telling his men, "Be a tiger, but be a smart tiger!"[10] During the coming months, Shepherd's leadership came under extreme scrutiny. Though a competent aviator, he would often be overwhelmed by the extraordinary missions asked of *Oriskany*'s aviators. To be certain, CAG Shepherd was a solid leader of men in combat. He was often overshadowed by the men under him, including the fearless and magnanimous Bryan Compton, the new commanding officer of VA-163. Competent, tough, and completely professional (he later became the first captain of USS *Nimitz* CVN-68),

Compton did not suffer fools. Never one to flaunt a false bravado, CAG Shepherd faced the impossible task of balancing unavoidable losses while at the same time providing enough victories to satisfy higher authorities and still provide a stable base for air wing morale.[11] Many of his subordinates complained loudly and bitterly, but the responsibility and heavy burden was shouldered by CAG Shepherd alone.

The surge in Rolling Thunder led to fewer available aircraft, which hampered the navy's ability to equip squadrons for combat, and *Oriskany* suffered several follow-on effects. Although the navy was in the process of fielding new aircraft, they could not operate from *Oriskany*, so she soldiered on with limited numbers of older aircraft. As the war ground on, there were fewer and fewer Crusaders for replacements. By 1967 the shortage meant one of *Oriskany*'s fighter squadrons traded in their bomb-capable F-8E Crusaders for earlier F-8C variants robbed from utility squadrons. Because higher headquarters could not make the decision, Cdr. Bob Rasmussen and Cdr. Cal Swanson made it for them. In true fighter pilot fashion, they rolled dice at the Miramar officers club during a happy hour in late January. VF-III lost and traded in their newer jets for less capable airframes. Because the F-8C did not have wing pylons for air-to-ground ordnance, it meant that *Oriskany*'s strikes had less firepower available to suppress North Vietnamese defenses. With Rolling Thunder reaching its peak, this became one of the underlying reasons behind their many losses in 1967.[12] New aircraft also meant even less time to train, as acceptance inspections took time, as did acquainting pilots with the different aircraft. As their training continued, Swanson recommended to Shepherd that Crusader pilots be allowed to lead strikes, thereby lessening the workload of the senior pilots in the attack squadrons. It was also a way for fighter pilots to earn medals, which until that time had been the exclusive purview of attack pilots. It seemed like a good idea, until Swanson led the air wing's last strike to Fallon, Nevada, and accidentally dropped a bomb on an Atomic Energy Commission building—*outside the actual bombing range*. It was an embarrassing event for Swanson, although Shepherd covered for him. In the end, the whole concept was quickly and quietly forgotten. Rolling Thunder remained an attack pilot's war.

While the men of *Oriskany* made final preparations for their return to Vietnam, the widening chasm over American involvement was ready to explode. The air war over North Vietnam became one of the main points of public controversy. Fueling the public's outcry was a series of articles published by Harrison Salisbury, the assistant managing editor of the *New York Times*. The North Vietnamese manipulated Salisbury's articles as part of their propaganda efforts to sway American support. At the same time, General Westmoreland's request for an additional 206,000 troops became public. The articles, coupled with greater troop commitments, fueled public outcry and led to further dissension within the Johnson administration. Antiwar protests continued to grow in size and scope, threatening to tear the country apart. On 15 April an estimated four hundred thousand antiwar protesters marched in New York City, with another one hundred thousand marching in San Francisco. Protesters marched from Central Park to the United Nations building to hear speeches by Martin Luther King Jr. and other antiwar leaders. It was Martin Luther King Jr.'s first open opposition to the war, and though civil rights leadership had been divided over violent versus nonviolent approaches, by the spring of 1967 they stood united on their opposition to the war. The intensity of the opposition began to sway members of the Johnson administration. By 1967 President Johnson's approval rating had plummeted to below 50 percent, and the term "credibility gap" began being used to describe the Johnson administration's penchant for deceiving the public. Even his closest advisors began to express their doubts. In early May, John McNaughton wrote to McNamara:

> A feeling is widely and strongly held that "the Establishment" is out of its mind. The feeling is that we are trying to impose some U.S. image on distant peoples we cannot understand (any more than we can the younger generation here at home), and that we are carrying the thing to absurd lengths. Related to this feeling is the increased polarization that is taking place in the United States with seeds of the worst split in our people in more than a century. . . . The picture of the world's greatest superpower killing or seriously injuring 1,000 noncombatants a week, while trying to pound a tiny backward nation into submission on an issue whose merits are wholly disputed is not a pretty one.[13]

Throughout, Johnson remained reluctant to admit the actual costs of the war. Although short-term bookkeeping allowed his administration to hide the true costs, the bill came due in the spring of 1967 as mounting government deficits and runaway inflation took hold.[14] Additionally, in 1965 President Johnson chose not to mobilize U.S. Reserves out of concern for the political ramifications. Instead, his administration upped conscription quotas. The end result was the same. The continued induction of up to forty thousand men each month quickly became the focal point for growing anger over civil rights and American involvement in Southeast Asia. The tinderbox of dissent and frustration exploded during the summer of 1967. In June riots broke out across the United States—Atlanta, Boston, Cincinnati, Buffalo, and Tampa. By the end of the summer, 159 race riots, coupled with anti-war protests, crippled the country. Popular culture at the time referred to the summer of 1967 as the "Summer of Love." In reality, it was violent and chaotic both in the United States and in Vietnam. *Oriskany* departed from Alameda on 16 June amid the tumult. As representatives of the society from which they were drawn, her crew was all too aware of the turmoil surrounding the war in Vietnam. With great apprehension, she arrived in Subic Bay on 2 July, and the crew made final preparations for combat.

Triumph at Phu Ly

Oriskany began her first line period of 1967 on 12 July. The pace of operations no longer allowed for warm-up periods, and her pilots immediately commenced flying armed reconnaissance missions in preparation for larger strikes near Hanoi and Haiphong. In the first two days, the air wing lost two airplanes and one pilot. One Skyhawk was so badly damaged that it was patched together and flown to the depot at Cubi Point. The air war had changed. No matter how ready the men of CVW-16 believed themselves to be, nothing could prepare them for the impending onslaught.

The air wing's reintroduction to the lethal North Vietnamese defenses mirrored events happening in America. Secretary McNamara's closest aide, John McNaughton, was killed along with his wife and youngest son in a tragic plane crash. Influential in the Americanization of the war, by 1967 McNaughton had begun expressing his doubts. In May he successfully advised President Johnson against granting General Westmoreland's request for an additional two hundred thousand troops. The loss of a close confidant with similar misgivings about the war left McNamara alone to face rallying hawks. In the week following McNaughton's death, America burned. Riots exploded in Harlem, the Bronx, and Newark. The Twelfth Street riots in Detroit resulted in five days of violence that left forty-three dead, over four hundred injured, and more than two thousand buildings destroyed before police, Michigan National Guard, and U.S. Army troops stopped the violence. The scale of the riot rivaled those of the New York City Draft Riots during the Civil War and the 1992 Los Angeles Riots. "The Long, Hot Summer," as it became known, sent shockwaves throughout the country.[15]

Likewise, the impending decimation of *Oriskany*'s ranks appalled the navy. During the tumultuous week following 16 July, tragedy befell their initial triumph. That same week, Rolling Thunder 57 started, adding sixteen targets, including an airfield, rail yards, ten bridges, and twelve barracks—all within the Hanoi and Haiphong restricted circles. But none of the targets were within the forbidden 10-mile inner circle around Hanoi. This escalation followed the same previous patterns—a cognizant attempt by President Johnson to prevent discussion by the hawks or doves concerning his conduct of the war. His decision ensured a partisan fight by August.[16] The air wing's arrival on the line coincided with Rolling Thunder 57, and the ship quickly settled into what the crew called the "Dr. Pepper 10-2-4 schedule" because of the regularity. With the majority of missions now being flown into the very center of North Vietnam's defenses, *Oriskany*'s long, hot summer had begun.

On 16 July vf-162's Lt. Cdr. Demetrio "Butch" Verich launched as part of the flak suppression element on an afternoon raid on the Phu Ly rail yards. As they approached the target, his division of Crusaders was attacked by a volley of three sams. Verich successfully outmaneuvered two but was hit by the third missile. For the second time in just eleven months, Verich ejected from his crippled Crusader. As he descended in his parachute, his aircraft crashed and exploded directly beneath him. With wind driving him toward the fireball, Verich pulled on his parachute risers to slip the parachute and steer himself away from the inferno. He landed on a steep, rocky hill covered with thick jungle and trees a scant 16 miles from Hanoi.

Lt. Dick Wyman and Cdr. Herb Hunter, Verich's wingmen, orbited overhead, attempting to coordinate a rescue. While they circled, Verich climbed several hundred yards up the slope, since North Vietnamese soldiers were already heading toward the wreckage. Then Wyman was hit by AAA. The 37 mm damaged his Crusader enough that he diverted to Da Nang. That left Cdr. Al Headly, VA-152's executive officer, and his wingman orbiting overhead, though they too had to leave by nightfall. Verich remembered, "I saw my wingman had fixed my position and would be back, but it was getting dark so I figured I wouldn't be rescued until morning. I thought the best thing would be to hide and then move after dark. I covered myself with branches and waited. The North Vietnamese were beating the bushes, some less than a hundred yards away." Throughout the night, he could hear soldiers yelling, dogs barking, and a strange sound like two pieces of bamboo being struck together rhythmically.[17] Verich unwittingly spent the evening next to the same 37 mm AAA battery that had damaged Wyman's aircraft. "I decided to move at dawn," said Verich. "But just as the sun was coming up, a jet passed overhead so I stayed where I was and waited."[18]

The jet that passed overhead was flown by VA-163's Lt. Cdr. Marv Reynolds, who took the rescue effort personally. Reynolds discovered the downed pilot was Verich after he recovered from the Phu Ly strike. Reynolds immediately began making the case for a rescue, convincing Cdr. Compton, then CAG Shepherd, and finally CTF-77, Rear Adm. Dave Richardson, who authorized the effort. At 0300 two A-4s and an E-1B launched to attempt to locate Verich and confirm his identity via code word. Reynolds left his wingman with the E-1B while he proceeded feet-dry to search the area. The sound of Reynolds's Skyhawk woke Verich. After Reynolds made several attempts to raise Verich on the radio, Verich replied to Reynolds's query with "Is this Marv?" The pair quickly conferred, and Reynolds told Verich they'd be back in half an hour.[19]

The rescue was on. Reynolds flew back to the gulf to refuel from an awaiting tanker while passing words to the E-1B to launch the CSAR. The Sea King from HS-2, flown by Lt. Neil Sparks and Lt. (junior grade) Robin Springer, began their precarious transit inland. As the helicopter passed Hon Ma Island they picked up an escort of four VA-152 Skyraiders led by Cdr. Allen Headley. Because Verich had been shot down in the heavily populated region south of Hanoi, the escorts had their work cut out for them. Reynolds and his wingman avoided three SAMS and withering AAA before they destroyed the closest 37 mm emplacement. Meanwhile, the Sea King made its way through the deep valleys, trying to pinpoint Verich. The crew could not see Verich through the trees, but as they passed over him, Verich fired a flare, which was noticed by one of the crew members. Sparks quickly turned the helicopter around and brought it to a hover overhead.

As the crew lowered the jungle penetrator, the helicopter came under intense ground fire. Though two crewmen, Teddy Ray and Al Masengale, returned fire, they could not suppress all of it, and rounds began tearing through the helicopter. One round hit just below Sparks, knocking out the generator, and then they lost the second generator. Another round exploded through the instrument panel. Then another round knocked out the automatic pilot, which made the helicopter difficult to control and almost impossible to hold in a hover. Another round destroyed the radio equipment in the nose. Without a radio, Sparks and Springer could not talk to their escorts or to Verich. Thinking quickly, Springer pulled out his own survival radio. Springer took off his helmet and put the radio up to his ear, allowing him to get the last bits of information they needed to recover Verich. Without an automatic pilot, Sparks struggled to keep the helicopter steady for the nearly twenty minutes required to hoist Verich aboard.[20] Verich missed the jungle penetrator on the first drop, but the second time it came down about 10 feet from him, and he was able to get to it. Sparks still managed to keep the helicopter in its precarious hover until Verich was aboard—a herculean task, as rough terrain surrounded the helicopter on all sides, and they were nearly 50 feet below the rim of a cliff wall.[21] With Verich finally aboard, the Sea King began its long flight back to the gulf.

The excitement didn't end with Verich's recovery. While the rescue unfolded, *Oriskany* aircraft conducted an early morning Alpha strike nearby. MiG-21s harassed the raid but were driven off by the TARCAP. As the strike headed for the gulf, another MiG-21 made an unobserved run on the F-8 escorts. Cdr. Bryan Compton saw the MiG launch an Alkali air-to-air missile, which, fortunately, missed. Compton still had a full load of eight Zuni rockets, which he shot at the MiG. The Zunis missed, and Compton pressed in for another attempt with his 20 mm cannons. Some 200 feet behind the MiG, Compton only managed to fire off thirty rounds before his cannons jammed. The MiG pilot broke off his engagement and returned to Phuc Yen. Compton summed up the experience by saying, "Pretty frustrating, a hamburger ready to eat, and no teeth!"[22]

Sparks and his crew stopped to refuel on USS *Worden* (CG-18) at the northern SAR station before heading for *Oriskany*. After dropping off Butch Verich, they returned to the *Hornet*, where awestruck sailors examined the damaged helicopter.[23] The rescue was a huge success, despite the damage. Verich successfully evaded the North Vietnamese for nearly fifteen hours before eventually being rescued. He survived overnight and, even more newsworthy, was the reason why—VF-162 became the first squadron to have two men shot down and rescued twice. Verich was summoned to Saigon for the "Five O'Clock Follies" to brief reporters on his harrowing experience. Both Reynolds and Sparks received the Navy Cross for their efforts during the rescue. Unfortunately, their success led to disaster the next day when another rescue attempt occurred in the same vicinity.

Tragedy at Co Trai

Tragedy befell VA-164 on 18 July as they struck the bridge at Co Trai, which had been bombed just five days earlier. On their ingress to the bridge, Lt. Cdr. Richard Hartman and Lt. (junior grade) Larry Duthie evaded several SAMs, losing altitude in the process. As they began climbing back to altitude, Hartman's Skyhawk was hit by 37 mm AAA. His airplane exploded, and he immediately ejected from the fireball. Hartman was so low that he only swung twice beneath his parachute before landing on a karst ridge 25 miles south of Hanoi, near Phu Lai. Because of the successful rescue the day before, a SAR mission was quickly authorized and launched from the northern SAR destroyer. Although Duthie attempted to climb and orbit overhead Hartman's position, he too was hit. Duthie headed for the gulf with his airplane on fire and smoke filling the cockpit. With no oxygen and failed hydraulics, Duthie stayed with the airplane because the engine still worked, and he was able to control it by flying with trim. After flying 12 miles toward the coast, his airplane became uncontrollable. The trim failed, and the Skyhawk rolled 135 degrees before beginning an uncontrollable dive. Duthie ejected near Nam Dinh in a region known as the Hourglass, some 45 miles southeast of Hanoi. Although Nam Dinh was closer to the coast and a rescue there would theoretically be easier, the densely populated city was in the midst of the heavily defended Red River Delta.[24] It also happened to be less than 10 miles from Hartman's position.

Now there were two aviators down, greatly complicating the rescue process. Rescue forces waited an inordinate amount of time for clearance to attempt the rescues. In the interim, a Sea King from HS-2 refueled at the northern SAR destroyer. The helicopter, Big Mother 67, was flown by Lt. John Bender and Lt. (junior grade) John Schloz with crew members Aviation Antisubmarine Warfare Technician 2nd Class David Chatterton and Aviation Antisubmarine Warfare Technician 3rd Class Wayne Noah. As the crew listened to the unfolding drama, permission was finally granted, and they began heading for Duthie.[25] The air force also launched two Jolly Green helicopters and four A-1E Sandys, though their transit from the border to Duthie's location took time, as they skirted around the highly defended and populated areas of the Red River valley.

Duthie came down through heavy trees along a karst ridge and quickly moved 100 yards uphill to avoid capture. After Duthie spent nearly four hours on the ground, the rescue forces arrived. Jolly Green 36 and 37 approached from the southwest, while Big Mother approached from the south. Four VA-152 Skyraiders escorting the Sea King were joined by two of the air force Sandys. The six A-1s, along with at least one VA-163 A-4, flown by Lt. Cdr. Mac Davis, went to work neutralizing guns and troops in the area. The on-scene commander, Maj. Ted Bronczyk, called Duthie and instructed him to light off a smoke flare as they escorted a helicopter in. According to Duthie, "The flare-smoke drifted down my arm to the ground, and then it slowly filtered uphill. Bender saw it coming into a little clearing and went into a hover there. Hearing the helicopter a ways up the hill, I made my way up it to the clearing. I got beneath the chopper, stood under it, and with one of my two radios (I had not lost any of my survival gear, as some reports say) I called and called." North Vietnamese gunners, who had been waiting for this exact moment, opened fire. Ground fire erupted from three sides—close enough for the crew to hear it over the noise of the engines and rotors as Bender settled into a hover.[26] Owing to the steep terrain and unpredictable wind gusts, Bender struggled to keep the helicopter in a hover so Chatterton could lower the jungle penetrator. Ground fire quickly damaged the helicopter and hit Chatterton in the chest. Unfortunately, Duthie was directly underneath the helicopter in an area where radio reception was not possible.[27] With Chatterton wounded and the crew unable to hear Duthie, the penetrator was never lowered.

Bender had no choice but to abort the rescue. He departed, flying over flat farmland and one of the hottest areas in an attempt to save time and, hopefully, Chatterton's life. VA-152's Lt. Hank Miller escorted the crippled helicopter out to sea. Big Mother made it to the SAR destroyer, but not before David Chatterton died of his wounds. Later, as sailors counted the twenty-eight bullet holes in the Sea King, they found two in the Plexiglas window adjacent to Bender's head.[28]

Duthie later recalled, "As Big Mother departed, Bronczyk called me and said to cool my heels a bit, but that they were bringing in another helicopter. I went back down the hill into the trees to wait. A guy with a rifle about 75 feet from me was in the trees on the other side of the clearing; why he didn't come over to capture me, I'll always wonder (and be thankful for)." In the meantime, the remaining Skyraiders continued suppressing AAA in the area. Sandys 1 and 2 were severely damaged within minutes. Low on fuel and flying heavily damaged aircraft, the pilots returned to their base in Thailand. Jolly Green 36 announced he was low on fuel and departed as well, leaving Sandys 3 and 4 escorting Jolly Green 37 at 8,000 feet. A quick fuel calculation by her crew showed they had just enough to make the attempt.

The call soon came, and Jolly Green 37, flown by Maj. Glenn York and 1st Lt. Billy Privatte, dived down to treetop height and began the mad dash for Duthie. Their descent rapidly built up airspeed, creating banging noises that the crew mistook for AAA. As York entered the clearing, he overflew Duthie. With small arms fire pummeling the helicopter, Privatte hung his head out the window and spotted Duthie. The helicopter's rotor blades took the top off a tree as York turned around and went into a hover. Privatte later said the small arms fire sounded like popcorn.[29] Seconds lasted a lifetime, and the crew had little choice but to hold their hover as Sgt. Theodore Zerbe ran the jungle penetrator down. Duthie ran back to the clearing and quickly jumped on as Zerbe began hauling him in. As soon as Duthie cleared the trees, York started flying away, with Duthie dangling beneath.

The day's tragedy continued to unfold. Low on fuel and having sustained battle damage, Sandys 3 and 4 departed for Thailand. With night fast approaching, Crown 4, the airborne command post and overall rescue coordinator, asked Jolly Green 37 to make one last attempt to pick up Hartman. Hartman had been in sporadic contact with rescue forces throughout Duthie's rescue and had been successfully evading the North Vietnamese. Major York agreed, despite the damage to his helicopter and a low fuel state. In support of this last attempt, *Oriskany* launched the equivalent of another Alpha strike to suppress the gun positions near Hartman. Escorted by *Oriskany* fighters, York flew south along the next karst ridge toward Hartman. Hartman did not come up on the radio, and the rescue force was called off after attempting to suppress the most intense ground fire they had seen that day. Hartman was left to survive the night and await another attempt at sunrise.

To conserve fuel, York climbed to 12,000 feet and headed west for Lima 36, an emergency landing strip in Laos. A MiG attempted to intercept them but missed due to their altitude. At Lima 36, York made an instrument approach in the dark in mountainous terrain, using his automatic direction finding (ADF) gear to home in on an Air America aircraft. Jolly Green 37 landed with low fuel lights on and damaged nose gear that wouldn't extend.[30] According to Duthie,

> Lima 36 was a weird and spooky place. We landed at the end of the runway with 70 pounds of fuel—not enough to air-taxi down the strip to the fuel area or to even go into a brief hover. With the help of some Hmong soldiers, Randy McComb, the PJ [air force pararescueman], hauled fuel in 55-gallon drums up to the bird and refueled it—with a hand-pump. Tons of work. Then York went back into North Vietnam (with that wounded bird) to rendezvous with some other Sandy A-1s in an attempt to rescue Dick. Before they left, York told me that if Dick Hartman wasn't rescued that afternoon, he wouldn't be coming out—which is what happened. York's Jolly Green was denied permission into the Navy's portion of RP VI.[31]

The day's toll included two Skyhawks, two severely damaged helicopters, four severely damaged A-IEs, and the life of one man. Rescue forces recovered one of the downed aviators, but they had left Dick Hartman. There were many heroes on that hellish day—the same day Newark and Plainfield, New Jersey, burned back in America. York was awarded the Air Force Cross. The other members of his crew, as well as the four A-IE pilots, all received Silver Stars. *Oriskany's* men performed other acts of heroism, and although they were not officially recognized, they prevented further disaster. It was a horrible day in a very long war.

Another hellish day was 19 July. On board *Hornet*, the death of Chatterton, in addition to the damage sustained by two of their helicopters, weighed heavily on the crew tasked with rescuing Hartman. Lt. Dennis Peterson and his copilot, Ens. Donald Frye, planned their upcoming mission carefully, intending to arrive overhead at daybreak and use the cover of darkness for safety.[32] In the predawn hours, VA-152 launched six Skyraiders from *Oriskany* to provide RESCAP and escort the rescue helicopter. During the evening, Lt. Pete Peters and Lt. J. P. O'Neill braved SAMS and AAA in their Crusaders in order to maintain contact with Hartman. Their efforts paid off, as Hartman evaded, periodically checking in to report on the intensive weapons buildup in his vicinity. At 0525 he made contact with the Skyraiders as they arrived overhead.

With a quick call, the rescue commenced. Peterson and his crew began their transit as six Skyraiders and ten Skyhawks from *Oriskany* pounded AAA positions. At 0640 Peterson instructed Hartman to pop smoke when the helicopter arrived overhead. The crew missed the smoke and overshot Hartman's position. As the helicopter swung back around, tragedy struck. One of the Skyraiders attempted to mark Hartman's position with a Zuni Rocket. At the same time, a cluster bomb dropped by one of the Skyhawks failed to open and exploded nearby. Peterson and his crew mistook the cluster bomb for the Zuni and flew directly over an unseen 37 mm AAA battery in the valley. The North Vietnamese held their fire until Peterson's helicopter was directly overhead. The Sea King was shot down in an immense fireball, killing Peterson, Frye, and Aviation Antisubmarine Warfare Technician 2nd Class William Jackson and Aviation Antisubmarine Warfare Technician 2nd Class Donald McGrane.

During the ill-fated rescue attempt, VA-164 lost their third aircraft in two days. Lt. Cdr. Bob Arnold, Lt. John Davis, and Lt. (junior grade) Barry Wood were providing flak suppression for the rescue. Following one of their attack runs with Zuni rockets, Wood noticed a rapid drop in his fuel level. Davis was also critically low on fuel, and the pair turned toward the coast. Davis believed that they could make it feet-wet to an available tanker, which he managed to do. With less fuel, Wood did not believe he could make it and opted to eject before his engine flamed out.[33] He ejected for the second time in six days, landing 8 miles offshore. Barry Wood was eventually recovered by a small boat from the SAR destroyer USS *Richard B. Anderson* (DD-786).

Cdr. Donald Wilson, the commanding officer of VA-152, attempted to escort another helicopter in, but after the loss of another Skyhawk and helicopter with its four crew members on top of the previous day's toll, Hartman's rescue was called off. Rear Adm. Richardson made the decision to leave Hartman before more men were killed trying to rescue him. The gut-wrenching decision was made even more tragic in the following days, as Hartman continued to evade capture in one of the most densely populated regions of North Vietnam. *Oriskany* aircraft contacted Hartman again on 20 July, informing him that a survival kit would be dropped for him. In his last words, he pleaded over his survival radio, "Please don't leave me." Lt. Cdr. Leon "Bud" Edney, one of Hartman's squadron mates, refused to be nominated for a Silver Star in recognition of his effort to drop supplies to Hartman, believing they had abandoned him.[34] Although men hoped that he had been captured, Richard Hartman never returned at the end of the war, and he was never seen in any POW camp. Given the ferocity of the fighting during his attempted rescues, it is likely Hartman was killed outright upon capture. But all that was in the future. All *Oriskany*'s men knew is that they'd abandoned one of their own to a horrible fate.

The Ghost Riders' losses over that two-day period hit Lt. Cdr. Bob Arnold particularly hard. As a senior flight leader in VA-164 he had handpicked the three other members of his division: Lt. Cdr. Dick Hartman, Lt. (junior grade) Larry Duthie, and Lt. (junior grade) Barry Wood. Arnold was quite proud of his division, which he gave the radio call sign "hoser flight." All the men were bachelors, and Arnold claimed they were destined to do great things during the upcoming cruise.[35]

Instead, after a week of combat his division ceased to exist. Hartman was missing. Duthie was evacuated due to injuries sustained on 18 July. Wood turned in his wings after ejecting for the third time in less than a year. He asked for and was given a transfer to the navy's riverine forces fighting in the Mekong Delta in South Vietnam.

Regrettably for *Oriskany*, the day's tragedies continued. As the Hartman rescue ended in heartbreak, *Oriskany* launched another Alpha strike against the bridge at Co Trai. For the second day in a row, the defenses surrounding the bridge claimed another air wing aircraft. Adding to the aura of Co Trai, VF-162 lost an aircraft on the same date in 1966. Cdr. Herb Hunter, a former member of the Blue Angels and new executive officer of VF-162, led the flak suppression element and was hit in the wing by 57 mm AAA. The hit ruptured the fuel tanks in his Crusader's wings and destroyed the aircraft's hydraulic systems. Hunter and his wingman, Lt. J. P. O'Neill, flew toward the gulf and what they believed was *Oriskany*. In reality, they were heading for *Bon Homme Richard*, steaming several miles closer to the coast.

Out of fuel, Hunter opted to risk a landing on *Bon Homme Richard*. However, due to the damage, Hunter could not jettison his ordnance, refuel in-flight, or raise the wing for landing. The variable incidence wing of Crusader was unique in that the entire wing rose to provide increased lift at lower landing speeds. Landing without it added exponential risk to Hunter's task. Hunter discussed his options with O'Neill, one of the most experienced Crusader pilots in the fleet, and he recommended repeatedly that Hunter eject. No one will ever know why Herb Hunter took the chance to save such a damaged aircraft. However, after one week of combat operations *Oriskany*'s loss rates exceeded the air wing's ability to resupply. In seven days, the air wing had lost seven aircraft, with an additional six severely damaged. Perhaps the chance to save a precious aircraft influenced Hunter to attempt the landing. According to Cdr. Bob Rasmussen, the commanding officer of VF-111, Hunter's brother-in-law, and fellow squadron mate from the Blue Angels, "He was just not about to let an aircraft that had a hole in one wing the size of a basketball, an asymmetric armament load of 1,000 pounds, practically zero fuel and a wing that could not configure for landing, get the best of him."[36] When Hunter attempted to land on *Bon Homme Richard*, his aircraft hit the deck too fast and hard enough to shear off the landing gear. His Crusader literally disintegrated on impact, skipped the arresting gear wires, and plunged over the side. Herb Hunter was found floating under the water in a partially deployed parachute. According to Rasmussen, "Given the circumstances, this was more than an even probability, and Herb Hunter likely realized this as much as anyone."[37] Herb Hunter's loss ripped through the air wing. It underscored just how deadly the skies over North Vietnam had become. If such an experienced pilot could be lost, what chance did the rest of them stand?

There was no respite for the air wing as losses continued. The day after the Hartman and Hunter heartbreak, *Oriskany* lost another two airplanes before shifting her schedule to become the nighttime carrier. The losses continued. A week after he'd helped orchestrate the rescue forces for Larry Duthie, Lt. Cdr. Mac Davis was killed during a nighttime armed reconnaissance mission. His squadron mate, Lt. Cdr. Dean Cramer, recalled the incident:

> It was a night mission, July 25, underneath the flares, and flares were about as useless as a candle. You couldn't find anything with a God damn flare. He dropped the flare, and theoretically, you'd see things under it. Well you couldn't see anything but shadows, everything else was a guess.
>
> He was sure he found a couple of trucks, but to this day we'll never know. He was with another guy. They dropped their bombs and decided to do night, low-level strafing runs under the flares.[38]

Following Davis's death, Dean Cramer performed the unenviable task of collecting Davis's personal items so they could be shipped home. A former sailor, Cramer rose through the ranks before eventually becoming the Saints' maintenance officer. Following Davis's death, Cramer directed the sailors who worked for him to change how they put names on the ready room chairs. Seating order was according to seniority in the squadron, with individual embroidered headrest covers denoting name and rank. When a pilot was lost, the covers had to be changed. With so many men being lost, Cramer told his sailors to start using Velcro name tags so they could be removed and changed as required.[39] To say that the losses caused anxiety among the air wing would be an understatement—it gnawed at them. In less than two weeks, they'd lost eleven planes, with another six seriously damaged. Four men were either dead or missing. Then, VAH-4 lost a Skywarrior on a simple ferry flight from Cubi Point. Two more men were added to the toll. Years later, Lt. Cdr. Bob Arnold summed up the feelings at the time: "The entire air wing was in a state of mild shock. Even the seasoned veterans from the prior cruise couldn't recall anything like the intensity of air defenses we were running into. Some of the pilot comments were: 'Jesus, there were so many gun flashes at the target it looked like Los Angeles at night—except it was daytime,' and 'Where the hell do they get all those missiles? They've got to be exhausted just pulling the trigger so often.'"[40]

Fire on the Flight Deck!

The need for carriers caused the navy to move another Atlantic fleet carrier to support the war. USS *Forrestal* (CVA-59) departed Norfolk, Virginia, on 6 June, arriving on Yankee Station on 25 July. Once on the line, her air wing flew strikes alongside *Oriskany*, *Bon Homme Richard*, and *Intrepid*. For an inexperienced East Coast air wing, they had been extremely fortunate: after four days of combat and nearly two hundred sorties, *Forrestal*'s air wing had yet to suffer a single loss. On 29 July, the day began like any day on Yankee Station as each ship continued the daily grind of launching missions. *Forrestal* launched one early morning Alpha strike and was preparing to launch her second when tragedy struck. Just before 1100, stray voltage accidentally fired a Zuni rocket from a Phantom. The errant rocket hit a Skyhawk's fuel tank, causing a chain reaction of explosions and fire on the flight deck. The fire quickly spread, fueled by over 40,000 gallons of aviation fuel, bombs, and other ordnance on her mission-ready aircraft. Vintage bombs being used because of ordnance shortages began to cook off, blowing holes in the flight deck, which allowed burning fuel and bombs to reach six decks below.[41] The resultant fire was among the worst in naval history and the greatest naval disaster of Vietnam.

Clouds of thick black smoke billowed into the air as explosions wracked *Forrestal*. With memories of *Oriskany*'s holocaust fresh on everyone's mind, ships on Yankee Station steamed to her assistance. All flight operations from Yankee Station ceased as *Oriskany*, *Intrepid*, and *Bon Homme Richard* quickly joined the numerous destroyers circling the stricken carrier. It was an unreal situation—*how could it be happening again?* Men could be seen jumping overboard into the sea from *Forrestal.* Helicopters from all three carriers swooped into assist and rescue men as they could.

One of *Oriskany*'s plane guard helicopters happened to be airborne when the conflagration began. The Seasprite, flown by Lt. David Clement, quickly closed on *Forrestal* to investigate the thick smoke. As he flew up the port side, the first explosion pounded the small helicopter as it engulfed *Forrestal*'s stern. Clement and his crew began flying down the ship's wake looking for survivors. Hovering proved difficult, however, as shockwaves and debris from explosions rained down around their helicopter. They quickly picked up five badly burned men and took them to *Oriskany.* On board *Oriskany,* men gathered hoses and firefighting foam to transfer to *Forrestal,* despite the risk it put them at should the equipment be needed. They also launched all the ship's whale boats to begin searching for survivors in the water.[42] It had been only nine months since their own holocaust, and *Oriskany*'s crew felt a special urge to help. Her men knew all too well the terror of being trapped on a burning ship at sea.

Helicopters made countless trips that day, transferring medical personnel and firefighting equipment to the stricken carrier. Lt. Cdr. Allan Addeeb, *Oriskany*'s senior medical officer (SMO), was on one of these helicopters—a fact unknown to Captain Holder. Allan Addeeb held a unique position in that he was a qualified naval aviator as well as a doctor. He got away with a lot under both Captain Holder and CAG Shepherd, as his skills were always in high demand.[43] Upon arrival, the helicopters dodged explosions and flying shrapnel to land on the badly listing, debris-covered flight deck. Once aboard, Addeeb began assisting *Forrestal*'s surgeon until the sick bay became clogged with smoke. Addeeb recommended that they begin evacuating wounded to *Oriskany,* and helicopters began the grim task of transferring *Forrestal*'s many injured sailors. Once these wounded started arriving, the only remaining doctor aboard *Oriskany* was quickly overwhelmed, necessitating Addeeb's return. Even after he arrived back aboard, the sheer numbers of horribly burned men quickly overwhelmed them. With more badly injured men arriving by the minute, Addeeb and his corpsmen set up a triage. Soon, dozens of men were lying in stretchers all over the sick bay.[44] The sight of *Forrestal*'s hideously burned men was hauntingly familiar for those who had survived the October fire. Sailors helped where they could, while Doctor Addeeb's medical department worked nonstop to provide basic care. Eventually, two more doctors arrived from *Intrepid* to help prepare casualties for transfer to the hospital ship *Repose* (AH-16) later that evening. Normally stationed off Da Nang, *Repose* steamed north to provide the advanced care so desperately needed.

While the fire on *Forrestal*'s flight deck was under control in an hour, fires continued to rage below decks. Sixteen World War Two era 1,000-pound bombs had been loaded on planes parked on the flight deck. Nine of them exploded in the fire, with catastrophic results.[45] More than twelve hours later, her crew brought the fires under control. The final cost was staggering: 134 dead and 161 seriously wounded. Twenty-one jets were destroyed, and another forty-three were damaged. It cost the navy $72.2 million to repair *Forrestal*, and she never returned to combat.[46] As with *Oriskany* nine months earlier, the loss of *Forrestal* with her men and aircraft further strained the navy's ability to sustain combat operations. In her absence, the lion's share was taken over by the older 27C class carriers currently on Yankee Station.

Following the *Forrestal* tragedy, Rear Adm. Richardson recommended that Seventh Fleet extend *Bon Homme Richard* on station. Her pilots had been flying missions since late February, and the thought of extending left many feeling hopeless.[47] Instead, they were given a reprieve and sailed for home as scheduled, leaving *Oriskany* as the primary attack carrier on Yankee Station. *Oriskany* duly shifted her schedule to become the white (daytime) carrier. In the long, hot summer, being the daytime carrier meant Alpha strikes, and lots of them—three a day—all at a time when Gallup polls reported that more than half of Americans disapproved of Johnson's handling of the war, and a nearly equal number thought the United States had erred in sending troops. *Oriskany*'s losses continued, because in reality, there were no easy targets, as every strike was "going downtown" in the middle of either Hanoi or Haiphong.

On 31 July *Oriskany* launched two Alpha strikes, one against Van Nhue and another against Thanh Lang. Years later, Lt. Cdr. Bob Arnold recalled the first Alpha strike of the day:

One particular target, the Van Nhue headquarters area, was located in the suburbs six miles southeast of downtown Hanoi. It was a series of barracks and associated auxiliary buildings that was supposed to be a headquarters for the big mugga muggas.... There was no easy way to get there, so it was decided to take a straight shot: coast in at "the crotch," head straight for downtown and roll in six miles short where the headquarters was located. Maybe, just maybe, the bad guys would hold their fire thinking we were headed downtown. That way, we could be on and off target before they brought in the big stuff. It didn't work. As one of the strike pilots said afterwards, "We caught them with their pants up!"

I was strike lead; my fifteenth combat mission. Shortly after we went feet dry, we started picking up flak and missiles. The strike group was hosed down all the way into the target area. As we approached the target the weather went sour. The initial report from the weather recce aircraft was low scattered clouds. By the time we arrived, the weather had worsened to low broken to overcast. When you could see through the clouds, every village looked the same. All the time, missiles were flying and black and white puffs of flak were appearing everywhere. The strike was aborted and we broke for home looking for targets of opportunity along the way. One F-8 fighter escort was lost to a SAM.[48]

The Crusader lost on this mission was the thirteenth plane lost by the *Oriskany*. Flown by VF-III's Lt. (junior grade) Charlie Zuhoski, the incident is illustrative of CVW-16 during 1967. In the previous months, every squadron in the air wing received replacements in the form of very junior aviators, fresh from flight training.[49] Typical of pilots thrown into the fray, they did not last long in the meat grinder. As part of an Iron Hand section during the barracks raid, Zuhoski was escorting a VA-164 Skyhawk performing the deadly mission. As his A-4 flight lead dueled with SAMs, their section quickly became targeted by other sites in the vicinity. As he climbed through 11,000 feet to avoid a volley of missiles, Zuhoski's Crusader was hit in the fuselage by a SAM. He ejected from the flaming wreckage and landed in the village of Ngu Nghi, 10 miles east of downtown Hanoi. Zuhoski was in his first fleet squadron, having joined the Sundowners four months prior. He was married on 3 June, less than two weeks before *Oriskany* departed for Vietnam. Now after two weeks of combat and fourteen missions, he faced nearly six years as a POW.

On 4 August the same headquarters reappeared on the target list, and Bob Arnold volunteered to lead the mission. He'd already planned and led the strike once and was familiar with the mission:

> The last minute planning went on until late that evening. I managed about four hours sleep (par for the course) before the briefings started. If there was one light moment it came when the air intelligence people pulled out the flak map, an enlargement of the target area. Where there were known flak sites they had put in colored pins—different colors for different caliber weapons and SAM sites. The map looked like someone had spattered several cans of different colored paint on it—the pins covered the entire target area. Somebody said "Oh, shit," and that broke the tension. What the hell, it didn't cost any more to laugh.[50]

The strike launched and used a different route from their previous attempt. Instead of flying directly to the target, they flew north of Haiphong, using mountains to mask their approach. The plan seemed to work, as not a shot was fired for the first twenty minutes prior to the target. Then, two minutes before reaching their roll-in point for the headquarters, chaos ensued. Arnold continued:

> Someone radioed, "Missile, one o'clock." No sooner had he finished broadcasting than the missile went over the strike group—long, brown and going like hell. Other transmissions filled the air. "Two missiles 11 o'clock."
>
> "Come left, break left."
>
> "Go down, go down."
>
> "Two missiles 3 o'clock."
>
> "Missiles 12 o'clock."
>
> By that time, I was nose down in a tight left hand spiraling dive. Two missiles went over me, I rolled right and pulled hard as another missile went by my left wing. . . . Nobody knew for sure how many missiles were fired at us in that two minute period. The low estimate was 30, the high 44. They were everywhere and kept coming. The result was a melee, but fortunately not a disaster.[51]

Only one Skyhawk, flown by Lt. Cdr. Marv Reynolds, was hit by a SAM. He managed to jettison his bombs and make it back safely, though the Skyhawk had to be craned off in Cubi Point. Bob Arnold and his wingman managed to find the headquarters and destroy it, so the air wing hopefully wouldn't have to go back.

Later that day, the air wing lost their fourteenth aircraft in three weeks. The ship was scheduled to come off the line in just three days. Aviators hoped to survive long enough to enjoy the respite, but fate intervened during an Alpha strike on the outskirts of Haiphong. As the strike package approached the target, a POL storage site at Luc Nong, a volley of four SAMs greeted them. The flight scattered as everyone evaded the missiles. Lt. (junior grade) Ralph Bisz tried vainly to outmaneuver the missiles but was hit at about 10,500 feet. His aircraft exploded and spun downward in a large ball of fire. The flaming wreckage burned out halfway through its plummet to the ground. Nobody saw a parachute, and no emergency beeper or voice communications were ever heard.

As with so many of the downed aviators, Ralph Bisz's status was simply not known. Men on the mission didn't believe he could have survived, but somewhere up the chain of officialdom, he was listed as captured. His wreckage had come down in the heavily populated Hai Duong Province, and if he had survived, he would have been quickly captured. The decision caused an extremely confusing situation, giving false hope to his family that he may have survived. In reality, the popular Bisz, who had survived crashing into his future skipper just days before miraculously surviving the fire (Tom Spitzer had perished after they became separated), was dead. His loss was one more among the many during the long, hot summer.

Oriskany shifted to night operations to finish out the line period. On 8 August she sailed for Cubi Point. During the next week, her crew craned off scores of damaged aircraft while men not on duty tried to enjoy some liberty. Cubi Point proved to be a good place for them to drown their sorrows as they tried to forget the painful memories of their first line period.

11

The Stennis Hearings and the
Climax of Rolling Thunder

AS ORISKANY'S MEN ENJOYED liberty in the Philippines, military leadership in the United States took part in a last-ditch effort to save the air war. In February 1966 the dovish Senate Foreign Relations Committee, led by Senator William Fulbright, exposed serious divisions within the foreign policy establishment. With testimonies from former general James Gavin and esteemed diplomat George Kennan, the committee grilled Ambassador Maxwell Taylor and Secretary of State Dean Rusk. National television coverage of the Fulbright hearings helped fuel public dissent and accelerated declining support of the war. By the summer of 1967, Secretary McNamara's disillusionment had turned into outright hostility toward the air war. From his vantage, the military continually promised more than it could deliver, and nowhere was this more apparent than in the failure of the POL campaign.[1]

McNamara's hostility left senior military leaders feeling betrayed. They felt that airpower had never been given a real chance to show what could be achieved and that halting the bombing was a mistake. If Rolling Thunder was scaled down, airpower would be seen as a failure, as would its leadership. The military believed they had never been given a chance to succeed because of political limitations. In short, they believed that the targeting policy as forced on them by civilian leaders had stopped Rolling Thunder from producing results, never mind the dogma associated with sortie counts. To block any efforts by McNamara to cut bombing or show that airpower had failed, military leaders turned to Senate hawks for support.

Members of the Senate Armed Services Committee, chaired by Senator John C. Stennis, established themselves as ardent supporters of the war. In August 1967 the hawkish Senate Preparedness Investigating Subcommittee began its own hearings, meant to be the equivalent of the Fulbright hearings. Preparations began in June 1967 and went public on 9 August. The Stennis hearings pitted Robert McNamara against the military leadership, including the JCS, over ongoing restrictions on the bombing of North Vietnam. According to the Pentagon Papers, "The subcommittee unquestionably set out to defeat Mr. McNamara. Its members were known for their hard-line views and military sympathies.... They viewed the restraints on bombing as irrational, the shackling of a major instrument which could help win victory."[2] On the day the hearings went public, the Johnson administration attempted to limit any fallout by adding sixteen extra targets and expanding armed reconnaissance missions while removing the restrictions surrounding Hanoi and Haiphong to include the buffer zone along the Chinese border. With restrictions lifted, the air war grew exponentially just in time for *Oriskany* to resume operations on Yankee Station.

As the hearings progressed, the public finally became aware of the deep divide between the Johnson administration and senior military leadership concerning the air war. During eight days of testimony, generals and admirals testified before the subcommittee, publicly airing their grievances concerning the conduct of the war. On average, the United states conducted thirty thousand sorties a month in Vietnam: seventeen thousand were flown against targets in South Vietnam, while thirteen thousand were flown in North Vietnam. Ninety percent of these sorties were armed reconnaissance attacks, none of which were at issue. The remaining 10 percent of sorties in North Vietnam, some thirteen hundred a month, were directed against fixed targets comprising the target list. The debate centered on this 10 percent. The master target list itself contained 427 targets, 359 of which had been recommended by the Joint Chiefs. Of that 359, 57 had yet to be authorized by the Johnson administration and became the focal point of the disagreement.[3] By the time Secretary McNamara testified on 25 August, the damage had been done. Having lost much of his original faith in the war, McNamara felt little need to justify his opposition to the war he helped orchestrate. In typical McNamara fashion, he belittled the importance of every target listed, rattling off numbers, facts, and figures to counter each target on the list.[4] However, in the end, comments like this sealed his fate: "I am perfectly prepared to admit that I may be very wrong in my recommendations on these targets, but I am not wrong in submitting to you that the approval of all these targets and the destruction of all of them would not make any material difference in the war, and that is my only point."[5] In his conclusion, McNamara still had the gall to say, "I don't believe that there is this gulf between the military leaders and the civilian leaders in the executive branch." He also claimed that pilots faced less risk at the height of 1967 than earlier in the war—a technicality, considering the number of sorties then being flown into Route Package VI.[6] McNamara's aloof testimony and the public nature of the hearings forced President Johnson to make a political decision to expand the air war. The subcommittee's summary report sided with the military and sharply criticized McNamara's reasoning, forcing the administration into an awkward position. Ultimately, the president felt compelled to overrule McNamara and expand the air war. By seeking the political middle ground, President Johnson satisfied no one, and his decision resulted in the loss of more American lives.[7]

Although the Stennis hearings achieved the desired result of exposing the divide between the Johnson administration and the military, it proved to be too little, too late. Public opinion about the war had been split evenly, but as the summer wore on, public support for Vietnam plummeted. Antiwar fervor reached an all-time high, fueled by comments from the hearings like Senator Stuart Symington's: "If the position as presented by the Secretary this morning is right, I believe the United States should get out of Vietnam at the earliest possible time and on the best possible basis; because with his premises, there would appear to be no chance for any true 'success' in this long war."[8] President Johnson eventually authorized the majority of the targets on the JCS's list. However, the divisiveness of the war, coupled with the upcoming Tet Offensive, eventually forced Johnson to halt Rolling Thunder and ultimately doomed his administration. The men fighting had no way of knowing this, of course. They continued to fly missions throughout the late summer and fall, paying the price in men and planes as their country struggled to comprehend its involvement in Vietnam.

Cutting the Arteries: Bridges and the Thermal Power Plant

Following liberty at Cubi Point, *Oriskany* returned to Yankee Station on 18 August. With the Stennis hearings still in progress, the air wing began striking the newly added targets. This escalation resulted in her pilots flying into "the center of hell with Hanoi as its hub. The area that was defended with three times the force and vigor that protected Berlin during World War II."[9] The heaviest air combat to date occurred on 21 August, with seven strikes (four air force and three navy) bombing targets in Hanoi. The coordinated raids were intricately planned, with each wave spaced exactly two minutes apart. *Intrepid*'s air wing struck Port Wallut and the Van Diem army depot, while *Constellation*'s air wing pounded the airfield at Kep and the rail yards at Duc Noi, just 5 miles from downtown Hanoi. This raid was intended as a diversion for *Oriskany*'s mission, tasked with destroying the Hanoi thermal power plant. Earlier in May, airplanes from *Bon Homme Richard* had damaged the power plant. As expected, the North Vietnamese repaired the facility, and it was again operational.

Cdr. Bryan Compton led *Oriskany*'s mission. He later recalled, "This was the first fixed target that we were scheduled to strike that was worth more than the cost of the ordnance we put into it. We were thus excited when we got a chance to devise a plan to take it out."[10] Planning commenced with Lt. Cdrs. Jim Busey, Dean Cramer, and Jerry Breast. Earlier in his career, Breast had performed initial testing on the AGM-62 Walleye and was intimately familiar with the weapon. To successfully destroy the plant, they needed near simultaneous impact of four Walleyes. Figuring they'd lose an airplane on their ingress, they planned for six. As they approached the target, the flight would fan apart and attack from different headings of the compass. Once the team completed planning, Compton briefed the mission up the chain of command to Seventh Fleet, Vice Adm. John Hyland. After the briefings, the strike was on standby until the plant reappeared on the target list.[11]

On 20 August they were notified that the mission was to be part of the next day's strikes. As planned, Compton led the mission, with Busey, Breast, Lt. Cdr. John Miles, Lt. (junior grade) Vance Schufeldt, and Lt. (junior grade) Fritz Schroeder. Cramer and Lt. (junior grade) Dave Carey were briefed as well in case anyone aborted. To minimize their exposure to the North Vietnamese defenses, they went without external fuel tanks. This decreased weight and drag, allowing them to fly faster. Because they expected the other six strikes to provide suppression and divert attention, they went with minimum Iron Hand and no AAA suppression elements. TARCAP and two Iron Hand aircraft held along the mountains south of Hanoi alongside their tankers. Because of this, Compton asked *Oriskany*'s navigator to move the ship as far north as possible, thus minimizing the distance they had to fly.[12]

On 21 August the mission launched as the third navy strike and fifth out of the day's seven waves. Miles aborted and was replaced by Cramer. Not surprisingly, Cramer took Carey's Skyhawk when his first aircraft developed issues. The flight of six flew over the coastline and topped off their fuel. With the other strikes occupying the North Vietnamese, they made it to their turn point before meeting any defenses— two SAMs launched from south of the city. As the flight split into two flights of three for their attack runs, the sprawling city came into view: the Doumer bridge across the Red River, Truc Bach Lake on the northwest side of the city, and the adjacent power plant. At that point AAA opened fire, concentrating on the southern elements. Compton recalled:

> Locking onto the target, I got a good picture of the west front of the power plant through my gunsight. Shifting to the Sony Scope [small television screen to monitor the Walleye's flight to the target], I could see the cross-hair locked on a window in the face of the building, so I "pickled" [to release ordnance] the weapon away. For some reason, nobody seemed to be tracking me with their guns now, so as I pulled away, I took a turn around the target and tried to get a picture or two with my hand-held camera. I could see three distinct impacts on the power plant, but could not see the other two.[13]

Busey and Cramer faced the preponderance of the defenses. Dean Cramer later recalled the mission:

> I was hit in my dive, my glide, by an 85-millimeter that exploded underneath and blew the plane inverted. I got back level, but the Walleye screen was all screwed up and I could hear the bomb, with a thin tin-like skin, tearing away from the plane. The 85-millimeter, and I didn't know this, put a hole in one wing, a small hole, which was bleeding fuel and leaving a white vapor trail behind me. Every God damn SAM and flak site in Hanoi, I'm convinced was shooting at me. I ducked six or eight SAMs, controlled SAMs. I flew up, there'd be one, and I'd go down and there'd be another. All the SAMs were in close, reasonable range and finally they just ran out. Then I

got complacent, flying straight and level, and a 37-millimeter shell blew a hole in the port wing, which caught fire. The wing's burning merrily and I say, "Okay, I'm hit, I'm on fire and coming out." We're on a tactical frequency, over Hanoi and I think nobody else can hear. Wrong.[14]

Knowing that the day and this mission would encounter heavy resistance, the discrete strike frequency was broadcast throughout the ship. *Oriskany*'s men stood transfixed by the events as they unfolded over the ship's loudspeakers. Busey was also hit, though he continued and got his Walleye on the power plant. The drama continued as Cramer calmly broadcast his intentions. With fuel streaming he became critically short on fuel. Both waiting tankers experienced problems, leaving Cramer desperate before he finally managed to rendezvous with a Skywarrior. Cramer's aircraft was so badly damaged that the tanker could only transfer 200 pounds. Because *Oriskany* was so far north, that much fuel was enough to get him to the ship.

Dean Cramer continued:

The ship clears me straight in, but unbeknownst to me, Busey's cleared straight in on a different frequency. So here we are both coming straight in, and I've got another problem. If I come in on a normal approach, the plane's going to flame out right over the fantail. So in my head, I decide to shoot a precautionary flameout. But I can't tell the *Oriskany* because nobody will ever approve it. I plan to come in at 2,000 or 3,000 feet, chop the power to idle, dump the nose down, and flare myself into the wire. As I decide, "Okay now," out from under my nose comes Jim. "Aw shit!" I pullout, say, "Okay Jim, you've got it." He says, "No, I'll take it around." "No Jim, you've got it." He says, "No, I'll take it around." "No, Jim, you've got it, and I'm already doing a 360 because I expect my wing will fall off when I trap and clobber the deck." Jim comes in and bolters, and I call up and say, "Sorry about that Jim, but you had your chance." By now, I'm back in position, drop the nose, flare the wire, and land. I look around and the God damn island has people all over it, and they're all waving. It's like family day, and on the flight deck is the admiral and the captain of the ship, and they're both waving. I park the airplane, climb out, and they're beating me on the back. Then I find out it's all been on the IMC.

The admiral gave all of us medicinal brandy, Christian Brother's brandy with cokes, two or three of those. A kid who had been a public affairs officer on Second Fleet staff is now a PAO on the Seventh Fleet staff, and I know him and he knows me, and he says, "Mr. Cramer, did you think about ejecting?" I said, "Eject? Hell no, the liberty's piss poor over there." Everybody laughs and I don't think anything about it. That night I write a letter to my wife—another day, a couple of hops—and about a week later I get a letter from her saying she just heard about me on television. Walter Cronkite picked it up.[15]

By all accounts, *Oriskany*'s part in the day's raids was a big success. The North Vietnamese defenses were ferocious, launching nearly thirty SAMs at the six Skyhawks, as well as AAA and small arms fire. Sailors counted 127 holes in the starboard wing of Jim Busey's Skyhawk. The wing was warped and buckled from the intensity of the flames. The end of the starboard horizontal stabilizer had been shot off, and the elevator had been ripped away by the airstream. Dean Cramer's Skyhawk suffered similar damage. Sailors stood in awe, gaping at damage that included a hole nearly 3 feet wide in the port wing.[16] Five jets made it to the power plant. Three hit the generator, and the other two hit the boiler, producing columns of heavy black and white smoke that rose high into the sky over Hanoi. Both Compton and Busey received the Navy Cross for the raid. Jerry Breast received the Silver Star, while the others received the Distinguished Flying Cross.

Despite *Oriskany*'s success, the day was very costly. The North Vietnamese fired over 150 SAMs at the seven raids.[17] Two air force F-105s were shot down. *Constellation*'s mission against the Doc Noi rail yard met with disaster. They intended to attack the rail station two minutes before VA-163 hit the power plant, and the four F-4 Phantoms and four A-6A Intruders were pummeled by the same defenses. AAA hit one Intruder on the ingress, though the crew continued to the target. A SAM hit the lead A-6 at the top of its dive, and the other Intruders narrowly missed hitting the crew as they swung in their parachutes. The crew was quickly captured. The remaining three airplanes bombed the rail yard and made a wide turn to the north to avoid bad weather. Unfortunately, the turn took them over Kep airfield, whose alert gunners had just been bombed. As the crews fled from the AAA at Kep, they unwittingly flew toward China. Before the flight could alert the lead Intruder of their proximity to China, they were attacked by Chinese MiGs, which downed two more aircraft. The last Intruder ducked into a nearby storm cloud to escape before the crew made their way back to the Tonkin Gulf—the sole survivors of a flight of four A-6s.[18]

Battle of the Electrons: Tragedy in Haiphong

Earlier in July, Admiral Sharp's staff developed a plan to isolate the port of Haiphong using a concentrated interdiction ring around the city. During early August, only 10 percent of the daily sorties were directed toward this effort. With the Stennis hearings ongoing, reconnaissance photos revealed an immense buildup of supplies on the docks and wharfs. As restrictions were lifted, *Oriskany*'s air wing found itself at the forefront of efforts to isolate the port city. They struck rail and road bridges while seeding coastal waterways with mines in an attempt to stem the movement of supplies out of the port city.

Unknown to the men flying these missions was that the North Vietnamese, with help from their Soviet advisors, discovered a way to defeat the navy's ALQ-51 self-protect jammers. The air force continuously upgraded their self-protect jammers, while the navy continued without updating the ALQ-51. By late August North Vietnamese SAM operators had become proficient enough to differentiate between the false returns of the ALQ-51 and actual targets.[19] In the measure/countermeasure battle of electrons, the North Vietnamese now had an advantage that they began to exploit with deadly results. Losses to SAMs suddenly spiked, and the navy never understood how or why. By August, air force aircraft were being hit once per one hundred SAM firings, while four navy aircraft were being hit per one hundred SAM firings.[20] In 1967 SAMs accounted for half of the navy's losses and one-third of the *Oriskany*'s. During the waning months of Rolling Thunder, the navy commissioned studies to understand why. Many theories were postulated: the terrain favored the air force; the larger numbers of aircraft per strike favored the air force; the F-105 was faster and thus better able to evade missiles. The reports completely ignored the importance of self-protect jammers. One report even stated that "there is no clear cut relationship between the use of this equipment and a subsequent decrease in SAM effectiveness."[21] In the end, it came down to the simple answer that the North Vietnamese had effectively countered the navy's electronic countermeasures.

On 31 August *Oriskany*'s air wing discovered the deadliness of this new North Vietnamese advantage. For the previous two days, the air wing struck targets in and around Haiphong. Cdr. Bryan Compton developed a ruse in which the strikes would go feet-dry south of Haiphong and fly inland several miles before making a hard right turn to bomb their target in Haiphong. It worked the first two days, but by the third day the North Vietnamese knew the pattern and set a trap.

On that fateful third day, *Oriskany* launched a strike against the rail bridge at Vat Cach. What should have been a twelve-plane strike quickly degraded to a ten-plane strike as squadrons struggled to keep planes flyable in the hectic tempo. VA-163 managed to launch six airplanes with a division led by Compton and Lt. Cdr. Hugh Stafford. Lt. Cdr. Dean Cramer followed with his wingman, Lt. Donovan Wood. VA-164 had their own division, led by Lt. Cdr. Richard Perry and Lt. John Davis. Shortly after going feet-dry, the North Vietnamese 285th Missile Regiment / Seventy-Third SAM Battalion ambushed the strike from a new site they relocated after the previous two days.[22]

Cramer saw two missiles launch and called for evasive maneuvers. The flight immediately broke apart as Skyhawks began defending. The SAM site was beneath the flight, and the men had mere seconds to react. Compton and his wingman pulled up and to the right, as did Cramer and Wood. Stafford and his wingman dove down, straight into the first missile. The SAM exploded directly in front of Stafford's Skyhawk. The force of the explosion blew Stafford out of his cockpit, still strapped to his ejection seat. The blast shattered his left arm and broke his collarbone and ribs. Immobilized, Stafford was fortunate to survive due to the automatic functions of his ejection seat, which deployed his parachute. He landed in a tree near a village and was quickly captured.

One of the many replacements who arrived in June, Lt. (junior grade) Dave Carey was also on his first deployment. The exploding SAM destroyed the engine of his Skyhawk, and Carey ejected as fire quickly consumed the aircraft. Carey landed in a rice paddy next to a village less than a mile from Stafford. Carey managed to raise Cramer on his survival radio as he flew by. Cramer advised him he couldn't get a helicopter in for the rescue and told Carey he'd see him "when it was all over."[23] Carey was also quickly captured and bound by villagers, who began chopping off his flight gear with a machete. The same SAM that brought down Stafford and Carey also severely damaged Cramer's and Wood's Skyhawks. Cramer's jet engine ingested warhead fragments, which destroyed it. Luckily, the engine held together long enough for him to make it back to *Oriskany*, where sailors replaced it.

The second missile targeted the division from VA-164. The SAM site was directly underneath them, giving them even less time to react. The missile came up nearly vertically and detonated directly under Perry's Skyhawk, with the blast rocking all four planes in the flight. The explosion blew large holes in the bottom of Perry's aircraft. With fuel streaming from his aircraft, Perry turned toward the water. His wingman, Lt. (junior grade) Mike Mullane, joined Compton and continued toward the target. Lt. John Davis and his wingman, Lt. (junior grade) George Schindlar, joined Perry to escort his mortally wounded Skyhawk. Perry calmly radioed he'd been hit and jettisoned his bombs and drop tanks as he flew to the gulf. Davis recalled:

> As he approached the shoreline, I could see fire start to emanate from the engine bay vents just forward of the fuselage break, and I told him so. He didn't respond on the radio (highly possible he'd lost electrical by this point). As he crossed the shoreline, Dick's plane started a right hand roll. I told him time to get out. His plane completed a full 360 degree roll, now about 1–1.5 miles offshore, and as it came through wings level, he ejected. The chute was immediately normal. As I remember, altitude was on the order of 10,000 feet.
>
> I set up an orbit with George around him. Some minutes passed. Then George reminded me that Dick should be up on the hand-held radio, and I concurred. I put full flaps down and slowed as much as possible (to just above buffet) and made a pass close aboard to Dick in his chute. He was limp and lifeless, and I'm certain he was dead at that point.
>
> After a long descent, Dick went into the water. He slowly went under, it was about five–ten minutes after water entry before the

helo got there. The helo sent a swimmer down to him, who surfaced and declared Dick KIA. The helo came under fire from shore batteries and retreated before Dick's body could be recovered. We learned when back on *Oriskany* that the swimmer had seen a large hole in Dick's chest.[24]

In a span of seconds, *Oriskany* lost three airplanes and three men. Two Skyhawks were destroyed by a single SAM. Another two aircraft were damaged. Perry, one of the most respected and beloved men in the air wing, was dead. To make matters worse, they had been unable to recover his body, leading to years of anguish for his family. Perry's loss was a tremendous blow to morale. He was dearly loved by all who knew him.[25] At the time of his death, Jessie Beck was sending so many care packages that the carrier onboard delivery (COD) aircraft often contained more mail bags for VA-164 than the rest of the ship and air wing combined.[26] To honor Perry's legacy, VA-164 began painting "Lady Jessie" on their commanding officer's aircraft. It became a point of pride and tradition for the squadron. Richard Perry's legacy would live on, and the squadron continued to honor his relationship with Jessie Beck. To be certain, the air war would continue, as would the losses. But after Perry's death, men continued on as if in a daze.

President Johnson called for an unscheduled news conference on 1 September in an attempt to contain the damage caused by the Stennis hearings. During the conference, Johnson denied any division among his advisors and overruled McNamara. Even worse than McNamara's public dressing-down was the subsequent escalation against his advice.[27] Despite the apparent removal of most restrictions, the exasperating on-again, off-again nature of Rolling Thunder continued. The Johnson administration extended peace feelers in mid-August at the same time it ratcheted up strikes on Hanoi. Then in September, McNamara ordered a cessation of strikes within the 10-mile circle around the city as a show of faith to the North Vietnamese. To keep peace talks quiet, the military wasn't informed of the reasoning. It was maddening. Hanoi complained loudly that Johnson was merely retargeting Haiphong instead of Hanoi and escalating, not deescalating, the war.

The high-water mark of these efforts to isolate Haiphong was 4 September. CAG Shepherd led the first strike against Haiphong's southern highway bridge. When they approached within 5 miles of the bridge, the sky erupted with bursts of 37 and 85 mm AAA. Twenty airplanes managed to drop four of the bridge's five spans, with VA-163's Lt. (junior grade) Ken Adams receiving credit for dropping two of them. The young aviator earned a Distinguished Flying Cross not only for his bombing but for saving his wingman from a volley of five SAMs. Over the next eleven days, *Oriskany* flew thirty Alpha strikes against targets near Haiphong, losing three aircraft in the process. Much to McNamara's chagrin, one of these targets included the port of Cam Pha, which he had vehemently argued against weeks earlier. On 10 September jets from *Coral Sea* and *Oriskany* pounded the port facility, leaving coal stocks burning. Newspaper headlines announced, "Jets Bomb North Viet Port for 1st Time."[28] Two days later, jets from the same carriers struck the very center of Haiphong, bombing warehouses and rail yards. By the end of the day, just one bridge remained standing—a span on the city's southern edge.[29] The focus on Haiphong resulted in one unintended, albeit favorable, consequence, of which the administration should have taken note. After nearly nine continuous days of strikes, the North Vietnamese began to run out of SAMs and ammunition. The large stockpiles of supplies lining the streets of Haiphong in August vanished. For the first time since Rolling Thunder began, strikes experienced fewer defenses due to the concentrated efforts.[30]

Unfortunately, the success would not last. Poor weather from the northeast monsoon, coupled with extended peace initiatives, gave the North Vietnamese a chance when they needed it most. In August the United States flew 11,634 sorties—the majority of them over Route Package VI. By September the totals had fallen to 8,540. John Colvin, the British consul general to North Vietnam from 1966 to 1967, later described the effects the campaign achieved. Upon leaving Hanoi in September, he concluded that North Vietnam "was no longer capable of maintaining itself as an economic unit nor of mounting aggressive war against its neighbor":

> The strength of the American bombing campaign of summer 1967 had rested not only on its weight but on its consistency, hour after hour, day after day. The strategy, as well as damaging or destroying—in ports, on railway lines, and on storage areas—the capacity

of the D.R.V. to feed itself and to maintain invasion, had also, for the first time, allowed the North Vietnamese no time to repair warmaking facilities. No sooner were they repaired than they were struck again; Tonkinese ingenuity had been defeated and, by the remorseless persistence of the campaign, their will eroded to near-extinction. But although some spasmodic bombing in the northeast quadrant took place after September, it was on a greatly reduced scale and frequently interrupted by long periods of inactivity during "peace initiatives," all illusory if not contrived, and anyway occasions when the campaign should have maintained, even increased, momentum.... Victory—by September 1967 in American hands—was not so much thrown away as shunned with prim, averted eyes.[31]

President Johnson and members of his administration were fully aware of all this but remained unable to make the politically tough decision to escalate the campaign and probably win the war. Walt Rostow sent President Johnson a top secret memorandum describing the impact of Rolling Thunder on Vietnam. He described how in early 1966 the North Vietnamese had been able to unload a freighter in less than ten days, but by August 1967 they required thirty-three days to offload the supplies. Over six hundred thousand people were now required to repair bridges and keep roads open. Those people were no longer working in the limited industrial base or in the fields to feed the country. Soviet aid skyrocketed from $100 to $700 million in 1967 as North Vietnam appeared to be on the verge of collapse.[32] With North Vietnam on the verge of collapse, Rolling Thunder might have succeeded, but that didn't happen (even though the bombing continued, albeit at lesser levels).

Pilots flying over North Vietnam paid for this gradualism in spades. Perhaps none paid more than the men of *Oriskany*. As she sailed for a port call in Sasebo on the island of Kyushu, Japan, McNamara's restrictions remained. As the Joint Chiefs and Admiral Sharp argued for more strikes, the North Vietnamese used the time to rearm and fortify their defenses for the next round. While in Japan, *Oriskany*'s pilot ranks, severely depleted during the previous line periods, began to receive replacements. The new pilots included Lt. Cdr. John McCain III, who volunteered for combat after surviving the inferno on *Forrestal*. McCain came from a navy family, and he followed in the steps of his father and grandfather, both of whom were famous admirals. His father would eventually replace Admiral Sharp as CINCPAC in July 1968. Unfortunately, these inexperienced replacements did not last long, as Johnson lifted the restrictions again in October. A quick glance at VA-163 tells the story. The squadron received three new replacements in Sasebo. By the end of October, one remained.

12

Black October

AT THE BEGINNING OF October 1967, the *New York Times* announced that U.S. casualties surpassed 100,000, with 13,643 killed and 86,635 wounded. The toll tripled over the next year as the American commitment peaked. As *Oriskany* sailed south from Sasebo, the JCS continued pressuring President Johnson to remove the restrictions around Hanoi. Following the Stennis hearings, Earle Wheeler, the chairman of the Joint Chiefs of Staff, suffered a heart attack. With Army Chief of Staff Gen. Harold Johnson filling in, the JCS presented McNamara with an updated target list. It included draft execute orders lifting the Hanoi ban and authorizing strikes on Phuc Yen.[1] McNamara demurred, and the restrictions stayed, allowing North Vietnam time to fortify its defenses. *Oriskany* arrived on Yankee Station on 5 October as the latest peace initiatives failed. That same day, ten MiGs attacked an incoming air strike from *Intrepid*. Outnumbered, the Skyhawk pilots fought for their lives during a ten-minute-long air battle north of the airfield at Kien An. Under pressure from conservatives, President Johnson was unwilling to pay the domestic political price for further failed peace talks and acquiesced to their calls for escalation. The next day, he approved six new targets in Haiphong, including the MiG base at Kien An. Three days later, the Tuesday luncheon approved another major escalation, and the air war accelerated.[2]

As a result of the heavy action and subsequent losses, the month quickly became known as Black October. Except for a two-day lull in the action due to Typhoon Carla, favorable weather allowed maximum efforts for the entire month. *Oriskany* flew two Alpha strikes each day, and, depending on the ship's status as the day or night carrier, nightly armed reconnaissance missions either preceded or followed them. The pace quickened and losses grew. On average, the air wing lost a plane every two days throughout October. While the losses could not compare with those of the first line period, they were still appalling. After four months of continuous combat, pilots realized the odds of surviving until another carrier relieved them. The tyranny of the present prevailed. False bravado masked the fact that men were terrified and tired from continuous combat. Superstitious by nature, pilots onboard *Oriskany* became even more so. Routine preflight rituals became dogma. VA-164 eventually lost three Skyhawks with "Lady Jessie" markings. VF-162 lost three Crusaders numbered 206, and pilots became reluctant to fly the replacement.[3] Even Dr. Addeeb began flying regular missions with VA-163. Cdr. Bryan Compton saw that he got the necessary carrier landing qualifications in August, and he became part of the Saints' roster. Each night, the air wing operations officer, Lt. Cdr. Buck Sheeley, called the squadrons to check the number of available aircraft and pilots. Before October VA-163's duty officer had duly responded, "Twelve pilots, plus Doc." By October it was no longer "plus Doc" but rather "thirteen pilots." Of course, Captain Holder didn't like it, but he didn't have any other choice except to try and limit him to tanker missions. Even then, Dr. Addeeb flew feet-dry during several of his nearly eighty missions.[4]

During October the personality conflict between CAG Shepherd and Bryan Compton finally came to a head. Shepherd realized his shortcomings more than anyone and put his confidence in his two attack squadron commanding officers and their senior strike leads. As did any mortal man facing death on a daily basis, Shepherd struggled with the enormity of the missions and the constant losses. The problem was that Compton was not an average aviator. He was the best, and fearless as well. Compton expected the same level of commitment from all men, but not everyone measured up to his standards, not even Shepherd. During a mission earlier in the cruise, a junior pilot screamed over the radio as volumes of AAA greeted them over their target. Compton tersely replied, "Shut up and die like a man."[5] Other stories involved Compton flying low and slow over estuaries near Haiphong, using his landing lights during twilight to identify ship names and nationality.[6] Compounding the issue was Compton's almost legendary status following the August power plant raid. Three of the four Navy Crosses awarded to the air wing during 1967 went to Compton and other Saints. Cdr. Doug Mow, VA-164's commanding officer, proved himself just as capable as Compton, though he too was often overshadowed by Compton. Intelligent and judicious, Mow offered a paternalistic leadership style that became the soft sell to Compton's hard sell. Together, their leadership helped pull the air wing through Black October, dominating the air battles and the strong personalities. It was a terrible and deadly time. Without them, it likely would have been much worse.

Rock Hodges

Two days after arriving on the line, the air wing lost one of its stalwart aviators. A veteran of all three cruises, Lt. Dave "Rock" Hodges was one of the most experienced and respected men in the air wing. The development of the Iron Hand mission is personified in his story. A former captain in the air force, Hodges previously flew B-47s. Following an interservice transfer, he became a lieutenant and joined VA-164. He often regaled the ready room with his stories of the Strategic Air Command, describing his transfer as having "escaped Curtis LeMay." (The cigar-chomping air force chief of staff earned his reputation by building the United States' nuclear forces from the ground up. A strategic bombing zealot, LeMay was well known for his strict regulations and demand for high performance by all men.) Cdr. Jack Shaw, VA-164's commanding officer in 1965 (and a colorful character himself), assigned Dave Hodges the call sign "Rock" after the 1963 Rock Hudson movie, *Gathering of Eagles*, about the air force.[7]

Rock Hodges quickly became the air wing's electronic warfare expert. A natural intellect, he began researching the new APR-25 and ALQ-51 as the equipment became available. Rock then taught his squadron mates and the air wing about the sounds and bearing information provided by the gear. As a result, his reputation grew. With the introduction of the Shrike missile, VA-164 became one of the first fleet squadrons to carry it. Once again, Rock naturally learned the intricacies of the missile and spread his knowledge. He personally developed many of the Iron Hand tactics used by the navy during the war. In particular, he realized that he could launch Zuni rockets to trick the SAM operators into shutting off their radars.[8] Doing so not only preserved precious Shrikes but increased their lethality, allowing him to hunt even more SAMs. Rock Hodges also realized that the North Vietnamese listened to their radio frequencies, so he'd call "Shotgun," the code word indicating that a Shrike had been fired. If the North Vietnamese were listening, they often shut down their radars. If they did not shut them down, he followed with an actual Shrike.[9]

Few could match Rock Hodges's tenacity in the air during Iron Hand missions. He was a tiger. Fighter pilots dreaded the thought of escorting him while he hunted SAMs.[10] One story from the second line period of 1967 cemented his celebrated status among the air wing. Rock Hodges was flying as part of a flak suppression element during a strike over Haiphong. As they neared the target, radar-controlled AAA began tracking him. With each air burst getting successively closer, Rock calmly radioed, "Nice shootin', soldier! Now take this!" Whereupon he rolled in and dropped his cluster bombs on the offending gun emplacements.[11] Men felt better knowing he was dueling with SAMs, suppressing the defenses so they could make it to the target.

On 7 October *Oriskany* launched a morning Alpha strike against the rail yards at Do Xa, just south of Hanoi. In order to suppress the defenses, the number of Iron Hand and flak suppression aircraft nearly outnumbered the bombers. As the raid neared the target, Rock Hodges began sparring with several SAM sites in the area. While he concentrated on one site, the North Vietnamese fired two missiles from a different site. Both missiles successfully tracked Hodges's Skyhawk, and he never saw them. Though the first SA-2 missed, the second missile hit him. His shattered Skyhawk rolled right and crashed into a ridgeline, taking with it one of *Oriskany*'s best and brightest. Hodges epitomized the warrior ethos, and, as it had with Perry, his loss resonated throughout the air wing. Now the air wing would be flying missions into the heart of the Iron Triangle without their preeminent SAM killer.

The next day, *Oriskany* launched a major effort against the MiG base at Kien An. Cdr. Bill Span, VA-164's executive officer, led the twenty-one-plane strike against the newly authorized target. Low clouds obscured the airfield until the last possible moment, though Span spotted it through a break in the weather. Barrage fire from 85, 57 and 37 mm AAA bracketed the opening. Miraculously, not an airplane was hit. Span put his bombs on the runway centerline, as did four other Skyhawks. Others destroyed the taxiways and aircraft revetments. The mission was a success and rendered a valuable MiG base unusable, though Phuc Yen still remained untouched. Unfortunately, the loss of a valuable E-1B Tracer spoiled the day. Following the Kien An mission, the early warning aircraft from VAW-11 landed at Chu Lai to refuel before the afternoon Alpha strike. Shortly after takeoff, the crew became disoriented in bad weather and crashed into the mountains northwest of Da Nang. The loss of the entire crew forced their small detachment to stand down for several days until a replacement aircraft and crew could be flown to the *Oriskany*.

On 9 October VA-164's Lt. (junior grade) Larry Cunningham was shot down for the second time that cruise. He held the unfortunate distinction of being the air wing's first loss in July, just weeks after joining VA-164. No one had seen him get hit during their first day, though he successfully managed to nurse his crippled Skyhawk back. With the recovery complete, the flight deck was fouled with sailors preparing airplanes for upcoming missions. As his squadron mates met on the flight deck to ascertain his status, Cunningham flew alongside and ejected. The *Oriskany*'s plane guard quickly rescued him. As he exited the helicopter, soaking wet from his recent swim, he asked his flight lead, Lt. Cdr. Denis Weichman, and Cdr. Bill Span, "How long is this cruise going to last?"[12] Four months later, he repeated the experience, this time ejecting near the SAR destroyer. Larry Cunningham would have more close calls before the month ended.

The War at Home and Phuc Yen

By mid-October the Johnson administration had seemingly lost control both in the United States and in Vietnam. On the political front, despite Secretary McNamara's efforts to the contrary, the Stennis hearings resulted in a steady escalation of the air war. Now, because of these escalations, doves were just as displeased as Hawks. On the home front, a week of antiwar protests occurred throughout the country, with clashes in Oakland, California, and on several college campuses. Despite a general disdain from the American public for campus revolutionaries, the number of protests continued to grow. As antiwar fervor increased, the protests grew more violent. Following the violence that marked the summer of 1967, the country was definitely on edge.

On 18 October air operations over North Vietnam came to a halt as Super Typhoon Carla swept through the South China Sea. At the same time (17 October in the United States), President Johnson overruled Secretary McNamara during their Tuesday luncheon. The meeting drew major media attention because the country realized another major escalation was in the offing. While Johnson continued to draw the line at mining Haiphong and bombing the Gia Lam airfield, he finally acquiesced to striking the MiGs at Phuc Yen. Unfortunately, because of poor weather, the strikes were postponed for several days. In the interim, the North Vietnamese concentrated their defenses around Hanoi. When the weather cleared, aviators faced the greatest concentration of air defense firepower of the war: fourteen AAA regiments and twelve separate AAA battalions totaling more than 1,000 guns, as well as twenty-six missile battalions with 156 launchers—more than 80 percent of North Vietnam's entire missile force.[13]

The skies began clearing on 21 October, and Rolling Thunder resumed. That same weekend, massive demonstrations crippled Washington DC. The demonstrations began at the Lincoln Memorial with as many as one hundred thousand people protesting the war. Later, at least fifty thousand marched on the Pentagon. Famous photographs of the day's events juxtaposed young protesters placing flowers in the gun barrels of soldiers guarding the Pentagon. The sight of thousands of mostly peaceful protesters being confronted by armed troops in the nation's capital did not reassure the country or the president.[14] Polarization threatened to tear the country apart, and unfortunately the worst was yet to come, as escalations approved the week prior had yet to occur. By the end of the week, virtually all military and economic targets in North Vietnam that could be considered significant would be bombed. Only five of the targets identified during the Stennis hearings remained untouched, and six of the seven MiG bases had been struck.

Around noon on 23 October, Seventh Air Force bases in Thailand and CTF-77 carriers on Yankee Station finally received approval to strike Phuc Yen, the VPAF's primary jet base and home of twenty frontline MiG fighters, as well as Air Defense Headquarters.[15] Located 11 nautical miles northwest of downtown Hanoi, the base remained the number six priority target recommended by the JCS. "Frag orders," or the abbreviated daily operations orders from the White House, directed four separate navy and air force strikes timed to hit the airfield at fifteen-minute intervals. The air force would lead the first two air strikes, bombing the runway, while the navy would follow with another two strikes, bombing taxiways and aircraft revetments. Morale among the pilots soared as the wings began planning and men volunteered to fly on such a historic mission.

Tuesday, 24 October, dawned hot and hazy with broken clouds as crews began briefing for their missions. F-105 Thunderchiefs from the 355th Tactical Fighter Wing (TFW) led the strikes. Per a contract known as "The Snoopy" (a daily message sent between the fighter wings in Thailand to coordinate mission details), F-4 Phantoms from the legendary Col. Robin Olds's Eighth TFW provided two strike flights and MiG CAPs to the 355th.[16] F-105s from the 388th TFW made the second strike wave. As they rocketed down Thud Ridge, F-105 pilots fought through moderate SAMs and AAA before hitting the airfield with 2,000-pound bombs. They cratered over half of the runway, while F-4 pilots dropped cluster munitions on revetments and parked MiGs. Wild Weasels destroyed three SAM sites near Hanoi, and an air force Phantom shot down a MiG-21. Two of the MiGs managed to get airborne during the first wave's bombing run and maneuvered behind the F-105s before the alert Phantom crew shot one of them down with their 20 mm gun pod.[17] Several of the sixty-four aircraft in the first two raids suffered damage, though none were lost. They exited the target area as the third wave from *Coral Sea* appeared.

CVW-15 aboard *Coral Sea* launched fifty-two aircraft led by their CAG, Cdr. James Linder. This package, consisting of thirty-six Skyhawks and sixteen Phantoms, crossed the coast northeast of Thanh Hoa and proceeded west before turning north to avoid Hanoi's heavy defenses. At a prearranged point, CAG split his strike package, taking half the planes to attack from the south, while the remainder flew on to attack from the north. Constant audio cues from SAMs and AAA forced pilots to turn off their RWR systems in order to hear radios that were becoming inaudible from constant MiG alerts and SAM warnings during the air force strikes. The southern group came under such intense fire from Hanoi that the aviators stopped trying to visually track SAMs and blindly jinked to their roll-in point.[18] As they dove on the airfield, two Phantoms providing TARCAP were hit by SAMs. The Skyhawks were met by a tremendous barrage of AAA. A terrified Skyhawk pilot called, "CAG's hit!" AAA knocked out Linder's radio, hitting his wingman and a division leader within the strike element. But Linder continued, successfully bombing the eastern taxiways and earning a Silver Star for his actions—*his second of three Silver Stars in three days*. As they pulled off target, the next group rolled in from the north. A thin cloud layer from 2,000 to 3,000 feet obscured their targets, and VA-155's Cdr. William Searfus circled his Skyhawks over the airfield until he found an opening that allowed him to successfully bomb the western taxiways.[19] *Coral Sea*'s airplanes formed up in a somewhat ragged stream headed southwest and low to clear the SAM range amid the relative safety of the mountains. As they proceeded out, they passed *Oriskany*'s air wing en route to Phuc Yen with the final wave.[20]

Oriskany launched a strike of twenty-three Skyhawks with twelve F-8 Crusaders as escorts, as well as eight Iron Hand aircraft. Led by VA-164's commanding officer, Cdr. Doug Mow, they also skirted the North Vietnamese defenses by flying around Hanoi. As with *Coral Sea*'s strike, the skies erupted as *Oriskany*'s aircraft left the relative safety of the mountains. The skies were marked with smoke trails from countless SAM launches as Crusaders rolled in for the suppression runs. All of *Oriskany*'s Skyhawks managed to hit the taxiways and revetments, despite the heavy resistance. VA-163's Lt. (junior grade) Vance Schufeldt was hit by a burst of 37 mm AAA as he pulled up following his attack, the only damage incurred in the strike.

The strikes on Phuc Yen required extraordinary efforts from the men tasked with suppressing the defenses. The North Vietnamese fired 107 SAMs on the 24th—nearly all in the vicinity of Phuc Yen. Initially, the Vietnamese missile controllers were confused by the different jammers used by air force and navy aircraft. The navy's ALQ-51 jammers were more easily countered, and as a result, they bore the burden of the SAMs fired. Thirty-two SAMs were fired at *Oriskany*'s aircraft during their six minutes over the airfield.[21] VA-164's Lt. Cdr. Denis Weichman led the *Oriskany*'s Iron Hand mission. His division of Skyhawks, plus their Crusader escorts, had their work cut out for them. Weichman and his Crusader wingman, Lt. Cdr. Dick Schaffert, quickly destroyed one of the fifteen confirmed SAM sites in the vicinity. As they hunted, multiple SAM launches forced the entire element down to lower altitudes, where AAA took its toll. Two Skyhawks were quickly hit, including Weichman's. With Schaffert in trail, Weichman attacked a second SAM site. As the pair defended against missiles from nearly every direction, Weichman's jet took more hits. Weichman's attack destroyed the site, but one burst of AAA destroyed the nose of his Skyhawk and knocked out his radio and navigational equipment. Weichman remembered, "Some shrapnel hit the nose of the airplane. The navigation system was lost. I became separated from the rest of the flight, and for the life of me, I couldn't remember how to get back to the gulf. My only navigation reference was visual, and I couldn't remember whether the sun came up in the east and set in the west, or vice versa."[22] With two sites destroyed and *Oriskany*'s aircraft out of harm's way, Schaffert led Weichman back to the gulf. Their recovery was uneventful, and once they were aboard *Oriskany*, sailors counted more than 140 holes in Weichman's Skyhawk. Weichman received the Silver Star for destroying two SAM sites during the raid, while Schaffert received the Distinguished Flying Cross for escorting him.[23]

Tactically and operationally, the strikes carried out on 24 October were successful. That the staffs of four geographically separate wings planned and executed joint raids involving over 150 aircraft was no small feat. Nearly every air force and navy aircraft involved in the strike hit its assigned target, rendering the runway unusable with eighteen direct bomb hits. The strikes destroyed five MiG-21s and five MiG-17s in their revetments, and one MiG-21 was shot down. Wild Weasels and Iron Hand escorts destroyed five SAM sites. Because most of the twenty MiGs then based at Phuc Yen had been caught on the ground and the remaining MiGs had fled to China, this proved a particularly stiff blow.

Following the strikes, the North Vietnamese immediately began filling the craters in an attempt to repair the runway. Although night-time air strikes by marine Intruder squadrons stationed at Da Nang hampered these efforts, the craters had been filled by daybreak on 25 October. More strikes were required to keep the base from becoming operational. Thus the next day would be a repeat, with the air force tasked to bomb the runway while the navy bombed aircraft revetments and facilities at the embattled airfield.

On the morning of 25 October, the 355th and 388th TFWs attacked Phuc Yen for the second time in twenty-four hours. Although they didn't have as many SAMs available, the Vietnamese added more AAA batteries during the evening. This meant that any strike was certain to meet heavy resistance. To execute their attack, the 355th split into four waves, crossing the runway at one-minute intervals. The second F-105 across the target was lost to AAA, and as they rocketed across the air field, tension was high—one Thud pilot accidentally fired an AIM-9 Sidewinder while dropping his bombs. The 388th TFW was jumped by eight MiG-17s, which managed to sneak behind the Thuds before being spotted. The last four-ship in the wave selected afterburner and broke into the MiGs. The flight jettisoned their ordnance, which coincidentally caused the MiGs to break off the engagement as they evaded the falling drop tanks and bombs. Air force pilots reported that the runway had indeed been repaired, though they succeeded in putting another four strings of bombs across the runway.

Coral Sea suffered a minor setback that morning when a Zuni rocket ignited during testing below decks. The rocket, the same type that had started the *Forrestal* fire, penetrated a bulkhead on the mess decks and critically injured nine sailors. Her sailors had taken heed from the *Oriskany* and *Forrestal* fires and quickly extinguished the blaze, allowing the ship to launch her morning strikes on schedule. Her air wing launched fifty-two aircraft, which followed the same westerly route as the day prior. They intercepted Thud Ridge to better protect them from the rugged Hanoi defenses, and the plan paid off. *Coral Sea*'s airplanes made it to the field unmolested and destroyed AAA emplacements and aircraft revetments without losing any aircraft.

Aboard *Oriskany*, CVW-16's raid also mirrored the previous day's strike, though they suffered one loss and several damaged aircraft. CAG Shepherd led twenty-three Skyhawks and twelve Crusaders on the long westerly route. Severe haze and broken clouds made it difficult to find the airfield as the strike package raced along the deck in unfamiliar terrain. As the strike package left the mountains, VA-164's Cdr. Bill Span watched with growing apprehension as CAG appeared to not see the airfield. With their RWR gear screaming audio alerts, warning him became impossible. AAA filled the sky, and Span feared that if they flew any farther, the entire raid would be unable to make their dive profiles, leaving them even more vulnerable to the AAA. With the airfield passing off their right wing, Span tersely announced he had the target in sight and began his attack—ahead of Shepherd.[24]

Before the main strike left the safety of the mountains, three Skyhawks from VA-163 detached from the larger package and flew ahead to begin individual Walleye attacks on the control tower, hangar, and Air Defense Headquarters. The A-4s were immediately targeted by the defenses. Four SAMs flew through their formation. As they dodged the missiles, Lt. (junior grade) Vance Schufeldt was hit by AAA for the second time in two days. Intent on mission success, Schufeldt proceeded to guide his first Walleye into the control tower, destroying it. He continued over the airfield and attacked the Air Defense Headquarters with his second Walleye. Throughout, Schufeldt recorded the mission with a hand-held camera, providing some of the only footage of the strike's success. The heavy defenses surrounding Phuc Yen made poststrike reconnaissance missions a near-suicidal task, and his pictures provided the only assessment of all four strikes. For his actions, Schufeldt was awarded the Silver Star.[25]

While the Walleye flight delivered their precision weapons, CVW-16's main strike group arrived overhead the airfield amid intense AAA. Barrage fire and SAMs quickly damaged two Skyhawks as they rolled in on their assigned revetments and the taxiway linking them to the runway. Bill Span's four-plane division destroyed three MiG-21s in their revetments. Lt. Cdr. John McCain was further credited with the destruction of two MiGs caught on the ground. Unfortunately, Lt. (junior grade) Jeffrey Krommenhoek, a recent replacement pilot for VA-163's depleted ranks, was last seen rolling in on his assigned target. No one saw him get hit, and the defenses did not permit a search of the area.

As with the previous day, the Iron Hand division faced stiff resistance. The North Vietnamese fired eighty-three SAMs during the four raids, thirty-six of them at *Oriskany*'s aircraft.[26] Lt. Cdr. Bob Arnold led four Skyhawks and four Crusader escorts in a mission that resulted in his second Distinguished Flying Cross in three days. AAA quickly damaged one of the escorts as they penetrated the western SAM rings in an attempt to draw SAMs away from the main group. Arnold had just destroyed one SAM site 2 miles west of Hanoi when another site fired two missiles at him. Arnold outmaneuvered the missiles and then attacked the offending site with his last Shrike.

Arnold's last attack forced the North Vietnamese to shut down their missile guidance radars, allowing *Oriskany*'s airplanes to successfully retire from Phuc Yen. As he followed them out of harm's way, Arnold flew over a previously unknown auxiliary fighter strip 15 miles west of Hanoi. Glancing down, he was startled to see a MiG parked near the end of the runway. Not willing to pass up such a lucrative target, Arnold delivered his remaining bombs on the hapless MiG.[27]

The hazy visibility and poor weather added to the confusion as airplanes escaped from Phuc Yen. Ever vigilant for MiGs, *Oriskany*'s TARCAP narrowly avoided disaster when Cdr. Cal Swanson fired a Sidewinder at an Iron Hand Skyhawk misidentified as a MiG-17. The Skyhawk pilot, Lt. (junior grade) Larry Cunningham, was saved by a timely break-left call from his wingman, VF-III's Lt. (junior grade) Carl Stattin. After being shot down twice already, Cunningham was not happy about this latest affront. It was bad enough that the North Vietnamese were trying to kill him daily, but to have a senior officer almost shoot him down was too much.[28] It was a terrible and deadly time, and stress began to take its toll—the last week of October is remembered as a blur by most. Men naturally flocked to the superiors who enhanced their chances at survival. Shepherd's difficulty in finding the target, plus the terse words between Span and himself that followed the mission, only added to the stress.[29]

The Power Plants

As always, events in Washington transpired to limit the Phuc Yen raid's impact. The second day of raids destroyed another ten MiGs and put another eighteen craters in the runway. Unfortunately, at the same time, the Tuesday luncheon removed authorization for further strikes on the MiG base while adding targets such as the Hanoi and Uong Bi power plants. This restriction allowed the North Vietnamese to begin repairing the airfield and fly in replacements for the twenty MiGs destroyed during the two days. Without the ability to maintain pressure on Phuc Yen, the effort was wasted. Nothing changed, and soon MiGs from Phuc Yen were attacking American aircraft with no fear of reprisal.

The low point of 1967 for CVW-16 was 26 October. The somber day marked the one-year anniversary of the hangar deck fire. But the men were too tired and too numb. They had simply suffered too much during the past months. For most, this day would be their fourth day in a row of strikes into Hanoi. As a result of the previous day's targeting luncheon, the air wing was tasked with destroying the Hanoi thermal power plant. Unlike the previous raid, which was a point of pride with VA-163, there was not enough time to design an elaborate raid as part of other strikes. The air wing would have to fight its way into Hanoi alone.

As pilots were briefed for the mission, they began comprehending the overwhelming defenses they faced. Following three days of strikes to Hanoi, Lew Chatham, the assistant strike operations officer, fully expected to lose pilots. Lt. Cdr. John McCain pleaded with Lt. Cdr. Jim Busey to be put on VA-163's flight schedule for the mission. Busey, who referred to McCain, the new guy, as "Gregory Green-Ass," relented. On board for less than a month, McCain was still too new to be apprehensive about the mission that lay ahead.[30]

That afternoon, *Oriskany* launched eighteen planes, led by Shepherd. The target lay in the very middle of Hanoi, and there was no easy way to minimize the risk. Shepherd led the strike west of the city, so if anyone was hit, at least they'd be flying toward the gulf. It also helped that they would be flying away from the setting sun, making life harder on the Vietnamese gunners. Shortly after going feet-dry, the defenses began tracking the strike. Flying at medium altitudes, the pilots were in the heart of the defenses. With RWR gear blaring in their helmets, pilots watched as the sky erupted with "intense and accurate" 57 and 85 mm AAA. McCain later recalled the raid: "The closer we came to the target the fiercer were the defenses.... We were now maneuvering through a nearly impassable obstacle course of antiaircraft fire and flying telephone poles. They [SAMs] scared the hell out of me. We normally kept pretty good radio discipline throughout a run, but there was a lot of chatter that day as pilots called out SAMs."[31]

As the strike approached the city center, poor weather once again conspired against Shepherd. Lt. Cdr. Buck Sheeley managed to find the power plant on the edge of Truc Bach Lake and talked Shepherd's eyes onto it. They were so close that Shepherd was again putting his dive profile at risk. Sheeley dove down, leading his wingman, VA-164's Lt. (junior grade) Frederic Knapp, through tracking AAA fire. Despite barrage fire blanketing their release altitude, Sheeley still destroyed the pumping station serving the power plant.

As the number three position in CAG's division, McCain made his dive on the target with a SAM warning screaming in his ears. He was hit immediately after dropping his bombs, and the blast blew off his starboard wing.[32] His Skyhawk plummeted in an inverted spin, and McCain ejected. The force of the ejection knocked him unconscious, breaking his right leg at the knee, his left arm, and his right arm in three places. McCain parachuted into Truc Bach Lake and came to as he plunged beneath the water. Using his good leg, he kicked off the bottom of the lake, only to sink again. On the third try, McCain managed to use his teeth to pull the inflation toggle on his life preserver and float to the surface. He was immediately set upon by angry locals, who swam out to drag him from the water. They proceeded to beat him—McCain was stroked with a rifle butt and eventually bayoneted before a North Vietnamese soldier arrived to control the crowd and haul him off to prison.

The Iron Hand division faced an impossible task as they fought to suppress the defenses. Lt. Cdr. Bob Arnold earned his third Distinguished Flying Cross in four days for his efforts. During planning, he identified the most dangerous SAM sites and assigned two to each of the Skyhawks. As the strike approached Hanoi, Arnold destroyed one SAM site 2 miles east of the city, following his Shrike to the site and bombing missiles on their launch rails. But the defenses were just too great. Before McCain was lost, a SAM brought down one of the flak suppression Crusaders flown by Lt. (junior grade) Chuck Rice, one of VF-162's August replacements. Rice saw two missiles tracking him as they began their bombing runs. His Crusader was loaded with bombs, and he didn't have enough airspeed to escape the first missile. Rice attempted the last-ditch evasive maneuver and thought he'd made it. As he rolled wings level, the missile impacted. He later recalled the experience:

> I daresay what I'm about to tell happened in no more than three to six seconds, but it seemed much longer. It hit, a tremendous jolt, and scared the shit out of me. Fire came into the cockpit. I got burned on my eyelids and neck and hands. I had vowed I would not jump out of an airplane as long as I had altitude and could make it go.... Well, it won't fly. "You're going to die." I said that out loud....
>
> I pulled. The next sensation I felt was a violent tumbling. I didn't feel the seat separate, the chute come out—just tumbling. Suddenly I'm in a totally different war than I was familiar with. The war I'd fought till this point involved the sound of my own jet engine and the radio voices of men either high-pitched panic or calm and cool,

with puffs of exploding flak outside my canopy, and the white contrails of jets streaming around.

Soon as I punched out, it's windy and I'm hearing all this noise. Flak and missiles exploding, the roar of bombs going off, the sound of the whole strike group, instead of just the sound of my engine. And the smell! Even that high up I could already smell North Vietnam. Night soil used as fertilizer. The country smelled like shit.

There I was. If you've ever seen a five-year-old kid who just lost his mother in a shopping mall, that's what you've got in that parachute floating down. Mrs. Rice's little boy, Chuckie, age twenty-four. It was the worst despair I'd ever felt in my life. And I started to cry. I said, "This can't be happening to me." Floating down. Tears pouring out of my eyes.[33]

As the strike group flew back to *Oriskany*, their numbness masked the toll. The strike had been successful, but it came at great cost. While the damaged power plant burned for days, men struggled to cope with the stress and constant losses. Lt. (junior grade) George Schindelar was Shepherd's wingman, and when he didn't see the target, it delayed their dive to the point they dove at too steep an angle. Schindelar had almost flown into the lake trying to pull out from a 65-degree dive, and he was livid. During his debrief, he angrily told both Doug Mow and Bill Span that he refused to fly again with CAG Shepherd. Both men calmly told him to be quiet, and he'd fly with whomever he was assigned. Rear Admiral Richardson was so pleased with the results that he told his staff to submit whoever led the strike for a Navy Cross. The whole incident left a bad taste in everyone's mouth and further polarized the air wing at a time when they could least afford it.

And so it went. The Alpha strikes continued twice a day, with missions to the Uong Bi power plant, the ferry at Kim Quan, and more. The days blurred together as men kept flying, believing North Vietnam to be on the brink of defeat. But the chance for victory, so close in September, had passed. The seeming fury unleashed by President Johnson proved to be nothing more than an impotent fit of rage.

13

In the End

IN EARLY NOVEMBER, THE northeast monsoon arrived in full force, signaling an end to the good weather that had enabled the crescendo of activity in October. At the time, the rains signified nothing more than the standard pause in Rolling Thunder. Few, if any, realized that before the weather cleared again in the spring, President Johnson would announce the end of Rolling Thunder and withdraw from the election. McNamara sent a private memorandum to Johnson recommending a freeze in troop levels and a halt to the bombing. He also recommended that the United States turn over the war to the South Vietnamese, which Johnson refused to do. No one will ever know if McNamara resigned or was forced out, but by the end of the month he had announced his resignation. His last day was 29 February 1968, and in the interim, the air war continued.

The air wing lost another Skyhawk before *Oriskany* sailed for Yokosuka, Japan. The crew enjoyed nine days of liberty as the ship underwent a series of inspections in preparation for a planned overhaul upon return to the United States. If they weren't already off-loaded in Cubi Point, damaged aircraft were flown to the NIPPI Repair Facility in Atsugi. With the inspections and repairs complete, the ship departed on 15 November, arriving on Yankee Station four days later.

Oriskany's fourth line period began with the entire region covered in low, thick clouds, which precluded most strikes except a few mining missions on the coastal waterways. Despite heavy losses in October, the VPAF continued to be very aggressive, and losses to MiGs increased. Instead of standing down, the VPAF soon reached parity, and the Americans' hard-fought advantageous edge began to erode. In November and December, the VPAF claimed nine U.S. aircraft to six of their own. By the end of December, all MiG fields except Cat Bi were serviceable, and MiG inventory actually rose.[1]

Tragedy on the Flight Deck

On the afternoon of 19 November, VF-III's Lt. Edwin Van Orden was killed in a tragic accident. Just three weeks earlier, the courageous Van Orden had saved Cdr. Bill Span during an Iron Hand mission as the air wing struck the Uong Bi power plant. The pair flew in low level along the mountains north of Haiphong, and Span had indications of active SAM sites radiating. By the time Span popped up to shoot his Shrikes, the North Vietnamese had already launched missiles at them. Van Orden dutifully called the missiles out to Span, who dived down to treetop level in an effort to evade. Two missiles narrowly missed him. Span then followed his Shrikes to the SAM sites and bombed them. As he left the area, other pilots noted the carnage wreaked as burning SA-2 missiles snaked around their launchers, causing further destruction. Unfortunately, Van Orden became separated from Span during their evasive maneuvering. They both made it back, and Van Orden apologized profusely for having lost sight of Span—the man he was supposed to be escorting. Span allayed Van Orden's fears by replying that he'd done everything right. Without Van Orden's timely radio call, Span never would have seen the missiles in time to evade them.[2]

Now, as *Oriskany* began its fourth line period, Ed Van Orden was launching on a maintenance test flight when disaster struck. His Crusader was the first aircraft to launch from the starboard catapult for the late-afternoon launch. Following the prelaunch checks, the catapult officer touched the deck to signal the launch; however, instead of sending Van Orden's Crusader flying off the bow, the catapult ripped the keel pin out of his aircraft and flung the empty bridle several hundred yards in front of the ship. Van Orden tried in vain to stop his aircraft. He secured the afterburner and locked his brakes as the Crusader slid down the length of the flight deck. It eventually stopped when the nose gear dropped into the safety net on the bow. Van Orden ejected at that moment.

Ejection seats of the period often killed or maimed as many men as they saved. Early ejection seats were not zero/zero, meaning capable of saving a man if he ejected at zero airspeed and zero altitude. The pilot had to eject above a certain airspeed and altitude for the seat to function properly. Van Orden's roommate, Lt. Cdr. Dick Schaffert, was scheduled as the F-8 safety observer for the launch and witnessed the accident. Schaffert later recalled:

The canopy came up and the seat shot upwards. The Martin-Baker [ejection seat] rocketed Ed up and slightly to the left. Nearing the top of his trajectory, the drogue chute came out and Ed seemed to tumble forward out of the seat. The main chute was coming out, but it was obvious Ed was going to hit the water before it was completely deployed. I was running out the Pri-Fly [primary flight control, or the control tower located in the island of the aircraft carrier] door and looking back over my left shoulder when he was still about 50 feet above deck level.

I ran down the six levels of stairs in the island. I was certain Ed would be in the water when I reached the flight deck. I ran out of the island through Flight Deck Control. There was an F-8 on the port cat, but it was shutting down and several people were running forward to the port bow. [Eventually, a flight deck chief scrambled up the side of Van Orden's Crusader and climbed into the cockpit to shut down the roaring jet engine.] The plane guard helo was pulling into a hover off the port bow and I was certain they would be picking up Ed. I ran to the rail behind the port blast deflector that was coming down. I watched for a swimmer to emerge from the helo, but then I saw two white shirts carrying a stretcher running toward the port bow.

Ed's parachute had snagged on the port gun tub and had swung him into the side of the ship. Green shirts were already pulling the shroud straps, and Ed, into the sponson when the stretcher guys got there. They immediately laid him face-up on the stretcher, lifted it to the flight deck and started across for the hatch to Flight Deck Control. His left arm was hanging down and I lifted it to his chest. I held it there as we ran across the deck, into Flight Deck Control, and descended the escalator to Sick Bay. The Corpsmen and Doc were there immediately and started working on him. I felt completely helpless standing there. When they took off Ed's mask and helmet, I became aware that his face was completely white!

It was only a few moments before one of the Corpsmen came over to me and said, "Sir, his neck was broken. He must have died immediately." For some reason, I checked my watch and noted that I had to get to Ready [Room] Three. I was already a few minutes late for my flight briefing. I met Skipper Rasmussen in the passageway between Sick Bay and Ready Three, which were almost adjacent on the *Oriskany*. I could only mutter quietly, "He didn't make it, Sir."[3]

Dick Schaffert then briefed and flew an uneventful night BARCAP. At 0130, he returned to their stateroom and began the gut-wrenching task of sorting through Van Orden's personal effects. It was a task that Schaffert had performed twice during the previous year, and he took the utmost care, knowing that Ed Van Orden's parents would be the next ones to open the boxes. As he sealed the mail in larger envelopes, Schaffert noted several letters from a Western Airlines stewardess. The budding romance had begun after a chance meeting in Tokyo as Van Orden, Schaffert, and Norm Levy arrived to ferry replacement aircraft to the Philippines. Schaffert continued: "Reading her letters to Ed, it was obvious something good was going on between them. Two days after Tooter Teague left Yankee Station with Ed's body, to be buried near his home in Arlington, Texas, I wrote her probably the saddest letter I ever had to write. I wrote it while manning the Alert Five in a Crusader on Oriskany's starboard cat."[4]

The investigation that followed revealed two factors contributing to Ed Van Orden's death. First, his Crusader had been launched 505 times, with a keel pin that was to have been replaced after 500 catapult launches. Second, the catapult had been worked on while *Oriskany* was in Yokosuka, and a valve that regulated the release of steam pressure had been improperly installed. The result was that the full force of pressure was released immediately instead of at a steady acceleration.[5] This overpressure ripped the already stressed attachment point out of Van Orden's Crusader, with disastrous results. Knowing this did little to ease the pain. Van Orden's loss hit the Sundowners particularly hard, as it seemed to be one more senseless loss in addition to the already staggering losses.

The next day, Dr. Allan Addeeb again proved his worth when VA-163's Lt. (junior grade) Denny Earl was hit during an armed reconnaissance mission. Small-arms fire tore through the left side of Earl's cockpit, shattering his left leg. Jim Busey was Earl's flight lead and didn't know if he'd make it due to blood loss. Addeeb was airborne, flying a tanker mission, and he overheard their conversation. Addeeb instructed Busey over the radio, telling him to have Earl inflate his anti-G suit to act as a tourniquet. That act stopped the blood loss and allowed Earl to make it back to *Oriskany*, where he landed in the barricade. Earl's return was captured by public affairs, eventually making national news. Addeeb later chided Busey for taking credit for the G suit tourniquet idea.[6]

When Addeeb landed following his tanker mission, he climbed down from the flight deck and proceeded to help operate on Earl. The ship's general surgeon began preparing for surgery as Addeeb swapped his flight suit for surgical scrubs. With Addeeb's assistance they repaired Earl's leg with several pins. With his leg repaired, Earl was evacuated, arriving in Pensacola, Florida, less than thirty-six hours after being wounded.

Iron Hand and a Duel with MiGs

Weather continued to limit operations throughout December. The air wing managed to fly two major strikes, one against storage caves at Nui Long and another that dropped a recently repaired span of the Haiphong Highway bridge. As a result, losses finally began to slacken.

The afternoon of 14 December resulted in one of the most storied aerial engagements of the war. While eight Skyhawks mined the Canal des Bambous between Hanoi and Haiphong, Lt. Cdr. Dick Schaffert single-handedly fought six MiGs to a draw. The mission was fraught with peril, as it was in the midst of the Red River Delta, halfway between the two cities, with plenty of AAA and SAMs and surrounded by MiG fields. Because VF-111 flew the older, non-bomb-capable F-8C, they primarily flew as Iron Hand escorts. On smaller missions such as this, only two Iron Hand A-4s would be required. They were almost always escorted by Cdr. Bob Rasmussen, VF-111's commanding officer, and Schaffert, the operations officer.[7] On that fateful day, Schaffert escorted Lt. (junior grade) Chuck Nelson, while Rasmussen escorted Lt. Cdr. Denis Weichman.

The mission launched at 1645. After a quick rendezvous, they proceeded feet-dry, flying westward into the setting sun. Shortly after crossing the coast, Red Crown began calling four bandits, the code word for hostile aircraft headed for the strike. A miscommunication led the radar controllers to believe that the Iron Hand package was the strike, which led to confusion, as the MiGs were in fact targeting Schaffert and Nelson.

Alerted by the calls, Schaffert remained vigilant as Nelson dueled with a SAM site. When Nelson pitched up to shoot a Shrike, he slowed down, forcing Schaffert to perform a "lag roll." At 18,000 feet, Schaffert rolled inverted to keep sight of Nelson. At that moment, he spotted two 923rd FR MiG-17s. Schaffert warned Nelson of the threat and dove to engage the MiGs. Schaffert leveled off from his dive at 11,000 feet, with the MiGs to the north and slightly above him.

As Schaffert turned toward the MiGs, the strike package fled for the gulf. Unfortunately, Nelson lost sight of everyone and radioed to tell Schaffert. Closing on the lead MiG's wingman, Schaffert fired an AIM-9D. Because the MiGs were turning toward Schaffert, the missile missed by about half the distance of the MiG's wingspan.[8] Unfortunately, during preflight checks, one of his four AIM-9 Sidewinders had failed and was removed by ordnancemen, leaving him with three. Now he was down to only two remaining missiles plus 20 mm cannons to fend off MiGs.

Schaffert continued to fight for an advantage against the pair of MiGs. As he climbed through 15,000 feet, he looked over his shoulder, hoping to spot Nelson, and instead he saw two more MiG-17s rapidly closing in behind him. Schaffert called for Chuck Nelson to escape while alerting Rasmussen and Weichman that he was fighting four MiG-17s. They were busy dueling with SAMs, and the TARCAP was still escorting the strike feet-wet, so no help was available as Schaffert began the fight of his life. Few men were as qualified as Schaffert for that day's battle. With more than 3,500 hours of flight time, he was on his 276th combat mission. He would need every bit of training, as well as luck, to survive. Schaffert also happened to be pressing his luck. During an arrested landing in October, the restraint system on his ejection seat failed, causing him to crash into the radar scope above the instrument panel. Unbeknownst to him, he'd suffered a fracture in his spine, as well as four herniated discs. The Sundowners were down to only nine pilots, so after a rest of two days, Schaffert was back flying. According to him, "it was 3 months before I was able to turn my head for more than one inch. Consequently, in order to check six [look behind him], etc. I had to lean forward in the seat and turn my body at the hips. Impossible to do that without unfastening the upper Koch fittings at the shoulders. So, that was added to my going feet dry check list." An ejection seat has six attachment points: two leg restraints, two lap belts, and two fittings on the shoulder. Flying in this manner meant that Schaffert was technically strapped in the ejection seat and thus the airplane. The problem was that the shoulder attachment points were attached to his parachute in the ejection seat. If Schaffert needed to eject, he likely would have fallen to his death without a parachute.[9]

For the next ten minutes, Dick Schaffert dueled the MiGs to a standstill. Knowing he couldn't turn with the MiG-17s, Schaffert fought vertically. Using his afterburner, Schaffert began a series of vertical maneuvers that drove him as high as 25,000 feet as he sought an advantageous position against the MiGs. One eight-G break turn pulled his oxygen mask off his sweat-soaked face. Alone over North Vietnam, he was now unable to call for help.

Fortunately for Schaffert, the VPAF MiGs fought as sections of two, giving the former gunnery instructor a fighting chance. Schaffert fired his second AIM-9, and although it appeared to guide, he never saw the result, as his attention was drawn to tracers streaming over his canopy. The second section had done some superb flying and was now blasting away behind him. According to Schaffert, "For a split second, I was at a loss as to what to do. If I pulled harder to try and force an overshoot, I would pull right up into the barrage of tracers sailing over my canopy."[10] Schaffert's training and experience paid off. He unloaded his Crusader, stomping bottom rudder as he dove away, cutting off and under the MiG's turn. The abrupt move caused his Crusader to accelerate. The move befuddled the MiG pilots, because his Crusader had seemingly vanished underneath them. Schaffert now had excess airspeed, which he used to climb back to 20,000 feet. Unable to match his climb, the MiGs broke off to the west. At this point, two MiG-21s joined the fight and launched four Atolls at Schaffert. The missiles missed, and the MiG-21 pilots appeared unwilling to join a fight that would have pitted six MiGs against a lone Crusader. Schaffert ignored the MiG-21s and continued down, using his afterburner to rapidly close the distance between himself and the MiG-17s for his third and final missile shot, which also missed. At a range of 800 feet, one of the MiGs pitched up in front of him. Schaffert squeezed the trigger for his 20 mm cannons, and, once again, fate intervened. His cannons fired one or two rounds before they jammed. The high-G maneuvering caused the pneumatic feeder system to malfunction, robbing Schaffert of a sure kill. Now he was weaponless and defensive as more tracers from the MiG leader flashed by.

Fortunately, one pair of MiGs fled, but the original section stayed and fought on. There was little Schaffert could do, since he was out of missiles, his guns were jammed, and he was unable to call on the radio. He performed yet another high-G defensive maneuver and climbed in a rolling maneuver with the MiGs. After the third series of rolling scissors (so named because it looks like a pair of scissors opening and closing), the lead MiG's wingman pitched out of the fight. Schaffert and the last MiG remained locked in their vertical duel, and finally after their sixth maneuver, Dick Schaffert decided to escape. After topping out at 5,000 feet, he dove down in afterburner. He barely pulled out in time, leveling off below 100 feet and 500 knots. To his surprise, the MiG pilot must have run short of fuel as well, since he declined to pursue Schaffert.[11] Desperately low on fuel, Schaffert turned for the gulf, having outfought six MiGs.

Chuck Nelson now found himself engaged by the MiG-17 that had pitched out of Schaffert's battle. He too outfought the MiG pilot, providing a continuous stream of radio calls as he forced the MiG on the defensive. Having escorted the main strike feet-wet and away from other MiGs, the TARCAP turned back to help. Drawn to Chuck Nelson's calls, VF-162's Cdr. Cal Swanson and Lt. Dick Wyman proceeded to Nelson's position. The other Iron Hand section was also en route. Although Rasmussen and Weichman were too late to help Schaffert, they arrived on the scene first. According to Rasmussen, "At this point, only one MiG was left, and he was hightailing it northwest at high speed and very low altitude, making high-G maneuvering turns."[12] Rasmussen misjudged his speed and overshot, giving Denis Weichman an opportunity. Despite having all his Shrikes and bombs on his Skyhawk, Weichman managed to make three gun passes, expending forty rounds of 20 mm ammunition before breaking off to give the fighters a chance.

When Swanson and Wyman arrived, the five pilots kept continuous pressure on the hapless MiG pilot. As soon as one plane came off its run, another replaced it. Wyman made one head-on pass, trading fire with the MiG. Surprised to see "the whole front end of his plane lit up when he fired," Wyman pitched up to avoid the MiG's cannon fire. When he rolled back into position, Swanson was making a pass on the MiG. The MiG pilot put up a good effort and quickly outturned Swanson, ending up on his tail and shooting. As Swanson and Wyman fought the MiG, Bob Rasmussen maneuvered into missile range and fired two AIM-9s, one of which narrowly missed Wyman. Rasmussen recalled the moment: "I fired my first Sidewinder and missed. It was likely out of the envelope. I fired the second moments later and it tracked but failed to detonate. At this point, there was probably more danger of friendlies running into each other than any possible danger from the MiG, who was just running for his life. There were a lot of our aircraft on the scene. Wyman fell in behind the MiG almost immediately after my second shot and brought him down.... Wyman just did a better job."[13]

Dick Wyman finally maneuvered into position and brought down the MiG-17 with a Sidewinder that tore off two-thirds of its left wing: "The airplane just whipped into something like a violent aileron roll and exploded in the air. Red fire streaked along the left side of the plane as it cartwheeled down into a rice paddy. There was a big ball of flame when it hit. We were barely fifty feet above the ground when the dogfight ended."[14] The entire sequence was caught on film by Chuck Nelson, who by this time had settled overhead and was taking pictures with a hand-held camera. His pictures of the green-and-brown MiG-17 during the swirling 70-mile dogfight became some of the most widely circulated pictures of the air war.[15]

The whole engagement lasted fourteen minutes. Schaffert was still climbing on his maximum-range profile when Wyman scored his kill. Schaffert's low fuel light was on, indicating 1,350 pounds of fuel as he flew down the Red River for *Oriskany*. Schaffert stated, "I probably cut it a little too close because I called the ball on *Oriskany* with only 200 pounds indicated. Final course was to the southeast and the Boss let me do a straight in." He was shutting down his airplane when Swanson and Wyman came rocketing by the carrier, doing a victory roll.

Schaffert received a Distinguished Flying Cross for his extraordinary defense of Nelson during their Iron Hand mission. A total of seven AIM-9s were shot, but only Wyman's actually worked. In true fighter pilot fashion, squadron mate Lt. Cdr. Pete Peters remarked dryly, "Damn it Dick. Four of those bastards to shoot at and you didn't get any?"[16] If U.S. missiles performed better, the score might have been higher. Dick Schaffert entered fighter pilot lore, becoming perhaps the only man to outfight six-to-one odds and live to fight another day. In the years following, Schaffert often wryly joked that his only consolation was that he got to witness Swanson and Wyman almost hit each other during their victory roll fly-by.[17]

The line period continued, with missions being flown despite the horrible weather. On 16 December Schaffert and his wingman, Lt. (junior grade) John Sande, were supporting a small strike led by Cdr. Bryan Compton near the same area of the previous air battle. Once again they encountered MiGs, this time two MiG-21s. The engagement proved uneventful, but Schaffert was flying the same Crusader that had served him so well two days prior. All aviators are superstitious, and Old Nick 106 had become something of a good-luck charm for Schaffert.[18] Upon the conclusion of that day's missions, *Oriskany* left the weather and the line period behind. Following a short stop in Cubi Point, she sailed for Hong Kong, where the crew enjoyed the holidays and a respite from the war. As with previous years, McNamara's routine stand-down for Christmas and the New Year gave the North Vietnamese ample opportunity to move supplies south and fortify their defenses in preparation for the inevitable resumption of bombing. Reconnaissance flights showed men and matériel moving south. Admiral Sharp complained loudly, but to no avail.

Wildman and Weichman

Oriskany returned to the line on 31 December amid the New Year bombing pause. Their focus shifted to Steel Tiger and the interdiction of supplies in Laos, though horrendous weather hampered their efforts. On 2 January 1968 the air war resumed. *Oriskany* teamed with *Coral Sea* and *Ranger* to interdict supplies. They mined rivers and struck transshipment points at Vinh and Thanh Hoa, ferries at Hai Duong and Dong Phong, and the rail yards at Hung Yen. The losses resumed as pilots ventured back over North Vietnam, and VF-III's Lt. (junior grade) Craig Taylor received a particularly rough welcome to the air wing. Taylor joined the Sundowners during the last port call and was shot down on his very first mission while escorting an RF-8. The rest of the air wing fared little better. The losses came so quickly that it seemed they were on track to repeat the heartbreak of July and October. In the first five days of the New Year, *Oriskany* lost five airplanes. After surviving the Hanoi power plant mission, George Schindelar survived yet another close call, ejecting during an armed reconnaissance mission. VF-162's Lt. (junior grade) Rich Minnich was killed by a SAM north of Haiphong. VA-163's Lt. (junior grade) Ralph "Skip" Foulks disappeared during a nighttime armed reconnaissance mission in the horrible weather. One of the few replacement pilots from early 1967 to have survived, Foulks was getting ready to celebrate his one-year wedding anniversary when they returned. He had already survived being shot down in late October, and his loss hit the Saints particularly hard.[19] The tyranny of the present prevailed once again. Men didn't believe they'd survive the two weeks until their scheduled departure, which seemed so close yet so far away.

Weather provided a reprieve from missions up north, but the pace continued as operations shifted to Laos. Lt. Cdr. Denis Weichman was hit by 23 mm AAA during a Steel Tiger mission. He was on his third pass over the target, a small bridge 10 miles north of Ban Don Pang, when he was hit. His engine began to vibrate, though he was able to fly across Laos and the southern portion of North Vietnam to the gulf. Weichman eventually lost control as fire from the damaged engine burned through control cables, forcing him to eject short of *Oriskany*. North Vietnamese junks moved in to capture him, although his squadron mates kept the boats at bay until an HS-6 Sea King arrived for the rescue. The helicopter, flown by Lt. Bob Wildman and Lt. (junior grade) Arne Bruflat, rescued Weichman and delivered him to *Oriskany*. This was the crew's third rescue in just two days, attesting to how many airplanes were being lost during the first week of 1968.[20]

The loss of the legendary Deny Weichman proved to be the last combat loss of the deployment. At 6 feet, 6 inches, Weichman was a giant of a man barely capable of squeezing into the cockpit of a Skyhawk. His quick smile and superb stick and throttle skills established him as a natural leader in the air wing. After flying Skyraiders, Weichman flew as an advisor to the South Vietnamese Air Force and eventually c-123 cargo planes for Air America, dropping operatives and supplies into North Vietnam in the early years of the war.[21] He eventually returned to the United States and transitioned to Skyhawks. A veteran of the 1966 *Oriskany* deployment, he survived the fire because he'd been flying at the time—his room was consumed by the fire. After surviving the heavy combat of 1967, Weichman went on to make aviation history, eventually flying 625 combat missions during the war. That record also resulted in him being one of the most heavily decorated aviators. By 1973, then Commander Weichman had received the Silver Star, five Distinguished Flying Crosses, forty-six Strike-Flight Air Medals, four individual Air Medals, six Navy Commendation Medals, and the Purple Heart, along with campaign and Vietnamese awards.[22]

Oriskany's fifth and final line period ended on 12 January as the ship sailed for Subic Bay. That afternoon, an awards ceremony was held on the hangar deck. Men stood as four admirals commemorated the fallen and lauded the air wing's accomplishments. In 1967 the navy had flown 77,000 sorties over North Vietnam. During 122 days of combat, *Oriskany* had flown over 9,500 of them, including 181 strikes into Hanoi or Haiphong. Her air wing suffered mightily as a result, losing over half their planes and almost a third of the pilots. Other air wings tauntingly referred to them as Bloody Sixteen. At the time, the survivors did not appreciate the moniker, though over the years it has become a badge of honor.

Proving he wasn't as bad as the aviators originally suspected, Captain Holder passed word to the ready rooms that he'd allow "informal parties" in the ready rooms. The pilots got rip-roaring drunk to celebrate their survival.[23] Two days later, they arrived in Subic Bay. Because *Oriskany* was scheduled for an overhaul, and the navy's losses in 1967 were so bad, available jet aircraft and equipment were off-loaded at Cubi Point to help replenish carriers remaining on Yankee Station. On 17 January *Oriskany* sailed for Yokosuka, where some of the air wing caught a flight from Tokyo to the United States. Pilots waited apprehensively as the marine base at Khe Sanh came under siege, and then the North Koreans captured USS *Pueblo* (AGE-2). After surviving seven months of combat, men feared they'd be fighting North Korea in the dead of winter instead of going home. To their relief, *Enterprise* took station in the Sea of Japan, and *Oriskany* continued home. She arrived in Alameda on 31 January amid anxious families and news of the Tet Offensive tearing through South Vietnam. The war had changed drastically.

The year 1967 should be remembered as the year that might have been. Rolling Thunder nearly succeeded, despite the ineptitude shown by the Johnson administration. The Pentagon Papers put it succinctly: "It was an unhappy, contentious time in which the decibel level of the debate went up markedly but the difficult decision was not taken—it was avoided."[24] In the end, the piecemeal targeting and the on-again, off-again nature of the bombing could not stop Communist efforts— especially with the blank check given North Vietnam by the Soviets and Chinese. Johnson's policy was costly, and the Stennis hearings did little to help. They further polarized the country and forced Johnson to expand the air war after the North Vietnamese had solidified their air defenses. By the end of 1967, the North had reached parity, and in 1968 the tables turned, with the VPAF downing more aircraft than they lost. The air battles of 1967 resulted in the heaviest action and losses of the war. *Oriskany* and Carrier Air Wing 16 were at the forefront each time.

Part 5

In Retrospect

Remember that you are an actor in a drama, of such a kind as the author pleases to make it. If short, of a short one; if long, of a long one. If it is his pleasure you should act a poor man, a cripple, a governor, or a private person, see that you act it naturally. For this is your business, to act well the character assigned you; to choose it is another's.

—Epictetus, *The Enchiridion*

14

1968, the Summer of Violence

As events careened out of control, 1968 became a watershed year for the United States. With the Vietnam War as the catalyst, the country came apart along racial, economic, and political lines. Following the violence of 1967, polarizing events happened so quickly during 1968 that the country had little time to digest and make sense of them before the next crisis occurred. The moderation and discussion required of the citizens of a republic did not take place.

It all began with the Tet Offensive. While the Johnson administration and media focused on the *Pueblo* crisis and the siege of Khe Sanh, the North Vietnamese launched an all-out offensive coinciding with the Tet holiday and cease-fire. As *Oriskany*'s men enjoyed their homecoming, fighting raged throughout South Vietnam. Tactically, the offensive was disastrous for the Communists. In South Vietnam, Viet Cong were killed by the tens of thousands, resulting in the destruction of the insurgent network as a separate fighting force. Northern Communists assumed key leadership positions in the south as fighting shifted from insurgency to conventional warfare. Strategically, the Tet Offensive delayed the Communists' timeline for unification, and the war would drag on for years as a result.

Despite these Communist setbacks, Tet proved to be the breaking point for the Americans. The offensive caught everyone, including the president, his advisors, and the military leadership, by surprise. The American public, tired after years of war and rhetoric, lost faith in the government. Tet provided ample evidence of Rolling Thunder's failure to influence the war in the south, if not the general failure of the U.S. effort. The Democratic Party began to abandon the war begun by President Kennedy, leaving Johnson alone to struggle in the morass. Thus, the Tet Offensive and subsequent fighting had a profound effect on the course of the war and American politics. Admiral Sharp bluntly recalled, "March 1968 was most definitely a traumatic month for official Washington on all counts, especially for President Johnson. Among other things, he was still faced with the tough problem of how to handle public reaction to the recent Tet offensive and the dwindling support for his war policies."[1] On 1 March the hawkish Clark Clifford replaced Robert McNamara as the secretary of defense. In the wake of Tet, President Johnson asked Clifford to review General Westmoreland's request for 25,000 additional troops, with options to increase the number to 206,000, including thirteen additional fighter squadrons. The next three days permanently altered the new secretary's outlook on the war. Clifford quickly realized that there had never been a plan for victory and a plan to end the war. Instead, the Johnson administration and military leadership hoped to wear down the North Vietnamese until they had had enough. Militarily, unleashing strikes against North Vietnam might have helped stop the offensive, but Clifford opposed this option due to the complete failure of strategic thinking within the administration. Then on 10 March the *New York Times* broke the explosive news that Westmoreland had asked for another 206,000 troops. While the true number was never intended to be 206,000, the damage was done. Johnson balked at the prospect of calling up the reserves and putting the economy on a wartime footing during an election year and in a time of great public dissent. Instead, he approved the deployment of an additional 24,500 men. On 22 March he also announced his decision to appoint Westmoreland as Army Chief of Staff as troop totals grew to 549,500—the highest total of the war.

The political situation quickly became untenable for President Johnson. On 13 March, three days after news of the troop request broke, Johnson narrowly defeated Eugene McCarthy in the New Hampshire presidential primary. The incumbent should have won handily, but instead he won by a mere 230 votes. The news stunned the world, as if McCarthy had actually won. The master politician had just been challenged by another Democratic candidate because of the discontent over Vietnam. Then on 16 March Robert Kennedy announced his candidacy.[2] Johnson began deliberating with his most trusted advisors, who told him the blunt truth. After weeks of agonizing, President Johnson was truly a broken and defeated man. He delivered a televised speech on the evening of 31 March, reaffirming the country's commitment to South Vietnam. Johnson closed by saying,

> With America's sons in the fields far away, with America's future under challenge right here at home, with our hopes and the world's hopes for peace in the balance every day, I do not believe that I should devote an hour or a day of my time to any personal partisan causes, or to any duties other than the awesome duties of this office—the Presidency of your country. Accordingly, I shall not seek, and I will not accept, the nomination of my party for another term as your President.[3]

The fallout from the speech was twofold and immediate. First and foremost, it completely upset the 1968 presidential election amid the domestic turmoil. Four days later, the assassination of Martin Luther King Jr. led to widespread riots throughout the country in what became known as the Holy Week Uprising. Johnson was forced to deploy army and National Guard troops to help restore order. Without King, non-violence gave way to Stokely Carmichael and the Black Power movement. Following the long, hot summer, violence became the election year norm.

With the presidential race wide open, Vice President Hubert Humphrey announced he would seek the presidency. Because of his association with Johnson and Vietnam, Humphrey faced stiff competition from Robert Kennedy. That changed following Kennedy's assassination on 5 June. Humphrey went on to win his party's nomination during the disastrous Democratic National Convention in Chicago. The whole convention was marred by the excesses of protesters and police alike, making Chicago yet another defining moment in 1968. Humphrey eventually gained in the polls before losing to Richard Nixon, who became the Republican nominee after the moderate Nelson Rockefeller withdrew from the race. Under the guise of states' rights and law and order, Nixon gained the white backlash vote and victory with help from right-wing Republicans and traditional Southern Democrats. Although the popular vote was close, the electoral vote proved decisive. Politics of reason gave way to politics of emotion, and moderation became a thing of the past after Richard Nixon realigned American politics in 1968. It was no surprise that after the violence of 1967 and 1968, American voters chose Nixon's promise of maintaining an orderly society over the promise of a Great Society coming apart at the seams. But that was all in the future. First, the country had to survive the pandemonium of 1968.

The second and more pressing issue for the men fighting in Vietnam was that during his speech, Johnson also announced the curtailment of strikes in North Vietnam. Once again, none of the military leadership, including Admiral Sharp, was advised of the decision to stop strikes the next morning.[4] Although he meant to restrict strikes north of the 20th parallel, Johnson never publicly stated or defined that limit. During his speech, Johnson said,

> Tonight, I have ordered our aircraft and our naval vessels to make no attacks on North Vietnam, except in the area north of the Demilitarized Zone where the continuing enemy buildup directly threatens allied forward positions and where the movements of their troops and supplies are clearly related to that threat. The area in which we are stopping our attacks includes almost 90-percent of North Vietnam's population, and most of its territory. Thus there will be no attacks around the principal populated areas, or in the food-producing areas of North Vietnam. Even this very limited bombing of the North could come to an early end—if our restraint is matched by restraint in Hanoi.[5]

Johnson's omission caused great confusion. With the worst weather in three years of Rolling Thunder finally clearing, Admiral Sharp had ordered strikes near the Thanh Hoa bridge, near the northern limits of Johnson's restriction. They occurred on 2 April. Sensational news reports on the strikes were used to show that Johnson had acted in bad faith. The very next day, orders came down restricting bombing to targets south of the 19th parallel.

The president's announcement emasculated Rolling Thunder. The primary focus shifted to interdicting supplies along the myriad of trails that composed the Ho Chi Minh Trail in Laos and in the panhandle. Sorties were now restricted to Route Packages I, II, and III, eliminating 98 percent of the targets on the master target list.[6] Because these areas contained no important or politically sensitive targets, military commanders were finally free of scrutiny from Washington—as long as strikes stayed within the prescribed areas. With less restrictive ROE in the lower route packages, free fire zones were established to maximize the advantage of air-to-air missiles and radar coverage provided by navy ships in the Tonkin Gulf. Sortie counts seemingly grew, in part because the SAMs stayed in Hanoi and Haiphong. Without the need for extra suppression aircraft, both services allocated these extra sorties to their interdiction efforts. By June the air force had doubled the number of sorties flown into Route Package I, flying six thousand missions into this small area. These efforts held little hope of stemming the tide, as North Vietnam used the partial halt to its full advantage. Men and matériel streamed south at unprecedented levels. While Johnson's announcement eventually produced a breakthrough in negotiations, the North Vietnamese continually delayed in order to replace losses incurred during the conventional fighting now taking place in South Vietnam. By the summer, imports into Haiphong had doubled the monthly average of 1967. POL stocks and general cargo became the priority as North Vietnam rebuilt its infrastructure and moved massive amounts of matériel south.[7] Free from any possible retaliatory strikes, VPAF MiGs returned from China, landing at newly repaired bases. With renewed aggressiveness, MiGs began harassing interdiction efforts before fleeing back to safety north of the 19th parallel. These hit-and-run tactics accounted for 22 percent of all U.S. losses in 1968, testifying to the changed nature of Rolling Thunder. Tough missions remained, although they were a far cry from the intensity of 1967. Nothing could compare to the missions flown into Route Package VI during late summer and fall of that year.

Despite the partial bombing halt, Rolling Thunder continued through the summer and fall of 1968. Communist officials stalled, stating they would not conduct negotiations while the bombing persisted. Then suddenly, Vietnamese officials finally agreed to meet with the Americans for preliminary talks. As a result, on 31 October President Johnson declared that all bombing would end at 0800 on 1 November in Washington (2 November in Vietnam). Although the bombing halt was purportedly linked to progress in the peace talks, the fact that they occurred days before the U.S. presidential election fooled no one. The JCS and military leadership correctly doubted that Rolling Thunder would resume under any circumstances. Thus, President

Johnson's announcement signaled the end of a very significant chapter in the history of U.S. involvement in the Vietnam War.

The year 1968 also proved to be a watershed year for both *Oriskany* and CVW-16, as both missed the conclusion of Rolling Thunder. The ship moved to Hunters Point Naval Shipyard in San Francisco on 8 February and began a massive nine-month overhaul. President Johnson ended Rolling Thunder the day after *Oriskany* left the shipyards. The carrier eventually made six more deployments, including four more to Yankee Station, before the United States stopped supporting South Vietnam. None of these would be as traumatic as the deployments made during the Rolling Thunder years.

Following its tremendous losses in 1967, the air wing was broken up. There is conjecture that the split occurred as a result of the horrendous losses, but this is simply not true. During this period of transformation in naval aviation, many squadrons were transitioning to newer airframes, which took precious time to train pilots and technicians. As a result, there weren't enough squadrons available to fill the ranks of deploying air wings. CVW-16 was split in order to fill the holes in other air wings deploying to Vietnam. Men who had already been through so much while flying from *Oriskany* found themselves preparing for an imminent return to combat. While *Oriskany* enjoyed some down time, the two Skyhawk squadrons, VA-163 and VA-164, joined CVW-21 on *Hancock*. These squadrons deployed in July 1968 for their fourth deployment in four years. The two Crusader squadrons, VF-111 and VF-162, remained stateside as part of CVW-16, while VA-152 transitioned to Skyhawks. CVW-16 eventually made one more deployment on USS *Ticonderoga* during 1969 before it was disestablished. Afterward, the remaining squadrons were redistributed among air wings headed to Southeast Asia. By 1975 all the squadrons except VF-111 had been shuttered, victims of bureaucratic budget cuts as carrier aviation transformed into the modern nuclear navy that emerged at the war's end. It was a quiet and ignominious end to a storied air wing.

15

The POWS

No STORY OF THE air war in Vietnam is complete without mentioning the plight of the POWs. While a full accounting is beyond the scope of this work, it deserves mention.[1] From 1964 to 1973, 771 men were imprisoned in Southeast Asia. The majority were aviators, shot down during Rolling Thunder. As professionals, these men differed from POWs of previous wars. Their average age was thirty-four. Nearly 80 percent had a college degree or higher.[2] These characteristics helped shape the men's resistance to the depravities of their captors. From the beginning, the North Vietnamese refused to treat downed pilots as prisoners of war, ignoring the Geneva Convention. Instead, they referred to pilots as "war criminals," guilty of committing crimes against the Vietnamese people during an illegal war of aggression. Because North Vietnam and the United States did not have diplomatic relations with each other, pilots simply vanished when shot down. North Vietnam did not allow inspections by the International Red Cross and refused to provide the names of men detained. The U.S. government simply had no idea who was imprisoned or dead.

Communist indoctrination was constant, as was systematic torture. North Vietnamese torture was exceptionally cruel, learned over years of colonial occupation and honed under the Communists. In the wake of World War Two, nationalist and Communist movements brought resentment to a boil, and American prisoners experienced that wrath during their captivity.[3] Unfortunately, the frequent bombing pauses followed by escalation only served to anger Communist captors, who alternated torture and leniency according to the shifting U.S. policy.[4] Extreme beatings were common. Prisoners were bound in tight ropes until their arms or legs were dislocated. Men faced solitary confinement or were left in leg irons for weeks on end—sometimes both. Medical treatment was often withheld, threatening men who had been grievously wounded during their ejections. This brutal treatment was intended to force prisoners to confess to war crimes or participate in staged propaganda activities. While military information was gathered from newer prisoners, its usefulness was minimal when compared to the overall goal of complete subjugation.

At the core of the prisoners' resistance was the Code of Conduct. Following the Korean War, the U.S. government learned of the shocking Chinese Communist treatment of POWs. Sociologist Albert Biderman's research into methods used to coerce information and false confessions led directly to the creation of the Code of Conduct, which outlined expected behavior of American service members.[5] While the code provided a framework to guide POW behavior, it quickly proved unrealistic as POWs experienced the Vietnamese wrath. Every man eventually reached his breaking point, no matter what the code said.

The overall POW experience can be divided into four distinct periods: the beginning, the torture era, the good guy era, and the homecoming. August 1964 until October 1965 marked the beginning, when early prisoners were housed with common Vietnamese criminals. As the initial trickle of shoot-downs turned into a flood, conditions worsened. In October 1965 guards discovered a list of policies and a master list of POW names while searching a cell; this discovery elicited a swift change in North Vietnamese policies.

The torture era lasted from October 1965 until the end of 1969. This brutal period consisted of torture and isolation as the North Vietnamese sought to use the prisoners for propaganda purposes. As the bombing escalated, so did the number of POWs: more POWs arrived in camps in 1967 than in all the other years. The climax of Rolling Thunder in October 1967 gave the POWs false hope that the end was near, and when President Johnson suddenly ended the campaign, they faced the darkest of times.

The good guy era began after the Nixon administration began a large public relations campaign to improve treatment of prisoners coupled with the death of Ho Chi Minh. Although the North Vietnamese attempted to stop the negative publicity and regain world opinion by improving prisoner conditions, they still branded the men as criminals, refusing them rights and recognition as POWs. Food rations improved from the starvation diet. Prisoners could suddenly communicate. POWS began to receive packages and letters from home. The Vietnamese even allowed them to write one letter per month. Torture and extortion were replaced by simple and "straightforward detention."[6]

The resumption of bombing during Operation Linebacker was the United States' attempt to stop the invasion of South Vietnam by the North in 1972 and marked the turning point for the last phase. It also marked a generational split between prisoners who endured years of brutality during the bombing pause and the new generation of pilots shot down after bombing resumed. Finally, with the signing of the Paris Peace Accords in 1973, the POWS began going home. Operation Homecoming lasted from February to April 1973, with transports airlifting prisoners out of Hanoi. POWS were released in the order of their shoot-down, traveling to Clark Air Force Base in the Philippines and then to Travis Air Force Base in California.

The Men

The fact that *Oriskany* and CVW-16 lost so many aircraft meant that a significant number of men became POWS. These men went on to play a critical role in the POW saga. CAG Stockdale is synonymous with the POW experience, and his leadership was crucial to the prisoners' survival. Cdr. Harry Jenkins became one of the first men to be tortured as the Vietnamese tightened the screws. Released early, Ens. David Matheny memorized the names of fellow prisoners to provide the first confirmation of who was actually alive in North Vietnam. Lt. Cdr. John McCain was the most seriously injured POW, yet he refused early release on the grounds it would provide the North Vietnamese even more propaganda value. Lt. (junior grade) Chuck Rice became one of a handful of men selected for special treatment by Cuban Communists. It is not possible to cover all of the prisoners or all their years of captivity. A short summation of the highlights will suffice, acknowledging that their story is one of incredible perseverance and bravery in the darkest of hours.[7]

James Stockdale is the central figure in the POW story. His leadership during the seven and a half years he spent in prison allowed a great many of the POWS to "return with honor." Unlike the leadership of the air war, POW leadership was a joint effort from the beginning. It was a conscious decision between Stockdale, the senior naval officer, and Lt. Col. James Robinson "Robbie" Risner, the senior air force officer. Both men were shot down within a week of each other in September 1965. These two men provided the wisdom and spirituality the POWs needed to survive the long years ahead.[8]

Stockdale was horribly injured during his September 1965 ejection. He suffered a broken back. His left knee was broken and sticking out at a ninety-degree angle when a mob of angry villagers attacked him upon landing. Stockdale talked doctors into not amputating his leg—a decision that likely saved his life, as it is doubtful he would have survived the operation. He arrived at Hoa Lo in downtown Hanoi on 12 September 1965 and was transferred for surgery to fix his mangled leg at the end of the month. After one surgery, another followed in early October 1965. At the end of the month, he was transferred back to Hoa Lo. Though he remained in isolation, his leadership began affecting his fellow POWs. As they tightened the screws on the others, the Vietnamese remained reticent to do Stockdale further harm. To date, he was their biggest prize. Stockdale alive was very valuable to the North Vietnamese, though in time he became the biggest thorn in their side.[9] He remained in isolation, slowly recuperating. Then in January 1966, while still hobbling around on crutches, Stockdale was finally introduced to torture. Locked in leg irons and tortured with ropes, Stockdale was forced to denounce the war. The torture reinjured his leg, giving him a reprieve from the famous Hanoi march in response to the POL strikes.

In early 1967 James Stockdale made his greatest impact yet. One of the prisoners had been forced to read Harrison Salisbury's inflammatory articles over the camp's loudspeakers. The articles were published in the *New York Times* in December 1966 after Salisbury was invited to Hanoi by the North Vietnamese. That his articles were manipulated as part of the North's propaganda efforts is important; however, they also provided a counterpoint to the five o'clock follies' sterile reporting on the air war and fueled dissension, something the POWs could not afford. Stockdale ordered prisoners to take a week in leg irons before agreeing to talk over the camp radio. This instruction "reflected his penchant for finding a middle ground between doctrinaire obedience to the Code of Conduct and a principled yet tenable standard of resistance."[10] Stockdale's guidance lifted morale at the time when it was needed most. He followed that first edict by promulgating a new set of policies that became the basis for POW resistance. Known by the acronym BACK US, they set the standard for the POWs' behavior until their release in 1973.

B—Bowing. Do not bow in public, either under camera surveillance or where non-prison observers were present.

A—Air. Stay off the air. Make no broadcasts or recordings.

C—Crimes. Admit to no "crimes," avoiding use of the word in coerced confessions.

K—Kiss. Do not kiss the Vietnamese goodbye, meaning show no gratitude, upon release.

US—Unity over Self.[11]

Time after time, men became despondent after failing to live up to the Code of Conduct during torture sessions. Therefore, Stockdale's guidance became the moral and legal compass for POW conduct. It was a set of orders that followed the intent of the code but in a manner that the men were able to follow.

Of course, the Vietnamese could not let the leadership and resistance provided by Stockdale stand unchallenged. The extensive bombing throughout the summer and fall of 1967 nearly caused prison officials to come unglued and led to the "Stockdale purge." They systematically tortured men to find who was issuing orders and providing crucial leadership under the BACK US program. By September 1967, as Stockdale's fellow aviators came so close to knocking Hanoi out of the war, the Vietnamese caught him communicating with another prisoner. The Vietnamese had their man. Stockdale later claimed he "felt like Jesus about to go on the cross."[12] They tortured him for three weeks, rebreaking his left knee in the process as they attempted to gain information on subordinates in the prisoner chain of command. Stockdale stalled by giving them a list of all the prisoners, 212 names in rank order, claiming they were the head of a snake. Cut off one, and the next would replace him. The Vietnamese elicited an apology, but he managed to obscure the key players. His resistance was becoming legendary, and he later recalled that at some point during the ordeal "some fellow, unknown prisoner, pretending to shake his bath rag dry, snapped in unmistakable code, 'GBUJS' for 'God Bless You Jim Stockdale.'"[13]

As the air war reached its high point in October 1967, the Vietnamese became anxious to stop any further resistance. They moved Stockdale and ten other "hard-liners" whom they viewed as the most influential and unmanageable prisoners to Alcatraz, a former colonial prison for France's most feared political opponents.[14] Each man sent there spent his entire time in solitary confinement in a 4-foot-square cell. When the ordeal was over, James Stockdale had spent four years in solitary confinement, two of them in leg irons. Yet his leadership of the POWs continued unabated. On the third anniversary of his shoot-down, Stockdale heard "the most meaningful citation I've ever received." As the other men in Alcatraz cleaned their waste buckets, they swished out in code, "Here's to CAG for three great years. We love you. We are with you to the end."[15]

In late January 1969, fellow Alcatraz inmate Harry Jenkins suffered from an attack of intestinal worms. To gain medical care for his fellow *Oriskany* pilot, Stockdale ordered a two-day hunger strike. Jenkins got the attention he needed, and Stockdale was hauled away to the famous Room 18 torture chamber at Hoa Lo. It was there that James Stockdale gained infamy. In less than twenty minutes of unusually harsh rope torture, the Vietnamese made him submit. The torture continued for two months as they elicited more information. Stockdale sensed that the Vietnamese wanted him to make a filmed propaganda statement, and his thoughts were confirmed when they arrived with soap and a razor, ordering him to clean himself up. Stockdale used the razor to give himself a reverse Mohawk, cutting his scalp badly in the process. When the Vietnamese decided to cover up his wounds with a hat, he then took a stool from his cell and proceeded to bludgeon his face with it. With his face a bloody pulp and his eyes swollen shut, he had thwarted their attempt. To keep the upper hand, Stockdale would "freshen" his wounds by beating his head against the walls. As Stockdale later recalled, he was "finally learning what Dostoevsky's 'underground man' knew: 'What a man craves is not a rationally desirable choice, but an *independent* choice.'"[16]

Torture continued throughout the summer of 1969, and through it all, Stockdale kept communicating, leading the POWs. Then in late August the Vietnamese caught him communicating again. He was sent back to Room 18 for more torture. As his captors whipped him in the face with a fan belt, Stockdale decided he would rather die than divulge details of the communication scheme. Left alone that night, Stockdale broke the cell's window and sliced his wrists with the shards. Panicked guards discovered him and summoned medics, who saved him. Stockdale was moved back to solitary confinement to heal. The incident happened shortly after Ho Chi Minh's death and after the press conference highlighting Vietnam's mistreatment of POWs. Losing one of their most valued senior prisoners would only bring further attention to the issue. From this point forward, things began to change for the better in the prison system.[17]

James Stockdale led the POW resistance to the end, even when it became apparent that other officers outranked him, as they were unwilling or unable to lead. Upon repatriation, Stockdale received the Medal of Honor not only for his incredible leadership but for his two episodes in Room 18 during 1969. Fellow inmate Dick Stratton summarized it best: "Jim Stockdale is a man for all seasons. Hanoi did not make the man; Hanoi provided the stage for him to play his finest role."[18]

After being shot down in November 1965, Cdr. Harry Jenkins became the first senior officer to proceed directly into torture. After his capture and a ten-day journey, he arrived at Hoa Lo, where his captors recognized his name from news articles in the *Stars and Stripes*. A week of torture and interrogation followed, with Jenkins sinking into despair over his inability to follow the Code of Conduct. Stockdale's leadership proved critical to Jenkins's survival. Men slowly developed a more realistic attitude toward the code and life as POWs under the Vietnamese. Having already served alongside Stockdale as one of his squadron commanders, Jenkins became an able deputy in the prison system. Considered a hard-liner by the Vietnamese, Jenkins was one of the eleven men moved to Alcatraz in the fall of 1967. During the good guy era, he was one of the extraordinary men to be placed in Cell Seven of Camp Unity. He was one of the ringleaders of the Church Riot of December 1970. When the Vietnamese hauled Jenkins and other senior officers away for more torture and interrogation, he helped turn the tide and improve the POW situation.

The tale of VF-III's Ens. David Matheny became very contentious. Shot down in early October 1967, the young aviator quickly became targeted for early release. As the Tet Offensive raged, the Vietnamese released three men to peace activists Daniel Barrigan, a Jesuit priest, and Howard Zinn, famed professor of history at Boston University and author of *A People's History of the United States*. The three men released were Matheny, air force Maj. Norris Overly, and Capt. Jon Black. The three received a red carpet sendoff in front of newsmen and Communist Party officials. To make things worse, the prisoners left behind had to listen to the events, plus recordings of the three men making confessions prior to their release.[19] Contempt for the men known as MOB (from the acronym formed by their last names) ripped through the prisoners. It was a blow to prisoner morale throughout the camps. The code forbade early release, and most POWs believed these men committed a grievous offense. To be certain, the issue was not a black and white one. Moral and legal arguments were made, often depending on whether a POW was a hard-liner or a pragmatist. The three men left without senior ranking officer (SRO) permission. Their act had opened a potential floodgate, threatening senior authority and POW unity at a time when the prisoners could least afford it.[20]

To the men's credit, they provided critical information to the U.S. government upon their return. Seaman Doug Hegdahl was a well-known prisoner who had been blown overboard from USS *Canberra* (CA-70) during a nighttime bombardment of North Vietnam. A strong swimmer, he survived and was rescued by fishermen. At first the Vietnamese believed him to be a covert operative, but they quickly realized that he was indeed a nineteen-year-old sailor. Because they believed him to be no threat, the Vietnamese gave him nearly free rein of the camp. They couldn't have been more wrong. With careful coaching from Cdr. Dick Stratton, Hegdahl began memorizing the names of all the POWs in the North.[21] Hegdahl was meant to leave but then was replaced by Overly. Hegdahl managed to teach Matheny seventy of the names before the swap occurred. Matheny eventually conveyed the names to officials in Washington. Upon his release in 1969, Hegdahl provided the remainder of the names. These men provided the first confirmation of who was alive and interned. Black also provided valuable information. Imprisoned at Hoa Lo, he gave analysts drawings of the camp's layout and even more names. This allowed photo interpreters to locate and plot the prison's location for the first time.

It is beyond me to pass judgment on these men. They broke faith with their fellow POWs, but in doing so, they provided their country information it needed to begin improving the plight of those still in Vietnam.

Shot down while attacking the Hanoi thermal power plant, John McCain was lucky to survive his ejection and subsequent capture. He remains the most grievously injured POW to survive imprisonment. The Vietnamese tortured him for four days in Hoa Lo before taking him to a rat-infested hospital room in central Hanoi. They realized the propaganda treasure they had captured and set about to capitalize on it as McCain passed in and out of consciousness. As his condition stabilized, the Vietnamese again tortured him for information—before treating his injuries. McCain spent an agonizing two hours in pain as doctors attempted to set his mangled right arm without anesthetic. Incapable of setting the bones, they eventually settled on wrapping him in a body cast. Unable to care for himself, McCain was guarded by a teenage boy who stole more of McCain's food than he fed him. Around this time, McCain's captors advised him that repair of his leg was contingent upon him being filmed to show his lenient treatment. McCain agreed, mostly as a way to let his family know he was alive, although he demurred when pressed for further statements. He was saved by a French Communist journalist who told the Vietnamese the short footage sufficed.[22] The Vietnamese eventually operated on his leg, leaving him in yet another cast and still bedridden.

At the beginning of 1968, McCain remained weak and unable to care for himself. He was transported to the Plantation, a prison used for propaganda by the Vietnamese, as they continued to focus on his special status as the son and grandson of famous admirals. Upon arrival, McCain shared a cell with two air force officers, Col. Bud Day and Maj. Norris Overly. Day, who also received the Medal of Honor for his actions as a POW, was nearly as badly injured as McCain. Day's strength proved to be a source of inspiration for McCain as Overly nurtured both injured men. Overly was released early, and Day was eventually transferred to another prison, leaving McCain in solitary confinement for the next two years. During the summer of 1968, McCain's father relieved Admiral Sharp to become CINCPAC, and the Vietnamese made more propaganda demands of him, even proposing early release. According to Bud Day, John McCain was the only person who qualified for early release due to his injuries, yet McCain resisted.[23] He would wait his turn according to the Code of Conduct and Stockdale. This propaganda failure incensed the North Vietnamese, who made John McCain pay, "singling him out for what was probably the harshest sustained persecution of any prisoner at the Plantation, lasting over a year, including an episode in September 1968 when over a span of four days his left arm was rebroken, he was trussed in ropes, and he was beaten 'every two to three hours' until he signed a confession of criminal wrongdoing and apology." That statement was about all they got out of the "crown prince." He fended off pressure to meet with delegations. He diverted his interrogators with useless information, once listing the offensive line of the Green Bay Packers as the members of his squadron.[24]

When McCain emerged from solitary, he became one of the primary leaders of the resistance both at the Plantation and later as a member of Cell Seven at Camp Unity. He perhaps withstood more than most men, although he firmly believes that the Vietnamese were unwilling to kill him because of his propaganda value.[25] This tenacity cost him dearly. John McCain's wounds never fully healed. Upon homecoming, he was still limping on his bad leg, although he left his new crutches behind, because as he remembered, "I wanted to take my leave of Vietnam without any assistance from my hosts."[26] His mangled right arm remains a full 2 inches shorter than the left.

Following his shoot-down on the same mission as John McCain, Lt. (junior grade) Chuck Rice entered his own special hell. As a new prisoner, Rice had yet to experience the torture and extortion that had reached inhuman lows. Because of this, he was singled out to prepare him for early release. It was not to be.[27] Transferred from Hoa Lo to the Zoo, Rice and twenty other men were randomly persecuted by a Cuban known as "Fidel." Fidel's goal was compliance, pure and simple, and it was achieved through brutal torture. This Cuban institutionalized water boarding and whippings with automotive fan belts. He also introduced confessions written in little blue books. Chuck Rice was one of the lucky ones, because not all men survived their encounters with Fidel. Even the Vietnamese were shocked by his excesses. The Cuban program slowly wound down, and Fidel lost influence. Chuck Rice summed up the later years in Zalin Grant's *Over the Beach*:

By 1970 the pressure had eased a bit. The publicity campaign spearheaded by the POW families, along with the attention the Nixon administration gave the problem, achieved results in terms of the kind of treatment we were given. . . . For the first time we were all together. A formal military structure was secretly established. The ranking officer, an air force colonel, was our camp commander. Rules and regulations were laid down. The communication system began working so well that it became bureaucratic and you almost resented it. In the first years we loved to have contact with other Americans. Now we were together and the military mentality began to reassert itself.[28]

These men all played a critical role in the POW experience. There were others from the air wing too. VMF(AW)-212's Capt. Harlan Chapman became the first marine POW. VF-III's Ens. George McSwain, described as "a tough hombre" by his fellow prisoners, was eventually broken during a wave of violent reprisals following an escape attempt by fellow inmates. VA-163's Lt. Cdr. Hugh Stafford's great sense of humor allowed him to tell countless jokes and puns, to the delight and amusement of his fellow inmates. One of his more famous puns played on the saying "A penny saved is a penny earned." Stafford invented a character named Benny who shaved off all the hair on his body. In his tale, Benny was struck by lightning and reduced to ashes, which were placed in a small jar. After luring fellow POWs with the story, Stafford would ask if they knew the lesson, to which he'd respond, "A Benny shaved is a Benny urned."[29]

The Families

The women and families left behind when their husbands and fathers went to fight in Vietnam also deserve special recognition. Residing at the various air stations in Alameda, Lemoore, and Miramar, they suffered silently, not only during Rolling Thunder, but throughout the war as their husbands continued to fly and fight in their chosen professional careers. In gallows humor, the wives were often referred to as "Cruise Widows," but that description and reality were only a moment's heartbreak away. The inevitable casualty notification could send their world into a tailspin, forever changing their lives. Events such as the fire on the hangar deck affected entire communities as grieving families struggled to cope with losses in their close-knit ranks. As the home of the Pacific Fleet's attack squadrons, Naval Air Station Lemoore in California bore the brunt. During Vietnam, Skyhawk losses were more than double those of any other naval aircraft. One hundred ninety-five navy A-4s were lost in combat, and seventy-seven more in operational accidents—31 percent of the navy's fixed and rotary wing losses during the war. The majority of them were flown by Lemoore-based pilots. The polarization tearing the country apart affected these pilots' wives too. No matter their political affiliation, these women supported their husbands through thick and thin. It took understanding and compassionate women to survive—and their attitudes had a direct impact on morale. Not all marriages survived the test.

The POW situation affected morale from the beginning, and the Johnson administration did little to help. With no official channels between Hanoi and Washington, there was no way for bureaucrats to confirm a pilot's status. Early on, the Johnson administration's policy was to keep quiet and avoid upsetting the North Vietnamese, who they feared would actually follow through with their threats of punishing the "criminals." Compounding the issue was the change in policy concerning captured men. As more men were captured in the early 1960s, the Johnson administration worried the public would begin questioning American involvement, so they changed the official phrasing from "captured or interned" to "detained."[30] Whether intentional or not, the change and the administration's overall stance did nothing to help the POWs or their families.

The wives of downed aviators immediately entered a bureaucratic purgatory. By naval regulations, families of a deceased serviceman were no longer authorized government quarters. So these wives not only lost their husbands but were kicked out of their homes by the navy. The POW issue only muddied the water further. If a pilot went missing, then the families were left in limbo. During the height of the air war in 1967, Capt. Howie Boydston, the commanding officer of Lemoore, began allowing wives to stay on base, no matter the regulation.[31] It was a small step, but one that held major implications, especially considering the entire support network available to the wives existed at their base. His support became influential in breaking the bureaucratic logjam at a time when the government told the families nothing.

Sybil Stockdale proved to be just as influential to the POWs as her husband, Jim Stockdale. She saw through the smokescreen and began to seek answers. When the U.S. government failed in its responsibilities, Sybil became energized. She knew that her husband and his fellow POWs were being tortured, and she was frustrated with the government's lack of answers. During a June 1968 interview with a reporter from *Look* magazine to discuss Jim's plight, she and a another wife decided that forming a national organization was the only way to achieve results. Thus began the National League of Families. In less than a month, they had 350 members in twenty-four chapters across the country, and the numbers continued to grow.

With Sybil as the national coordinator, the League of Families began highlighting the POW issue. In less than a year, the organization influenced the new Nixon administration to act. The black POW/MIA flag that is now a common sight to many Americans became the league's symbol as it gained momentum. Sybil and other wives began visiting American officials in Washington and Vietnamese officials in Paris. Sybil Stockdale later recalled one of her visits to Washington in July 1969:

> I couldn't help liking Secretary Laird. He'd ended the "keep quiet" policy and had the guts to talk about the truth of the prisoners' treatment in public. I secretly felt that the organizational efforts of us wives and families on a national level had been influential in forcing our government to join us in speaking out publicly. One official in the Defense Department told me they knew they'd better join us or we were going to mop up the floor with them. That was exactly how I wanted them to feel.[32]

That was the power of Sybil Stockdale. She and the other women caused the Nixon administration to place pressure on the North Vietnamese, highlighting their inhumane treatment of the prisoners to the world. This in turn forced the Politburo to change its stance on the POWs.[33] The navy eventually awarded her the Public Service Medal. She remains the only wife ever to receive such an award.

Marilyn Elkins serves as an additional example of how the war touched these women's lives. Her husband, Lt. Frank Elkins, was killed during a nighttime armed reconnaissance mission in October 1966. As they had just married, she was not living on base, and she was dependent on the few things government representatives could tell her. Two months after her husband was declared missing, she struggled with the reality of it all.

> By December, I had lost twenty-five pounds. I was down to a hundred and must have looked horrible, but I never glanced at a mirror. It made people uncomfortable to be around me. I was young, my husband was missing and if they told you they were sorry, you were liable to cry, and they didn't want to see you cry. But if they ignored it and didn't say anything, they came across as callous. Shirley's husband, Jack, who was in Squadron 162, returned home after the fire. She was afraid for me to see him, afraid it would make things worse, Jack coming back, Frank not with him. He finally came around to the house but didn't know what to say or do. I was in a period of suspended disbelief, a time capsule. You talk yourself into believing what you want to believe and ignore any fact that doesn't fit in.[34]

Marilyn Elkins soon found herself ensnared in the political issues surrounding the POW and MIA movement as well as American involvement in Vietnam. Some members of the League of Families would not talk to politicians simply because they were doves with an antiwar stance. It didn't help that the hawks often used the same issue to further their own political agendas.[35] Very few viewed the issue in an objective manner. Marilyn continued to hope that Frank Elkins was alive. She wrote and mailed packages, despite the continually changing rules about what could be said in letters. She eventually became disenchanted with the POW issue, as very little reason was put into the debate.

Marilyn Elkins waited for years to discover her husband's fate. Was he alive in the prisons, or had he indeed perished? At one point, because the U.S. government could not do it, she traveled to Paris to query officials at the North Vietnamese Embassy. She eventually moved to Paris and began making daily trips to the embassy to ask the Vietnamese if they had any information about her husband. After more than two months, they quietly told her he was dead.[36] But whom could she trust? The navy officially listed Frank Elkins as MIA. They could not confirm otherwise, and that status remained. In 1973 Marilyn published her husband's diary under the title *The Heart of a Man* in an attempt to raise awareness of the POW and MIA issue. Operation Homecoming was under way, and there was still no official accounting of him. Zalin Grant's *Over the Beach* does an epic job of covering the impacts on this young woman as she struggled to make sense of the morass. The Vietnamese eventually returned Frank Elkins's remains in 1990.

Oriskany's POWs and their families epitomize the service and sacrifice that occurred during Vietnam. As Stuart Rochester and Frederick Kiley, the authors of *Honor Bound*, conclude, the POW story "remains one of the few truly shining moments of that troubled era."[37] Upon homecoming, these men and their families felt the weight of their suffering drain from their bodies—what Lt. Cdr. Hugh Stafford later called a "profound, bottomless fatigue."[38] Some men picked up their former lives easily, while others struggled. Some returned to their wives and enjoyed long marriages, while others returned to failing marriages that succumbed to the trauma. On the whole, most did remarkably well, considering the severity and longevity of their confinement.[39] Some of the men came home to enjoy further success. Jim Stockdale received the Medal of Honor, was promoted to admiral, and eventually led various academic institutions. Later, he became Ross Perot's running mate in the 1992 presidential election, in part out of his loyalty to Perot for the man's outstanding help to Sybil Stockdale and the National League of Families. John McCain also entered politics, eventually becoming a senator from Arizona and a primary candidate during an unsuccessful presidential bid. It is no stretch to say that the POWs from *Oriskany* and CVW-16 had a greater impact on modern U.S. history than they could have ever imagined while imprisoned in North Vietnam.

16

"Because Our Fathers Lied"

The Vietnam Syndrome—No More Vietnams

THE WAR IN VIETNAM may be over, but it is still being fought over. As those who struggled with the policy decisions during Rolling Thunder came to learn, any dispassionate and objective appraisal on the subject of Vietnam is almost impossible.[1] History continues to show that the arguments made for and against the Vietnam War during that chaotic time continue to resonate in postwar histories. Literary work on the subject is immense. No other conflict in U.S. history has resulted in so many published works assessing and assigning blame or justifying the effort. This is especially true with regard to the air war. All too often, these histories are emotional, anecdotal, and argumentative. They convey the author's polarized passions but do little to explain them. Instead, they follow preconceived personal views or experiences, either dove or hawk, radical leftist or conservative. What does it all mean? What lessons, if any, can be learned?

Forty years after the fall of Saigon, Americans have failed to come to terms with Vietnam because they can agree neither on what happened nor why. The wound still festers. As noted columnist George Will observed, "So powerful were—are—the energies let loose in the sixties that there cannot now be, and may never be, anything like a final summing-up. After all, what is the 'final result' of the Civil War? It is too soon to say."[2]

Conversely, President Johnson's biographer, Robert Caro, noted, "Time equals truth. There is no one truth, but there are an awful lot of objective facts and the more facts you manage to obtain, the closer you will come to whatever truth there is."[3] With Caro's comments in mind, it is possible to examine Rolling Thunder and the American failure in Vietnam. It is beyond the scope of this book to examine and render judgment on all the lessons stemming from this troubled era. However, a cursory examination reveals several objective observations.

The United States failed to stop the Communist takeover of South Vietnam, as well as of neighboring Laos and Cambodia. Some will argue that the United States did not lose the war. While this is true, it is also deceptive. Upon signing the Paris Peace Accords, the United States withdrew all forces but agreed to leave nearly 160,000 North Vietnamese troops in the South. These same critics will point to the success of Operation Linebacker as an example of the success and proper use of airpower, never mind the fact that the war and the stated goals of the Nixon administration were different from Johnson's during Rolling Thunder. While the United States never suffered a defeat in Vietnam, it was certainly not willing to pay the price for victory. This is perhaps the greatest tragedy of Rolling Thunder. The bombings' unintended consequences had a greater impact on the war's outcome than did their declared rationales in 1965. The campaign proved to be a colossal misjudgment, worsened by civilian decision makers.[4] A full-blown air campaign as argued for by Admiral Sharp and the Joint Chiefs likely would not have produced a satisfying conclusion, as the political cost would have been too high both at home and abroad.[5] As it was, Rolling Thunder polarized world opinion against the United States while providing Hanoi with a rallying point for its populace. It also gave the Communists a tremendous bargaining chip with a growing POW population. These effects on American foreign policy with regard to the Defense Secretary Caspar Weinberger and later Gen. Colin Powell doctrines that guided America through the end of the Cold War have been well documented.

Less understood or readily acknowledged is the war's effect on the modern American military. After signing the Paris Peace Accords in 1973, President Nixon did away with the draft and adopted a professional standing military. Prior to assuming command in Vietnam, General Westmoreland had originally favored a volunteer military. By the time he became the Army Chief of Staff, he opposed it. Westmoreland fought with Nixon until he was told, "We are going to have an all-volunteer army, or we're not going to have an army at all."[6] Nixon's impetus for an all-volunteer military was based on the willingness of the aviators flying and fighting in Vietnam.[7] The air war over

North Vietnam was fought by professionals like the men flying from *Oriskany*, who had a vested interest in seeing a successful conclusion to the war. While the United States became further divided over its involvement in Vietnam, the pilots taking part in Rolling Thunder saw the late summer of 1967 as the decisive point of the air campaign. Aviators intensified their efforts, despite the limitations placed on them. Squadrons suffered even more casualties, which caused greater frustration with the war, yet they persisted in their attempts to stop North Vietnam's support of the war in South Vietnam. The controversial conscription during the war, coupled with the efforts of the aviators both in the air and as POWs, gave President Nixon a solid reason to implement the professional military that exists today.

Adopting a volunteer military transformed the U.S. military into a highly trained professional organization. It solved many of the issues that plagued the Vietnam era. Training became a priority. Lessons learned from Rolling Thunder led to the fabled Ault Report and the creation of Top Gun, the Naval Fighter Weapons School. The air force followed with its own weapons school. This led to massive training by both services at secretive, remote training ranges in the western deserts of Nevada and California. The training provided to today's aviators is simply unfathomable to the men who flew in Vietnam.

Only time will tell if the change to a volunteer force is successful. The perceived benefit of an all-volunteer military was the virtual guarantee that future military intervention could never again upset American society and domestic programs. It has inadvertently led to a warrior caste and divorced Americans from their country's foreign policy. In the case of both wars in Iraq and Afghanistan, it led to the very real issue of having a military, but not the populace, at war. The volunteer force succeeded during a time when Johnson and McNamara were trying and failing to protect domestic programs during a time of war.

Domestically, the impacts of Rolling Thunder and the war in Vietnam were equally far reaching. The immense cost of Rolling Thunder as a part of the estimated $167 billion spent on the war dealt an immense blow to the economy. Johnson's decisions to simultaneously finance the war and his Great Society without raising taxes resulted in double-digit inflation and a federal debt that wreaked havoc on the American economy and lowered living standards well into the 1990s.

Politically, Rolling Thunder and Vietnam forever destroyed bipartisanship. They also destroyed Americans' faith in their government, calling into question the integrity, honesty, and competence of its leaders. The Watergate scandal was the final blow.

Despite it all, there is still a positive lesson that can be drawn. Although the experience will forever color the national psyche, the United States can't have another Vietnam, because it has already had it.

Strategic Failures

Though he inherited the budding conflict in Vietnam, President Johnson and his administration are primarily responsible for the decisions that escalated the U.S. military's commitment in Vietnam while at the same time imposing the limits with which that military power could be applied throughout Indochina. It was Johnson and his staff who continually sought the middle ground, trying to look tough on Communism while in reality fighting the war in such a manner that they actually strengthened North Vietnamese resistance.[8] Because Johnson and his staff insisted on such close control, other programs, both foreign and domestic, suffered. Vietnam became all encompassing, overshadowing critical events the administration failed to act upon. The Six-Day War in the summer of 1967 was a case in point. As McNamara struggled with daily targets for Rolling Thunder, the crisis in the Middle East exploded—and we are still living with the consequences today. Rolling Thunder and Vietnam were the products of bad decisions by well-intentioned though arrogant—and ignorant—individuals.[9]

It is unrealistic, however, to blame the Johnson administration for all these failings, as the senior military leadership also deserves a significant portion of the blame. In the books *The Wrong War* by Jeffrey Record and *Dereliction of Duty* by H. R. McMaster, both authors conclude that while the Joint Chiefs of Staff, Pacific Command, and Military Assistance Command Vietnam were not well served by their civilian superiors, they also failed to serve their country well. These men not only supported the administration's decision to enter an open-ended land war in Asia but also submitted, without effective protest, to civilian-imposed restrictions on military operations that they believed would cripple any chance for a decisive end to the war in Vietnam. Rather than confront the White House and the secretary of defense and place their careers on the line, these men chose to go along with civilian decisions they regarded as ruinous to any prospect for victory and as likely to cause an unnecessary loss of American lives. Even worse, they did so knowing that no one in the chain of command was really competent to critique their performance. Neither Johnson nor McNamara had a complete understanding of military affairs, and the chairman of the Joint Chiefs, Gen. Earle Wheeler, had spent his career as a staff officer with no combat acumen.[10]

Military leaders at all levels owe a duty to their troops to use them wisely and not squander their lives. They also have a duty to obey their superiors' orders. Advising elected officials and obeying unwise decisions is a thankless, difficult duty that during the Vietnam War and Operation Rolling Thunder had tragic consequences.[11] Service leadership continually told political leaders that the military could achieve results against a country that presented a poor target for a strategic bombing campaign. These men molded the war to suit their doctrine, viewing the war as a conventional conflict in which the enemy required essential logistical support, not as an insurgency. The United States contributed to its own defeat in Vietnam by fighting the war it wanted to fight, rather than the one at hand.[12] Service leadership fought in Vietnam in the same manner as they learned to fight in World War II, by attempting to wreck the North Vietnamese economy in order to produce a prostrate enemy. They never paused to consider whether or not their perception of the war was correct or if it even conformed to that of the country's civilian leadership.[13] The military was prepared to fight the Soviet Union. Its war strategy, tactics, and weapons were developed and implemented for that purpose. Planning and conducting limited military operations against an insurgency in a Third World country in support of a corrupt, unstable South Vietnamese government with a monolithic mindset doomed American involvement in Vietnam.

This failure of American strategy in Vietnam found its roots in the development of thermonuclear weapons. Many military professionals in the late 1950s and early 1960s believed that previous notions of strategy and force were rendered obsolete by these superweapons. These same strategists believed that the fear of escalating conflicts that could possibly culminate in nuclear war would prevent total war on the scale of World War II. Thus nuclear weapons and the associated premise of limited war had an extremely corrosive effect on the U.S. military, which became focused on defense economics and the attempt to achieve the maximum deterrent at the least cost. Throughout this period, the Department of Defense became preoccupied with technical, managerial, and bureaucratic concerns. It was this preoccupation that led to the sortie counts in the air war and the body counts in South Vietnam—measures of effectiveness that in reality measured very little and reflected America's arrogance during the early stages of its involvement in Vietnam. These numbers became strategic dogma and further served to mask the real American goals. The cost was high. When the country needed it the most, the senior leadership of the military was incapable of providing what the nation needed the most, a coherent national strategy for Southeast Asia.

Ultimately, the American involvement in the Vietnam War was predestined by a vast misjudgment of the character and culture of Southeast Asia, Vietnam, and the Vietnamese. More than any other single factor, it was this blindness that brought the American effort to its disastrous conclusion. Having never really looked at Vietnam for what it was, U.S. leaders never saw, until far too late, either the true nature of the enemy or the fatal weakness of the regime and society they tried, and failed, to save.[14] The American failure in Vietnam was a result of arrogance, hubris, and general faith in America's superior technology to carry the day. This disdain for the difficulties and complexities of the cultures that the United States faced in Vietnam led America to completely misjudge the character of the war. In short, cultural ignorance of Vietnam and Southeast Asia guaranteed American failure.

The failure of American strategy in Vietnam meant that any part of that strategy was doomed to fail, no matter how successful it may have been at the tactical level.[15] This strategic failure was further compounded by the mismanagement and interservice squabbling that typified Rolling Thunder. These failures put American men in a no-win situation, forcing them to make increasingly tough decisions for which there was no good outcome, and the experiences of *Oriskany* and Carrier Air Wing 16 during Rolling Thunder are one of the more tragic examples. The cost of flawed strategic leadership was paid in blood by the men who served in Vietnam and ultimately by the South Vietnamese when America stopped supporting them after the passage of the Church-Case Amendment in June 1973. In reality, it proved to be the beginning of a greater tragedy, as the crisis continued throughout the 1970s. Communism and genocide swept through Laos and the killing fields of Cambodia. Anyone associated with former governments or the military were purged—killed or forced to serve time in reeducation camps. The resultant flood of refugees fleeing this persecution served as a stark reminder of the continued cost of this failure. Noted author and naval aviator Stephen Coonts summarized it best: "The length and scope of America's involvement in Vietnam make it a national disaster. The cost both in human terms and dollars makes it a disgrace."[16]

Appendix 1

1965 WESTPAC

Homeport departure/return: San Diego 5 April 1965–16 December 1965

Seventh Fleet in-chop/out-chop: 27 April 1965–6 December 1965

Port calls: Pearl Harbor 17–20 April; Subic Bay 27 April–4 May; Subic Bay 3–9 June; Yokosuka 24 July–5 August; Subic Bay / Hong Kong 11–29 September; Hong Kong 23–27 October; Subic Bay 27–29 November; Pearl Harbor 10 December

Line periods: 8–31 May; 11 June–18 July; 10 August–10 September; 30 September–18 October; 29 October–25 November

Total: 141 days on the line

Table 1. 1965 Squadrons

Squadron	Aircraft	Call Sign
VMF(AW)-212 (Lancers)	F-8E	Sea Grape
VF-162 (Hunters)	F-8E	Super Heat
VA-163 (Saints)	A-4E	Old Salt
VA-164 (Ghost Riders)	A-4E	Magic Stone
VA-152 (Wild Aces)	A-1H/J	Locket
VAH-4 Det G (Four Runners)	A-3B	Holly Green
VFP-63 Det G (Eyes of the Fleet)	RF-8A	Cork Tip
VAW-11 Det G (Early Elevens)	E-1B	Over Pass
HU-1 Det 1 Unit G (Pacific Fleet Angels)	UH-2A	

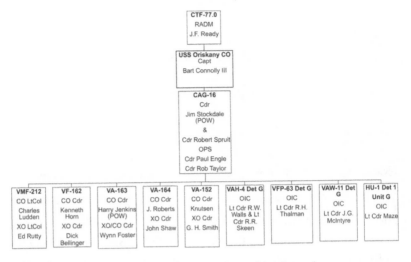

USS *Oriskany* and CVW-16 leadership, 1965. Created by the author.

Combat Losses: 15

26 August 1965

A-1H (139720, AH 592) of VA-152; Lt. (junior grade) Edward Davis, POW

A flight of A-1s was on a nighttime armed reconnaissance mission, looking for trucks along coastal roads close to the DMZ. Near Xuan Noa, 15 miles from the DMZ, the flight lead spotted a suspected truck park and initiated a dive bombing attack. Davis's aircraft was hit by AAA, and he bailed out. His wingman saw no chute or postcrash signal and reported that it was unlikely that Davis had survived. Davis was reported KIA, though he survived and was captured. Davis was repatriated in 1973.

29 August 1965

A-1H (134619, AH 586) of VA-152; Lt. Edd Taylor, KIA

Taylor was shot down by intensive AAA while providing a CAP for a downed F-105F pilot near Son La in RP V. The Skyraider crashed in almost exactly the same spot as the Thunderchief. The Vietnamese had set a trap for Taylor, as the F-105 pilot, Capt. W. D. Sherman, was captured immediately after Taylor was shot down. Taylor's remains were returned in April 2000.

RF-8A (146828, PP 919) of VFP-63; Lt. Henry McWhorter, KIA

McWhorter was killed north of Vinh. He and his wingman encountered heavy AAA at 8,000 feet. After taking evasive action, his wingman reported McWhorter's aircraft flying wings level, without canopy and ejection seat. Damage around the cockpit indicated that AAA may have fired the seat and probably killed the pilot. The landing gear came down as a result of damage to the hydraulic systems, and the aircraft entered a gentle glide until it crashed. McWhorter's remains were returned in February 1987.

6 SEPTEMBER 1965

A-4E (152042, AH475) of VA-164; Lt. James Burton, recovered

Burton's Skyhawk was hit by 37 mm AAA during an air strike against Hai Yen naval base near Thanh Hoa. Burton climbed immediately in order to reach the coast before his engine failed. Ninety seconds later, with fuel streaming and his aircraft on fire, Burton's hydraulics failed, causing him to lose control of the aircraft. He ejected less than 1 mile from shore and was rescued by a HU-16 amphibian.

8 SEPTEMBER 1965

RF-8A (146825, PP 918) of VFP-63; Lt. (junior grade) Robert Rudolph, KIA

Oriskany lost its second photo Crusader when Rudolph was hit by AAA while looking for SAM sites near Thanh Hoa. Soon after crossing the coast he and his wingman were targeted. His wingman watched Rudolph roll inverted and the canopy fall away but lost sight of him due to his own evasive maneuvering. He was unable to see if Rudolph ejected before crashing 15 miles northeast of Thanh Hoa. Though SAR efforts were launched, they were unsuccessful. Rudolph's remains were returned in December 1988.

9 SEPTEMBER 1965

A-4E (151134, AH352) of VA-163; Cdr. James Stockdale, POW

When weather precluded a strike against the Thanh Hoa bridge, Stockdale ordered his flight after secondary targets. He and Cdr. Wynn Foster decided to bomb railroad sidings 15 miles south of Thanh Hoa. After making his first pass, Stockdale was hit by 57 mm AAA. Due to his low altitude, Stockdale ejected, landing in the village of Tin Gia, and was immediately captured. Stockdale was repatriated in 1973 and later awarded the Medal of Honor for leading the American POW resistance.

5 OCTOBER 1965

F-8E (150848, AH 227) of VF-162; Lt. (junior grade) Rick Adams, recovered

Cdr. Richard Bellinger and his wingman, Adams, were flying BAR-CAP during a strike on a bridge near Kep. While crossing the coast at 30,000 feet, east of Haiphong, Bellinger saw two SAMs streaking toward them. Although he radioed a warning, Adams never heard it and took no evasive action. One of the missiles exploded just behind Adams's aircraft, causing damage to the tail surfaces and a fire in the fuselage. Adams flew his damaged Crusader 40 miles before it eventually exploded. He ejected through the inferno and was rescued by a helicopter and flown to USS *Galveston* (CLG-3) for medical attention.

31 OCTOBER 1965

A-4E (151173, AH 466) of VA-164; Lt. Cdr. Richard Powers, KIA

The increasing SAM threat caused the air force and navy to cooperate in an effort to find a solution. *Oriskany* detached two RWR equipped A-4s to Takhli to fly as pathfinders for F-105s. Powers led eight F-105s on a strike against a SAM site near Kep as part of a larger mission involving sixty-five air force and navy airplanes. While bombing the SAM site, his aircraft was hit and burst into flames. He climbed and banked suddenly, ejecting at less than 200 feet. Although captured by Vietnamese, nearby PRC troops overpowered them and executed Powers. He received the Navy Cross for this mission. Powers's remains were returned by the North Vietnamese in November 1987.

5 NOVEMBER 1965

F-8E (150665, WD 106) of VMF(AW)-212; Capt. Harlan Chapman, POW

VMF(AW)-212 lost its first pilot while bombing a bridge at Hai Duoung, 30 miles east of Hanoi. Chapman's F-8 took a direct hit from 57 mm AAA during his dive. As the aircraft began tumbling, Chapman's shoulder was dislocated. In spite of this, he was able to eject and was photographed descending in his chute by an RF-8A during its reconnaissance pass. Enemy defenses made a rescue impossible. He was immediately captured, becoming the first marine POW in North Vietnam. Chapman was repatriated in February 1973.

7 November 1965

A-4E (150071, AH 343) of VA-163; Lt. Cdr. Charlie Wack, recovered

A flight of *Oriskany* A-4s attacked a SAM site 10 miles southwest of Nam Dinh. Wack was hit by AAA during his dive. He continued his bombing run and managed to fly 12 miles out to sea before ejecting. Wack was picked up by an HU-16 amphibian. He received the Silver Star for this mission.

9 November 1965

A-1H (137566, AH 590) of VA-152; Lt. Cdr. Paul Merchant, recovered

A section of A-1s were on a nighttime armed reconnaissance mission when they found trucks 35 miles southeast of Vinh. During the attack Merchant was hit by AAA that damaged his engine. He jettisoned his ordnance and flew toward the gulf. After his engine failed, he glided the remainder of the distance, ditching his aircraft in the dark just off the coast. He was rescued by a UH-2 Seasprite from USS *Gridley* (DLG-21) just as North Vietnamese boats arrived to capture him.

13 November 1965

A-4E (151067, AH 340) of VA-163; Cdr. Harry Jenkins, POW

Jenkins and his wingman, Lt. (junior grade) Vance Schufeldt were searching for supplies on a river near Dong Hoi. As the river appeared unnavigable, they decided to bomb a nearby road junction. While en route to their new target, they flew over the village of Xuan Noa and spotted signs of recent vehicle activity. While flying low to inspect the area, Jenkins was hit by 37 mm AAA. He immediately lost control and ejected. Though SAR efforts were attempted, he was captured immediately. All four of the A-1s that took part in the SAR effort were damaged by small arms fire. Jenkins was repatriated in February 1973.

17 November 1965

F-8E (150675, WD 103) of VMF(AW)-212; Capt. Ross Chaimson, recovered

On 17 November *Oriskany*, along with other carriers, went back
to the Hai Duong bridge with disastrous results. Within thirty
minutes, CVW-16 lost three of the four planes lost on this strike.
Numerous others received significant damage and were able to
fly back to *Oriskany*. After previously surviving a ramp strike in
October, Chaimson's F-8 was the first aircraft lost. Hit by 37 mm
AAA during his bomb run, his electrical system failed, and he was
unable to release his bombs. Even though he deployed his emergency backup generator, it failed to work. As he flew back alone,
he attempted to land on USS *Bon Homme Richard* but ran out of
fuel before he was able to. Chaimson was recovered by a UH-2 Seasprite from the carrier.

A-4E (151083, AH 350) of VA-163; *Lt. Cdr. Roy Hap Bowling,* KIA

Bowling was the pilot of the second aircraft lost by *Oriskany* on this
mission. The operations officer of VA-163, he had just dropped a load
of Mk-82 Snake Eye bombs on the bridge and was flying a low-level,
high-speed egress when his aircraft was hit by AAA. The horizontal tail
plane departed his aircraft, and he rolled to the right and impacted the
ground. Amazingly enough, Bowling managed to eject but did not
survive the ejection. Bowling's remains were returned to a presidential commission visiting Hanoi in March 1977.

A-1H (135244, AH 588) of VA-152; *Lt. Cdr. Jesse Taylor,* KIA

Twenty-five minutes after Bowling crashed, a section of A-1s from
Oriskany arrived to provide RESCAP. One of the Skyraiders was piloted
by the CVW-16 operations officer, Taylor, who volunteered to fly the mission. He was struck by AAA while searching for Bowling. He attempted
to fly back to sea but crashed in coastal marshes southwest of Haiphong.
Taylor was posthumously awarded the Navy Cross for this mission,
and USS *Jesse Taylor* (FFG-50) was named after him. Taylor's remains
were returned by North Vietnam in December 1975.

Operational Losses: 9

27 FEBRUARY 1965

F-8E (BuNo Unknown) of VMF(AW)-212; *1st Lt. Glenn Bollenbach, recovered*

A-4E (151171) of VA-164, *Lt. James Burton, recovered*

Bollenbach had a midair collision with a flight of A-4 Skyhawks during a flight in marginal weather. Burton ejected and was recovered. Bollenbach landed at NAS Miramar with a damaged wing.

16 MAY 1965

F-8E (150931) of VF-162; Maj. Robert Bell, KIA

Bell, an air force pilot on an exchange tour with VF-162, was killed during a tragic accident at Bien Hoa air base. Following a CAS mission over South Vietnam, Bell had a hung bomb, which prevented him from landing aboard *Oriskany*, and he diverted to Bien Hoa to have it downloaded. His Crusader was parked adjacent to several rows of B-57B Canberra bombers, each loaded with bombs for upcoming missions. For unknown reasons, one of these bomb-laden Canberras exploded. The rest quickly followed, with explosions rocking the flight line. Ten B-57s were destroyed, as well as Bell's F-8 and fifteen A-1s. More than thirty helicopters and A-1s were damaged by the flying debris. Twenty-seven men, including Bell, were killed.

25 MAY 1965

A-3B (138947, ZB610) of VAH-4; Lt. Cdr. Richard Walls (Pilot), recovered, Lt. (junior grade) Jerry Adams (BN), recovered; Lt. (junior grade) Ignatus Signorelli (3CM), recovered, Lt. (junior grade) Frank Tunic (4CM), recovered

Walls and his crew were launching on a tanker mission when the catapult bridle hook broke during the catapult shot. The Skywarrior trundled down the deck and over the bow. A previous wheels-up landing in November 1962 had caused a hook fracture that went undetected until this mishap. Both Walls and Adams broke their legs in the incident. *Oriskany*'s Seasprite picked up three crew members, while the fourth was rescued by USS *Boyd* (DD-544). Tunic was ship's company.

30 JUNE 1965

A-1H (139708, AH588) of VA-152; Lt. Cdr. Eric Schade Jr., recovered

The engine failed on Schade's A-1 as he was being catapulted off the ship for a strike mission. He escaped the sinking aircraft and was picked up by USS *Perkins* (DD-877), which returned him in exchange for 35 gallons of ice cream.

18 July 1965

A-4E (151089, AH346) of VA-163; Lt. Art Avore, KIA

The engine of Avore's Skyhawk failed as he was catapulted off *Oriskany* for a mission over South Vietnam. The aircraft sank within seconds, and he was unable to escape.

21 July 1965

A-1H (139636, AH 589) of VA-152; Lt. Edd Taylor, recovered

Taylor bailed out of his A-1 when the engine failed during a check flight following maintenance. Taylor came down 10 miles from the ship and was recovered by *Oriskany*'s Seasprite. Taylor was killed during a CSAR mission on 29 August.

10 August 1965

A-1J (142012, AH 586) of VA-152; Lt. (junior grade) Lawrence Mailhes, KIA

Mailhes failed to return from a night RESCAP mission over the Gulf of Tonkin near Tiger Island. The cause of his loss was never discovered, and his remains were never recovered

17 October 1965

F-8E (149198, WD 105) of VMF(AW)-212; Capt. Ross Chaimson, recovered

This was the first of four aircraft lost by VMF(AW)-212. Chaimson struck the ramp while attempting to land following a BARCAP mission at night and in bad weather. Exactly a month later, he ejected from another F-8.

17 November 1965

F-8E (150875, WD 113) of VMF(AW)-212; 1st Lt. Gary Peil, recovered

In addition to the terrible losses incurred by CVW-16 on their Hai Duong mission, they lost another aircraft that evening, the second of the day for VMF(AW)-212. Similar to Chaimson's incident a month prior, Peil struck the pitching flight deck at night and in bad weather following a night BARCAP. Luckily, Peil survived the accident and was picked up by whaleboat from USS *McKean* (DD-784). Peil spent almost twenty-five minutes in the water and nearly succumbed to exhaustion while trying to disentangle himself from his parachute before he was rescued.

Personnel Casualties

Airman John Federico of VF-162 was accidentally wounded by 20 mm fire from an F-8 in April. Ordnancemen had failed to de-arm the aircraft, and while sailors performed maintenance, the guns fired. Federico had bullets pass through both his forearms, though they miraculously missed hitting his torso. Federico was sent to Clark AFB and then on to the United States to recover.

Airman Tom Prezorski of VA-163 drowned after being blown overboard during flight operations on 5 May 1965.

Damaged Aircraft

17 May 1965

F-8E (150346, WD112) of VMF(AW)-212; Pilot Unknown

Lost LAU-33 pod during the catapult launch, damaging the unit horizontal tail (UHT).

21 May 1965

A-1H (139610) of VA-152; pilot unknown

Hit by ground fire over South Vietnam.

14 June 1965

A-4E (151083, AH350) of VA-163; pilot unknown

Hit by ground fire over South Vietnam.

A-4E (151055) of VA-163; pilot unknown

Hit by ground fire over South Vietnam.

17 June 1965

F-8E (150672) of VF-162; pilot unknown

Hit by ground fire over South Vietnam. Aircraft required depot repair at NAS Cubi Point.

19 June 1965

A-4E (151194) of VA-164; pilot unknown

Hit by ground fire.

A-1J (142051) of VA-152; pilot unknown

Hit by ground fire.

24 June 1965

A-1H (137502) of VA-152; pilot unknown

Hit by ground fire.

25 June 1965

F-8E (150913) of VMF(AW)-212; pilot unknown

Hit by ground fire, causing a dent in the left fuselage below the cockpit.

30 June 1965

F-8E (150913, WD 104) of VMF(AW)-212; Capt. Ross Chaimson

After the Alpha strike against the Vinh airfield, Chaimson was unable to extend his nose gear. He made an emergency landing at Da Nang, causing extensive damage to the intake. The aircraft was left in Da Nang.

A-1H (139702) of VA-152; pilot unknown

Hit by ground fire.

2 July 1965

A-4E (BuNo unknown) of VA-163; Lt. (junior grade) Dick Pennington

Hit by AAA during Nam Dinh oil facility strike. Shell removed top 6 inches of tail.

12 July 1965

A-4E (151179) of VA-164; pilot unknown

Hit by ground fire.

10 August 1965

A-4E (151187) of VA-164; Cdr. James Stockdale

Hit by AAA during a strike on Son La army barracks. Significant damage to the starboard wing.

11 August 1965

A-1H (137576) of VA-152; pilot unknown

Hit by ground fire. Minor injuries.

15 August 1965

F-8E (150306, WD 115) of VMF(AW)-212; pilot unknown

Aircraft hit by ground fire, causing a large hole in the bottom fuselage.

20 August 1965

F-8E (150344, WD113) of VMF(AW)-212; pilot unknown

Aircraft hit by ground fire. Small hole in starboard droop.

23 August 1965

A-4E (151183) of VA-164; Lt. (junior grade) Ken Kreutzman

Hit by ground fire during the strike of a suspected SAM site near Kep, causing significant damage to the starboard wing.

A-4E (BuNo unknown) of VA-163; Lt. (junior grade) Charlie Stender

Hit by 57 mm AAA during a strike of a suspected SAM site near Kep. The shell traveled down the intake, destroying the engine. Stender flew his burning aircraft back to the *Oriskany*. The airplane was craned off for depot repair at Cubi Point.

A-4E (BuNo unknown) of VA-163; Lt. Cdr. Bill Smith

Hit by AAA during a strike of a suspected SAM site near Kep, causing significant damage to the starboard wing.

A-4E (BuNo unknown) of VA-163; Lt. (junior grade) John Shore

Hit by 57 mm AAA during a strike of a suspected SAM site near Kep. Shell hit just behind canopy but did not explode.

A-4E (BuNo unknown) of VA-163; pilot unknown

Hit by AAA during the strike of a suspected SAM site near Kep, causing significant damage to the starboard wing.

F-8E (150340, WD114) of VMF(AW)-212; pilot unknown

Aircraft hit by AAA. During recovery, pilot overstressed port droop, outer wing panel, and starboard droop.

25 August 1965

F-8E (150902, WD114) of VMF(AW)-212; pilot unknown

Hit by ground fire, damaging port fuselage, fuel cell, and engine.

F-8E (149198, WD105) of VMF(AW)-212; pilot unknown

Hit by ground fire, causing damage to starboard outer wing panel.

31 August 1965

F-8E (150932, WD101) of VMF(AW)-212; pilot unknown

Hit by ground fire while strafing PT boats. A bullet hit the metal frame and ricocheted out of the cockpit, shattering the windscreen.

F-8E (150665, WD106) of VMF(AW)-212; pilot unknown

Hit by ground fire while strafing PT boats, damaging the port droop.

2 SEPTEMBER 1965

F-8E (150921) of VF-162; pilot unknown

Hit by ground fire.

4 SEPTEMBER 1965

F-8E (150925, WD103) of VMF(AW)-212; Lt. Col. Charles Ludden

Hit by AAA while strafing a gun emplacement on the coast at Cape Falaise. The Crusader took hits in the nose, wing, and cockpit. Ludden received serious shrapnel wounds in the face, arms, and leg, rendering him momentarily unconscious. Small fragments penetrated his visor and lodged in Ludden's left eyeball and orbital area of the right eye. He regained consciousness and control of the aircraft at approximately 500 feet, although Ludden overstressed the Crusader, causing serious damage. Ludden made it back to *Oriskany*, where he was grounded through the remainder of the line period. Aircraft required repair at Cubi Point depot.

5 SEPTEMBER 1965

F-8E (150654, WD107) of VMF(AW)-212; pilot unknown

Hit by ground fire, causing damage to starboard landing gear door, fuselage, and UHT.

6 SEPTEMBER 1965

A-4E (BuNo unknown) of VA-163; Cdr. Harry Jenkins

Hit by enemy ground fire, causing major damage. Aircraft was stricken.

5 OCTOBER 1965

A-1H (BuNo unknown) of VA-152; pilot unknown

Hit by enemy ground fire.

F-8E (BuNo Unknown) of VF-162; pilot unknown

Hit by 100 mm AAA during armed reconnaissance mission.

7 October 1965

A-4E (151162) of VA-164; pilot unknown

Hit by ground fire, causing major damage.

F-8E (149192, WDIII) of VMF(AW)-212; pilot unknown

Hit by AAA. Hole in port wing. Aircraft required depot repair at NAS Cubi Point.

F-8E (150913) of VMF(AW)-212; pilot unknown

Hit by AAA, damaging starboard fuselage and forward fuel tank.

9 October 1965

F-8E (150926, WD102) of VMF(AW)-212; pilot unknown

Hit by ground fire. Shell trajectory took it through the bottom right-hand side of intake through the top. Aircraft required depot repair at NAS Cubi Point.

10 October 1965

A-4E (BuNo Unknown) of VA-163; pilot unknown

Hit by 85 mm AAA while attacking bridge near Nga Son on Highway 10.

12 October 1965

A-4E (151157) of VA-164; pilot unknown

Hit by ground fire.

13 October 1965

A-4 (BuNo unknown) of VA-163; pilot unknown

Hit by ground fire while attacking trucks near Ninh Binh.

15 October 1965

A-4 (BuNo unknown) of VA-163; pilot unknown

Hit by ground fire while attacking a bridge on Highway 1A.

17 October 1965

F-8E (150875, WD113) of VMF(AW)-212; pilot unknown

Hit by ground fire, damaging leading edge of vertical stabilizer.

F-8E (150344) of VMF(AW)-212; pilot unknown

Hit by enemy ground fire, damaging starboard fuselage electrical compartment.

F-8E (150306, WD115) of VMF(AW)-212; pilot unknown

Hit by ground fire. Damage to starboard fuselage.

A-4E (BuNo unknown) of VA-163; pilot unknown

Hit by ground fire during RESCAP.

A-4E (BuNo unknown) of VA-163; pilot unknown

Hit by ground fire.

A-4E (BuNo unknown) of VA-163; pilot unknown

Hit by 85 mm AAA during an Alpha strike in Thai Nguyen province.

18 OCTOBER 1965

A-1J (142051) of VA-152; pilot unknown

Hit by ground fire, causing substantial damage.

31 OCTOBER 1965

F-8E (150902, WD104) of VMF(AW)-212; pilot unknown

Hit by AAA, causing damage to tail. Shell fragments also penetrated afterburner, necessitating replacement.

F-8E (150913) of VMF(AW)-212; pilot unknown

Hit by AAA, damaging port fuselage, fuel cell, and engine. Aircraft required depot repair at NAS North Island.

F-8E (150340) of VMF(AW)-212; pilot unknown

Hit by ground fire.

A-4E (151152) of VA-164; Lt. John Davis

Hit by ground fire during low-level Alpha strike on bridge at Bac Giang. Small arms fire destroyed the refueling probe tip.

A-1H (BuNo unknown) of VA-152; pilot unknown

Hit by ground fire while performing RESCAP for Alpha strike at Bac Giang.

F-8E (BuNo unknown) of VF-162; pilot unknown

Hit by ground fire while performing TARCAP for Alpha strike at Bac Giang.

A-4E (BuNo unknown) of VA-163; pilot unknown

Hit by ground fire on flak suppression run during Alpha strike at Bac Giang.

1 November 1965

A-4E (151194) of VA-164; pilot unknown

Hit by ground fire, causing major damage.

2 November 1965

A-4E (151159) of VA-164; pilot unknown

Hit by ground fire, causing major damage.

3 November 1965

A-4E (BuNo unknown) of VA-164; pilot unknown

Hit by ground fire during armed reconnaissance mission near Bac Giang.

5 November 1965

F-8E (150902, WD104) of VMF(AW)-212; pilot unknown

Hit by ground fire during Alpha strike on Hai Duong, damaging outer wing.

F-8E (150654, WD107) of VMF(AW)-212; pilot unknown

Hit by AAA during Alpha strike on Hai Duong, damaging port main landing gear and gear door.

A-4E (BuNo unknown) of VA-164; pilot unknown

Hit by 85 mm AAA during Alpha strike on Hai Duong.

A-4E (BuNo unknown) of VA-164; pilot unknown

Hit by ground fire during Alpha strike on Hai Duong.

A-4E (BuNo unknown) of VA-163; pilot unknown

Hit by ground fire during Alpha strike on Hai Duong.

7 November 1965

A-1H (134563, AH584) of VA-152; Lt. Gordon Wileen

Hit by AAA during CSAR. Wileen lost his hydraulics and was unable to lower the landing gear. He made a wheels-up landing at Da Nang.

8 November 1965

F-8E (150902) of VMF(AW)-212; pilot unknown

Lost LAU-33 pod on the catapult shot, damaging the UHT.

A-4E (BuNo unknown) of VA-164; pilot unknown

Hit by AAA during strike on Uong Bi.

9 November 1965

A-4E (BuNo unknown) of VA-163; pilot unknown

Hit by ground fire during armed reconnaissance mission near Hoa Binh.

F-8E (BuNo Unknown) of VMF(AW)-212; pilot unknown

Hit by 37 mm AAA.

10 November 1965

F-8E (150654, WD107) of VMF(AW)-212; pilot unknown

Hit by AAA, damaging port ventral fin and fuel cell.

12 November 1965

A-4E (BuNo unknown) of VA-164; pilot unknown

Hit by AAA during Alpha strike on Nam Sach bridge in Hai Duong province.

13 November 1965

A-1H (137520) of VA-152; pilot unknown

Hit by ground fire, causing substantial damage.

A-1H (139810) of VA-152; pilot unknown

Hit by ground fire, causing substantial damage.

A-1H (135244, AH588) of VA-152; pilot unknown

Hit by ground fire, causing substantial damage.

A-1H (134515) of VA-152; pilot unknown

Hit by ground fire, causing substantial damage.

A-4E (BuNo unknown, AH460) of VA-164; pilot unknown

Hit by ground fire.

17 November 1965

A-1H (139695, AH591) of VA-152; Lt. Cdr. Eric Schade

Hit by AAA while performing RESCAP for Bowling following the Hai Duong raid. Damage to port wing included twenty-five holes. Subsequent hard landing on *Oriskany* further damaged the aircraft, and it was stricken from the records.

F-8E (149153, WDIII) of VMF(AW)-212; Capt. Samuel Dolan

Hit by AAA during the strike on Hai Duong bridge. Shell fragments damaged Dolan's hydraulic lines, making operation of the variable incidence wing and in-flight refueling impossible. With a perilously low fuel state, a landing aboard ship was the only option. Fast approach speeds resulted in an exceptionally hard landing, which destroyed the fuselage fuel tank and various fuel lines and control cables. Aircraft craned off for depot repair at NAS Cubi Point. Dolan was injured during the hard landing.

F-8E (150902, WDII4) of VMF(AW)-212; pilot unknown

Hit by ground fire, causing damage to port electrical equipment compartment.

F-8E (150340) of VMF(AW)-212; pilot unknown

Hit by ground fire, causing damage to port wing tip.

A-4E (BuNo unknown, AH341) of VA-163; pilot unknown

Hit by ground fire.

A-4E (BuNo unknown, AH349) of VA-163; pilot unknown

Hit by ground fire.

A-4E (BuNo unknown, AH460) of VA-164; pilot unknown

Hit by ground fire.

18 NOVEMBER 1965

A-IH (BuNo unknown) of VA-152; pilot unknown

Hit by ground fire during an armed reconnaissance mission in Quang Binh province.

21 NOVEMBER 1965

A-4E (BuNo unknown) of VA-163; pilot unknown

Hit by ground fire while attacking trucks during an armed reconnaissance mission near Nghe An.

A-1 (BuNo unknown) of VA-152; pilot unknown

Hit by ground fire while attacking a bridge in Thanh Hoa province.

A-4E (BuNo unknown) of VA-164; pilot unknown

Hit by ground fire while attacking a road north of Bac Giang pass in Laos.

23 NOVEMBER 1965

F-8E (BuNo unknown) of VF-162; pilot unknown

Hit by ground fire during weather reconnaissance mission over Haiphong harbor.

25 NOVEMBER 1965

F-8E (149190) of VMF(AW)-212; pilot unknown

Hit by ground fire while attacking bridge at Dong Trieu in Quang Ninh province. Destroyed starboard UHT.

Appendix 2

1966 WESTPAC

Homeport departure/return: Alameda 26 May 1966–16 November 1966

Seventh Fleet in-chop/out-chop: 11 June 1966–8 November 1966

Port calls: Pearl Harbor 1–6 June; Yokosuka 14–21 June; Subic Bay 26–27 June; Subic Bay 30 July–5 August; Subic Bay 10–15 September; Hong Kong 17–23 September; Subic Bay 28 October–3 November

Line periods: 30 June; 8–27 July; 6 August–7 September; 24 September–26 October

Total: 87 days on the line

Table 2. 1966 Squadrons

Squadron	Aircraft	Call Sign
VF-111 (Sundowners)	F-8E	Old Nick
VF-162 (Hunters)	F-8E	Super Heat
VA-163 (Saints)	A-4E	Old Salt
VA-164 (Ghost Riders)	A-4E	Magic Stone
VA-152 (Wild Aces)	A-1H/J	Locket
VAH-4 Det G (Four Runners)	A-3B	Holly Green
VFP-63 Det G (Eyes of the Fleet)	RF-8A	Cork Tip
VAW-11 Det G (Early Elevens)	E-1B	Over Pass
HU-1 Det 1 Unit G (Pacific Fleet Angels)	UH-2A	

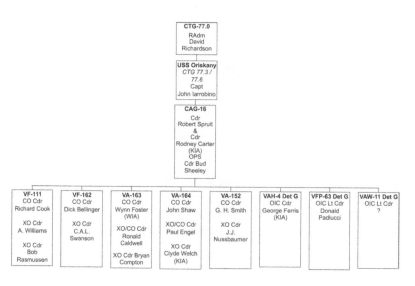

VF-111 CO Cdr Richard Cook XO Cdr A. Williams XO Cdr Bob Rasmussen	VF-162 CO Cdr Dick Bellinger XO Cdr C.A.L. Swanson	VA-163 CO Cdr Wynn Foster (WIA) XO/CO Cdr Ronald Caldwell XO Cdr Bryan Compton	VA-164 CO Cdr John Shaw XO/CO Cdr Paul Engel XO Cdr Clyde Welch (KIA)	VA-152 CO Cdr G. H. Smith XO Cdr J.J. Nussbaumer	VAH-4 Det G OIC Cdr George Ferris (KIA)	VFP-63 Det G OIC Lt Cdr Donald Padlucci	VAW-11 Det G OIC Lt Cdr ?

USS *Oriskany* and CVW-16 leadership, 1966. Created by the author.

Combat Losses: 16

12 JULY 1966

F-8E (15092, AH 203) of VF-162; Lt. (junior grade) Rick Adams, recovered

Adams was flying TARCAP during a strike on the Dong Nham POL facility 20 miles northeast of Haiphong. SAMs forced the strike into small arms range, and his aircraft was hit in the tailpipe by small arms fire. The fire spread quickly through the entire aircraft, forcing him to eject. He was picked up by an SH-3 Sea King after spending forty-five minutes on the ground. Adams had been shot down by a SAM during the 1965 cruise and thus became the first aviator to survive being shot down twice. As a result he was reassigned to a stateside post.

14 JULY 1966

F-8E (150908, AH 202) of VF-162; Cdr. Richard Bellinger, recovered

Bellinger, the commanding officer of VF-162, was shot down by a MiG-17 flown by Ngo Duc Mai while escorting an air strike against storage facilities at Nam Dinh. His flight of three F-8s was engaged by MiG-17s 25 miles south of Hanoi. The starboard wing of his Crusader was badly damaged by cannon fire. When his hydraulics failed, he diverted to Da Nang rather than attempt a landing aboard

Oriskany. Unable to in-flight refuel, he ejected after running out of fuel 16 miles from Da Nang. Bellinger was rescued by an HH-43 Husky from Da Nang.

19 JULY 1966

F-8E (150919, AH 210) of VF-162; Lt. Terry Dennison, KIA

Dennison was flying TARCAP for a strike against the heavily defended Co Trai bridge when he was hit by an SA-2. Over thirteen missiles were fired during the raid, and his aircraft was hit at 12,000 feet and immediately destroyed. The wreckage came down near Hoang Xa, 18 miles south of Hanoi. Dennison's remains were returned in March 1974.

23 JULY 1966

A-4E (152100, AH 301) of VA-163; Cdr. Wynn Foster, recovered

Foster, the commanding officer of VA-163, was leading an armed reconnaissance mission against a POL storage site 7 miles north of Vinh when he was hit in the cockpit by a 57 mm shell. Shrapnel from the shell destroyed the cockpit and severed his right arm just below the shoulder. Bleeding profusely and losing consciousness, Foster managed to fly his crippled aircraft out to sea and eject over the SAR destroyer, USS *Reeves* (DLG-24). He was rescued by a boat from the destroyer. Foster was evacuated from there to *Oriskany* and eventually stateside.

28 JULY 1966

A-4E (152077, AH 407) of VA-164; Ens. George McSwain, POW

McSwain was on an Iron Hand mission to destroy a SAM site reported at the mouth of the Song Ca River near Vinh. After firing his Shrike missiles at the site, McSwain began climbing to regain altitude. After reaching 12,000 feet, his airspeed had diminished to less than 200 knots when an explosion rocked his aircraft. The aircraft fell out of control, possibly as a result of its stalling. The North Vietnamese claimed that an AAA battery protecting a SAM site downed his aircraft. McSwain was released from captivity in March 1973.

7 AUGUST 1966

A-1H (139701, AH 501) of VA-152; Lt. Charles Fryer, KIA

Fryer was hit in the port wing by small arms fire while strafing a train during an armed reconnaissance mission 35 miles north of Vinh, near

Qui Vinh. Although he reached the coast, Fryer did not survive the ditching off Cape Bouton.

11 AUGUST 1966

F-8E (150880, AH 112) of VF-111; Lt. (junior grade) Cody Balisteri, recovered

Balisteri was on an armed reconnaissance flight over coastal islands when his F-8 was hit by ground fire 10 miles south of Hon Gai. The aircraft immediately caught fire, and Balisteri ejected when it became uncontrollable. He was picked up by an SH-3 Sea King from HS-6.

13 AUGUST 1966

F-8E (150866, AH 113) of VF-111; Lt. Cdr. Norm Levy, recovered

Levy was on an armed reconnaissance mission when he was shot down in the same area as Balisteri. AAA hit Levy's Crusader as he attacked fuel barges. Without hydraulics, his aircraft became uncontrollable, and he ejected. He was rescued 5 miles east of Dao Cat Ba by an SH-3 Sea King from HS-6.

18 AUGUST 1966

F-8E (150300, AH 211) of VF-162; Lt. Cdr. Demetrio "Butch" Verich, recovered

Verich was hit during an armed reconnaissance mission 15 miles northwest of Vinh. He was pulling up from his third bombing run on a bridge and barges on a river when he was hit by small arms fire. He flew toward the coast, and when his aircraft became uncontrollable, he ejected just offshore. He was rescued by a HC-1 SH-2 Seasprite from USS *Halsey* (DLG-23).

28 AUGUST 1966

A-1H (135231, AH 506) of VA-152; Cdr. Gordon H. Smith, recovered

Smith, the commanding officer of VA-152, was hit by AAA while flying along the coastline near Van Yen, 25 miles south of Thanh Hoa. Hit in the fuselage, his A-1 began burning rapidly. He bailed out but struck the tail as he fell away from the Skyraider. Fortunately, his parachute deployed before Smith hit the water, and he was picked up by an HC-1 Seasprite from USS *Halsey* (DLG-23).

31 AUGUST 1966

RF-8G (146874, AH 602) of VFP-63; Lt. Cdr. Tom Tucker, recovered

The officer-in-charge of VFP-63's detachment was shot down while attempting to photograph a foreign oil tanker and other ships in Haiphong harbor. As he approached Quang Yen, 5 miles northeast of Haiphong, his aircraft was hit by 37 mm AAA. Tucker lost control and ejected only 1,500 feet over Haiphong Harbor. He landed in a shipping channel less than 150 yards from the shore. An SH-3 from USS *Kearsarge* flew at less than 50 feet and under constant fire from vessels and shore batteries to attempt the rescue. The operation was successful, and Tucker was recovered in one of the most dangerous and highly photographed rescue missions of the war.

5 SEPTEMBER 1966

F-8E (150896, AH 106) of VF-111; Capt. Wilfred Abbott (USAF), POW

Abbott's section of Crusaders was attacked by two MiG-17s of the 923rd Fighter Regiment (FR) near Ninh Binh. Although the North Vietnamese claimed both aircraft, only Abbott's aircraft was shot down. His right leg was broken during the ejection, and although it was operated on by the North Vietnamese, it took over two years to heal. He was repatriated in March 1973.

6 OCTOBER 1966

F-8E (150924, AH 201) of VF-162; Lt. Cdr. Richard Leach, recovered

Leach was escorting an RF-8 Crusader during a reconnaissance mission over Hon Gai harbor. Midway through the mission, his low fuel light came on as the result of a fuel leak. Both aircraft immediately flew toward the sea, but Leach ejected after running out of fuel 70 miles south of Hon Gai. He was recovered by a navy helicopter.

8 OCTOBER 1966

A-1H (137629, AH 510) of VA-152; Lt. Jack Feldhaus, MIA

During an armed reconnaissance mission 25 miles southwest of Thanh Hoa, both Feldhaus and Lt. (junior grade) Fred Guenzel were hit by extremely heavy ground fire as they entered heavy clouds. Feldhaus radioed that he'd been hit by ground fire and that his right wing was on fire. Guenzel never saw Feldhaus again, though he reported a fireball on the ground that he believed to be an aircraft crash. Feldhaus's last radio transmission was a garbled "I'm getting out." Guenzel and another aircraft searched the area amid increasing ground fire and deteriorating weather without success. They saw no parachute and heard no emergency signals. Surveillance continued during the succeeding days but revealed nothing. Feldhaus was declared MIA. In 1977 the secretary of the navy issued a presumptive finding of death. Feldhaus's remains were recovered in June 2000.

12 OCTOBER 1966

A-4E (152075, AH 411) of VA-164; Lt. Frank Elkins, MIA

Elkins was on a nighttime armed reconnaissance mission when his section was engaged by a SAM site near Tho Trang, 45 miles southwest of Thanh Hoa. Elkins saw the missile launch and began evasive maneuvering. He was either hit by the SA-2 or impacted the ground while trying to outmaneuver the SAM. In 1990 Elkins's remains were returned by the Vietnamese.

14 OCTOBER 1966

A-1H (139731, AH 511) of VA-152; Ens. Darwin Thomas, KIA

Thomas was on a nighttime armed reconnaissance mission 25 miles southwest of Thanh Hoa when his section spotted several trucks. He began his rocket attack and was killed when he failed to pull out of his dive. His remains have not been recovered.

Operational Losses: 14

11 APRIL 1966

A-4E (150137) of VA-163; Ens. Daniel Kapner, KIA

Kapner was killed during a training flight shortly before the 1966 deployment. During a long-range strike from *Oriskany* to Marine Corps Air Station Yuma, Arizona, he became fixated on his target and flew into the ground.

10 JUNE 1966

A-4E (151085) of VA-163; Lt. Cdr. John Miles, recovered

VA-163 lost its second jet during *Oriskany*'s transit when Miles ejected during aerial refueling west of Hawaii. Fuel streamed out of the refueling basket and was sucked down Miles's engine, where it exploded. Miles ejected into the Pacific and was rescued by *Oriskany*'s Seasprite.

29 July 1966

A-4E (152095) of VA-164; Lt. (junior grade) Donovan Ewoldt, KIA

Ewoldt was killed in between line periods in a tragic training accident. He flew into the water while attempting in-flight refueling at night in marginal weather.

23 August 1966

F-8E (150907, AH101) of VF-111; Lt. (junior grade) Rich Meadows, recovered

Beginning 23 August, there was a string of five accidents in four days involving *Oriskany* aircraft. Meadows launched at midnight for a BAR-CAP mission. His engine failed shortly after launching, forcing him to eject. At 0011, USS *Frank E. Evans* (DD-754) was sent to investigate a flare fired by Meadows. He was recovered by a helicopter from the destroyer after spending twenty minutes in the water and returned to *Oriskany* at 0655.

25 August 1966

A-4E (152084, AH401) of VA-164; Lt. (junior grade) William Bullard, KIA

Bullard was killed when his aircraft flew into water following a night catapult shot. He was launching on a nighttime armed reconnaissance mission when the accident occurred.

A-1H (135236, AH502) of VA-152; Lt. (junior grade) Jim Beene, recovered

On the same night Bullard was killed, a faulty catapult shot resulted in the loss of this Skyraider. The holdback parted, and the catapult didn't fire, allowing the aircraft to trundle off the flight deck. Jim Beene ditched off the starboard bow and was recovered by *Oriskany*'s Seasprite.

26 August 1966

An A-4E Skyhawk ran over ABE3 Richard Story on the flight deck. The accident crushed his right hand and badly bruised his right side.

27 August 1966

A-4E (152093, AH403) of VA-164; Ens. Barry Wood, recovered

While on a nighttime armed reconnaissance mission, an electrical failure over North Vietnam forced Wood to eject in the Gulf of Tonkin. He ejected at 0510 and was rescued by a Seasprite at 0613.

27 AUGUST 1966

A-4E (150079, AH314) of VA-163; Lt. (junior grade) John Schroeder, recovered

In a repeat of the previous evening, a Skyhawk returning from a nighttime armed reconnaissance mission suffered an electrical failure, forcing the pilot to eject in the gulf. The failure occurred during Schroeder's night approach to land on the carrier. He ejected at 0346 after becoming disoriented due to a lack of instruments. He was rescued by a motor whaleboat from USS *Buck* (DD-761) two hours later.

16 SEPTEMBER 1966

UH-2B (152196, UP51) of HC-1; Lt. Cdr. Dale Barck, recovered; Ens. Daniel Kern, recovered; Petty Officer William Thoday, recovered

Despite high winds and heavy seas, three *Oriskany* Seasprites helped rescue crew members of the British freighter *August Moon*, then aground on Pratas Reef in the South China Sea. During the rescue, a 65-foot wave knocked a helicopter into the sea. Quick reactions from the other helicopters saved all three crewmen, and the entire operation succeeded without loss of life.

5 OCTOBER 1966

A-1H (137610, AH513) of VA-152; Lt. (junior grade) Jim Beene, KIA

After surviving his previous ditching on 25 August, Beene was lost when his aircraft disappeared in a thunderstorm 15 miles south of Hon Mat Island. An oil slick was found on the surface of the water in the vicinity. His remains were not recovered.

23 OCTOBER 1966

A-4E (150072, AH 312) of VA-163; Cdr. Ronald Caldwell, recovered

Ens. Ralph Bisz and Caldwell, the commanding officer of VA-163, were returning from a nighttime armed reconnaissance mission when they collided while orbiting before their descent for landing. Caldwell ejected after his engine failed and was rescued by the destroyer USS *Hamner* (DD-718). Bisz landed at Da Nang air base with 2 feet of his port wing and aileron missing.

26 OCTOBER 1966

Fire broke out on the hangar deck of the ship. Six A-1s and seven A-4s were on the flight deck, having been readied for night operations, before bad weather canceled the launch. Ordnance on the aircraft, including magnesium parachute flares, had to be downloaded and stored. As the flares were being stowed in a temporary storage compartment, one of them ignited due to mishandling. Flames and toxic fumes spread rapidly throughout the ship. A total of thirty-six officers and eight sailors were killed in the fire, including twenty-four aviators from the air wing and two doctors. Three A-4s were damaged, and one A-4E (151075) and two UH-2S (149774/150183) were destroyed.

Ship's company casualties as a result of the hangar bay fire:

Lt. (junior grade) Dewey Alexander	Administration Department
Lt. (junior grade) Ramon Copple	Supply Department
Cdr. Richard Donahue	senior medical officer
Journalist Seaman Robert Dyke	Administration Department
Lt. Cdr. Omar Ford	Operations Department
Lt. Frank Gardner	Gunnery Department
Lt. Cdr. William Garrity	chaplain
Seaman James Gray	Deck Department
Cdr. Jack Harris	Carrier Division 9 Staff
Airman Apprentice Greg Hart	Administration Department
Lt. (junior grade) James Hudis	Air Department
Cdr. Harry Juntilla	Operations Department
Lt. (junior grade) James Kelly Jr.	Security Division
Seaman James Lee	Administration Department
Lt. Cdr. Walter Merrick	chaplain
Boatswains Mate 3rd Class Donald Shanks	Deck Department
Boatswains Mate 3rd Class Alvin Shifflet Jr.	Deck Department
Lt. (junior grade) Frank Tunick	Supply Department
Fireman William Wallig	Administration Department

Air Wing 16 casualties as a result of the hangar bay fire:

Lt. (junior grade) Cody Balisteri	VF-III
Lt. Joselyn Blakely Jr.	HC-I
Ens. Charles Boggs	VF-162
Lt. (junior grade) James Brewer	VA-164

Cdr. Rodney Carter	commander, CVW-16
Lt. (junior grade) William Clements	VAW-11
Lt. Cdr. George Farris	officer-in-charge, VAH-4
Lt. John Francis	VAW-11
Lt. Julian Hamond	VF-111
Lt. Lloyd Hyde	flight surgeon, CVW-16
Lt. (junior grade) William Johnson	VA-164
Ens. Daniel Kern	HC-1
Lt. Cdr. Norman Levy	VF-111
Aviation Maintenance Administration Airman David Liste	VA-152
Lt. (junior grade) William McWilliams III	VF-111
Lt. Clarence Miller	VA-163
Lt. Cdr. Clement Morisette	VA-163
Cdr. John Nussbaumer	executive officer, VA-152
Lt. (junior grade) Gerald Siebe	HC-1
Lt. Cdr. James Smith	VAH-4
Lt. (junior grade) Thomas Spitzer	VA-163
Lt. Cdr. Daniel Strong	VA-164
Ens. Ronald Tardio	VA-163
Cdr. Clyde Welch	executive officer, VA-164
Lt. (junior grade) James Welsh	HC-1

Personnel Casualties

Aviation Electrician 3rd Class Edwin Dilks, VA-164
Aviation Boatswain's Mate 3rd Class Charlie Stone fell overboard from a small liberty boat while returning to *Oriskany* in Subic Bay on 10 September 1966. His body was not recovered.

Damaged Aircraft

2 JUNE 1966

A-4E (151098) of VA-163; Lt. (junior grade) Wayne Cypress

After a late wave-off call from the landing signals officer (LSO), Cypress suffered an in-flight arrestment. His Skyhawk suffered significant damage when it slammed onto the flight deck.

6 JULY 1966

A-1H (137629, AH510) of VA-152; pilot unknown

Aircraft hit by ground fire while conducting CAS near Dinh Tuong. Two bullet holes in port wing.

A-1H (139752) of VA-152; pilot unknown

Aircraft hit by ground fire while conducting CAS near Bien Hoa, resulting in a small hole in the port aileron.

8 JULY 1966

F-8E (150880, AH112) of VF-111; pilot unknown

Lost LAU-33 pod on the catapult shot, damaging the port UHT.

12 JULY 1966

A-4E (151087) of VA-163; Lt. Fredrick Mitchell

Hit by ground fire, resulting in a small hole in the starboard wing.

14 JULY 1966

F-8E (150917, AH205) of VF-162; Lt. Jack Kilpatrick

Landing gear collapsed during arrested landing.

16 JULY 1966

A-4E (150072, AH312) of VA-163; Cdr. Ronald Caldwell

Nose wheel sheared during carrier landing.

23 JULY 1966

A-4E (151124) of VA-163; Lt. (junior grade) Peter Munro

Aircraft hit by ground fire, causing fire and damage to aircraft wiring and hydraulics.

24 JULY 1966

A-1H (135231, AH506) of VA-152; pilot unknown

Aircraft hit by ground fire during armed reconnaissance mission near Ha Tinh in Route Package II. Damage included a small hole in the propeller.

A-1H (139970) of VA-152; pilot unknown

Aircraft hit by ground fire during armed reconnaissance mission near Tinh Giah in Route Package IV, causing a hole in the starboard fuselage.

27 July 1966

F-8E (150920) of VF-162; pilot unknown

Nose gear collapsed on arrestment, damaging the tailpipe.

F-8E (150899, AH206) of VF-162; pilot unknown

Nose gear collapsed on arrestment, damaging the tailpipe.

F-8E (150911, AH207) of VF-162; pilot unknown

Crusader damaged during catapult shot.

28 July 1966

A-4E (151075) of VA-163; Lt. Cdr. William Smith

Aircraft hit by 57 mm AAA while attacking railroad cars in RP IV. Shrapnel pierced the tailpipe, resulting in fire damage to empennage and several holes through the port horizontal stabilizer. One shell went through the starboard wing fuel tank. Shrapnel through the port engine access door resulted in severed hydraulic lines and the emergency landing gear cable.

29 July 1966

F-8E (149203, AH200) of VF-162; Cdr. Cal Swanson

Nose gear collapsed on landing following a BARCAP.

8 August 1966

A-4E (151086, AH301) of VA-163; Lt. (junior grade) Peter Munro

Aircraft hit by ground fire during armed reconnaissance mission near Hai Ninh in RP IV, resulting in a 3-by-4-foot hole through the starboard wing. Saved by a KA-3B that continuously refueled him until landing aboard *Oriskany*.

9 August 1966

A-4E (152086) of VA-164; pilot unknown

Aircraft suffered a hard landing following an armed reconnaissance mission, resulting in collapsed nose gear and a ruptured drop tank.

10 August 1966

A-4E (BuNo unknown) of VA-163; pilot unknown

The port slat ripped off the Skyhawk during violent evasive maneuvers to avoid radar-guided AAA during a rail facility strike near Nam Son in RP IV.

A-4E (152037) of VA-163; Cdr. Ronald Caldwell

Aircraft hit by ground fire, causing damage in bottom fuselage and several holes in the horizontal stabilizer.

16 August 1966

F-8E (150306) of VF-111; pilot unknown

Hit by ground fire.

17 August 1966

RF-8G (146871) of VFP-63; Lt. Andre Coltrin

Aircraft hit by ground fire during a photo reconnaissance mission, damaging fuel system, pitot static system, and port wingtip.

F-8E (150913) of VF-162; pilot unknown

AIM-9 accidentally came off during a BARCAP, damaging the UHT.

20 August 1966

A-4E (152076) of VA-164; pilot unknown

Aircraft hit by 37 mm AAA while attacking AAA sites near Nghe An in RP III. Damage included large holes in the external fuel tank and wing.

23 August 1966

A-3B (138971) of VAH-4; Lt. Cdr. George Farris, Lt. (
junior grade) Ignatius Signorelli

Aircraft suffered a broken tail hook while landing at 0325 in the morning. The arresting gear cross-deck pendant also broke in the accident. Lt. (junior grade) Raymond Shreena lost his right leg at the knee, and AO1 James Johnston lost both legs when the number 4 cross-deck pendant whipped around the flight deck.

24 August 1966

A-1H (BuNo unknown) of VA-152; pilot unknown

Aircraft hit by ground fire during an armed reconnaissance mission near Nhu Xuan in RP IV, resulting in several bullet holes in the port wing.

28 August 1966

A-4E (152074, AH405) of VA-164; Lt. John Davis

Aircraft hit by 37 mm AAA during an armed reconnaissance mission near Cat Ba Island. One hit in the starboard wing resulted in one hole the "size of a beach ball." Davis was unable to land aboard *Oriskany* and diverted to Da Nang, where he made a rather sporty arrested landing.

A-1H (137610, AH 513) of VA-152; pilot unknown

Aircraft hit by ground fire during an armed reconnaissance mission in mountainous terrain west of Thanh Hoa, damaging the starboard wing.

29 AUGUST 1966

A-1H (137610, AH 513) of VA-152; pilot unknown

Aircraft hit by ground fire while conducting an armed reconnaissance mission southwest of Thanh Hoa, damaging the engine cylinder and distributor.

30 AUGUST 1966

A-1H (139728, AH 514) of VA-152; pilot unknown

Aircraft hit by ground fire while conducting an armed reconnaissance mission along the coast in RP IV, damaging the centerline drop tank and port fuselage.

31 AUGUST 1966

A-4E (152061) of VA-164; pilot unknown

Aircraft hit by ground fire during an armed reconnaissance mission in mountainous terrain northwest of Thanh Hoa in RP IV. Hit in the starboard horizontal stabilizer.

5 SEPTEMBER 1966

F-8E (149211, AH 112) of VF-111; Lt. Randy Rime

Aircraft damaged by gunfire from a MiG-17. Rime was injured by flying Plexiglas, and his aircraft was severely damaged during landing.

8 SEPTEMBER 1966

A-4E (152061) of VA-163; Cdr. Bryan Compton

Aircraft hit by enemy ground fire while attacking trucks 10 miles west of Thanh Hoa in RP IV, resulting in a small hole in the port wing.

F-8E (150921, AH 204) of VF-162; pilot unknown

Aircraft damaged by 37 mm AAA while bombing a bridge on Highway I in Ha Tinh in RP II.

A-4E (149658) of VA-163; pilot unknown

Aircraft hit by ground fire while attacking trucks during an armed reconnaissance mission in RP IV. Aircraft sustained hits in the rudder and vertical stab.

RF-8G (146871) of VFP-63; pilot unknown

Aircraft hit by ground fire during a photo reconnaissance mission in RP II.

24 SEPTEMBER 1966

A-1H (134575) of VA-152; pilot unknown

Aircraft hit by ground fire during an armed reconnaissance mission in RP III. The aircraft sustained several hits, causing minor damage to the port wingtip.

A-1H (139728, AH 514) of VA-152; pilot unknown

Aircraft hit by enemy ground fire while attacking barges along the coast of RP III, causing minor damage to starboard aileron.

25 SEPTEMBER 1966

A-4E (152048) of VA-164; pilot unknown

Aircraft nose wheel collapsed on landing after a tanker sortie.

26 SEPTEMBER 1966

A-4E (150131) of VA-163; Lt. (junior grade) Peter Munro

Nose tire exploded during landing, resulting in a failure of the nose landing gear.

A-4E (151087) of VA-163; Lt. (junior grade) Louis Nordbye

For the second time that day, the nose tire exploded during landing, resulting in a failure of the nose landing gear.

A-1H (137622) of VA-152; pilot unknown

Aircraft hit by ground fire while bombing a bridge in RP IV. Aircraft hit in the main wing spar and was stricken.

27 SEPTEMBER 1966

A-4E (150134), of VA-163; pilot unknown

Aircraft hit by ground fire while attacking PT boats in the port of Cam Pha.

A-4E (152083) of VA-164; Lt. Cdr. Richard Perry

Aircraft hit in the nose section by 37 mm AAA while attacking a SAM site. The shell destroyed the nose of the aircraft, and debris struck the tail, while some was ingested into the engine. The blast tore through the cockpit and injured the pilot's foot.

A-4E (152092, AH402), of VA-164; pilot unknown

Aircraft hit by ground fire while attacking a pontoon bridge in RP II.

A-4E (152087, AH404), of VA-164; pilot unknown

Aircraft hit by AAA while attacking POL barges in the port of Cam Pha.

29 SEPTEMBER 1966

A-4E (151139) of VA-163; Lt. Cdr. John Miles

Aircraft hit by 85 mm AAA while attacking a bridge along Highway I in RP III. Hit resulted in a large hole in the bottom of the starboard wing and a small hole in the starboard intake.

30 SEPTEMBER 1966

A-4E (151075) of VA-163; Lt. Cdr. Cecil Tulley

Aircraft hit by enemy ground fire, resulting in a large hole through the port wing.

A-1H (134575) of VA-152; pilot unknown

Aircraft hit by ground fire while strafing barges off the coast of RP II, damaging the main landing gear and hydraulic lines.

A-1H (139752) of VA-152; pilot unknown

Aircraft hit by 37 mm AAA while strafing barges off the coast of RP II. Damaged fuselage and bottom of the port wing spar.

I OCTOBER 1966

A-4E (152049) of VA-164; pilot unknown

Aircraft was launching on an Iron Hand mission when one of its MK 83 bombs fell off during the catapult stroke. The bomb punched a hole in the port wing.

Aircraft hit by 57 mm AAA during a nighttime armed reconnaissance mission in RP IV. Damage included a hole in the centerline drop tank, one hole in the engine access door, and one in the port intake.

8 OCTOBER 1966

A-1H (139752) of VA-152; Lt. (junior grade) Fred Guenzel

Lt. Jack Feldhaus and Guenzel were on an armed reconnaissance mission 25 miles southwest of Thanh Hoa when both aircraft were hit by extremely heavy ground fire. Guenzel's aircraft was hit by 14.5 mm automatic weapons fire, causing severe damage, including a 10-inch hole in the starboard wing. The hit also destroyed all bomb racks on that wing.

10 OCTOBER 1966

A-1H (135371) of VA-152; pilot unknown

Aircraft hit by ground fire while attacking a bridge in RP III, causing light damage to the starboard flap.

11 OCTOBER 1966

A-1H (139641) of VA-152; pilot unknown

Aircraft hit by ground fire while attacking a bridge in RP III, resulting in a small hole in the port wing.

14 OCTOBER 1966

A-4E (152048) of VA-164; pilot unknown

Following a nighttime armed reconnaissance mission in RP II, the nose landing gear collapsed on landing, causing moderate damage to the nose of the aircraft.

20 OCTOBER 1966

A-1H (137622) of VA-152; pilot unknown

Aircraft hit by ground fire while strafing a barge off the coast of RP III, resulting in a small hole in the edge of the starboard wing.

21 OCTOBER 1966

A-4E (152035) of VA-164; pilot unknown

Aircraft hit by bomb fragment while attacking barges off the coast of RP IV. Fragment punctured the starboard wing.

23 OCTOBER 1966

A-4E (149998) of VA-163; Ens. Ralph Bisz

Bisz and Cdr. Ronald Caldwell suffered a midair collision at night 20,000 feet overhead *Oriskany*. Caldwell ejected, and Bisz landed at Da Nang air base with 2 feet of the port wing and aileron missing.

24 OCTOBER 1966

A-4E (152088) of VA-164; pilot unknown

Nose wheel collapsed during carrier landing upon completion of an armed reconnaissance mission, causing moderate damage to the nose of the aircraft.

Appendix 3

1967–1968 WESTPAC

Homeport departure/return: Alameda 16 June 1967–31 January 1968

Seventh Fleet in-chop/out-chop: 26 June 1967–23 January 1968

Port calls: Pearl Harbor 20–21 June; Cubi Point 2–12 July; Cubi Point 9–16 August; Sasebo 19 September–1 October; Yokosuka 6–15 November; Cubi Point 18–23 December; Hong Kong 24–30 December; Cubi Point 14–17 January 1968

Line periods: 14 July–7 August; 18 August–15 September; 5 October–2 November; 20 November–16 December; 31 December 1967–11 January 1968.

Total: 122 days on the line

Table 3. 1967–68 Squadrons

Squadron	Aircraft	Call Sign
VF-111 (Sundowners)	F-8C	Old Nick
VF-162 (Hunters)	F-8E	Super Heat
VA-163 (Saints)	A-4E	Old Salt
VA-164 (Ghost Riders)	A-4E	Magic Stone
VA-152 (Wild Aces)	A-1H/J	Locket
VAH-4 Det G (Four Runners)	KA-3B	Holly Green
VFP-63 Det G (Eyes of the Fleet)	RF-8A	Cork Tip
VAW-11 Det 34 (Early Elevens)	E-1B	Over Pass
HU-1 Det 1 Unit G (Pacific Fleet Angels)	UH-2A	

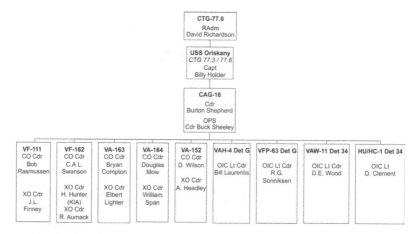

USS *Oriskany* and CVW-16 leadership, 1967. Created by the author.

Combat Losses: 30

14 JULY 1967

A-4E (152049, AH 407) of VA-164; Lt. (junior grade) Larry Cunningham, recovered

Oriskany suffered its first loss on its first day. Cunningham was hit by AAA while attacking barges on a river near Gia La, 15 miles southeast of Vinh. His A-4 was hit in the nose, and parts were sucked into the engine. By the time he made it to *Oriskany*, his aircraft was on fire. Unable to land aboard the ship, he ejected alongside and was recovered by an SH-2.

15 JULY 1967

A-1H (135288, AH 504) of VA-152; Lt. (junior grade) Rob Cassell, KIA

Cassell was killed during an armed reconnaissance mission along the coast near Thanh Hoa. He began attacking small boats and barges near the village of Hon Ne and was hit by small arms fire from the boats. Cassell radioed that he'd been hit, and his aircraft crashed into the water shortly thereafter. His remains have not been recovered.

16 JULY 1967

F-8E (150925, AH 201) of VF-162; Lt. Cdr. Demetrio "Butch" Verich, recovered

Verich's second shoot-down occurred while three Crusaders were on a flak suppression mission for the strike on the Phu Ly rail yard. Approaching the target, his division was targeted by SAMs. Although he successfully evaded two missiles, a third SA-2 struck his aircraft as he descended through 5,000 feet. Verich ejected, landing 16 miles from Hanoi. After spending fifteen hours on the ground, most of it in the vicinity of a 37 mm emplacement, Verich was rescued by an HS-2 Sea King from *Hornet*.

18 July 1967

A-4E (151986, AH 404) of VA-164; Lt. Cdr. Richard Hartman, POW, died in captivity

A-4E (151175, AH 415) of VA-164; Lt. (junior grade) Larry Duthie, recovered

18 July was a bad day for VA-164 as they struck the bridge at Co Trai. Before reaching the bridge, Hartman and his wingman, Duthie, evaded several SAMs that drove them to lower altitudes. Before they could climb to safer altitudes, Hartman was hit by 37 mm AAA. With his aircraft on fire, he ejected at 1,000 feet. Because of the successful recovery of Verich the day prior, a SAR mission was organized while Duthie attempted to orbit over Hartman's position.

Duthie was quickly hit by the same AAA battery. He headed for the gulf with his airplane on fire, smoke filling the cockpit and no oxygen. Both hydraulic systems failed, though Duthie stayed with it, as he had a good engine and he could control the plane by flying with trim. He flew another 12 miles before his Skyhawk became uncontrollable. Duthie ejected near Nam Dinh in a region known as the Hourglass, some 45 miles southeast of Hanoi. It also happened to be approximately 10 miles from Hartman.

The first rescue attempt for Duthie was aborted due to heavy ground fire. After several helicopters and their fixed-wing escorts were damaged by ground fire, Larry Duthie was finally rescued by an HH-3 from Detachment 1, 37 Aerospace Rescue and Recovery Squadron (ARRS), while rescue efforts for Hartman were postponed until the following day.

19 July 1967

A-4E (152034, AH 401) of VA-164; Lt. (junior grade) Barry Wood, recovered

F-8E (150899, AH 206) of VF-162; Cdr. Herb Hunter, KIA

On 19 July SAR efforts for Richard Hartman resumed as six A-1s from VA-152 escorted another Sea King to his position. The RESCAP was also covered by A-4s, one of which was hit. Wood was hit in his fuel tank as he made a rocket attack. The leak went unnoticed until Wood realized he didn't have enough fuel to return to *Oriskany*. Wood jettisoned his remaining ordnance and flew toward the coast. After running out of fuel, he ejected 8 miles offshore and was recovered by a small boat from the SAR destroyer USS *Richard B. Anderson*. This was Wood's second ejection in six days and his third in less than a year. Due to this fact, he requested and was granted a transfer to the navy's riverine force.

When the helicopter arrived to rescue Hartman, it unwittingly flew over previously unnoticed AAA emplacements. The SH-3 was shot down, killing everyone aboard. After the loss of a Skyhawk, this helicopter and its four crewmembers, and the previous day's toll, Hartman's rescue was called off. Hartman remained in radio contact throughout and was able to evade capture for over three days. He was killed upon being captured or died in POW camp shortly thereafter. His remains were returned in March 1974. The remains of the helicopter crew were returned in 2012.

The bridge at Co Trai was attacked again as Hartman's rescue fell apart. Hunter, the executive officer of VF-162, led the flak suppressors and was hit in the wing by 57 mm AAA. The hit ruptured the fuel tanks in his Crusader's wings and caused a partial loss of hydraulics. Hunter attempted to land on *Bon Homme Richard* with his wing in a lowered position. His aircraft hit the deck too fast and hard enough to shear off the landing gear. The Crusader broke apart on impact, skipped the arresting gear wires, and plunged over the side. Hunter was found floating under the water in a partially deployed parachute.

20 July 1967

A-4E (150097, AH 312) of VA-163; Lt. Russell Kuhl, recovered

Kuhl was shot down during a series of strikes on the My Xa POL storage facility 15 miles northwest of Haiphong. He was hit by 37 mm AAA, and his engine began vibrating. Shortly thereafter, Kuhl radioed that his cockpit was filling with smoke before his radio quit. He flew toward the SAR destroyer and ejected. He was rescued by an HH-3 from the 37 ARRS, whose crew witnessed the ejection before rescuing him. Kuhl was flown back to *Oriskany* and eventually transferred to the Oakland Naval Hospital due to neck injuries sustained in the ejection.

25 JULY 1967

A-4E (149961, AH 304) of VA-163; Lt. Cdr. Don "Mac" Davis, KIA

Davis was lost on a nighttime armed reconnaissance mission near Ha Tinh, 20 miles south of Vinh. After spotting a convoy of trucks, Davis and his wingman began strafing under the light of parachute flares. It is unclear whether he was shot down by small arms fire or simply flew into the ground. After two failed attempts, his wreckage was finally located, and his remains were recovered in 1997.

31 JULY 1967

F-8C (146984, AH 110) of VF-111; Lt. (junior grade) Charles Zuhoski, POW

Zuhoski was the thirteenth plane lost by *Oriskany* during her first line period. The escort for a Skyhawk flying the deadly Iron Hand mission, Zuhoski evaded one volley of missiles and was climbing through 11,000 feet when his Crusader was hit by another, unseen SAM. With his Crusader on fire, he ejected and landed in the village of Ngu Nghi, 10 miles east of Hanoi. He was repatriated in March 1973.

4 AUGUST 1967

A-4E (150052, AH 313) of VA-163; Lt. (junior grade) Ralph Bisz, KIA

Bisz was shot down while attacking a POL storage site at Luc Nong. His flight was attacked by a SAM site 8 miles northwest of Haiphong. The site launched a volley of four missiles, and his aircraft was struck at about 10,500 feet. Remnants of the aircraft were observed falling in a large ball of fire before crashing. No one in his flight saw a parachute, and no emergency beeper or voice communications were received. It was assumed that Bisz had been killed when the missile struck. However, the navy officially listed him as captured. Between 1988 and 2004 joint U.S. and Vietnamese teams conducted investigations and surveyed the crash site. The remains of an unknown pilot were exhumed from the local cemetery, and a positive identification was finally made in 2008.

31 AUGUST 1967

A-4E (152028, AH 315) of VA-163; Lt. (junior grade) Dave Carey, POW

A-4E (149975, AH 310) of VA-163; Lt. Cdr. Hugh Stafford, POW

A-4E (151991, AH 402) of VA-164; Lt. Cdr. Richard Perry, KIA

On the third consecutive day of strikes into Haiphong, *Oriskany* launched ten Skyhawks from both VA-163 and VA-164 to bomb the railway bridge at Vat Cach. Thirteen miles southwest of Haiphong, the formation was ambushed by an unknown SAM site.

One SAM exploded directly in front of Stafford and his wingman, Carey. The force of the explosion blew Stafford out of his cockpit, still strapped to his ejection seat. Though badly injured, he survived due to the automatic functions of the ejection seat, which deployed his parachute. The explosion destroyed the engine of Carey's Skyhawk, and he ejected as the aircraft was consumed by fire. Both were quickly captured and eventually repatriated in March 1973.

The same volley of SAMs also hit the VA-164 Skyhawks. The missile that hit Perry's aircraft came up near vertically, directly underneath him, and was not seen until the last possible moment. It detonated under Perry's aircraft, causing severe damage. Streaming fuel, he turned toward the sea and jettisoned his external stores. Two miles off the coast, Perry's Skyhawk began an uncontrolled right-hand roll. As the plane rolled upright, he ejected. Perry was seen hanging limply in his parachute, and when he entered the water, he never resurfaced. Though a helicopter arrived on scene, Perry's body was entangled in the parachute lines, and the North Vietnamese were shelling the helicopter with mortars. The rescue swimmer was forced to leave Perry's body in the water. His remains were returned in February 1987.

5 OCTOBER 1967

F-8C (146938, AH 114) of VF-111; Ens. David Matheny, POW

Matheny was lost on a strike against a pontoon bridge at Nho Quan, 20 miles southwest of Nam Dinh. Matheny was in a turn at 10,000 feet when his aircraft was either hit by AAA or suffered a catastrophic engine failure. He glided as far as he could toward the coast, ejecting at the last minute over a karst ridge several miles inland. He was surrounded and captured before a SAR attempt could be launched. Matheny was released in February 1968, along with two other officers, as part of a propaganda campaign by the North Vietnamese. When released, he provided the first confirmation of many American POWs.

7 October 1967

A-4E (152086, AH 413) of VA-164; Lt. David Hodges, KIA

Hodges was killed during an Iron Hand mission 15 miles south of Hanoi. While dueling with several SAM sites, his flight spotted the launch of two SA-2 missiles, which began guiding toward them. Hodges was slow to respond and probably never saw the missiles. The first SA-2 missed, but the second missile struck his aircraft. His Skyhawk burst into flames, rolled right, and crashed into a karst near Hoang Xa. No ejection was attempted. His remains were recovered in 1995 and 1996.

9 October 1967

A-4E (152085, AH 416) of VA-164; Lt. (junior grade) Larry Cunningham, recovered

After surviving his previous shoot-down on 14 July, Cunningham had just bombed a pontoon bridge at Nao Quan and was crossing the coastline when his engine suddenly quit. He attempted to restart the engine several times but was forced to eject after descending through 3,000 feet. He was rescued by a helicopter from USS *Fox* (DLG-33). It is likely that his aircraft was struck by small-arms fire while he was attacking the well-defended bridge.

18 October 1967

A-4E (152048, AH 402) of VA-164; Lt. Cdr. John Barr, KIA

Barr was part of an Iron Hand flight protecting a strike on the Haiphong shipyards. As they engaged a well-defended SAM site near the port, his Skyhawk was hit by AAA and exploded. No parachute was seen. Barr's remains were returned by the Vietnamese in 1988 and 1989.

22 October 1967

A-4E (150116, AH 306) of VA-163; Lt. (junior grade) James Dooley, KIA

Dooley was shot down during an Alpha strike on the Haiphong railway yards. Although he successfully dropped his bombs, his aircraft was hit and streaming fuel. After climbing to 6,000 feet, his aircraft began a descending turn before crashing into the Cua Cam River. Despite the heavy defenses, Cdr. Bryan Compton circled the heavily defended area no fewer than eight times looking for Dooley. No attempt at ejection was seen, nor have any remains been located or recovered.

24 October 1967

A-4E (149963, AH 311) of VA-163; Lt. (junior grade) Ralph "Skip" Foulks, recovered

Foulks was also shot down while bombing the Haiphong railway yards. He had just bombed the target and was south of Haiphong, heading for the coast at 6,500 feet, when he was hit by AAA. Though he lost his engine, Foulks was able to glide 3 miles out to sea before ejecting. He was recovered by a navy helicopter after spending several minutes in the water.

25 October 1967

A-4E (150086, AH 315) of VA-163; Lt. (junior grade) Jeffrey Krommenhoek, MIA

Krommenhoek was shot down during the second day of strikes on the Phuc Yen airfield. This was the last of four air force and navy waves, and *Oriskany*'s strike encountered ferocious defenses. Krommenhoek was last seen rolling in on his target, an aircraft revetment north of the embattled airfield. A search of the area after the raid was not possible, given the numerous defenses. Krommenhoek was declared KIA ten years later. Although wreckage has been recovered, no remains have been identified.

26 October 1967

F-8E (150310, AH 206) of VF-162; Lt. (junior grade) Chuck Rice, POW

A-4E (149959, AH 300) of VA-163; Lt. Cdr. John McCain III, POW

Oriskany lost two aircraft while bombing the Hanoi thermal power plant on the afternoon of 26 October. Rice was part of the flak suppression element and was hit by a SAM as his flight accelerated ahead of the strike package. He was hit while inverted at 15,000 feet as he attempted to outmaneuver the first of two missiles. His port wing was blown off, forcing him to eject. Rice landed in Hanoi and was immediately taken prisoner. He was repatriated in March 1973.

McCain was in the lead division and was struck by either AAA or a SAM immediately after he dropped his bombs. The explosion blew off McCain's starboard wing while he was close to the ground, and he was lucky to eject in time. Both his arms and his right leg were broken during the ejection, and McCain almost drowned when he landed in Truc Bach Lake next to the target.

McCain was captured and eventually repatriated in March 1973. McCain's father became CINCPAC in July 1968, and McCain's status as the son and grandson of famous navy men was used by the Vietnamese for propaganda purposes.

2 NOVEMBER 1967

A-4E (151985, AH 414) of VA-164; Lt. (junior grade) Frederic Knapp, KIA

Knapp was lost during an armed reconnaissance mission north of Vinh. After spotting trucks near Cho Giat, Knapp began a Zuni rocket attack from 9,000 feet and flew into the ground. He never attempted to eject and is believed to have been killed during the dive. Villagers near the crash site recovered his remains and buried him nearby. In 1982 the Vietnamese returned Knapp's identification card, but his remains have not been located.

5 DECEMBER 1967

F-8C (146907, AH 102) of VF-111; Lt. Jay Meadows, recovered

Meadows was escorting a reconnaissance mission in RP III when he was hit by small-arms fire over Highway 1A. The hit went unnoticed until he suddenly lost one of his flight controls. Hydraulic fluid was seen streaming from the aircraft, which eventually caught fire. Meadows flew to the southern SAR destroyer before losing his remaining flight controls and his engine. He ejected near the destroyer and was recovered by a navy helicopter.

1 JANUARY 1968

RA-3B, (144847) of VAP-61. Lt. Cdr. James Dennison, MIA; Lt. (junior grade) T. H. Hanley, MIA; PHCS H. H. Herrin Jr., MIA

On New Year's Day, a photo reconnaissance Skywarrior on detachment from Naval Air Station Agana in Guam to *Oriskany* was catapulted for a mission over North Vietnam. The crew was on a nighttime infrared reconnaissance mission looking for truck traffic. Although the mission was flown under radio silence, it was under continuous radar surveillance. The plane was hit by ground fire and turned toward the sea. The aircraft went down 30 miles off the coast at approximately 17°40'N and 107°10'E. Although an extensive search was conducted, it was terminated with negative results.

2 JANUARY 1968

F-8C (146989, AH 106) of VF-111; Lt. (junior grade) Craig Taylor, recovered

Taylor had just joined VF-111 a week prior and was on his first combat mission, escorting an RF-8 mission near Thanh Hoa. AAA hit his aircraft and destroyed his engine, although he was able to glide as far as the coast. His aircraft eventually stalled, and he ejected 7 miles off the coast. A section of Skyhawks provided protection from North Vietnamese vessels in the area while he waited for a helicopter to rescue him.

4 JANUARY 1968

F-8E (150865, AH 206) of VF-162; Lt. (junior grade) Rich Minnich, KIA

Minnich was part of a TARCAP for an airstrike against a bridge at Hai Duong. A SAM struck his Crusader while they orbited near the target at 15,000 feet. His wingman, Lt. J. P. O'Neil, watched as Minnich's Crusader caught fire and spun to the ground, crashing 10 miles north of Haiphong. Minnich's remains were returned in December 1985.

5 JANUARY 1968

A-4E (150131, AH 303) of VA-163; Lt. (junior grade) Ralph "Skip" Foulks, KIA

Although he survived his 24 October 1967 shoot-down, Foulks was lost during a nighttime armed reconnaissance mission 25 miles south of Nam Dinh. After spotting a convoy of trucks, his section began their bomb runs. His flight lead lost sight of him, and Foulks was either shot down or flew into the ground while on his bomb run. His remains were returned by the Vietnamese in December 1988.

11 JANUARY 1968

A-4E (151152, AH 404) of VA-164; Lt. Cdr. Denis Weichman, recovered

Weichman was shot down during a Steel Tiger mission. He was on his third pass over a small bridge 10 miles north of Ban Don Pang when his aircraft was hit by ground fire. With his engine vibrating excessively, he flew across Laos and North Vietnam to the Tonkin Gulf. He eventually lost control as fire burned through control cables, forcing him to eject short of *Oriskany*. It has been misreported that he broke his leg during the ejection. He was rescued by an HS-6 Sea King and was back flying the next day.

Operational Losses: II

6 May 1967

F-8E (149193 AH 211) of VF-162; Lt. Lee Prost, KIA

Prost was killed on a training flight off the California coast shortly before *Oriskany* deployed. He had a wing unlocked caution light, and his Crusader's wing came off in midflight as he strafed a spar towed by *Oriskany*. His body was not recovered.

12 July 1967

A-4E (150102) of VA-164; Lt. Barry Wood, recovered

Wood was launching on a training sortie while *Oriskany* sailed from Subic Bay to Yankee Station when his Skyhawk was catapulted with insufficient airspeed. He ejected safely, and the aircraft crashed into the sea in front of *Oriskany*. Wood was recovered by *Oriskany*'s Seasprite. Barry Wood ejected six days later for the third time in a year.

20 July 1967

F-8E (150916) of VF-162; Lt. (junior grade) James Nunn, recovered

As he was preparing to be catapulted off *Oriskany* for a RESCAP mission, Nunn inadvertently took his hand off the throttle to signal to the catapult officer. At that moment, the catapult fired, causing the throttle to pull back. With no power on the aircraft, he had insufficient airspeed to fly, and the aircraft flew into the water. Amazingly, Nunn ejected underwater and was rescued, although he suffered a fractured neck.

28 July 1967

KA-3B (142658) of VAH-4; Ens. Bruce Patterson, KIA; Aviation Electrician 2nd Class Charles Hardie, KIA; Lt. Cdr. Don Kentopp, recovered

Two crewmembers were killed when their KA-3B suffered a dual engine failure during a nighttime logistics flight from *Oriskany* to Cubi Point. With thunderstorms in the Tonkin Gulf, Kentopp attempted to fly over them. Climbing through 40,000 feet, both engines flamed out in the vicinity of 15°30'N and 276°0'E. Unable to restart the engines, the crew bailed out of the aircraft. Hardie blew the hatch, and both he and Patterson successfully bailed out. Kentopp's parachute got stuck on the seat, and he did not escape the airplane until it had reached 15,000 feet.

Fortunately, Kentopp was spotted by a patrolling aircraft and rescued by a boat from the American merchant ship SS *Fairport*. Patterson and Hardie were lost at sea. It is believed that, due to altitude, Patterson and Hardy died shortly after bailout.

8 SEPTEMBER 1967

F-8C (146929, AH 212) of VF-111; Lt. Cdr. Donald Baker, recovered

Baker was on an armed reconnaissance mission among the islands east of Haiphong when he suffered an electrical failure. 146929 had a record of generator failures, which was not uncommon in the F-8C. Compounding the problem was that his emergency electrical backup failed as well. Baker elected to eject alongside *Oriskany* due to the fact that he was low on fuel and uncertain about how much fuel he had available, and a flame-out at the ramp carried disastrous consequences. He was recovered by *Oriskany*'s Seasprite.

10 SEPTEMBER 1967

A-4E (150047, AH313) of VA-163; Lt. Dale Landreth, recovered

Landreth was launching for a tanker mission when his engine failed during the catapult shot. Landreth ejected safely, and the aircraft crashed into the sea in front of *Oriskany*. He was rescued by a Seasprite after spending two minutes in the water.

11 SEPTEMBER 1967

F-8E (150910) of VF-162; Lt. Jack Shaw, recovered

While on an armed reconnaissance mission in RP IV, Shaw realized that two of his bombs couldn't be dropped. Rather than risk landing on the *Oriskany*, he was diverted to Da Nang. Due to navigational errors, he ran out of fuel prior to reaching Da Nang and ejected.

8 OCTOBER 1967

E-1B (148132) of VAW-11. Lt. (junior grade) Andres Zissu, KIA; Lt. (junior grade) Norman Roggow, KIA; Lt. (junior grade) Donald Wolfe, KIA; Aviation Electronics Technician Chief Roland Pineau, KIA; Journalist Seaman Raul Guerra, KIA

After refueling to support the afternoon Alpha strike, the crew took off from Chu Lai in poor weather and proceeded toward Da Nang. Radar contact was lost as the aircraft approached Da Nang. Contact was briefly reestablished, showing the aircraft dangerously off course near mountainous terrain 10 miles northwest of Da Nang. The crew acknowledged emergency instructions to turn before radio and radar contact were lost again. A SAR mission was launched in the poor weather, and wreckage was eventually discovered at the base of a cliff. Due to the impossibility of the terrain, the crew's remains, except for Guerra, were not recovered until August 2005. To this date, his remains have not been recovered.

21 OCTOBER 1967

KA-3B (142655) of VAH-4; Lt. Cdr. Donald Albright, recovered; Lt. (junior grade) William Skinner Bombardier Navigator, recovered; Personnelman 2nd Class Ralph Estes III (3CM), recovered; Aviation Electrician 2nd Class William Lindsay (4CM), recovered

A KA-3B was launching from NAS Cubi Point for a logistics mission to *Oriskany*. During the takeoff roll, the pilot fired the jet-assisted take-off (JATO) bottles, and one of the starboard bottles came off after ignition. The burning rocket bounced off the starboard main mount and hit the starboard engine, causing the engine to flame out. Albright attempted to keep the plane flying but ditched just off Grandy Island. All four crewmembers escaped with limited injuries.

19 NOVEMBER 1967

F-8C (147004, AH102) of VF-111; Lt. Edwin Van Orden, KIA

Van Orden was killed while launching a postmaintenance check flight. The catapult fired with too much pressure and ripped the bridle attachment off his Crusader. He managed to stop his Crusader just as the nose dropped over the bow. Although the aircraft remained on the deck, Van Orden ejected. He struck a gun tub along the deck edge shortly after his parachute deployed and was killed on impact.

1 JANUARY 1968

A-4E (151133) of VA-164; Lt. George Schindelar, recovered

Schindelar suffered a total electrical failure while on a mission over Laos. The failure eventually locked his flight controls, and he ejected over the gulf. He was picked up by USS *Valley Forge* (LPH-8).

Personnel Casualties

12 OCTOBER 1967

Aviation Ordnanceman 3rd class D. A. Lash, KIA.
Lash was killed in an operational accident onboard *Oriskany*.

18 OCTOBER 1967

Aviation Structural Mechanic 3rd Class Richard Woynarski, KIA
Woynarski of VA-164 was killed when an aircraft tire he was inflating
exploded.

Combat-Damaged Aircraft

14 JULY 1967

A-4E (BuNo unknown) of VA-164; pilot unknown

AGM-12B caught fire after being hit by ground fire. Ordnance was jettisoned without further damage.

15 JULY 1967

A-4E (149964, AH 301) of VA-163; Cdr. Bryan Compton

Aircraft was hit by ground fire during a strike on a storage depot at
Ha Tinh. Damage included a 4-inch hole in the underside of the starboard wing. The aircraft was repaired enough to be flown to Cubi
Point for further repair.

16 JULY 1967

F-8E (150879) of VF-162; Lt. Dick Wyman

Wyman was hit by 37 mm AAA during a RESCAP mission. Aircraft had
sixteen holes in afterburner and empennage, forcing him to divert to
Da Nang.

F-8C (150925) of VF-111; pilot unknown

Aircraft hit by an SA-2 during a TARCAP mission for a strike near Phu
Ly, resulting in a 3-foot hole in the afterburner.

18 JULY 1967

A-1H (139641) of VA-152; pilot unknown

Aircraft hit by ground fire while attacking an ammo storage area in
Ha Binh province in RP VIb. One round hit the canopy.

A-4E (150131, AH 303) of VA-163; Lt. (junior grade) Kenneth Adams

Aircraft hit by SA-2 while attacking AAA sites during a strike southeast of Thanh Hoa in RP IV, damaging centerline drop tank.

30 JULY 1967

A-4E (150028, AH311) of VA-163; Lt. Cdr. Jerry Breast

Aircraft hit by 37/57 mm AAA during a strike on Bac Giang transshipment center in RP VIB. Damage included shrapnel holes in starboard slat.

1 AUGUST 1967

A-4E (151994, AH412) of VA-164; pilot unknown

Hit by ground fire en route to Tien Nong storage area in RP VIB. Aircraft took hits in canopy, radome, starboard wing, and starboard bomb racks.

2 AUGUST 1967

A-4E (149975, AH310) of VA-163; Lt. (junior grade) Kenneth Adams

Aircraft was hit by 37 mm AAA during strike on Loi Dong near Haiphong. Damage included a 2-by-5-inch hole in the port wing.

4 AUGUST 1967

A-4E (150083, AH305) of VA-163; Lt. Cdr. Marv Reynolds

Aircraft hit by an SA-2 during strike on Haiphong. Damage included one 16-by-20-inch hole in starboard wing root and multiple holes in port empennage and tailpipe. Aircraft craned off in Cubi Point.

20 AUGUST 1967

A-4E (150116, AH306) of VA-163; Cdr. Bryan Compton

Aircraft hit by 37 mm AAA during a strike on Brandon Bay. Damage included numerous small fragmentation holes in starboard empennage. Over 2 feet of starboard aileron was shot off.

21 AUGUST 1967

A-4E (150132, AH300) of VA-163; Lt. Cdr. Dean Cramer

A-4E (150028, AH311) of VA-163; Lt. Cdr. James Busey

Cramer's aircraft was severely damaged by 37/57 mm AAA during VA-163's Hanoi thermal power plant raid. Damage included thirty-seven holes 1 inch diameter or smaller, six holes 4 inches in diameter, and five holes in the port wing, the largest of which measured 38 by 18 inches. The port aileron had five holes, the largest 12 by 13 inches. Dean Cramer was injured.

Busey's aircraft was also severely damaged, with 115 holes 1 inch diameter or smaller, nine holes 8 by 5 inches. The starboard wing had three holes, the largest 8 by 41 inches. Fire also warped and buckled the starboard wing. The end of the starboard horizontal stabilizer and all of the starboard elevator were shot off.

22 August 1967

A-4E (BuNo unknown) of VA-163; pilot unknown

Nose landing gear collapsed on landing following a strike on Song Van.

27 August 1967

A-4E (152083) of VA-164; pilot unknown

Aircraft hit by ground fire during an armed reconnaissance mission near Ha Tinh in RP II. Shrapnel damaged the centerline drop tank, main landing gear doors, and ALQ-51 equipment.

A-1H (134569) of VA-152; pilot unknown

Aircraft hit by ground fire while attacking AAA emplacements near Tho Pac in RP II, resulting in a shattered windscreen and two holes in the starboard wing.

29 August 1967

A-4E (151152, AH404) of VA-164; pilot unknown

Aircraft hit by ground fire during the Iron Hand mission against the SAM site at Thu Do in RP VIB.

A-4E (151196) of VA-164; pilot unknown

Aircraft hit by AAA during strike on Dong Coi bridge in RP VIB, damaging port wing and fuselage.

31 August 1967

A-4E (149972, AH302) of VA-163; Lt. Cdr. Dean Cramer

A-4E (150131, AH303) of VA-163; Lt. Donovan Wood

Cramer's aircraft was hit by SAM fragments during the disastrous mission against the bridge at Vat Cach. The jet engine ingested shrapnel, which destroyed it.

Wood's aircraft was also hit by fragments from the same missile. Damage included multiple holes in the port slat, the largest measuring 2 inches.

A-4E (152035) of VA-164; pilot unknown

This Skyhawk was hit by AAA during an armed reconnaissance mission near Tinh Gia in RP III. Damage included one hole in the starboard wing.

1 SEPTEMBER 1967

A-1J (142030) of VA-152; pilot unknown

Aircraft damaged by ground fire during an armed reconnaissance mission along Highway 4A in RP IV. A single bullet damaged the port engine cowling.

2 SEPTEMBER 1967

A-4E (149982, AH314) of VA-163; pilot unknown

Aircraft damaged when fins came off a bomb and punctured the wing.

3 SEPTEMBER 1967

A-4E (151070, AH305) of VA-163; Lt. (junior grade) Gordon Hunter

Aircraft hit by 37 mm AAA during a strike on the Thanh Hoa bridge in RP IV. Damage included a 3-inch hole in the starboard wing root and an 8-inch hole on top of the starboard wing.

5 SEPTEMBER 1967

F-8C (146931) of VF-111; pilot unknown

Aircraft hit by ground fire while attacking WBLCs in Haiphong harbor.

9 SEPTEMBER 1967

F-8E (150888) of VF-162; pilot unknown

Aircraft hit by ground fire during a strike on railroad cars at Tinh Gia in RP III. Damage included one hole in the starboard leading edge flap.

A-4E (150006, AH312) of VA-163; Lt. Vance Schufeldt

Aircraft hit by ground fire during an armed reconnaissance mission in RP IV, resulting in damage to the centerline drop tank and a 3-inch hole in the starboard wing.

10 SEPTEMBER 1967

EA-1F (BuNo unknown) of VAW-13; pilot unknown

Aircraft suffered an electrical fire while jamming.

A-4E (150061, AH310) of VA-163; Lt. (junior grade) John Schroeder

Aircraft hit by 37 mm AAA during a strike on a bridge at Phuong Din. Shrapnel hit the leading edge of the port intake, damaging the engine.

A-4E (152085, AH416) of VA-164; pilot unknown

Aircraft hit by ground fire during an armed reconnaissance mission along Highway IA in RP II. Damage included several holes along the leading edge of the starboard wing.

11 SEPTEMBER 1967

A-4E (150131, AH303) of VA-163; Cdr. Bryan Compton

Aircraft hit by ground fire while bombing a bridge near Haiphong. While exiting the target area, Compton's aircraft sustained three hits in the starboard wing and rudder and on top of the fuselage.

13 SEPTEMBER 1967

A-4E (149971, AH304) of VA-163; Lt. Vance Schufeldt

Aircraft damaged by ground fire while suppressing AAA for a strike on Phuong Din in RP II. Damage included a small hole in the bottom of the port wing, with an 8-inch exit hole on top.

A-4E (151098) of VA-164; pilot unknown

Aircraft hit by ground fire while bombing construction equipment in RP III. Damage included one small hole in the fuselage.

17 OCTOBER 1967

A-4E (151985, AH414) of VA-164; pilot unknown

Aircraft hit by 37 mm AAA during a strike on a storage depot in the port of Haiphong, damaging the port slat.

22 October 1967

F-8E (149151, AH211) of VF-162; Lt. Cdr. Richard Leach

Aircraft hit by AAA during a strike on Haiphong. Damage included holes in the wing and landing gear doors. Aircraft craned off in Cubi Point.

23 October 1967

A-4E (151152, AH404) of VA-164; pilot unknown

Aircraft hit by 57 mm AAA while searching for WBLCs near Cam Pha.

24 October 1967

A-4E (149982, AH314) of VA-163; Lt. Vance Schufeldt

Aircraft hit by 85 mm AAA during Alpha strike on Phuc Yen. Damage included one 5-by-1-inch hole in the starboard wing, one hole in the starboard nose, and a shattered windscreen.

A-4E (151194, AH406) of VA-164; Lt. Cdr. Denis Weichman

Aircraft hit by 85 mm AAA during an Iron Hand mission for an Alpha strike on Phuc Yen.

A-4E (151985, AH414) of VA-164; pilot unknown

Aircraft hit by 37 mm AAA during an Iron Hand mission for an Alpha strike on Phuc Yen. Tail section extensively damaged.

25 October 1967

F-8C (147004, AH102) of VF-111; pilot unknown

Aircraft hit by ground fire while escorting an Iron Hand Skyhawk during strikes on Phuc Yen. Damage included six holes in the tail section of the aircraft.

A-4E (150006, AH312) of VA-163; Lt. (junior grade) Kenneth Adams

Aircraft damaged by SAM during a strike on Phuc Yen. Damage included buckling and multiple holes in the starboard fuselage.

A-4E (149971, AH304) of VA-163; Lt. Cdr. Dean Cramer

Aircraft hit by 37 mm AAA during a strike on Phuc Yen. Damage included one hole in the starboard horizontal stabilizer.

26 October 1967

A-4E (152083) of VA-164; pilot unknown

Aircraft hit by AAA during an Alpha strike on the Hanoi thermal power plant. Damage included three holes in the starboard aileron and one hole in the top of the fuselage.

27 OCTOBER 1967

A-4E (149964, AH311) of VA-163; Cdr. Ed Lighter

Aircraft damaged by SAM while bombing Highway 6 in Hoa Binh Province. Damage included fifteen holes in the forward fuselage and starboard wing.

29 OCTOBER 1967

F-8E (150879, AH205) of VF-162; Lt. Cdr. Richard Leach

Aircraft hit by SAM during a strike on Cho Ben. Aircraft suffered "large gaping holes" in the fuselage. Aircraft craned off in Cubi Point.

20 NOVEMBER 1967

A-4E (152203, AH300) of VA-163; Lt. (junior grade) Denny Earl

Aircraft hit by ground fire. A bullet entered the port side of the cockpit, shattering Earl's leg before destroying the rudder pedals. Earl was subsequently evacuated to the hospital at Naval Air Station Pensacola.

12 DECEMBER 1967

A-4E (150006, AH312) of VA-163; Lt. (junior grade) Gordon Hunter

Aircraft hit by ground fire in the vicinity of Ninh Binh in RP IV. Bullet entered port side of the cockpit and lodged in the instrument panel.

15 DECEMBER 1967

A-4E (150026, AH305) of VA-163, Lt. Cdr. Dean Cramer

Aircraft hit by ground fire near Quong Suoi, damaging the horizontal stabilizer.

16 DECEMBER 1967

A-4E (149664, AH311) of VA-163, Lt. Cdr. Earle Jackson

Aircraft hit by 85 mm AAA near Hon Gai. Damage included six shrapnel holes in the starboard fuselage.

2 JANUARY 1968

A-4E (151191, AH307) of VA-163, pilot unknown

Aircraft hit by ground fire while attacking railroad cars on an armed reconnaissance mission in RP IV. Damage included a 2-inch bullet hole in the port wing and a large tear where the round exited.

A-4E (151154) of VA-163, pilot unknown

Aircraft hit by ground fire while attacking WBLCs along RP IV, resulting in damage to the port wing.

4 JANUARY 1968

A-4E (150056) of VA-164, pilot unknown

Aircraft hit by 37 mm AAA while attacking a ferry in RP VIB. Damage included an 8-by-12-inch hole in the port wing.

A-4E (150026, AH305) of VA-163; pilot unknown

Aircraft hit by 37 mm AAA while attacking railroad cars near Nam Sach in RP VIB. Damage included two 12-inch holes in the port fuselage and two 12-inch holes in the tail and horizontal stabilizer.

6 JANUARY 1968

A-4E (150006, AH312) of VA-163; pilot unknown

Aircraft hit by 85 mm AAA during an armed reconnaissance mission in RP IV, damaging the port horizontal stabilizer.

A-1H (134567) of VA-152; pilot unknown

Aircraft experienced a fire in the cockpit during a RESCAP mission.

Appendix 4

Chronological History of Rolling Thunder

Rolling Thunder 1 (20 February 1965)

Canceled due to political unrest in South Vietnam. It was to have been an attack on Quang Khe naval base and Dong Hoi air base barracks.

Rolling Thunder 2, 3, and 4

Also canceled. Also had the same targets as Rolling Thunder 1.

Rolling Thunder 5 (2 March 1965)

By 2 March 1965 conditions in South Vietnam had stabilized to the point that Washington authorized Rolling Thunder 5 with South Vietnamese participation. USAF aircraft struck the ammunition depot at Xom Bong, and the VNAF struck the Quang Khe naval base. Rolling Thunder operations came with strict guidance. Targets were to be attacked on the specified day by the specified number of sorties, and they could not be reattacked later. Targets were clearly stated, with a limited number of alternates if bad weather covered the primary target. The navy did not participate in the opening strikes, as naval aircraft were covering the marine landings at Da Nang.

Rolling Thunder 6 (15 March 1965)

This involved attacks on targets in the southern part of North Vietnam. The USAF struck an ammunition depot at Phu Qui and the navy struck a radar installation on Tiger Island, 20 miles off the coast. Rolling Thunder 6 included the first participation by naval aircraft.

Rolling Thunder 7 (19–25 March 1965)

Rolling Thunder 7 began the release of weekly target packages. Washington gave the on-site commander discretion to choose the day of the attack within the specified week based on local conditions. Five targets, including barracks at Vu Con, were listed. Additionally, the participation of South Vietnamese aircraft was no longer required. Armed reconnaissance missions also began, although the numbers remained so limited as to be of little use.

Rolling Thunder 8 (26 March–1 April 1965)

Targets selected for this package consisted of radar sites providing coverage of North Vietnam, while the VNAF struck an army barracks. All targets were below the 20th parallel, except the radar station on the island of Bach Long Vi, which was 75 miles off the coast. The navy struck this radar station on 26 March, but it was not destroyed. Four aircraft were lost when it was attacked again on 29 March.

Rolling Thunder 9 (2–8 April 1965)

This package began concentrating on lines of communication in the southern half of North Vietnam. Strikes included attacks on the Thanh Hoa and Dong Phuong bridges. The Thanh Hoa bridge was attacked for the first time on 3 April 1965, resulting in the loss of two F-105s. This phase also resulted in the first photographs of a North Vietnamese SAM site 15 miles southeast of Hanoi.

Rolling Thunder 10 (9–16 April 1965)

Lines of communication remained the emphasis during this package, with strikes against bridges at Qui Vinh and Khe Khien. The number of armed reconnaissance missions increased to twenty-four missions per day.

Rolling Thunder 11–14 (17 April–12 May 1965)

Targeting lines of communication continued during these packages, as did North Vietnamese Army bases south of the 20th parallel.

Bombing Pause (12–18 May 1965)

Initiated in order to collect information and evaluate the results of Rolling Thunder.

Rolling Thunder 15 (18–24 May 1965)

The resumption of bombing resulted in one raid north of the 20th parallel against army barracks at Quang Suoi. The remaining missions were armed reconnaissance missions flown in specified areas.

Rolling Thunder 16 (25–31 May 1965)

Armed reconnaissance sorties flown during a twenty-four-hour period were increased to forty, with no more than two hundred per weekly package. The total number of sorties flown against North Vietnam in May increased to 4,000 from 3,600 during April.

Rolling Thunder 17 (1–7 June 1965)

Armed reconnaissance sorties increased to 260 per week.

Rolling Thunder 18–47 (8 June–24 December 1965)

The emphasis on transport and military targets continued as the campaign began its gradual expansion. Small numbers of targets north of the 21st parallel were struck. Restricted and prohibited areas around Hanoi and Haiphong as well as the buffer zone along the Chinese border were established. The JCS exempted Iron Hand missions from the overall sortie limitations. Total sorties flown during 1965 numbered 55,000.

Bombing Pause (24 December 1965–31 January 1966)

After the Viet Cong announced a Christmas "truce" in South Vietnam, Secretary of State Dean Rusk proposed suspending bombing operations for twenty-four hours. It was hoped that North Vietnam would respond in kind, and bombing would then be suspended to allow for peace talks.

Rolling Thunder 48 (31 January–28 February 1966)

The campaign resumed; however, operations were limited due to poor weather during February. Armed reconnaissance sorties were restricted to below the 21st parallel.

Rolling Thunder 49 (1–31 March 1966)

Weather continued to cancel missions, although permission was given for missions over most of North Vietnam. The total number of sorties flown during March was eight thousand.

Rolling Thunder 50 (1 April–8 July 1966)

The initial plan proposed strikes against two types of targets: the entire POL system and major industries in the northeastern portion of North Vietnam. Planning began for eleven specific industrial targets and the POL system; however, concern in Washington delayed the attacks. Authority to attack the POL system was eventually given, though permission was not given to strike targets until 29 June 1966. Armed reconnaissance was allowed over all of North Vietnam, including Route Package VI, except for the restricted areas. The total number of sorties flown during April increased to ten thousand.

Rolling Thunder 51 (9 July–11 November 1966)

POL continued to be the primary target of this package, with the addition of several small bridges and one bypass. CINCPAC promulgated a plan of action in late July to maximize destruction of North Vietnam's remaining elements; however, the only targets allowed by Washington for Rolling Thunder 51 were bridges. Armed reconnaissance along the northeastern rail line forced its closure for most of September and October. Sortie totals were raised to 13,000 per month.

Rolling Thunder 52 (12 November 1966–23 January 1967)

This package expanded the target list to include power stations, cement plants, and steel works, but these targets were disallowed and removed from the list before they could be attacked. The total number of sorties flown during 1966 was 148,000.

Bombing Pause (24–26 December 1966 and 31 December 1966–2 January 1967)

A cease-fire was directed for Christmas and the New Year, though CINCPAC asked that it be for no longer than forty-eight hours to limit North Vietnam's advantage.

Rolling Thunder 53 (24 January–22 February 1967)

The previous target list was continued with minor changes. Extremely bad weather precluded full-scale attacks on fixed targets and greatly reduced armed reconnaissance sorties.

Rolling Thunder 54 (23 February–22 April 1967)

In all, sixteen targets deemed vital to North Vietnamese industry were added to the target list. They included the Thai Nguyen steel works plant north of Hanoi, the Haiphong cement works, and several power stations. Estuaries and inland waterways up to the 20th parallel were listed as candidates for mining. The middle of April generally marked the end of bad weather over North Vietnam, and by 21 April all the Rolling Thunder 54 targets had been struck.

Rolling Thunder 55 (23 April–1 May 1967)

On 23 April the execute order for Rolling Thunder 55 was received. Armed reconnaissance operating areas remained constant, while the overall fixed targets increased dramatically. For the first time, selected targets were authorized for strike within the 10-mile circle around Hanoi. This included airfields at Kep and Hoa Lac, the power transformer in the center of Hanoi, and other industrial targets in the city. By 28 April all but one of the targets had been struck.

Rolling Thunder 56 (2 May–19 July 1967)

Good weather over North Vietnam permitted maximum effort against all authorized targets. Ten new targets were added, including a power plant in the center of Hanoi. Rolling Thunder 56 concentrated on the supply lines connecting Hanoi and Haiphong to Communist China, with the overall purpose of isolating Haiphong from Hanoi and both cities from the rest of North Vietnam.

Bombing Pause (23–24 May 1967)

A cease-fire was enforced for twenty-four hours in observance of Buddha's birthday.

Rolling Thunder 57 (25 May 1967–1 June 1968)

The summer of 1967 resulted in the heaviest bombing of North Vietnam during Rolling Thunder. Sixteen new targets, all in Route Package VI, were added. In a political move prior to the Stennis hearings, President Johnson added more targets to the list in August. The main effort was the continued attempts to isolate Hanoi and Haiphong, although by the end of August, Washington had again placed all targets in Hanoi on a restricted status. Sortie totals for August 1967 were 11,634. During September seventeen new targets were added to the list. In October eight more were added, and the restriction placed on targets in Hanoi was lifted. More targets were added in November, but monsoon season hindered the campaign. No new targets were added during December, but targets on the list were hit when weather permitted. Weather was the dominant factor influencing operations throughout North Vietnam in December. The total number of sorties flown during 1967 was 122,960, with another 9,740 of these against targets in Route Package VI.

Bombing Pause (24–25 December 1967)

Twenty-four-hour cease-fire enforced for observation of Christmas.

Bombing Pause (31 December 1967–2 January 1968)

On 30 December South Vietnam announced a New Year cease-fire. It included a twelve-hour extension that the South Vietnamese government had added in response to an appeal made by Pope Paul VI to make 1 January 1968 a "Day of Peace."

Rolling Thunder 57 (Continued)

Weather during the first three months of 1968 curtailed operations over North Vietnam. February's weather was the worst of any month during Rolling Thunder. There was an average of only three days per month on which strikes could be accomplished. Eight more targets were added to the list during this time. On 31 March President Johnson announced the curtailment of Rolling Thunder. Bombing was restricted to North Vietnam's transportation system below the 19th parallel.

Rolling Thunder 58 (2 July–1 November 1968)

Sortie rates continued at the same rate as before but were restricted to Route Packages I, II, and the southern portion of III. This meant that the bombing was extremely heavy in this area, and the transportation system was heavily hit. Rolling Thunder ended on 1 November 1968.

Notes

1. Rolling Thunder and the Numbers Game

1. Goldstein, *Lessons in Disaster*, 97–98.

2. Goldstein, *Lessons in Disaster*, 132.

3. McMaster, *Dereliction of Duty*, 82. McNamara told Johnson, "Divide and conquer is a pretty good rule in this situation. And to be quite frank, I've tried to do that in the last couple of weeks and it's coming along pretty well" (82).

4. The Pentagon Papers, Part IV.C.1, iii. Gradualism can be traced to a series of papers written in March 1964. Perhaps the most important was a policy statement produced by McGeorge Bundy. Known as National Security Action Memorandum (NSAM) 288, this document established the Johnson administration's policy in Southeast Asia (see The Pentagon Papers, Part IV.C.1, 40–56).

5. Following the failed Bay of Pigs Invasion and the Cuban Missile Crisis, President Kennedy and his staff developed a distinct distrust for the JCS. They believed the military would have pushed the country into war with the Soviet Union had the president and his advisors not been so resolute. This experience colored their thinking and helped reinforce what they witnessed during Operation Yankee Team.

6. DESOTO is an acronym for DEHAVEN Special Operations off Tsingtao. USS *DeHaven* (DD-727) conducted the first patrol in 1962 in response to China following the tense standoff between Taiwan and mainland China.

7. Goldstein, *Lessons in Disaster*, 133.

8. Hanyok, "Skunks," 39. See also Moise, *Tonkin Gulf*.

9. Goldstein, *Lessons in Disaster*, 156.

10. *Hearings by the Preparedness Investigating Subcommittee of the Committee on Armed Services*, United States Senate, 90th Cong., 1st sess. (testimony of Hon. Robert S. McNamara, Secretary of Defense, 25 August 1967), pt. 4, 303.

11. U.S. Navy Intelligence Lessons Learned in Vietnam, 15 January 1974, folder 2, box 2, pp. 5–6, Andrade Collection, https://vva.vietnam.ttu.edu/repositories/2/digital_objects/619866.

12. Sharp, *Strategy for Defeat*, 122.

13. The Pentagon Papers, Part IV.C.7.a, provides background on the decisions leading up to the POL strikes.

14. The Pentagon Papers, Part IV.C.7.a, 141–43.

15. The Pentagon Papers, Part IV.C.7.a, 179.

16. Hanyok, *Spartans in Darkness*, 236.

17. The Pentagon Papers, Part IV.C.7.a, 178.

18. Carrier aircraft are severely restricted by weight requirements. Bringing back unused ordnance means less fuel in order to meet the weight limit required to safely land.

19. Westmoreland, *A Soldier Reports*, 144.

20. Berger, *The* USAF *in Southeast Asia*, 75; Smith, *Rolling Thunder*, 80.

21. Pribbenow, "The -Ology War," 181.

22. Oral history transcript, Robert S. McNamara, interview 1 (I), 1 August 1975, by Elspeth D. Rostow, pp. 53–54, LBJ Library Oral Histories, https://www.discoverlbj .org:443/item/oh-mcnamarar-19750108-1-90-4.

23. For discussion on this topic, see McNamara and Van De Mark, *In Retrospect*; McNamara et al., *Argument without End*; Hendrickson, *Living and the Dead*; and Sorley, *Westmoreland*.

24. See Barlow, *Revolt of the Admirals*. The cancelation of USS *United States* in 1949 brought the debate to a head, resulting in the "Revolt of the Admirals." The incident started a debate, still ongoing, in the American military about the role of strategic bombing, nuclear weapons, and the unification of military command under civilian leadership.

25. Smith, *Rolling Thunder*, 225.

26. Smith, *Rolling Thunder*, 111.

27. Rasmussen, email to the author, 27 July 2005.

28. Foster, *Captain Hook*, 132.

29. McRae, "U.S. Navy," app. A, p. 5. The actual number of aircraft lost during the campaign is difficult to determine, as definitions of combat and operational losses varied by service. For example, an aircraft shot down by AAA on a combat mission is considered a combat loss, while an aircraft lost while launching at the beginning of a combat mission is considered an operational loss. Almost one-third of all navy losses during the Vietnam War were a result of operational accidents, which took their toll in both men and machines. It is generally accepted that 850–900 aircraft were lost during the three years of Operation Rolling Thunder.

30. McRae, "U.S. Navy," chap. 2, p. 13.

31. Smith, *Rolling Thunder*, 120.

2. The Environment

1. Cima, *A Country Study*, 242–43.

2. Prados, "The '65 Decision"; Pribbenow, *Victory in Vietnam*, 165–66. In August 1964 three of eleven VPAF regiments were radar units. Forty-four radars were confirmed and sixteen suspected by February 1965, figures that grew by another 50 percent in three months and 2.5 times over the next year.

3. Hanyok, *Spartans in Darkness*, 235.

4. Hanyok, *Spartans in Darkness*, 236.

5. Michel, *Clashes*, 2.

6. Hanyok, *Spartans in Darkness*, 261; Whiting, *Chinese Calculus*, 170. The actual number of American aircraft lost to Chinese pilots may never be known, as China

gave credit to North Vietnam to deny an American excuse for retaliation. Likewise, the United States often failed to note the loss of American aircraft that had been downed by China so that the Chinese could not confirm any potential wrongdoing, such as violations of Chinese airspace.

7. Zhang, "The Vietnam War," 756.

8. Zhang, "The Vietnam War," 756.

9. Prados, "The '65 Decision."

10. Pribbenow, "The -Ology War," 176.

11. Pribbenow, "The -Ology War," 177.

12. Shershnev, "No One Is Forgotten."

13. Shershnev, "No One Is Forgotten."

14. Pribbenow, "The -Ology War," 177.

15. Shershnev, "No One Is Forgotten."

16. Pribbenow, "The -Ology War," 184.

17. Hanyok, *Spartans in Darkness*, 261.

18. Davies, USN F-4 *Phantom*, 75.

19. Hanyok, *Spartans in Darkness*, 262.

20. Michel, *Clashes*, 169.

21. Sharp, *Strategy for Defeat*, 66.

22. Levinson, *Alpha Strike Vietnam*, 28.

23. Uhlig, *Vietnam*, 50.

24. Nichols and Tillman, *On Yankee Station*, 20.

25. Michel, *Clashes*, 139.

3. The Naval Air War

1. *Order of Battle for Carriers and Carrier-Based Squadrons in the Western Pacific (WestPac) and Vietnam 1964–1975*, https://www.history.navy.mil/research/library /research-guides/wars-conflicts-usnavy.html#anchor13254. Twenty-one aircraft carriers (fifteen CVA and six CVS) participated in Rolling Thunder. Although the antisubmarine carriers participated, their lack of a full air wing, including fighters, precluded many operations over North Vietnam. They complemented operations by hosting the helicopter squadrons so critical to CSAR.

2. Francillon, *Tonkin Gulf Yacht Club*, 45.

3. Levinson, *Alpha Strike Vietnam*, 26.

4. The time required from budget approval authorizing construction of a new carrier to her first deployment exceeded four years, so the only carriers commissioned during the war were laid down prior to its start. Today's supercarriers were laid down during the war but were unavailable until after the fall of Saigon.

5. Michel, *Clashes*, 27. For an example of how this shortage affected the navy, see McBride, *Shang Log*, which chronicles the USS *Shangri-La*, a World War Two–era carrier during her last cruise of the war. The ship was beset by mechanical and morale issues throughout its nine-month cruise.

6. Holloway, "Tactical Command and Control of Carrier Operations," in Naval Historical Center, *Command and Control*.

7. Foster, *Captain Hook*, 54.

8. VA-164, *Command History, 1967*, 28.

9. Only two Medals of Honor were awarded to naval aviators flying jets in. One went to Cdr. Jim Stockdale for his leadership of American POWs. The other was awarded posthumously to Lt. Cdr. Michael Estocin for his actions during two separate Iron Hand missions in the vicinity of Haiphong in April 1967.

10. The Fire Can and Fan Song radars are the NATO code names for Union equipment. The Fire Can radar controlled AAA, while the Fan Song radar controls the SA-2 missile.

11. VA-163, *Command History, 1966*, 32.

12. Thornborough and Mormillo, *Iron Hand*, 20.

13. VF-162, *Command History, 1967*, II-3.

14. Brown, email to the author, 11 October 2009; VF-162, *Command History, 1967*, II-2.

15. VF-162, *Command History, 1967*, II-3.

16. The F-8 community was the exception. The plane was the last fighter equipped with cannons, and its pilots continued to train and hone gunnery skills developed at the Fleet Air Gunnery Unit (FAGU) in the early 1960s.

17. See Michel, *Clashes*. Much has been written and debated about the reasoning behind USN and USAF loss rates during air-to-air combat in Vietnam. It is generally accepted that the "Loose Deuce" formations flown by navy fighters were superior to the air force's "Fluid Four." Michel provides perhaps the most unbiased and comprehensive in-depth look at the air war. He explains the differences in tactics, including the lessons learned from Rolling Thunder and how it led to the creation of Top Gun, the navy's air-to-air tactics school, and the air force's tactics school at Nellis Air Force Base.

18. Hershberg, *Marigold*, 88. The ICC used a fleet of tired Boeing 307 Stratoliners. The lumbering four-engine propeller planes were painted white with a blue stripe, identifying them as neutral. Unfortunately, they often found themselves caught between the United States and North Vietnamese. The flight between Tan Son Nhut, Phnom Penh, and Gia Lam in Hanoi was fraught with danger. It drove pilots and stewardesses to drink and shattered the nerves of those who remained, as most quit after experiencing the flight—it was that dangerous. Because of the ICC flights, Washington was compelled to impose more ROE to ensure the safety of foreign diplomats.

19. Naval Air Systems Command, "Report," 20. See also Westrum, *Sidewinder*.

20. Morgan, "Dragon in the Sky."

21. Morgan, "Dragon in the Sky"; Nichols and Tillman, *On Yankee Station*, 88.

22. Zaloga, *Soviet Air Defence Missiles*, 57.

23. Naval Air Weapons Center China Lake, California, is the home of operational and weapons testing for naval aviation. Its remote location, far from prying eyes, allowed testing against actual Soviet equipment during the Cold War.

24. Michel, *Clashes*, 38.

25. Price, *Rolling Thunder*, 50.

26. Price, *Rolling Thunder*, 3, 50.

27. Price, *Rolling Thunder*, 57.

28. Pribbenow, "The -Ology War," 183.

29. Morgan, "Orphans of the 7th Fleet."

30. Morgan, "Orphans of the 7th Fleet."

31. Morgan, "Orphans of the 7th Fleet." See also Jones, "The Most Highly Decorated."

32. Marcy, *Sundowner Days*, 34.

33. Sherwood, *Afterburner*, 292.

34. Sherwood, *Afterburner*, 293.

35. Stockdale, *Thoughts*, 64. Stockdale paraphrases Tom Wolfe's article in this 1988 speech. Wolfe, *The Truest Sport*, 525–56.

36. Nichols and Tillman, *On Yankee Station*, 34.

37. Arnold, "A Trip to the Suburbs."

38. Michel, *Clashes*, 120.

39. Levinson, *Alpha Strike Vietnam*, 176.

40. Michel, *Clashes*, 168.

41. Rasmussen, email to the author, 27 July 2005.

42. Michel, *Clashes*, 168.

43. For multiple accounts of this disastrous policy, see Levinson, *Alpha Strike Vietnam*.

44. Elkins, *The Heart of a Man*, 107–8.

45. Nichols and Tillman, *On Yankee Station*, 42.

46. Nichols and Tillman, *On Yankee Station*, 35.

47. Foster, email to the author, 19 September 2005.

48. Holloway, "Tactical Command."

49. Rasimus, *When Thunder Rolled*, 104.

4. Gradual Beginnings

1. Cosmas, MACV, 219.

2. Hendrickson, *The Living and the Dead*, 69.

3. McMaster, *Dereliction of Duty*, 332–33.

4. Levinson, *Alpha Strike Vietnam*, 241.

5. Lawson, *Carrier Air Group Commanders*, 35.

6. Levinson, *Alpha Strike Vietnam*, 58.

7. Stockdale, *In Love and War*, 89.

8. Stockdale, *In Love and War*, 89.

9. Brown, email to the author, 8 July 2013.

10. Text of speech from Sharp, *Strategy for Defeat*, 97–99.

11. Stockdale, *In Love and War*, 91.

12. Grant, *Over the Beach*, 31–32.

13. Foster, *Captain Hook*, 107.

14. Stockdale, *In Love and War*, 91.

15. Foster, *Captain Hook*, 37.

16. USS *Oriskany*, Deck Log, Wednesday, 5 May 1965; "U.S. Sailor Drowns in Sea," *Stars and Stripes*, 12 May 1965; Foster, *Captain Hook*, 37.

17. Headquarters Military Assistance Command Vietnam, MACV *1965 Yearly Summary*, 12; Schlight, *The War*, 45; Ryder, *"Lead,"* 214. Tom Meredith led the development and fielding of air force civil engineers, known as Prime Base Emergency Engineer Force (BEEF) and Rapid Engineer Deployable, Heavy Operational Repair Squadron, Engineer (RED HORSE) units. They have provided heavy construction and engineering support since this incident.

18. USS *Oriskany*, Deck Log, Tuesday, 25 May 1965; Carrier Air Wing 16, *Command History, 1965*, 35.

19. Foster, *Captain Hook*, 37.

20. Marcy, *Sundowner Days*, 43.

21. Foster, *Captain Hook*, 59.

22. Levinson, *Alpha Strike Vietnam*, 38.

23. Cable from Sullivan (Vientianne) to Admiral Sharp, CINCPAC, 4 June 1965, Air America and Civil Air Transport Collection, University of Texas at Dallas, http://www.utdallas.edu/library/uniquecoll/speccoll/aamnote/aam65.pdf.

24. In April 1965 F-4s from VF-96 engaged Chinese MiG-17s over Hainan Island. The incident was extremely controversial due to the fact that it occurred within Chinese airspace. The Johnson administration was terrified of PRC intervention, and the event was classified so that it would not publicly antagonize the Chinese. The PRC insisted that an F-4 had been downed by a "guided missile" fired by one of the other F-4s involved and that they had lost no aircraft. Most Americans believed the Chinese were lying, but in fact, they were closer to the truth than Washington. Events rapidly overtook the April engagement, and the historical record was left confused. This was due to the honest inability of the aviators to accurately recount what happened, as well as political revisionism, which dictated that no dogfights had occurred over Hainan. Seventh Fleet credited VF-96 with scoring the first MiG kill of the war, a misplaced honor.

25. Burgess and Rausa, *US Navy A-1 Skyraider Units*, 29.

26. Air America, *Command History, 1965*, http://www.utdallas.edu/library/uniquecoll/speccoll/aamnote/aam65.pdf, 15.

27. Stockdale quoted in Lawson, *Carrier Air Group Commanders*, 101.

28. "Downed Flier Swapped for Ice Cream," *Stars and Stripes*, 3 July 1965.

29. VMF(AW)-212, *Command Chronology, 1965*, II-10-2.

30. "Spotter Lauds Navy Pilots," *Stars and Stripes*, 1 September 1965.

5. The War Heats Up

1. CINCPACFLT, Staff Analysis Study 12-65, enclosure 1, table 1.

2. Wolfe, *Mauve Gloves*. Tom Wolfe was the first to mention the joke in publication, although the joke is referenced in many postwar publications concerning naval aviation; see Levinson, *Alpha Strike*; and Nichols and Tillman, *On Yankee Station*.

3. Mersky, *F-8 Crusader Units*, 27.

4. Lawson, *Carrier Air Group Commanders*, 101.

5. Foster, *Captain Hook*, 80.

6. Levinson, *Alpha Strike Vietnam*, 40.

7. CINPACFLT, Command History, 1966, 31 January 1967, 135, folder 2, box 8, Sedgwick Tourison Collection, Vietnam Center and Archive, Texas Tech University.

8. VMF(AW)-212, *Command Chronology 1965*, II-12-1.

9. Quoted in Levinson, *Alpha Strike Vietnam*, 43.

10. Foster, *Captain Hook*, 102.

11. Foster, *Captain Hook*, 108.

12. Levinson, *Alpha Strike Vietnam*, 83.

13. Although marine squadrons have been a continuous part of carrier air wings since World War Two, marines do not typically lead them. In 2006 Col. Douglas Yurovich assumed command of CVW-9, the first marine since Ludden.

14. Holloway, *Aircraft Carriers*, 204; Wildenberg, *Gray Steel*, 241–46; Hooper, *Mobility*.

15. Holloway, *Aircraft Carriers at War*, 204.

16. Holloway, *Aircraft Carriers at War*, 204.

17. Holloway, *Aircraft Carriers at War*, 206.

18. "New Champ in Taking Ammo Aboard," *Stars and Stripes*, 24 September 1965.

6. The Bridge Campaign

1. Van Staaveren, *Gradual Failure*, 190.

2. Mersky, "Belly," 27.

3. Lt. Cdr. Dan Macintyre and Lt. (junior grade) Allen Johnson claimed a MiG-17. The MiG was flown by Nguyen Van Bay from the 923rd FR. Though his aircraft was severely damaged, he survived the war with many victories, among them a VF-111 Crusader in 1966. He retired from the VPAF in 1991.

4. CINCPACFLT, Staff Analysis Study 12-65, 4.

5. Hirsch, *Two Souls*. The North Vietnamese threw Halyburton, a southerner, into a cell with Maj. Fred Cherry, an African American air force pilot. Cherry had been severely wounded, and by forcing Halyburton to care for Cherry, the North Vietnamese hoped to break both men. Instead, they became friends who depended on each other to survive the ordeal.

6. CINCPACFLT, *The United States Navy in the Pacific Fleet 1965*, 161.

7. Price, *Rolling Thunder*, 67-70.

8. CINCPACFLT, Staff Analysis Study 12-65, 5.

9. Barnhill, "SAM Killer Mission," 8.

10. National Security Agency, Southeast Asia / POW-MIA Affairs, https://www.nsa.gov/public_info/_files/vietnam_powmia_docs/DocC.pdf.

11. CINCPACFLT, Staff Analysis Study 12-65, 5.

12. CINCPACFLT, Staff Analysis Study 8-68, B-1-3.

13. Barnhill, "SAM Killer Mission," 8.

14. Pararescueman James Pleiman received the Silver Star for jumping into the water to rescue Huggins during a nine-minute gun battle. He was KIA during a similar rescue four months later.

15. VA-163, *Command History, 1966*, 25.

16. Smith quoted in Burgess and Rausa, *U.S. Navy A-1 Skyraider Units*, 31.

17. Burgess and Rausa, *U.S. Navy A-1 Skyraider Units*, 31.

18. Smith quoted in Burgess and Rausa, *U.S. Navy A-1 Skyraider Units*, 32.

19. Burgess and Rausa, *U.S. Navy A-1 Skyraider Units*, 33.

20. Galdorisi and Phillips, *Leave No Man Behind*, 239.

21. Smith quoted in Burgess and Rausa, *U.S. Navy A-1 Skyraider Units*, 35.

22. Morgan, "Orphans of Seventh Fleet," 30.

23. Smith quoted in Burgess and Rausa, *U.S. Navy A-1 Skyraider Units*, 35.

24. USS *Oriskany*, Deck Log, Saturday, 6 November 1965. *Oriskany* steamed on a variable course of 300–330° for several hours to steam closer as the rescue unfolded. Captain Connolly turned into the wind to recover the aircraft and then sailed south. The log also shows entries for launching RESCAP A-1s during nonflying periods. Burgess and Rausa, *U.S. Navy A-1 Skyraider Units*, 36. The story was told during a 1990 reunion of air wing members and has appeared in several publications since. There are several versions, and each differs due to the haze and chaos of combat. The one common theme is of Captain Connolly sailing *Oriskany* into treacherous shoal-waters to help the pilots.

25. Foster, *Captain Hook*, 124.

26. Pribbenow, "The -Ology War," 178.

27. Pribbenow, "The -Ology War," 178.

28. Jenkins quoted in Levinson, *Alpha Strike Vietnam*, 36–42.

29. VA-152, *Command History, 1967*, 4.

30. Moore and Galloway, *We Were Soldiers*, 14.

31. USS *Oriskany*, Deck Log, Wednesday, 17 November 1965; "Martha Raye Wows All Hands at Sangley," *Stars and Stripes*, 25 November 1965.

32. Moore and Galloway, *We Were Soldiers*, 14. In November and December 1965, Western Union simply handed telegrams over to Yellow Cab drivers to deliver to families.

33. Foster quoted in Levinson, *Alpha Strike Vietnam*, 80.

34. Hershberg, *Marigold*, 13.

35. Foster quoted in Levinson, *Alpha Strike Vietnam*, 81.

36. Levinson, *Alpha Strike Vietnam*, 133.

37. Moore and Galloway, *We Were Soldiers*, 323.

38. The Pentagon Papers, Part IV.C.7.a, 21.

39. Hershberg, *Marigold*, 65.

7. The POL Campaign

1. VA-164, *Command History, 1966*, 7. Both the navy and air force held an advantage over the other services. Quality recruitment, coupled with the very real possibility of being drafted and sent into the meat grinder, led many young men to join these services. It was not enough to fill the ranks, however. See Sherwood, *Black Sailor*.

2. Foster, email to the author, 19 September 2005.

3. Foster, "The Saints of VA-163."

4. VA-163, *Command History, 1966*, 12.

5. "US Gets Bad Deal in Bombs," *Denver Post*, 17 April 1966, 6. A Pat Oliphant editorial cartoon published on 20 April 1966 spoofed McNamara's response that the bomb shortages were baloney.

6. Van Staaveren, *Gradual Failure*, 264.

7. VA-163, *Command History, 1966*, 33.

8. Of five brothers, three became naval aviators during World War Two. That two brothers commanded the same ship was a first in naval history. See the obituary in the *Boston Globe*, 25 October 2006.

9. A quick read of any books in the bibliography quickly uncovers the pervasive "us vs. them" mentality. Fifty years later, the mentality is still insidious and colors many memories of the time.

10. Schaffert, email to the author, 22 July 2010.

11. Schaffert, email to the author, 22 July 2010.

12. Marcy, *Sundowner Days*, 41.

13. USS *Oriskany*, Deck Log, Thursday, 7 July 1966; Bob Pearl, email to the author, 10 June 2010.

14. "Joint Chiefs Ask Raids on Haiphong Fuel, Oil," *Denver Post*, 13 March 1966.

15. Uhlig, *Vietnam*, 37. McNamara also directed that the most experienced pilots be used, that good weather be maximized to promote accuracy, and that the axis of attack should be carefully considered.

16. David Kraslow, "Bomb Decision 'Leak' Probed," *Denver Post*, 29 June 1966, 14.

17. Van Staaveren, *Gradual Failure*, 295.

18. Elkins, *The Heart of a Man*, 49.

19. CVW-16, *Command History, 1966*, 11.

20. Waechter, letters to the editor, RNPA *Contrails*, August 2008, 7; Mersky, *F-8 Crusader Units*, 31.

21. "A Feeling for Freedom," *Time*, 29 July 1966.

22. U.S. Air Force, Weapons Systems Evaluation Group, *Air-to-Air Encounters in Southeast Asia, Volume I*, Event 1-38, 272–74; O'Connor, *MiG Killers*, 50.

23. U.S. Air Force, Weapons Systems Evaluation Group, *Air-to-Air Encounters in Southeast Asia, Volume I*, Event 1-38, 274; Foster, *Captain Hook*, 177.

24. U.S. Air Force, Weapons Systems Evaluation Group, *Air-to-Air Encounters in Southeast Asia, Volume I*, Event 1-38, 274; Foster, *Captain Hook*, 177.

25. U.S. Air Force, Weapons Systems Evaluation Group, *Air-to-Air Encounters in Southeast Asia, Volume I*, Event 1-38, 274; O'Conner, *MiG Killers*, 50.

26. U.S. Air Force, Weapons Systems Evaluation Group, *Air-to-Air Encounters in Southeast Asia, Volume I*, Event 1-38, 276; O'Conner, *MiG Killers*, 50.

27. Foster, *Captain Hook*, 178.

28. Schaffert, email to the author, 30 June 2010.

29. Elkins, *The Heart of a Man*, 62.

30. Foster, "The Will to Survive," *Approach*, December 1966, 4.

31. Foster, "The Will to Survive," *Approach*, December 1966, 4.

32. Foster, "The Will to Survive," *Approach*, December 1966, 4.

33. Foster, "The Will to Survive," *Approach*, December 1966, 5.

34. Foster, "The Will to Survive," *Approach*, December 1966, 5.

35. Foster, *Captain Hook*, 189.

36. Elkins, *The Heart of a Man*, 68–69. Frank Elkins's wife changed names throughout when publishing the journal. Foster is called Falcon.

37. Foster, *Captain Hook*, 193.

38. CVW-16, *Command History, 1966*, 15.

39. Elkins, *The Heart of a Man*, 77.

40. Engel, email to the author, 10 November 2009.

41. Gray, *The Warriors*, 28.

42. Nichols and Tillman, *On Yankee Station*, 45.

43. Nichols and Tillman, *On Yankee Station*, 46.

44. Giberson, "The Legend."

45. Nichols and Tillman, *On Yankee Station*, 47.

8. The Battle Increases

1. Zaloga, *Red SAM*, 19. This figure is confirmed by CINCPACFLT, Staff Analysis Study 8-68, and CINCPACFLT, Staff Analysis Study 4-68.

2. Schaffert, email to the author, 30 June 2010.

3. VA-163, *Command History, 1966*, 33.

4. Schaffert, email to the author, 30 June 2010.

5. Galdorisi and Phillips, *Leave No Man Behind*, 275.

6. CVW-16, *Command History, 1966*, 19.

7. Galdorisi and Phillips, *Leave No Man Behind*, rescue synopsis, http://raunchyredskins.us/lnmb%20rescues/Levy.pdf.

8. CVW-16, *Command History, 1966*, 19.

9. Mersky, *F-8 Crusader Units*, 53.

10. VA-152, *Command History, 1967*, 7.

11. CVW-16, *Command History, 1966*, 20.

12. CVW-16, *Command History, 1966*, 22.

13. CVW-16, *Command History, 1966*, 22.

14. Galdorisi and Phillips, *Leave No Man Behind*, 277–78.

15. Galdorisi and Phillips, *Leave No Man Behind*, 277–78.

16. Galdorisi and Phillips, *Leave No Man Behind*, 277–78.

17. CINCPAC, *Command History, 1966*, 502; McNamara and Van De Mark, *In Retrospect*, 245–46; Van Staaveren, *Gradual Failure*, 303–4.

18. VA-163, *Command History, 1966*, 31.

19. U.S. Air Force, Weapons Systems Evaluation Group, *Air-to-Air Encounters in Southeast Asia, Volume I*, Event 1-43, 301–3.

20. O'Connor, *MiG Killers*, 52. The Vietnamese eventually operated on his leg, and he spent four months in a cast. After that, it took two years, with help from his cellmate and fellow POWs, for him to achieve use of his leg.

21. Rime, email to the author, 26 January 2014; O'Connor, *MiG Killers*, 52.

22. Rime, email to the author, 26 January 2014; O'Connor, *MiG Killers*, 52.

23. CVW-16, *Command History, 1966*, 11.

24. USS *Oriskany*, Cruise Book, 1966, 148; USS *Oriskany*, Deck Log, 16 September 1966.

25. USS *Oriskany*, Cruise Book, 1966, 147.

26. "Shipping Firm Thanks Oriskany for Rescue," *Stars and Stripes*, 25 September 1966.

27. Davis, "Stopping by Carlin," 15.

28. No longer a casino, the Riverside still stands next to the Truckee River in downtown Reno. It has been renovated with loft-style apartments, while the ground floor houses an upscale restaurant overlooking the river. The Jessie Beck Elementary School is not too far away, named after one of Nevada's leading businesswomen.

29. Kling, *The Rise*, 9.

30. Davis, "Farewell Lady Jessie," 14.

31. CINCPACFLT, *Command History, 1966*, 3.

32. Zaloga, *Soviet Air Defence Missiles*, 61.

33. Zaloga, *Soviet Air Defence Missiles*, 57.

34. CVW-16, *Command History, 1966*, 15.

35. Davis, email to the author, 22 October 2010.

36. CVW-16, *Command History, 1966*, 16.

37. USS *Oriskany*, Deck Log, 9 July 1966.

38. USS *Oriskany*, Deck Log, 23 August 1966; Maxwell, email to the author, 7 October 2010. Farris went through a Fleet Naval Aviator Evaluation Board (FNAEB) as a result of this incident. Farris had transitioned to A-3s after flying the A-1 and had been slow to learn the intricacies of flying the new airframe. Sadly, Farris was killed in the fire on 26 October.

39. USS *Oriskany*, Deck Log, Sunday, 2 October 1966; rescue summary, http://raunchyredskins.us/Operations/Combat%20sar.htm.

40. CVW-16, *Command History, 1966*, 16.

41. U.S. Air Force, Weapons Systems Evaluation Group, *Air-to-Air Encounters in Southeast Asia, Volume I*, Event 1-54, 355–59; O'Connor, *MiG Killers*, 53.

42. U.S. Air Force, Weapons Systems Evaluation Group, *Air-to-Air Encounters in Southeast Asia, Volume I*, Event 3-40, 68.

43. "Skyraider Downs MiG over North," *Stars and Stripes*, 11 October 1966.

44. Maxwell, interview with the author, October 2005. Continued in email to the author, 21 August 2010.

45. Schaffert, email to the author, 2 July 2010. This version can be verified by watching a Public Affairs movie shot during Secretary McNamara's visit. See http://research.archives.gov/description/85446.

46. The Pentagon Papers, Part IV.C.7.a, 150.

47. Van Staaveren, *Gradual Failure*, 304.

48. Grant, *Over the Beach*, 91.

49. Schaffert, email to the author, 30 June 2010. I have searched all the *Peanuts* strips for 1966 and have been unable to find this comic strip. Further searches through the Pacific edition of *Stars and Stripes* revealed no strip. It is likely that the

cartoon had been published on *Oriskany* either in the ship's newspaper or, more probably, in the ship's air plan. The air plan is the schedule of the daily flights from the carrier. The front contains the schedule, while the back contains pertinent notes, including a schedule of the day's nonflying events. Every day, each carrier in the navy publishes an air plan, which includes a cartoon, a tradition that is still upheld in naval aviation. The cartoons are frequently copies of original work, with new captions drawn in.

50. The Pentagon Papers, Part IV.C.7.a, 166.

51. Isaacs, *Vietnam Shadows*, 39–40.

9. Fire!

1. Foster, *Fire on the Hangar Deck*, 8–10.

2. Foster, *Fire on the Hangar Deck*, 47.

3. "A Carrier's Agony," *Life*, 25 November 1966.

4. "Agony of the Oriskany," *Time*, 4 November 1966.

5. Foster, *Fire on the Hangar Deck*, 62.

6. Foster, *Fire on the Hangar Deck*, 58.

7. Foster, *Fire on the Hangar Deck*, 66–67.

8. Foster, *Fire on the Hangar Deck*, 68.

9. Foster, *Fire on the Hangar Deck*, 106–7.

10. "A Carrier's Agony."

11. Dick Schaffert has written a letter to Norm Levy every Memorial Day since the fire. Schaffert, interview with the author, February 2012.

12. CVW-16, *Command History, 1966*, 34.

13. Foster, *Fire on the Hangar Deck*, 83.

14. "A Carrier's Agony."

15. CVW-16, *Command History, 1966*, 34.

16. Foster, *Fire on the Hangar Deck*, 100.

17. "A Carrier's Agony."

18. Foster, *Fire on the Hangar Deck*, 104.

19. "Fire in Hangar Bay One," *All Hands*, February 1967.

20. CVW-16, *Command History, 1966*, 36.

21. Foster, *Fire on the Hangar Deck*, 81.

22. "A Carrier's Agony."

23. "A Carrier's Agony."

24. Foster's *Fire on the Hangar Deck* places Meadows in his stateroom, while the CVW-16 Command History claims he was in the cockpit. Jay Meadows is deceased, so I was unable to confirm which story is correct. Other members of the air wing seem to remember him having climbed out of the cockpit prior to his heroics, but for most, their memories of the day are centered on what happened to them.

25. Schaffert, email to the author, 6 July 2012. After being blown into the hangar bay, Dick Schaffert dutifully made his way to VF-111's ready room and then to the flight deck to man the alert. It was while manning the alert that he witnessed the beginning of Meadows's heroics.

26. CVW-16, *Command History, 1966*, 37.

27. Schaffert, email to the author, 6 July 2012. The Navy and Marine Corps Medal is the second highest noncombat medal for bravery awarded to members who distinguish themselves by heroism not involving conflict with an enemy. It is typically awarded for actions involving great risk of one's own life. Other awardees include Cdr. Francis Brown, Lt. Howard Petty, Lt. (junior grade) Robert Williamson, Chief Warrant Officer Orville King, Aviation Electrician Chief Petty Officer John Johnson, Aviation Boatswain's Mate 2nd Class Henry Brooks, Aviation Boatswain's Mate 2nd Class John Clark, Aviation Boatswain's Mate 3rd Class Walter Fletcher, Storekeeper 3rd Class Romey Rose, Airman Francis Soave, Airman Michael Pardi, and Airman Tillman Bennett.

28. Foster, *Fire on the Hangar Deck*, 77.

29. Foster, *Fire on the Hangar Deck*, 78.

30. Quoted in "Fire in Hangar Bay One."

31. "Agony of the Oriskany." A complete version of the text can be found in U.S. Seventh Fleet News Release 645-66, 28 October 1966, "Highlights of Rescue Operations during Oriskany Fire," p. 5, folder 8, box 1, Ridgeway Collection.

32. Elkins, *Heart of a Man*, 72.

33. USS *Forrestal* never returned to combat, and the fire aboard USS *Enterprise* occurred after Rolling Thunder, during the lull in the air war before Operation Linebacker.

10. Long, Hot Summer

1. Headquarters Pacific Air Force, *Air Tactics*, 7.

2. For further information on this failed Italian-Polish peace initiative, see Hershberg, *Marigold*.

3. U.S. Air Force, Weapons Systems Evaluation Group, *Air-to-Air Encounters in Southeast Asia, Volume I*, Event 1-68, 415–55; Rasimuss and Olds, *Fighter Pilot*, 271–82.

4. Headquarters Pacific Air Force, *Air Tactics*, 7.

5. Van Staaveren, *Gradual Failure*, 143; Jacobsen, "Washington's Management of the Rolling Thunder Campaign," in Naval Historical Center, *Command and Control*; O'Connor, *MiG Killers*, 63.

6. CINCPACFLT, Staff Analysis Study 8-68, 5.

7. VA-164, *Command History, 1967*, 2.

8. Sheeley, interview with the author, Virginia Beach, Virginia, October 2009. Buck Sheeley was eventually given command of VA-152, which he led through their transition to A-4 Skyhawks and eventual deployment aboard USS *Shangri-La*.

9. Schaffert and Brown, email to the author, 17 August 2011.

10. Schaffert and Brown, email to the author, 17 August 2011.

11. Schaffert and Brown, email to the author, 17 August 2011.

12. Brown, email to the author, 11 October 2009.

13. The Pentagon Papers, Part IV.C.6.b, 147–56.

14. McNamara, interview, 23.

15. See McLaughlin, *The Long, Hot Summer*.

16. The Pentagon Papers, Part IV.C.7.b, 80.

17. Dittman, "Downed Pilot Eludes N. Viet's Dogs," *Stars and Stripes*, 20 July 1967.

18. Dittman, "Downed Pilot."

19. Davis, email to the author, 27 April 2013.

20. Galdorisi and Phillips, *Leave No Man Behind*, 306.

21. Dittman, "Downed Pilot."

22. U.S. Air Force, Weapons Systems Evaluation Group, *Air-to-Air Encounters in Southeast Asia, Volume I*, Event 3-341, 386; O'Connor, *MiG Killers*, 90.

23. Galdorisi and Phillips, *Leave No Man Behind*, 306.

24. Duthie, "Flightbag"; Span, interview with the author, Virginia Beach, Virginia, October 2009. Larry Duthie eventually returned to Vietnam and visited the Hourglass. Locals informed him that the area was used to relocate high-ranking Communist officials during the war. The defenses usually avoided firing upon airplanes to avoid drawing attention, but once the rescues began, aviators discovered how heavily defended the area was.

25. Duthie, email to the author, 19 January 2017; Galdorisi and Phillips, *Leave No Man Behind*, 307.

26. Duthie, email to the author, 19 January 2017; Galdorisi and Phillips, *Leave No Man Behind*, 307.

27. The radio antenna was located on top of the fuselage and thus masked any reception directly underneath the Sea King. Duthie, email to the author, 18 January 2017.

28. Duthie, "Flightbag"; Duthie, email to the author, 19 January 2017.

29. Duthie, "Flightbag"; Duthie, email to the author, 19 January 2017.

30. Frisbee, "Valor."

31. Anxious to repeat the success of Verich's rescue, Admiral Richards denied the attempt. Duthie, email to the author, 19 January 2017.

32. Galdorisi and Phillips, *Leave No Man Behind*, 308.

33. VA-164, *Command History, 1967*, 12; CINCPACFLT, Staff Analysis Study 4-68, A-VI-1; Span, interview with the author, October 2009; Duthie, email to the author, 22 January 2017.

34. Span, interview with the author, October 2009.

35. Duthie, email to the author, 22 January 2017.

36. Rasmussen, email to the author, 28 July 2006.

37. Rasmussen, email to the author, 28 July 2006.

38. Levinson, *Alpha Strike Vietnam*, 204.

39. Mersky, *US Navy and Marine Corps*, 50.

40. Arnold, "A Trip."

41. The rocket hit future Senator John McCain's Skyhawk, puncturing his drop tank before going over the side and impacting the water.

42. USS *Oriskany*, Deck Log, 29 July 1967.

43. Addeeb, *Oral History*, 17.

44. Freeman, *Sailors to the End*, 210; Addeeb, *Oral History*, 18.

45. Freeman, *Sailors to the End*, 273.

46. U.S. Navy, Judge Advocate General, "USS *Forrestal* (CVA-59) Fire Investigation," 3.

47. Gray, *Rampant Raider*, 273.

48. Arnold, "A Trip."

49. Days after this, another Sundowner pilot, John Laughter, earned a Distinguished Flying Cross during an alpha strike on the Hanoi battery plant. With little more than one hundred hours in the F-8, he took the lead after his wingman, Lt. Cdr. Dick Schaffert, suffered radio failure. Laughter kept the pair on station between Phuc Yen and the strike package while they dodged SAMs.

50. Arnold, "A Trip."

51. Arnold, "A Trip."

11. The Stennis Hearings and the Climax

1. Van Staaveren, *Gradual Failure*, 300–307.

2. The Pentagon Papers, Part IV.C.7.b, 90.

3. Draft Memo: Vietnam Data and Progress Indicators from Bundy to McNamara, 13 October 1967, 2, folder 4, box 8, Berman Collection.

4. The Pentagon Papers, Part IV.C.7.b, 95.

5. *Hearings by the Preparedness Investigating Subcommittee*, pt. 4, 303.

6. *Hearings by the Preparedness Investigating Subcommittee*, pt. 4, 352.

7. The Pentagon Papers, Part IV.C.7.b, 92.

8. Ted Sell, "McNamara Says Raids Alone Can't End War," *Washington Post*, 26 August 1967.

9. Broughton, *Going Downtown*, 105.

10. Quoted in Mersky, *US Navy and Marine Corps*, 50.

11. Mersky, *US Navy and Marine Corps*, 50.

12. Mersky, *US Navy and Marine Corps*, 50.

13. Quoted in Kilduff, *Osprey Air Combat*, 121.

14. Quoted in Levinson, *Alpha Strike Vietnam*, 208.

15. Quoted in Levinson, *Alpha Strike Vietnam*, 209.

16. VA-163, *Command History*, 1967, B-4.

17. CINCPACFLT, Staff Analysis Study 8-68, B-1-24. Navy raids reported 93–105 missiles fired during their strikes. Air force raids reported 31–46 firings.

18. Tannenbaum, "Papa Wasn't." Two A-6s were shot down by two Chinese 52nd FR pilots, Han Ruijie and Chen Fengxia. The only survivor, Lt. Robert Flynn, was captured by the Chinese and held in solitary confinement in Beijing until 1973. Flynn remained adamant until his death in 2014 that the aircraft never entered Chinese airspace. The Chinese returned the ashes of his pilot, Jimmy Buckley, in 1975. Of the eight men shot down that day, two remain MIA.

19. Pribbenow, "The -Ology War," 179.

20. CINCPACFLT, Staff Analysis Study 8-68, 27.

21. CINCPACFLT, Staff Analysis Study 8-68, 38. See also CINCPACFLT, *Attrition of U.S. Aircraft*, 9.

22. Pribbenow, "The -Ology War," 179.

23. Capt. Dave Carey, 10 November 2011, D145.1I, Vietnam Center and Archive 2011 Guest Lecture Series, Vietnam Center Collection, Vietnam Center and Archive.

24. Davis, email to the author, February 2013.

25. In the course of researching this book, I was continually struck by the amount of grief stemming from this episode. During the many interviews I conducted, this topic often resulted in hushed silence followed by quiet tears. Forty-five years following his death, it is still too painful for many veterans to discuss.

26. Span, interview with the author, October 2009.

27. The Pentagon Papers, Part IV.C.7.b, 100.

28. "Jets Bomb N. Viet Port for 1st Time," *Stars and Stripes*, 13 September 1967.

29. "Jets Bomb 8 New Haiphong Targets," *Stars and Stripes*, 14 September 1967.

30. Schaffert, email to the author, 13 June 2010. Dick Schaffert described putting on an air show with Lt. Cdr. Foster Teague. Because the North Vietnamese had no ammunition to shoot with, they stayed around and flew "some fancy passes."

31. Colvin, "Hanoi in My Time," 152–53. Colvin argues that the supplies used for the Tet Offensive had already been off-loaded and moved down the Ho Chi Minh Trail before September 1967.

32. W. W. Rostow to President Lyndon B. Johnson, memo, Bombing of North Vietnam, 18 October 1967, folder 9, box 2, Veteran Members of the 109th Quartermaster Company (Air Delivery) Collection.

12. Black October

1. The Pentagon Papers, Part IV.C.7.b, 103.

2. The Pentagon Papers, Part IV.C.7.b, 113.

3. Grant, *Over the Beach*, 214.

4. Addeeb, *Oral History*, 21.

5. Span, interview with the author, October 2009.

6. Kilduff, *Osprey Air Combat*, 121. Similar stories can be found in McCain and Salter, *Faith of My Fathers*.

7. John Davis, email to the author, 8 February 2013.

8. Cdr. Paul Engel had been stationed at NAWC China Lake prior to assuming command, and because of this, VA-164 had a close working relationship with engineers there. This allowed the squadron to develop tactics in conjunction with experts there. These tactics then spread to squadrons deploying to Vietnam.

9. Span, interview with the author, October 2009.

10. Laughter, Schaffert, Brown, email to the author, 8 February 2013.

11. Davis, email to the author, 12 February 2013.

12. Span, interview with the author, October 2009.

13. Pribbenow, "The -Ology War," 193.

14. The Pentagon Papers, Part IV.C.7.b, 114; William Chapman, "179 Arrested as Violence Takes Over," *Washington Post*, 22 October 1967. Fewer than eighty people were injured, a surprisingly small number, considering the raw emotions of all involved.

15. As the largest MiG base and its proximity to Hanoi, Phuc Yen was essentially

at what became "Bullseye." As the PIRAZ developed, threat warnings were given via radio, referencing a direction and distance from Hanoi and Phuc Yen. It proved an easy-to-use system allowing pilots to quickly determine if an airborne MiG posed a threat. A simple call, "Bandits launching, Bullseye!" would set aviators on edge.

16. Eighth Tactical Fighter Wing, *History*, 207.

17. This marked the first use of a QRC-248 IFF interrogator on the EC-121 College Eye. The QRC-248 secretly interrogated a MiG's IFF gear, allowing the EC-121 to covertly track it and thus provide fighters with precise threat locations. The system's use had been contested by members of the intelligence community who believed the risk of discovery far outweighed the gain. The system provided the Phantom with perfect warning calls.

18. Schulte, "The Raids," 2.

19. Searfus was posthumously awarded the Distinguished Flying Cross for this mission. The next day he led CVW-15's strike and earned a Silver Star. The awards were presented posthumously, as he was killed one month later in a tragic accident.

20. Schulte, "The Raids," 3.

21. CINCPACFLT, Staff Analysis Study 8-68, 17; Pribbenow, "The -Ology War," 193.

22. Weichman, as quoted in Levinson, *Alpha Strike Vietnam*, 131.

23. Schaffert, email to the author, 19 April 2013; Span, interview with the author, October 2009.

24. Span, interview with the author, October 2009.

25. VA-163, *Command History, 1967*, 13.

26. CINCPACFLT, Staff Analysis Study 8-68, 17; Span, interview with the author, October 2009.

27. Span, interview with the author, October 2009.

28. Schaffert, email to the author; Span, interview with the author, October 2009. After this incident, Cunningham's squadron mates kept a close watch on him in port. Inevitably after a few drinks, he always wanted to punch Swanson.

29. Span, interview with the author, October 2009.

30. McCain and Salter, *Faith of My Fathers*, 186.

31. McCain and Salter, *Faith of My Fathers*, 188.

32. McCain claims in his book that he was shot down by an SA-2, while the VA-163 *1967 Command History* claims he was brought down by 85 mm AAA. The National Archives data are inconclusive, saying "cause of loss unknown." North Vietnam credited their leading missile officer, Sixty-First Battalion's Nguyen Xuan Dai, with the shoot-down, later awarding him the title of Hero of the People's Armed Forces. Whatever brought McCain's airplane down, he likely never saw it, as he was too busy flying and egressing from the target area.

33. Grant, *Over the Beach*, 208.

13. In the End

1. Headquarters Pacific Air Force, *Air to Air Encounters*, 23.

2. Span, interview with the author, October 2009.

3. Schaffert, email to the author, 22 April 2013.

4. Schaffert, email to the author, 22 April 2013.

5. Laughter and Schaffert, email to the author, 19 April 2013; USS *Oriskany*, Deck Log, Sunday, 19 November 1967.

6. Addeeb Oral History, 15.

7. Schaffert, email to the author, 22 March 2013.

8. Schaffert, email to the author, 22 April 2013. Schaffert's engagement has been extensively retold. According to Schaffert, he first debriefed it to John Quisenberry for the initial Top Gun syllabus. It was included in a 1968 article for Ling-Temco-Vought and another briefing for OP-05 in the Pentagon in 1974. He was interviewed for Tillman's *MiG Master* and Gilchrest's *Crusader!* The most accurate version was given to the History Channel for its *Dogfights* show in 2006.

9. Schaffert, email to the author, 7 June 2017.

10. Thompson, "Ten Minutes of Terror."

11. Schaffert, email to the author, 23 April 2013.

12. O'Connor, *MiG Killers*, 103.

13. O'Connor, *MiG Killers*, 103.

14. O'Connor, *MiG Killers*, 103.

15. VA-164, *Command History, 1967*, 13; VF-162, *Command History, 1967*, II-2.

16. Quoted in Mersky, *F-8 Crusader Units*, 52.

17. Schaffert, email to the author, 22 April 2013.

18. Schaffert email to the author, 18 June 2010; Tillman and Van Der Lugt, *Aviation Elite Units*, 89.

19. The losses were equally hard on sailors tasked with maintaining the aircraft. During the last two line periods of the 1967–68 cruise, VA-163 sailors spent nearly three hundred man-hours repairing seven combat-damaged Skyhawks— this does not include total maintenance hours required nor all the losses incurred, as some damaged aircraft required repairs beyond the squadron's ability. VA-163 *Command History, 1967*, D-2.

20. Rescue summary taken from HS-6 squadron webpage, http://raunchyredskins .us/Operations/Combat%20sar.htm.

21. Span, interview with the author, October 2009.

22. Denis Weichman biography taken from his change of command pamphlet, http://a4skyhawk.org/?q=3e/va153/weichman-va153-1973co.htm.

23. Grant, *Over the Beach*, 253.

24. The Pentagon Papers, Part IV.C.7.b, 1.

14. 1968, the Summer of Violence

1. Sharp, *Strategy for Defeat*, 222.

2. The Pentagon Papers, IV.C.b, 186.

3. Pentagon Papers, IV.C.b, 202–3.

4. Grant, *Strategy for Defeat*, 226; The Pentagon Papers, IV.C.b, 194. Terrified of potential leaks, the administration advised the ambassadors to Australia, New Zealand, Thailand, Laos, the Philippines, and South Korea only. Though Thieu and Ky were consulted, there was little they could do.

5. The Pentagon Papers, IV.C.b, 198.

6. Headquarters Pacific Air Force, *Rolling Thunder January 1967–November 1968*, 27.

7. Headquarters Pacific Air Force, *Rolling Thunder January 1967–November 1968*, 32.

15. The POWs

1. The POW saga is well documented in Rochester and Kiley's *Honor Bound* and Hubble's *POW*. The Stockdales' book, *In Love and War*, serves as the ultimate telling of the POW experience.

2. The IQ of these highly educated men was 135 or more. Rochester and Kiley, *Honor Bound*, 422; Howes, *Voices*, 7; and Gaither, *With God*, 119.

3. Rochester and Kiley, *Honor Bound*, 1.

4. Rochester and Kiley, *Honor Bound*, 12.

5. Biderman, "Communist Attempts to Elicit False Confessions from Air Force Prisoners of War," *Bulletin of the New York Academy of Medicine*, September 1957.

6. Rochester and Kiley, *Honor Bound*, 539; Stockdale and Stockdale, *In Love and War*, 430–31.

7. Rochester and Kiley, *Honor Bound*, 596.

8. Yablonka, "Vice Admiral James Bond Stockdale."

9. Rochester and Kiley, *Honor Bound*, 130.

10. Rochester and Kiley, *Honor Bound*, 297.

11. Stockdale and Stockdale, *In Love and War*, 245–53; Rochester and Kiley, *Honor Bound*, 298.

12. Stockdale and Stockdale, *In Love and War*, 266–77; Rochester and Kiley, *Honor Bound*, 307.

13. Rochester and Kiley, *Honor Bound*, 308.

14. Stockdale and Stockdale, *In Love and War*, 278; Rochester and Kiley, *Honor Bound*, 327.

15. Stockdale and Stockdale, *In Love and War*, 285.

16. Stockdale and Stockdale, *In Love and War*, 336.

17. Stockdale and Stockdale, *In Love and War*, 349–59.

18. USNI blog, 3 July 2013, "Review of Lessons from the Hanoi Hilton," http://blog.usni.org/2013/07/03/review-of-lessons-from-the-hanoi-hilton.

19. Rochester and Kiley, *Honor Bound*, 367.

20. Rochester and Kiley, *Honor Bound*, 369.

21. Doug Hegdahl's story is amazing and worthy of more space than available here. Dick Stratton realized that Hegdahl had memorized the entire Gettysburg Address, forward and backward. He began coaxing Hegdahl to memorize names so he could be released early and provide the names to the world. Doug Hegdahl memorized names and shoot-down dates, as well as family members, to the tune of "John Jacob Jingleheimer Schmidt." Recently retired, Hegdahl taught for years at the Navy Survival School in San Diego, where he shocked students with his ability to still recite names.

22. McCain and Salter, *Faith of My Fathers*, 197.

23. Rochester and Kiley, *Honor Bound*, 363.

24. Rochester and Kiley, *Honor Bound*, 363.

25. McCain and Salter, *Faith of My Fathers*, 225–26.

26. McCain and Salter, *Faith of My Fathers*, 342.

27. Rochester and Kiley, *Honor Bound*, 399.

28. Grant, *Over the Beach*, 272.

29. Rochester and Kiley, "A Chronology."

30. Rochester and Kiley, *Honor Bound*, 99.

31. Levinson, *Alpha Strike*, 225.

32. "Return with Honor," *The American Experience*, http://www.pbs.org/wgbh /amex/honor/sfeature/sf_stockdale.html.

33. Declassified Vietnamese Communist Party documents show that the Politburo issued a special resolution outlining special instructions to improve the treatment of prisoners. See *1969 Collected Party Documents*, 303–5, translated for CWIHP by Merle L. Pribbenow, http://www.wilsoncenter.org/publication/e-dossier-no-30 -treatment-american-pows-north-vietnam/.

34. Grant, *Over the Beach*, 100.

35. Grant, *Over the Beach*, 172.

36. Grant, *Over the Beach*, 246–49.

37. Rochester and Kiley, *Honor Bound*, 592.

38. Powell, "Honor Bound."

39. Rochester and Kiley, *Honor Bound*, 592.

16. "Because Our Fathers Lied"

The quote used for this chapter's title is from Rudyard Kipling's poem "Common Form," in *Epitaphs of the War*: "If any question why we died, tell them, / because our fathers lied."

1. The Pentagon Papers, Part IV.C.7.b, 203–4.

2. Isserman and Kazin, *America Divided*, 294; Will, *Reassessing the Sixties*, 8.

3. Luscombe, "10 Questions for Robert Caro."

4. Record, *The Wrong War*, x.

5. Record, *The Wrong War*, 121.

6. Sorley, *Westmoreland*, 234.

7. Sherwood, *Afterburner*, 293.

8. Record, *The Wrong War*, xix.

9. Record, *The Wrong War*, x.

10. Sorley, *Westmoreland*, 106.

11. Nichols and Tillman, *On Yankee Station*, xiv.

12. Record, *The Wrong War*, xix.

13. Clodfelter, *The Limits of Airpower*, 101.

14. Isaacs, *Vietnam Shadows*, 177.

15. Smith, *Rolling Thunder*, 239.

16. Coonts in foreword to Nichols and Tillman, *On Yankee Station*, xii.

Glossary

Alert-Five: A manned fighter, sitting on the catapult ready to launch within five minutes. Used to intercept potential threats to an aircraft carrier. Also Alert-Fifteen and Alert-Thirty, which denote the time allowed from initial notification to being airborne.

Alpha strike: Large strike involving virtually all of a carrier's tactical aircraft, typically to one target and sometimes in coordination with another carrier.

ALQ-51: Deception jammer designed for self-protection of tactical aircraft. Fitted as standard in A-3, A-6, and RA-5C aircraft. "Shoehorned" into A-4, F-4, and F-8. See **shoehorn**.

Atoll: The NATO designation for the Soviet K-13 missile, the counterpart of the AIM-9.

ball: A series of lights providing glide slope indication used as a visual aid to landing on the aircraft carrier. During each landing, a pilot is told to "call the ball," whereupon he confirms that he can or cannot see the visual signals and is responding to them before landing.

bandit: A known enemy aircraft. See **bogey**.

barricade: A gigantic nylon net that catches damaged aircraft in midair.

bingo: A predetermined amount of fuel needed to return to base or an alternate airfield.

bogey: An unknown, possibly enemy aircraft.

bolter: An aircraft that has missed the arresting cables while attempting to land aboard the aircraft carrier.

break: A maximum performance turn used for defense against SAMs or aircraft.

bureau number (BuNo): Akin to a serial number. Each naval aircraft is assigned a number by the Bureau of Aeronautics when purchased. By referencing an aircraft's BuNo, it is possible to determine the manufacturer, date of manufacture, and other pertinent information.

CAG: Commander Air Group (wing). Up until 1962, air wings were known as air groups and commanded by a senior commander who had previously commanded a squadron. In spite of the change in terminology, air wing commanders were referred to as CAG in honor of the tradition. See CVW.

CALL SIGN: A unique identification used when communicating via radio. Ships, squadrons, and pilots were assigned a call sign to prevent the enemy from knowing their true identity.

CAP: Combat air patrol, an air patrol over a specified area for a prescribed purpose. For example, a rescue combat air patrol to help rescue a downed aviator is referred to as a RESCAP.

CHOP (in-chop/out-chop): The NATO code word for CHange of OPerational control. In-chop refers to a unit joining a fleet or area of operations. Out-chop means that unit has departed a fleet or area of operations.

COOK OFF: The premature detonation of ordnance, usually due to extreme heat associated with exposure to fire. Also known as thermally induced firing.

CVW: Carrier Air Wing. Combination of squadrons aboard each aircraft carrier, led by a senior commander. See CAG.

division: A flight of four aircraft made up of two sections. Called a 4-ship in the air force. See **section**.

Dixie Station: Point off the coast of South Vietnam in the Gulf of Tonkin designated for carrier operations over South Vietnam. Once sufficient numbers of aircraft arrived in South Vietnam, the navy was alleviated from the need to operate from Dixie Station. See **Yankee Station**.

Fan Song: NATO code name for the Soviet SNR-75 missile guidance radar associated with the SA-2 surface-to-air missile. The radar was capable of tracking one aircraft and guiding three missiles at once. See **SA-2**.

feet-wet: The radio call made when transiting from over land to over water flight.

feet-dry: The radio call made when transiting from over water flight to over land flight.

flak-trap: An ambush using AAA. An unsuspecting pilot would be drawn toward a previously unknown and concealed AAA position, which would open fire when the aircraft overflew it. The North Vietnamese often used fake SAM sites for this purpose.

frag-orders: Abbreviated daily operating orders that are transmitted from higher headquarters to subordinate units to direct daily activities. Also known as "FragO," "Frag-Ord," or "Fragmentary Orders."

general quarters: An announcement via a warship's speakers directing the crew to man their battle stations. The crew will remain at this condition of readiness, prepared for immediate combat.

in-country: Common phrase used to denote air operations in South Vietnam.

International Control Commission (ICC): An international force of Canadians, Polish, and Indian personnel responsible for enforcing the 1954 Geneva Accords.

Iron Hand: Code name for missions flown against SAM sites. Flown by an A-4 Skyhawk or A-6 Intruder carrying Shrike missiles. Known as Wild Weasel in the air force.

Iron Triangle: Nickname for the highly defended area between Haiphong, Hanoi, and Thanh Hoa.

jink: An irregular flight path with constantly changing altitude and direction. Used to prevent a predictable flight pattern, making it difficult for gunners to track a plane.

Loose Deuce: A tactical formation flown by a flight leader and wingman. Mutually supportive and flexible.

Mk 82/83/84: 500-, 1,000-, and 2,000-pound general purpose bombs used during Vietnam.

PIRAZ: Positive Identification and Radar Advisory Zone. An area over North Vietnam in which navy ships or air force early warning aircraft could monitor via radar and provide advisories to U.S. aircraft.

Red Crown: Code name of the ship performing PIRAZ duties in the Gulf of Tonkin. See **PIRAZ**.

RESPOT: The action taken to move aircraft on the flight deck. Generally done in preparation for launching or recovering aircraft. Prior to launching, aircraft will be moved aft to clear the catapults on the forward flight deck. Prior to recovery, aircraft will be moved forward to clear the landing area.

RHAW gear: Radar homing and warning equipment that points out the direction of radars and warns of changes in missile launch and guidance status. Also RWR (Radar Warning and Receiving).

route packages: Six arbitrary geographic areas established in North Vietnam to allow for better coordination between navy and air force strikes.

SA-2: NATO code name for the Soviet-built S-75 surface-to-air missile, a radar-guided high-altitude missile that could reach Mach 2.5 and carried an 86-pound warhead. See **Fan Song**.

section: A flight of two aircraft. Called a 2-ship in the air force. See **division**.

shoehorn: Navy operation to install the ALQ-51 deception system in small tactical aircraft that had not been designed to carry it.

Shrike (AGM-45): An air-to-surface antiradar missile fired at SAM sites. See **Iron Hand**.

Sidewinder (AIM-9): Air-to-air heat-seeking missile.

skids: Wheeled dollies used to move ordnance about the flight deck.

TACAN: Tactical Air Navigation system. A device in an aircraft that gives range and bearing to a radio signal.

TF-77 (Task Force 77): The US Navy's carrier force in the Gulf of Tonkin. Commander Task Force 77 (CTF-77) directed Yankee Station activity, with several carrier groups (CARGRUS) under its command.

Thud Ridge: The nickname given to a 12-nautical-mile, 5,000-foot-high ridgeline northwest of Hanoi. The ridge ran parallel to the Red River and was a useful navigation point. It also provided terrain masking from North Vietnamese radars.

TRAP: Naval aviation slang referring to an arrested landing onboard an aircraft carrier. Naval aircraft use a tailhook to catch a cable or cross-deck pendant on the flight deck in an arrested landing, which allows the aircraft to rapidly decelerate.

up north: Common navy aircrew phrase used to designate North Vietnam. See **in-country.**

VA (Attack Squadron): Attack squadrons on *Oriskany* flew A-4 Skyhawks or A-1 Skyraiders. Their primary functions were bombing or attacking military targets.

VECTOR: A navigation service during which a radar controller directs an aircraft via heading and distance.

VF (Fighter Squadron): Fighter squadrons on *Oriskany* flew F-8 Crusaders. Their primary function was to protect the attack aircraft from MiGs. Although it was not their primary mission, fighters could carry air-to-ground ordnance to relieve the burden on the limited numbers of attack aircraft.

VMF(AW) (Marine Fighter Squadron, All Weather): The marine fighter squadron on *Oriskany* flew F-8 Crusaders.

Walleye (AGM-62): TV-guided air-to-surface glide bomb introduced in March 1967. The pilot could see the target and guide the weapon through a TV lens installed in the nose of the weapon.

WESTPAC: Acronym for Western Pacific. Phrase used by sailors to describe any cruise in the western regions of the Pacific Ocean.

Yankee Station: Spot in the Gulf of Tonkin south of Hainan Island at which carriers maintained position for strikes into North Vietnam. Yankee Station was located at 17°30'N by 108°30'E. See **Dixie Station.**

Bibliography

Archival and Unpublished Sources

Air America. *Command History, 1965.* William M. Leary Papers, History of Aviation Collection, Special Collections Department, Eugene McDermott Library, University of Texas at Dallas, http://www.utdallas.edu/library/specialcollections/hac/cataam/notebooks/aam65.pdf.

Carrier Air Wing 16. *Command History, 1966.* Washington DC: Naval History and Heritage Command.

CINCPACFLT. *Attrition of U.S. Aircraft in the SAM Envelope of Route Package VI North Vietnam, July 1967 through March 1968.*

———. Staff Analysis Study 1-67. *Combat Attrition of Carrier-Based Aircraft during 1966 (U) of 13 February 1967.*

———. Staff Analysis Study 4-68. *Combat Attrition of Carrier-Based Aircraft during the Second Half of 1967(U) of 14 May 1968.*

———. Staff Analysis Study 8-68. *An Analysis of SA-2 Missile Activity in North Vietnam from July 1965 through March 1968 (U).*

———. Staff Analysis Study 9-67. *Recovery of Downed Carrier Based Aircrews (U) of 11 Sep 1967.*

———. Staff Analysis Study 12-65. *Attacks on SA-2 Sites 27 July–8 November 1965.*

———. Staff Analysis Study 16-66. *Attacks on Major Bridges in North Vietnam by U.S. Naval Aircraft (U) of 27 December 1966.*

———. *The United States Navy in the Pacific Fleet 1965.* Sedgwick Tourison Collection.

———. *Command History, 1966.* 31 January 1967, 135, folder 2, box 8, Sedgwick Tourison Collection.

Defense Prisoner of War, Missing Personnel Office (DPMO). "U.S. Accounted-For from the Vietnam War: Prisoners of War, Escapees, Returnees and Remains Recovered; Report for: United States Navy." 29 September 2009.

Drake, Ricky J. "The Rules of Defeat: The Impact of Aerial Rules of Engagement on USAF Operations in North Vietnam, 1965–1968." Master's thesis, Air University, 1992.

Drew, Dennis M. "Rolling Thunder 1965: Anatomy of a Failure." Master's thesis, Air University, 1986.

Ellsworth, John K. "Operation Rolling Thunder: Strategic Implications of Airpower Doctrine." Master's thesis, U.S. Army War College, 2003.

HC-I. *Command History, 1966.* Washington DC: Naval History and Heritage Command.

———. *Command History, 1967.* Washington DC: Naval History and Heritage Command.

Herman, Jan. "Oral History with LCDR (ret) ALLAN ADDEEB." 25 October 2005. U.S. Navy Medical Department Oral History Program, Washington DC.

Hewitt, William A. "Planting the Seeds of SEAD: The Wild Weasel in Vietnam." Master's thesis, Air University, 1992.

LBJ Presidential Library, University of Texas, Austin
     LBJ Library Oral Histories

McRae, Michael. "U.S. Navy, Marine Corps, and Air Force Fixed-Wing Aircraft Losses and Damage in Southeast Asia (1962–1973)." Center for Naval Analysis, Operations Evaluation Group. CRC 305, 1976.

Moeller, Michael. "The Sum of Their Fears: The Relationship between the Joint Targeting Coordination Board and the Joint Force Commander." Master's thesis, Air University, 1994.

Myers, Timothy J. "Paul Doumer Bridge: A Study of Leadership." Master's thesis, Air University, 1986.

National Archives and Records Administration. Combat Air Activities Files (CACTA), Record Group 218 (documents all Vietnam sorties flown during the period October 1965–December 1970)

Naval Air Systems Command. "Report of the Air to Air Missile System Capability Review July–November 1968" (the Ault Report). Washington DC: Naval History and Heritage Command. https://www.history.navy.mil/research/histories/naval-aviation-history/ault-report.html.

Naval Historical Center. *Command and Control of Air Operations in the Vietnam War.* Papers presented at the "Colloquium on Contemporary History," 23 January 1991.

———. *Dictionary of American Naval Fighting Ships.* https://archive.org/details/dictionaryofamer02wash.

Naval History and Heritage Command, Washington DC

The Pentagon Papers. Officially titled "Report of the Office of the Secretary of Defense Vietnam Task Force." National Archives, Washington DC. https://www.archives.gov/research/pentagon-papers.

Russell, James S. "Report of the Panel to Review Safety in Carrier Operations," 1967. Washington DC: Naval History and Heritage Command.

Schulte, Dick. "The Raids on Phuc Yen Air Field, NVN." Unpublished memoir, 2013.

Stewart, Henry P. "The Impact of the USS Forrestal's 1967 Fire on United States Navy Shipboard Damage Control." Master's thesis, Command and General Staff College, 2004.

U.S. Air Force. Directorate, Force Development and Analysis DCS Plans Tactical Air Command. *Summary of USAF Aircraft Losses in SEA.* June 1974. Defense Technical Information Center, http://www.dtic.mil/dtic/search/search.html.

———. Weapons Systems Evaluation Group. *Air-to-Air Encounters in Southeast Asia.*

Volume I, Account of F-4 and F-8 Events prior to 1 Mar 67. October 1967. Defense Technical Information Center, http://www.dtic.mil/dtic/search/search.html.

———. Weapons Systems Evaluation Group. *Air-to-Air Encounters in Southeast Asia. Volume II, F-105 Events prior to 1 Mar 67.* September 1968. Defense Technical Information Center, http://www.dtic.mil/dtic/search/search.html.

———. Weapons Systems Evaluation Group. *Air-to-Air Encounters in Southeast Asia. Volume III, Events from 1 Mar 67–1 August 67 and Miscellaneous Events.* February 1969. Defense Technical Information Center, http://www.dtic.mil/dtic/search/search.html.

———. Weapons Systems Evaluation Group. *Air-to-Air Encounters in Southeast Asia. Volume IV, Analysis.* April 1968. Defense Technical Information Center, http://www.dtic.mil/dtic/search/search.html.

U.S. Navy. Operational Evaluation Group. "Justification of the Air Effort in North Vietnam." 1 September 1967.

U.S. Navy. Judge Advocate General. "USS *Forrestal* (CVA-59) Fire Investigation." 19 September 1967. http://www.jag.navy.mil/library/jagman_investigations.htm.

USS *Oriskany. Command History, 1965.* Washington DC: Naval History and Heritage Command.

———. *Command History, 1966.* Washington DC: Naval History and Heritage Command.

———. *Command History, 1967.* Washington DC: Naval History and Heritage Command.

———. *Command History, 1968.* Washington DC: Naval History and Heritage Command.

———. *Cruise Book, 1965.* Washington DC: Naval History and Heritage Command.

———. *Cruise Book, 1966.* Washington DC: Naval History and Heritage Command.

———. *Cruise Book, 1967–68.* Washington DC: Naval History and Heritage Command.

———. Deck Logs, April–December 1965. Washington DC: Naval History and Heritage Command.

———. Deck Logs, May–November 1966. Washington DC: Naval History and Heritage Command.

———. Deck Logs, June 1967–January 1968. Washington DC: Naval History and Heritage Command.

VA-152. *Aviation Historical Summary, October 1964–March 65.* Washington DC: Naval History and Heritage Command.

———. *Aviation Historical Summary, April 1966–September 1966.* Washington DC: Naval History and Heritage Command.

———. *Command History, 1967.* Washington DC: Naval History and Heritage Command.

VA-163. *Command History, 1966.* Washington DC: Naval History and Heritage Command.

———. *Command History, 1967.* Washington DC: Naval History and Heritage Command.

VA-164. *Aviation Historical Summary, April 1966–September 1966*. Washington DC: Naval History and Heritage Command.

———. *Command History, 1966*. Washington DC: Naval History and Heritage Command.

———. *Command History, 1967*. Washington DC: Naval History and Heritage Command.

VF-111. *Command History, 1966*. Washington DC: Naval History and Heritage Command.

———. *Command History, 1967*. Washington DC: Naval History and Heritage Command.

VF-162. *Aviation Historical Summary, April 1965–September 1965*. Washington DC: Naval History and Heritage Command.

———. *Aviation Historical Summary, September 1965–April 1966*. Washington DC: Naval History and Heritage Command.

———. *Command History, 1967*. Washington DC: Naval History and Heritage Command.

Vietnam Center and Archive, Texas Tech University, Lubbock

Dale Andrade Collection

Larry Berman Collection (Presidential Archives Research)

James Ridgeway Collection

Sedgwick Tourison Collection

Veteran Members of the 109th Quartermaster Company (Air Delivery) Collection

VMF(AW)-212. *Command Chronology, 1965*. Washington DC: Naval History and Heritage Command.

VMF(AW)-212. *WESTPAC-ORISKANY*. Washington DC: Naval History and Heritage Command.

Published Sources

Arnold, Bob. "A Trip to the Suburbs." *Hook*, Winter 1990, 48–50.

Barlow, Jeffrey. *Revolt of the Admirals: The Fight for Naval Aviation 1945–1950*. Washington DC: Naval Historical Center, 1995.

Barnhill, Gary. "SAM Killer Mission." *Daedalus Flyer*, Fall 2006, 7–8.

Bell, Kenneth. *100 Missions North: A Fighter Pilot's Story of the Vietnam War*. Dulles VA: Brassey's, 1993.

Berger, Carl. *The USAF in Southeast Asia, 1961–1973: An Illustrated Account*. Washington DC: Office of Air Force History, 1984.

Biderman, Albert. "Communist Attempts to Elicit False Confessions from Air Force Prisoners of War." *Bulletin of the New York Academy of Medicine* 33, no. 9 (September 1957): 616–25.

Broughton, Jack. *Going Downtown: The War against Hanoi and Washington*. New York: Orion Books, 1988.

———. *Thud Ridge*. Philadelphia: Lippincott, 1969.

Burgess, Richard R., and R. Rausa. *us Navy a-1 Skyraider Units of the Vietnam War.* Osprey Combat Aircraft no. 77. London: Osprey Publishing, 2009.

Cima, Ronald. *A Country Study—Vietnam.* Washington DC: Federal Research Division, Library of Congress, 1987.

Clayton, Pete. "The Mighty 'O.'" *Hook*, Spring 1978, 18–23.

Clodfelter, Mark. *The Limits of Airpower: The American Bombing of North Vietnam.* New York: Free Press, 1989.

Colvin, John. "Hanoi in My Time." *Washington Quarterly* 4, no. 2 (Spring 1981): 136–54.

Cosmas, Graham A. *MACV: The Joint Command in the Years of Escalation 1962–1967.* Washington DC: Center of Military History, 2006.

Davies, Peter. *USN F-4 Phantom II vs VPAF MiG-17/19.* Oxford: Osprey Publishing, 2009.

Davis, John. "Farewell Lady Jessie." *Hook*, Spring 1988, 14.

———. "Stopping by Carlin, Nevada." *Hook*, Spring 1988, 15.

Duthie, Larry. "Flightbag" (Letters to the Editor). *Naval Aviation News*, Winter 2014, 4.

Eighth Tactical Fighter Wing. *History, 01 October–31 December 1967,* vols. 1 and 2. Montgomery AL: Air Force Historical Research Agency.

Elkins, Frank. *The Heart of a Man.* New York: W. W. Norton and Company, 1973.

Foster, Wynn F. *Captain Hook: A Pilot's Tragedy and Triumph in the Vietnam War.* Annapolis: Naval Institute Press, 1992.

———. *Fire on the Hangar Deck: Ordeal of the* Oriskany. Annapolis: Naval Institute Press, 2001.

———. "The Saints of VA-163." *Hook*, Winter 1990, 36–45.

———. "The Will to Survive." *Approach*, December 1966, 4–6.

Francillon, Rene J. *Tonkin Gulf Yacht Club: US Carrier Operations off Vietnam.* Annapolis: Naval Institute Press, 1988.

Freeman, Gregory A. *Sailors to the End: The Deadly Fire on the* USS Forrestal *and the Heroes Who Fought It.* New York: Harper Collins, 2002.

Frisbee, John L. "Valor: Down in the Delta." *Air Force Magazine*, July 1992.

Gaddis, John. *George F. Kennan: An American Life.* New York: Penguin Press, 2011.

Gaddy, David W. *Essential Matters: A History of the Cryptographic Branch of the People's Army of Viet-Nam, 1945–1975 with a Supplement on Cryptography in the Border Guard (Formerly the Armed Public Security Forces) 1959–1989.* Washington DC: Center for Cryptologic History, National Security Agency, 1994.

Gaither, Ralph, and Steve Henry. *With God in a POW Camp.* Nashville: Broadman Press, 1973.

Galdorisi, George, and Thomas Philips. *Leave No Man Behind: The Saga of Combat Search and Rescue.* Minneapolis: Zenith Press, 2009.

Giberson, Art. "The Legend of the Cubi Cat." *Wings of Gold*, Winter 2006, 27–28.

Gilbert, Kelly. "Fire in Hangar Bay One!" *All Hands*, February 1967.

Goldstein, Gordon. *Lessons in Disaster: McGeorge Bundy and the Path to War in Vietnam.* New York: Holt Publishing Company, 2008.

Grant, Zalin. *Over the Beach: The Air War in Vietnam.* New York: W. W. Norton and Company, 1986.

Gray, Glen. *The Warriors: Reflections on Men in Battle.* New York: Harcourt Brace, 1959.

Gray, Stephen R. *Rampant Raider: An A-4 Skyhawk Pilot in Vietnam*. Annapolis: Naval Institute Press, 2007.

Hanyok, Robert J. "Skunks, Bogies, Silent Hounds, and the Flying Fish: The Gulf of Tonkin Mystery, 2–4 August 1964." *Cryptologic Quarterly* 19, no. 4 (Winter 2000 / Spring 2001): 1–55.

———. *Spartans in Darkness: American SIGINT and the Indochina War 1945–1975*. Vol. 7, *The NSA Period: 1952–Present*. U.S. Cryptologic History Series 6. Washington DC: Center for Cryptologic History, National Security Agency, 2002.

Headquarters Military Assistance Command Vietnam. *MACV 1965 Yearly Summary*. Washington DC: GPO.

———. *MACV 1966 Yearly Summary*. Washington DC: GPO.

———. *MACV 1967 Yearly Summary*. Washington DC: GPO.

Headquarters Pacific Air Force. *Air Tactics against NVN Air Ground Defenses December 1966–1 November 1968*. CHECO (Contemporary Historical Examination of Current Operations) Report. Washington DC: GPO, 1969.

———. *Air to Air Encounters over North Vietnam 1 July 1967–31 December 1968*. CHECO (Contemporary Historical Examination of Current Operations) Report. Washington DC: GPO, 1969.

———. *Rolling Thunder March–June 1965*. CHECO (Contemporary Historical Examination of Current Operations) Report. Washington DC: GPO, 1966.

———. *Rolling Thunder July 1965–December 1966*. CHECO (Contemporary Historical Examination of Current Operations) Report. Washington DC: GPO, 1967.

———. *Rolling Thunder January 1967–November 1968*. CHECO (Contemporary Historical Examination of Current Operations) Report. Washington DC: GPO, 1969.

———. *Rolling Thunder 17 November 1967*. CHECO (Contemporary Historical Examination of Current Operations) Report. Washington DC: GPO, 1967.

Hendrickson, Paul. *The Living and the Dead: Robert McNamara and Five Lives of a Lost War*. New York: Knopf, 1996.

Hershberg, James G. *Marigold: The Lost Chance for Peace in Vietnam*. Washington DC: Woodrow Wilson Center Press, 2012.

Hirsch, James S. *Two Souls Indivisible: The Friendship That Saved Two POWs in Vietnam*. Boston: Houghton Mifflin, 2005.

Hobson, Chris. *Vietnam Air Losses, USAF, USN and USMC Fixed Wing Aircraft Losses in Southeast Asia, 1961–1973*. Forest Lake MN: Specialty Press / Midland Publishing, 2001.

Holloway, James L., III. *Aircraft Carriers at War: A Personal Retrospective of Korea, Vietnam, and the Soviet Confrontation*. Annapolis: Naval Institute Press, 2011.

Hooper, Edwin. *Mobility, Support, Endurance: A Story of Naval Operational Logistics in the Vietnam War 1965–1968*. Washington DC: GPO, 1972.

Howes, Craig. *Voices of the Vietnam POWs: Witnesses to Their Fight*. New York: Oxford University Press, 1993.

Hubble, John. *P.O.W.: A Definitive History of the American Prisoner-of-War Experience in Vietnam, 1964–1973*. New York: Reader's Digest Press, 1976.

Isaacs, Arnold. *Vietnam Shadows: The War, Its Ghosts, and Its Legacy.* Baltimore MD: Johns Hopkins University Press, 1997.

Isserman, Maurice, and M. Kazin. *America Divided: The Civil War of the 1960s.* Oxford: Oxford University Press, 2000.

Jones, Robert. "HC-7: The Most Highly Decorated Squadron in Vietnam?" *Foundation* 11, no. 2 (Fall 1990): 91–97.

Kamps, Charles T. "The JCS 94-Target List: A Vietnam Myth That Still Distorts Military Thought." *Aerospace Power Journal,* Spring 2001, 67–80.

Kilduff, Peter. *Osprey Air Combat: Douglas A-4 Skyhawk.* London: Osprey Books, 1983.

Kling, Dwane. *The Rise of the Biggest Little City: An Encyclopedic History of Reno Gaming.* Reno: University of Nevada Press, 2000.

Kurlansky, Mark. *1968: The Year That Rocked the World.* London: Vintage Books, 2005.

Lawson, Robert L. *Carrier Air Group Commanders, the Men and Their Machines.* Atglen PA: Schiffer Military History, 2000.

Levinson, Jeffrey L. *Alpha Strike Vietnam: The Navy's Air War, 1964 to 1973.* Novato CA: Presidio Press, 1986.

Lomperis, Timothy J. "Giap's Dream, Westmorland's Nightmare." *Parameters,* June 1988, 18–32.

Luscombe, Belinda. "10 Questions for Robert Caro." *Time,* 21 May 2012.

Marcy, Freeman. *Sundowner Days: Recollections of a Fighter Pilot.* Book on-line, http://clarecarver.com/freeman/#oriskanycruise.

Marolda, Edward J. *By Sea, Air and Land: An Illustrated History of the U.S. Navy and the War in Southeast Asia.* Washington DC: Naval Historical Center, 1994.

McBride, James J. *Shang Log: 1970 WestPac (Vietnam) Cruise, USS Shangri-La (CVS-38), CVW-8, VA-12.* Santa Fe NM: Paper Tiger, 1999.

McCain, John, and M. Salter. *Faith of My Fathers.* New York: Random House Publishing Company, 1999.

McLaughlin, Malcolm. *The Long Hot Summer of 1967: Urban Rebellion in America.* New York: Palgrave Macmillan, 2014.

McMaster, H. R. *Dereliction of Duty.* New York: Harper Collins, 1997.

McNamara, Robert S., James G. Blight, and Robert K. Brigham. *Argument without End: In Search of Answers to the Vietnam Tragedy.* New York: Perseus Books Group, 1999.

McNamara, Robert S., and Brian Van De Mark. *In Retrospect: The Tragedy and Lessons of Vietnam.* New York: Vintage Books, 1996.

Mersky, Peter. "Belly: The Story of a MiG Killer." *Foundation* 31, no. 2 (Fall 2010): 23–34.

———. *F-8 Crusader Units of the Vietnam War.* Osprey Combat Aircraft no. 7. London: Osprey Publishing, 1998.

———. *US Navy and Marine Corps A-4 Skyhawk Units of the Vietnam War.* Osprey Combat Aircraft no. 69. London: Osprey Publishing, 2007.

Mersky, Peter B., and N. Polmar. *The Naval Air War in Vietnam.* Annapolis: Nautical and Aviation Publishing Company of America, 1981.

Michel, Marshall. *Clashes.* Annapolis: Naval Institute Press, 1997.

Middleton, Drew. *Air War Vietnam.* New York: Bobbs-Merrill Company, 1978.

Moise, Edwin. *Tonkin Gulf and the Escalation of the Vietnam War*. Chapel Hill: University of North Carolina Press, 1996.

Moore, Harold G., and Joseph Galloway. *We Were Soldiers Once . . . and Young*. New York: Random House, 1992.

Morgan, Rick. "Dragon in the Sky: A History of VAW-13/VAQ-130, Part 1." *Hook*, Spring 2002, 23–34.

———. "Orphans of 7th Fleet: The Story of HC-7/CSAR." *Hook*, Fall 1998, 32–41.

Moser, Don. "A Carrier's Agony—Hell Afloat." *Life*, 25 November 1966.

Nalty, Bernard C. *Tactics and Techniques of Electronic Warfare: Electronic Countermeasures in the Air War against North Vietnam 1965–1973*. Washington DC: Office of Air Force History, 1977.

Newman, Rick, and D. Shepard. *Bury Us Upside Down: The Misty Pilots and the Secret Battle for the Ho Chi Minh Trail*. New York: Presidio Press, 2006.

Nichols, John, and Barrett Tillman. *On Yankee Station: The Naval Air War over Vietnam*. Annapolis: Naval Institute Press, 1987.

O'Conner, Michael. *MiG Killers of Yankee Station*. Friendship WI: New Past Press, 2003.

Olds, Robin S., with Christina Olds and Ed Rasimus. *Fighter Pilot: A Memoir of the Legendary Ace Robin Olds*. New York: St. Martin's Press, 2010.

Olson, James, and R. Roberts. *Where the Domino Fell: America and Vietnam 1945–1990*. New York: St. Martin's Press, 1991.

Powell, Stewart. "Honor Bound." *Hook*, Summer 2013, 27–33.

Prados, John. "The '65 Decision: Bombing Soviet SAM Sites in Vietnam." *VVA Veteran*, January/February 2006, http://archive.vva.org/archive/TheVeteran/2006_01/index.htm.

Pribbenow, Merle L., II. "The -Ology War: Technology and Ideology in the Vietnamese Defense of Hanoi, 1967." *Journal of Military History*, January 2003, 175–200.

———. *Victory in Vietnam: The Official History of the People's Army of Vietnam, 1954–1975*. Lawrence: University Press of Kansas, 2002.

Price, Alfred. *Rolling Thunder through Allied Force, 1964–2000*. Vol. 3 of *The History of US Electronic Warfare*. Alexandria VA: Association of Old Crows, 2000.

Rasimus, Edward J. *When Thunder Rolled: An F-105 Pilot over North Vietnam*. Novato CA: Presidio Press, 2003.

Record, Jeffrey. *The Wrong War: Why We Lost in Vietnam*. Annapolis: Naval Institute Press, 1998.

Rochester, Stuart, and Frederick Kiley. "A Chronology of Vignettes by and about POWs 1964–1973." *HOOK*, Summer 2013, 42–47.

———. *Honor Bound: American Prisoners of War in Southeast Asia, 1961–1973*. Washington DC: Historical Office, Office of the Secretary of Defense, 1998.

Ryder, C. C. *"Lead, Follow, or Get the Hell out of the Way!": The Life and Career of Brigadier General Tom Meredith, USAF, Ret.; the Father of "Prime Beef" and "Red Horse"; An Authorized Biography*. Victoria BC: Trafford, 2003.

Schlight, John. *The War in South Vietnam: The Years of the Offensive, 1965–1968, The*

United States Air Force in Southeast Asia. Washington DC: Office of Air Force History, Air Force History and Museums Program, 1999.

Sharp, U. S. Grant. *Strategy for Defeat: Vietnam in Retrospect*. Novato CA: Presidio Press, 1978.

Shershnev, Nikolay. "No One Is Forgotten, Nothing Is Forgotten." *VVA Veteran*, July/August 2006, http://archive.vva.org/veteran/0606/veteran0606.html.

Sherwood, John D. *Afterburner: Naval Aviators and the Vietnam War*. New York: New York University Press, 2004.

————. *Black Sailor, White Navy*. New York: New York University Press, 2007.

Smith, John T. *Rolling Thunder: The Strategic Bombing Campaign, North Vietnam, 1965–1968*. Walton on Thames: Air Research Publications, 1994.

Sorley, Lewis. *Westmoreland: The General Who Lost Vietnam*. New York: Houghton Mifflin, 2011.

Stockdale, Jim. *Thoughts of a Philosophical Fighter Pilot*. Stanford CA: Stanford University Press, 1995.

————. *A Vietnam Experience: Ten Years of Reflection*. Stanford CA: Hoover Institution Press, 1984.

Stockdale, Jim, and Sybil Stockdale. *In Love and War*. Annapolis: Naval Institute Press, 1990.

Tannenbaum, Fred. "Papa Wasn't a Rolling Stone . . . He Was a Pukin' Dog." *Hook*, Fall 2001, 15–27.

Thompson, Warren. "Ten Minutes of Terror." *Flight Journal*, December 2003, 10–14.

Thompson, Wayne. *To Hanoi and Back: The U.S. Air Force and North Vietnam 1966–1973*. Washington DC: Smithsonian, 2000.

Thornborough, Anthony, and F. Mormillo. *Iron Hand: Smashing the Enemy's Air Defences*. Somerset: Patrick Stephens Limited, 2002.

Tillman, Barrett. *MiG Master: Story of the F-8 Crusader*. 2nd ed. Annapolis: Naval Institute Press, 1990.

Tillman, Barrett, and Henk Van Der Lugt. *Aviation Elite Units: VF-11/111 "Sundowners" 1942–95*. Oxford: Osprey Publishing, 2010.

Timberg, Robert. *Nightingale's Song*. New York: Simon and Schuster, 1995.

Time. "Agony of the Oriskany." 4 November 1966.

Time. "A Feeling for Freedom." 29 July 1966.

Uhlig, Frank, Jr. *Vietnam: The Naval Story*. Annapolis: Naval Institute Press, 1986.

U.S. Congress. Senate. Committee on Armed Services. Subcommittee on Preparedness Investigating. *Investigation of the Preparedness Program on the U.S. Tactical Air Power Program*. 90th Cong., 2nd sess., 1968.

————. Senate. Preparedness Investigating Subcommittee of the Armed Services Committee. *Air War against North Vietnam*. 5 pts. 90th Cong., 1st sess., 1967.

U.S. Pacific Command. *Report on the War in Vietnam (as of 30 June 1968) Report on Air and Naval Campaigns against North Vietnam and Pacific Command-Wide Support of the War June 1964–July 1968*. Washington DC: GPO, 1968.

Van Staaveren, Jacob. *Gradual Failure: The Air War over North Vietnam, 1965–1966*. Washington DC: GPO, 2002.

———. *Interdiction in Southern Laos, 1960–1968*. Washington DC: GPO, 1993.

Waechter, Bill. Letters to the Editor. *RNPA Contrails*, August 2008, 7.

Webb, James. "Heroes of the Vietnam Generation." American Enterprise Institute, July/August 2000, http://www.jameswebb.com/articles/military-and-veterans /heroes-of-the-vietnam-generation.

Westmoreland, William C. *A Soldier Reports*. New York: Doubleday and Company, 1976.

Westrum, Ron. *Sidewinder: Creative Missile Development at China Lake*. Annapolis: Naval Institute Press, 2013.

Whiting, Alan S. *The Chinese Calculus of Deterrence*. Ann Arbor: University of Michigan Press, 1975.

Wildenberg, Thomas. *Gray Steel and Black Oil: Fast Tankers and Replenishment at Sea in the U.S. Navy, 1912–1995*. Annapolis: Naval Institute Press, 1996.

Will, George. Foreword to *Reassessing the Sixties: Debating the Political and Cultural Legacy*, edited by Stephen Macedo. New York: W. W. Norton, 1997.

Wolfe, Tom. *Mauve Gloves & Madmen, Clutter & Vine*. New York: Farrar, Straus and Giroux, 1976.

———. *The Truest Sport: Jousting with Sam and Charlie*. Library of America, Reporting Vietnam, *vol.* 1. New York: Literary Classics of the U.S., 1998.

Yablonka, Marc. "Vice Admiral James Bond Stockdale: Vietnam War Hero and Indomitable Spirit at the Hanoi Hilton." *Vietnam Magazine*, August 2006. http://www.historynet.com/vice-admiral-james-bond-stockdale-vietnam-war -hero-and-indomitable-spirit-at-the-hanoi-hilton.htm.

Zaloga, Steven. *Red SAM: The SA-2 Guideline Anti-Aircraft Missile*. New York: Osprey Publishing, 2007.

———. *Soviet Air Defence Missiles, Design, Development and Tactics*. Surrey: Janes Information Group Limited, 1989.

Zhang, Xiaoming. "The Vietnam War 1964–1969: A Chinese Perspective." *Journal of Military History* 60, no. 4 (October 1996): 731–62.

Index